Norman
Mark's
CHICAGO

Norman Mark's

CHICAGO

Walking,
Bicycling,
& Driving
TOURS
of the City

Norman Mark

CHICAGO
REVIEW
PRESS

To Grace, who walks with me through life;
to Joel, who can walk the walk and talk the talk;
to Geoff, who hears the music; and
to Anne, who finds the fun and the love.

Library of Congress Cataloging-in-Publication Data

Mark, Norman
  (Chicago)
  Norman Mark's Chicago: walking, bicycling & driving tours of
  the city/photographs by Mitchell Canoff; foreword by Mike
  Royko—Fourth edition.
      p.   cm.
  Includes index.
  ISBN 1-55652-197-9 (pa) : $12.95
  1. Chicago (Ill.)—Tours. I. Title. II. Title: Chicago
F548.18.M33   1993
917.73'110443—dc20   93-25222
                                                                CIP

Fourth Edition
Published by Chicago Review Press, Incorporated
814 North Franklin Street
Chicago, Illinois 60610

ISBN 1-55652-197-9
Printed in the United States of America

5 4 3 2 1

CONTENTS

FOREWORD

by Mike Royko

In fine detail and entertainingly, Norman Mark is going to tell you what you can expect to see while walking in various parts of Chicago. But it is the unexpected that can turn an ordinary stroll into something memorable.

Every time I take a walk, I expect to see something unexpected. I don't know what it will be, of course, but I do know that it or he or she will be there.

Depending on the part of town, it might be an imaginative panhandler, reciting a dramatic story of hardship.

Always listen them out. It's worth the time and a few coins. Most tell such good lies, you'll be amazed they avoided becoming advertising executives.

My favorite was Willie the Weeper, who sobbed and wailed and tore his hair while telling strangers that he needed train fare to get his penniless little brothers and sisters (waiting at Union Station) back home, wherever that was.

If you asked him for specifics, he wailed louder, bent as if in agony, and his answers were so racked with hiccups and gulps that he was incoherent.

But the tears were somehow real-huge, glistening drops that poured down his cheeks and soaked his shirt. They were irresistible. At the end of the day, the weeper usually had enough in his pockets to fly a family to Vegas for a weekend.

The last time I saw Willie, he had grown both as a performing artist and a physical specimen. I told him: "Kid, I gave you a dollar when you were just a tyke. Now you are six feet tall. You ought to consider getting a new act."

He choked off a sob, wiped away a tear, and said: "Hey man, beat it or I'll stomp you."

Which reminds me of a prudent rule in taking Chicago walks. Norman Mark will advise you not to carry large sums of money. That's good advice. But do not carry too little, either. Chicago respects the work ethic, and if someone goes to the trouble of trying to rob you, he might be damned disappointed and frustrated if you produce only 65 cents.

Twenty or thirty dollars is a small price to pay to avoid having your hair parted down to the nose.

Not that you should walk in constant dread. I've lived here all my life and have been robbed only once, not counting when my local tax bills arrive. Just avoid dark deserted streets at night, neighborhoods that are obviously mean, and lawyers' offices, and you should be just fine.

Chicago's taverns are among the world's finest and friendliest, and you shouldn't hesitate to visit them. They can provide some of the best unexpected sights. I once saw a man lift a jukebox and dance with it. In another, I saw a woman win a bet by eating the contents of a one-gallon jar of pickled pig's feet, and that was long before Paul Newman did the same with hard-boiled eggs. If you cheer for the home team on TV, don't order fancy mixed drinks or try to cash a check, avoid expressing liberal views on racial or political matters, and don't call the bartender "fellow" or "my good man," you will be accepted. But a little common sense is required. Don't wander into just any tavern when your feet get tired and your throat dry. Don't ever walk into a bar from which people or bottles are being thrown. Keep out if you have to climb over somebody lying in the entrance.

While you are walking, someone might unexpectedly try to sell you something. It might be a flashy wristwatch, a flashy young woman, a flashy young man, or tickets to a church raffle. As a general rule, decline politely and keep walking. Whatever he is selling, you can probably get it cheaper at a regular retail outlet, or even free if you have decent teeth and bathe regularly.

Someone might unexpectedly rush up to you and shake your hand near an elevated train station or a factory gate. Don't be alarmed. He is a candidate for office, and if you assure him that you think he is wonderful and your entire family is voting for him, he'll be happy and will go bother somebody else.

If somebody unexpectedly walks up to you and tries to hand you a dollar, it probably means that it is election day in Chicago, you are near a polling place, and he is a precinct captain. Just tell him you have already voted somewhere else and he'll leave you alone. On the other hand, he might raise the offer to $2, in which case you will have to make up your own mind.

When in Rome, you might get away with it. But around here, it isn't a good idea to get loudly amorous at the sight of a good-looking woman. You'll be mistaken for a fiend and might wind up being charged with a dozen or so unsolved sex crimes. Or she might just spray your face with Mace.

A few other simple rules: stay out of strange pool halls; don't intervene in domestic quarrels that spill into the street; and never argue with a Chicago cop. Nelson Algren, the city's finest writer, once advised against eating in places called "Mom's." I would advise against eating in the swinging restaurants with cutesy-poo names and enough ferns to hide Tarzan.

Visitors will find that Chicago, while having much that is beautiful, has its share of the ugly. Try not to be offended. It is what gives this city so much of its character. And nobody ever explained this as well as Algren:

"It isn't hard to love a town for its greater and lesser towers, its pleasant parks or its flashing ballet. Or its broad and bending boulevards, where the continuous headlights follow, one dark driver after the next, one swift car after another, all night, all night and all night. But you never truly love it till you can love its alleys too. Where the bright and morning faces of old familiar friends now wear the anxious midnight eyes of strangers a long way from home."

Have a nice walk.

PREFACE

I have once again finished the research and writing of this book. Chicago is bigger, better, cleaner, and more fun than the first time around in 1977.

Years ago, when I was a member of the Chicago Council on Foreign Relations Visitor's Bureau, I would scribble directions and suggestions for tourists. After they went off on a Chicago adventure, I would ask myself why someone didn't write a book that did that.

About this same time, I walked from the mid-North side to the *Chicago Daily News*, where I was a feature reporter. When I arrived, I told my editor we could get a good story by just walking through Chicago and talking to people. And so, almost every year, we did just that. We explored Lincoln Avenue, Milwaukee, and Clark Street until that great paper died.

After this book was published, we discovered that it must be rewritten every three or four years to keep the walks up to date. Each time, I tell myself that Chicago has changed more than it ever has. And it's changed again, getting more modern, picking up the pace, tearing down buildings, throwing up skyscrapers, replacing yesterday's hip restaurant with today's hot trend.

What has stayed the same is the people. Chicagoans are still the friendliest, strangest, most humorous, and different collection of folks in America.

This book presents the city in a way I think that Chicago should be shown to everyone—tourist, casual visitor, suburbanite, and city dweller.

Immediately after your first walk, you'll begin to know Chicago under its skin, where it lives, breathes, and smells.

The single most important fact to remember about Chicago is this:
People came here to make money.
They stay here to make money.
Money—and power or clout—runs this town.
Novelist Henry B. Fuller wrote that Chicago was "the only great city in the world to which all its citizens have come for the avowed purpose of making money. There you have its genesis, its growth, its object; and there are but few of us who are not attending to the object very strictly."

They tell the story of Augustus Swift, the Chicago packer, who asked his son, George, then age five, how much was 12 plus 13. The child didn't know and cried, "That's too hard for a little boy."

Swift yelled, "Now, George, listen! If you had 12 cents and I gave you 13 cents, how much would you have?"

George beamed and said, "Oh, a quarter, of course! Why didn't you say you meant money?"

Chicago doesn't lust after fads the way New York does. The city isn't as diffuse or as vague as Los Angeles is. We don't breathe as well as Denver is supposed to, we aren't as smugly or energetically liberal as is San Francisco, we aren't convinced we know what America is the way Dallas or Washington, D.C. do, and we do not have great scenery locked in our back yards like Portland or Seattle. Then again, Chicago isn't as dead as Indianapolis or Cincinnati or as vacant as Milwaukee.

But Chicago does revere the individual—the late Mayor Richard Daley telling reporters to kiss his ass when questioned about city contracts awarded to his family, and Mike Royko's daily columns filled with outrage and respect.

Chicago individuals—Daniel Burnham saving the lakefront; Al Capone slaking our thirst for beer and violence; Clarence Darrow defending the loathed; Jane Addams decreeing that poverty wasn't a sin; Montgomery Ward battling for our parks; Marshall Field saying the customer is always right and meaning it; and some guy saying he's fed up working for someone else and becoming a restaurant or bar owner.

Chicago traditions include:

■ Political corruption. There were charges of vote fraud during Chicago's first mayoral election in 1837, and they have continued ever since. By 1856, there were 1,500 more votes cast than there were eligible voters in town.

■ Immorality. It was said in 1857 that one resident of a Chicago whorehouse had been neither sober nor outdoors for five years, and had been nude for three of them.

■ Telling it true. A local headline about a hanging once blared, "Jerked to Jesus." Another legendary headline is alleged to have proclaimed, "Headless Body of Blond Found."

■ A desire to be first, the best, the biggest, the worst, the richest, and the most powerful.

Before venturing into this wonderful, beautiful, outrageous, crazy, hilarious, vicious, silly hell of a town, most people have a few basic questions:

1. Is it safe?

Chicago is safer than you believe it is. Chicago's crime statistics usually go down—which means only that the statistics are going down, not necessarily that there are fewer actual crimes.

You will be walking through a big city, so be sensible.

A good cop once gave me this advice: don't hold your purse as if it contains a million dollars. If you do, someone might believe you and take it away.

If you are walking down a street and you do not feel safe, you may be right. Quickly return to the better-lit main streets. Or immediately walk down the middle of that street.

Women, young or old, should not walk alone at night. It is preferable to have a companion during the daytime.

Do not worry about the crime syndicate. Although 1,000 syndicate-related deaths occurred from 1919 to 1967, The Boys seldom take amateurs for rides.

Your safety has been a major factor in the creation of these walks. Local residents and police were constantly consulted about the routes. I want my kind of town to welcome you. And I want you to experience Chicago as a town of incredible ethnic diversity and joyous experiences.

You can only know a city by walking through it. Chicago responds to the casual stroller better than most cities.

2. What should I wear?

If you will walk close to the lake, it will generally seem cooler than the weather forecast indicates. If it is winter, dress warmer than you think you ought to. If it is summer, dress in lighter clothes than the joking TV weatherforecasters indicate. If it is raining, wait. It will probably stop before the day ends.

3. How can I find my way?

Chicago has a simple street system. Except for some old, diagonal, Indian trails, such as Lincoln or Milwaukee Avenues, Chicago streets form a grid pattern. State and Madison is zero, with numbers going up to the north, south, east, and west of that. If the numbers are going down, you are heading toward the center of the city. If they are going up, you are gradually leaving town.

4. Is it necessary to act like a Chicagoan while walking?

No. However, if you want to, you may talk through your nose, believe you know everything, dress a little out of style, and every so often say, "Yah, but the city works."

Start taking these walks. You are going to love this town.

—*Norman Mark*

1 SOUTH MICHIGAN AVENUE WALK

Buckingham Fountain to the Cultural Center: What a way to start!

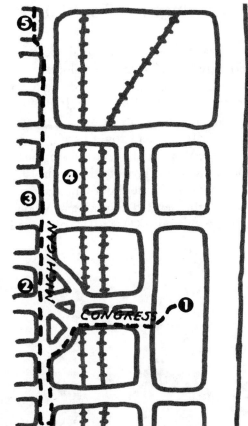

1. Buckingham Fountain
2. Auditorium Building
3. Orchestra Hall
4. Art Institute
5. Chicago Public Library
   (Cultural Center)

Time: About 2 hours, less if you walk quickly.

To get there: Take a #2, #126, or #149 bus to Congress Parkway, also known as the Eisenhower Expressway, get off and walk east to the fountain, about a block away. Or take a #145, #148, or #154 bus, get off at Congress and Michigan, walk east two blocks past the equestrian statues to the fountain. Or take the subway to Van Buren or Harrison, walk to Congress, and then go east.

If you drive: Exit Lake Shore Drive either at Balbo, turning right on Columbus, or at Jackson, turning left on Columbus. Look immediately for a parking space. If you do not find one, go east on Congress (Eisenhower Expressway), bear right and, just over the bridge as you near the refurbished equestrian statues, take a right and park in the city's underground lot. Be sure to lock your car and hide valuables in the trunk.

Buckingham Fountain and Grant Park

We begin at Buckingham Fountain because all explorations of Chicago should begin at its lakefront, its glory.

Buckingham Fountain is, according to some Chicagoans, the largest and best fountain in the world. It probably isn't, but who needs an argument on this point? Any Chicagoan will mention Buckingham Fountain with reverent tones usually reserved for descriptions of the Vatican, the White House, or Buckingham Palace.

The fountain was given to the city in 1927 by Kate Sturges Buckingham, whose grandfather built Chicago's first grain elevator and whose father built the elevated train system. Modeled after the Latona Basin in the gardens of Louis XIV's palace of Versailles, and sitting in a section

Buckingham Fountain

of Grant Park also modeled after Versailles, Buckingham Fountain is 280 feet across the bottom of the pool. That's twice as big as the French original, so there!

The four identical pairs of 20-foot bronze sea horses by French sculptor Marcel Loyau were meant to symbolize the four states that border Lake Michigan. This is not an important fact. I have lived in Chicago most of my life and never knew what those things were meant to be. Now that I know, my appreciation of the fountain has not changed one bit.

The central spout shoots 135 feet in the air, and the pool contains 1.5 million gallons of water, which pump through 133 jets at about 14,000 gallons per minute. What's more important than all those mind-boggling statistics is the fact that Buckingham Fountain can become your personal pleasure spot on earth, where man's and nature's beauty combine in a unique manner for you. The fountain has a delicate, cooling, lung-filling, inspiring beauty all its own, a lakefront jewel set off by a comprehensible skyline.

The fountain operates daily from May 1 to September 30, 11:30 a.m. to 10 p.m. with major, no-holds-barred, challenge-the-rainbows color displays from 9 to 10 p.m. For many years, the display was hand operated from a control station beneath the fountain. Now it's all done by computers, but it's still something to see. As a matter of fact, the fountain is so beloved by Chicagoans that it is safe to say you haven't really visited Chicago until you have looked at it at least once.

Face the skyline; to your right a very long block away stands the Petrillo Bandshell, where there are many free summer concerts. Taste of Chicago, and the Country, Blues, Jazz, and Gospel fests occur in this general area throughout the summer months. Whenever Chicagoans go to the lakefront for a fest, food will accompany the events. Often it will be delicious, occasionally it will be overpriced, and almost always there will be long lines during peak hours. But the music will be terrific—and free!

Less than a half mile from you, just south of the bandshell, Robert Bartlett flew the largest hand-launched kite, a monster 83 feet long with 820 square feet of cloth. It happened on April 24, 1974, as part of the WIND-AM Annual Kite Fly.

Now walk west, toward the skyline along Congress Parkway. Notice, to your right, the seated, brooding, nine-foot statue of Abraham Lincoln, created by Augustus Saint-Gaudens.

The similarity in appearance to the Lincoln Monument in Washington, D.C., stems from the fact that both statues, and most Lincoln statues, were based on the 1860 plaster life masks done of his hands and face by Leonard Volk. However, Saint-Gaudens created this statue partially from memory. He saw Lincoln waving from a carriage during his inauguration and walked by the president's body when he lay in state after his assassination.

Although Saint-Gaudens finished the statue in 1908, it wasn't installed until after his death because his original wax model was destroyed by fire.

Then there was controversy over where to put the statue. John Crerar, a well-known philanthropist, had left the city $2.5 million to build a library and $100,000 for a statue of Lincoln. Some thought the statue should be directly across the street from the library, then at Michigan and Randolph, but one of the South Park commissioners decided that a "court of presidents" would be a better idea. So the Lincoln statue was put in its current spot in Grant Park, and the Park District still has plans to complete the court of presidents by the year 2000 or so, by which time, one hopes, there will be more great presidents from whom to choose.

When I last took this walk, there were beautiful beds of flowers leading to the statue. This area once looked rather seedy and untended. Thank you, Chicago Park District, for the improvements.

Continue west, strolling past the equestrian statues on each side of Congress Plaza. They were created by Ivan Mestrovic and unveiled in

Mestrovic's strong equestrian statue on Congress Plaza

October 1929. Marvel at the strength they portray and remember: the artist wants the viewer to use his or her imagination and add the missing bow and arrow or spear.

Mestrovic was a shepherd in Croatia before being sent to Vienna to study. He became a very successful sculptor, and completed these bronze castings in his studio in Zagreb in 1928, two years after his first visit to Chicago. They are considered his finest works. Mestrovic left Yugoslavia when the communists took over and was the artist-in-residence at Notre Dame University until his death in 1962.

Turn left (south) on Michigan Avenue and continue to walk along Grant Park.

You will quickly notice a sexy, topless statue to the south. The woman, a goddess, has just struck a chord on her lyre. She is standing on a globe with wild beasts transfixed by the power of her music. The statue is a tribute to Theodore Thomas, and it proclaims that "scarcely any man in any land has done so much for the musical education of the people as did Theodore Thomas in this country. The nobility of his ideals. . . ." Well it does go on. The statue is quite sensuous. Perhaps musical education was sexier when Thomas was conductor of the world-famous Chicago Symphony.

Thomas conducted the Chicago Symphony for 13 years until his death in 1905, just three weeks after Orchestra Hall was dedicated. Originally, this statue was on the east side of Michigan Avenue, facing Orchestra Hall.

The sculptor, Albin Polasek, was a Czechoslovakian furniture maker who became so adept at wood carving that he made his models in wood rather than in clay even after he studied in Pennsylvania and Rome. He eventually became head of the sculpture department of the School of the Art Institute.

Up ahead, you'll also see the Augustus Saint-Gaudens 1987 statue of General John A. Logan. The statue honors the Illinois Congressman who, it was said, was "an ambitious civilian who was always on time for wars." However, its lasting fame occurred Wednesday, August 28, 1968, when Chicago had a "police riot" and peace marchers (or hippies or yippies) attempted to climb the statue and were beaten by police. This occurred during the Democratic Convention when protesting crowds surged in front of the Conrad Hilton. The police brutally responded with nightsticks in full view of network television cameras. Writer Shana Alexander described the scene this way: "The baby-blue helmeted police operate like a wolf pack, cutting out one or two demonstrators at a time from the swirling, heaving throng and pounding them into the pavement of Michigan Avenue as the mob with an inarticulate roar falls back into the bright green park. . . ."

Conrad Hilton Hotel

Cross the street to the Conrad Hilton, the subject of a recent $180 million restoration. This grand old hotel is now looking better than it did when it opened in 1927 as the 3,000-room Stephens Hotel. The Hilton became luxurious army barracks for a while, and now has 1,543 rooms, many with two baths.

Look up to the top three floors, known as The Towers, where corporate executives have their own lobby, concierge, honor bar, and twice-daily maid service.

At the very top, there are the Imperial Suites, and their names can be justified because Queen Elizabeth slept there in 1959 during her trip to open the St. Lawrence Seaway. They were added to the hotel by helicopters, which plunked down the prefabricated suites prior to the royal visit. The suites cost $1,500 a night, but that includes spectacular views of the lake and two bedrooms.

For a mere $4,000 a night ($6,000 for two nights on the weekend), you could rent the Crown Imperial Suite, with three bedrooms, five baths, an enormous living room with a grand piano and a see-through fireplace that looks into the study/bar, and a jacuzzi capable of comfortably seating six close friends. The suite comes complete with a butler in a formal tuxedo and a downstairs maid wearing a tasteful black dress with white lace collar and cuffs. On the weekends, the price of the suite includes a dinner for 20 or cocktails for 50. Don't worry, the dining room table can seat that many. The hotel offers free use of a chauffeured limousine with the suite.

By the way, in case the president should want to use the suite, there is a private switchboard that is already hooked up to lines going directly to the White House. In fact, according to those who know the Hilton, this is the *only* hotel in Chicago cleared by the Secret Service for presidential visits because the president can have an entire floor. So, if the president is in town overnight, this is where he'll probably be.

If you are hungry or thirsty, there are five restaurants in the Hilton: Buckingham's, which has a gourmet menu and a harpist; the Pavillion, which is open round the clock; the Lakeside Green, which offers high tea at 3 p.m. and musical entertainment Saturday evenings; the Fast Lane, a deli; and Kitty O'Shea's, an Irish tavern with the requisite beers on tap—Guinness, Harp, Ryan's, and Murphy's.

Before leaving the Hilton, do look around the ornate lobby just behind the front middle entrances. It features murals on the ceiling and gorgeous soft carpeting. This grande dame cleans up quite nicely.

Next turn north, and notice the Blackstone Theater, at 60 East Balbo. It has been a professional theater since it opened for business on New Year's Day, 1910, when there were 34 similar theaters in Chicago. By the time DePaul University purchased it from the Shubert Organization in 1988, there were only three such theaters in Chicago. The Blackstone, once home to Helen Hayes, Geraldine Page, Alfred Lunt, Lynn Fontanne, and Ethel Barrymore, was on its way to becoming a parking lot. Now, after spending more than $1 million to restore it, the Blackstone is safe as the home of the DePaul Theater School.

Sheraton-Blackstone Hotel

After crossing Michigan at Balbo, walk west toward the Blackstone Theater a few feet and enter the Sheraton-Blackstone Hotel, to be greeted by a lobby with huge chandeliers, sculptured plaster, and wood. Reflect for a moment that no one will ever build a lobby like this again (and perhaps try to imagine why anyone would want to in the first place).

In the Mayfair Theater (formerly a ballroom), you will find *Shear Madness*, a delightful comedy-mystery about a murder near a barber shop. The first act sets up the mystery, then the audience joins in for questions during the second act and actually helps solve the murder. This play has become a little gold mine for Marilyn Abrams and Bruce Jordan, the two actors who discovered it one summer years ago. The Chicago production, which celebrated its 10th anniversary on September 22, 1992, holds the Guinness record as the second longest running nonmusical play in American history. First place goes to the Boston production of the same play.

In 1990, when the Boston production surpassed *Life with Father* and made it into the record book, other Guinness record holders gathered here to celebrate. The hotel welcomed the fastest talker (682 words/minute), the fastest tap dancer (28 taps/second), the best balancer of cigar boxes (211 on his chin), and the man who held the record for pogo stick jumping under water. On that day, he merely juggled and yodeled while on a pogo stick—it would have been inconvenient to flood the ballroom.

Just off the lobby, to your left, you'll also see Joe Segal's Jazz Showcase, where six nights a week you can hear some of the finest musicians. The greats that have played this room include Dizzy Gillespie, Art Blakey, and Wynton Marsalis. The showcase, which has been in existence for more than 45 years, has been in this location for more than 13 years. If you're looking for Chicago jazz in a fine setting, you've found it.

This hotel has been the temporary home of 10 presidents during various campaigns and visits. But it is remembered historically as the site of the original smoke-filled room, suite 404-5-6. Around 2 a.m. on a warm evening in 1920, Warren G. Harding was called to these rooms and was told that the nomination for president might be his. He was then told, "We think you should tell us, on your conscience and before God, whether there is anything that might be brought up against you that would embarrass the (Republican) party. . . ."

Many presidential candidates would have been insulted at the suggestion contained in that order, but Harding took about 10 minutes, perhaps considering his mistress(es), his illegitimate child, or the rumor that he had Negro blood. Harding said there wouldn't be any impediment to his becoming president.

Later, *The New York Times* described Harding as "the firm and perfect flower of cowardice and imbecility of the Senatorial cabal," but that didn't prevent him from being elected and leading the second most scandal-prone Republican administration in American history. Historically, first place would have to go to Ulysses Grant. At least before the arrival of Richard Nixon in the White House.

Columbia College

Walk diagonally across the lobby, down some stairs, and out the Michigan Avenue door. Turn left (north), continue up Michigan Avenue to Columbia College at 624 North Michigan. Primarily a school of the arts, it is the place to attend if you wish to major in theater, film, music, dance, art, photography, television, radio, journalism, fiction writing, or arts management. The school has always embraced an open admissions policy, giving the student who has special talents a second chance. Here ACT and SAT test scores are optional for entrance.

Its triumphs, according to the *Chicago Tribune*, include a film department that is considered among the best in the nation and whose students have won three Student Academy Awards in the last decade; a literary anthology, *Hair Trigger*, that beat out Harvard's in a national competition; a dance center in Uptown (a neighborhood six miles to the north of where you are standing) with its own resident company plus the Center for Black Music Research, and a television department that produced its own soap opera for cable systems. Undergraduate tuition in 1993 was $6,564; for comparison sake, the University of Chicago tuition for the same year was more than $18,000.

That Columbia exists at all is a tribute to one man, Mirron "Mike" Alexandroff, who became the college president in 1963, when it had only 175 students and instructors earned $3 per class. It now has nearly 7,000 students. Alexandroff, a bigger-than-life personality, retired in August 1992.

Spertus Museum of Judaica

Continuing north, you will soon stand before the Maurice Spertus Museum of Judaica, at 618 South Michigan.

This museum has a permanent room dedicated to the memory of the 6 million Jews killed in Nazi Germany, the Bernard and Rochelle Zell Holocaust Museum, which displays, among other things, a concentration camp uniform and soap made from human fat.

The Artifact Center, designed for students grades 1 through 12, offers a chance to visit a re-creation of an archaeological dig in the Middle East, including a 3,000-year-old marketplace, an Israelite house, and a workshop. Mornings are reserved for groups, but the center is open for visitors Sunday through Thursday, 1:30 to 4:30 p.m.

The museum, with its many visiting exhibits, is open Sunday through Thursday, 10 a.m. to 5 p.m.; Friday, 10 a.m. to 3 p.m.; closed Saturday. Admission is $3.50 for adults; $2.00 for seniors and children.

I once took a course in Jewish mysticism there. One of the most memorable fables concerned Rebbe Zusia, who said before he died, "When I shall face the celestial tribunal, I shall not be asked why I was not Abraham, Jacob, or Moses. I shall be asked why I was not Zusia."

After a moment or two to ponder whether you are entirely the person you really are, continue walking to the north.

Americana Congress Hotel

You'll shortly arrive at a second Columbia College building, with the Museum of Contemporary Photography on the first and mezzanine floors of 600 South Michigan. The museum is free and open to the public year-round except during August. Founded in 1984, with a permanent collection of 3,400 prints from 440 photographers, it is unique in the Midwest for its exclusive commitment to photography.

Next, continue north and find the Americana Congress Hotel, at 532 South Michigan. It was here that industrialist J. Pierpont Morgan is supposed to have imbibed a bit much and fallen into the crystal fountain. The presidential suite, complete with a bathroom larger than most hotel rooms, is available for $500 a day.

Auditorium Theater

Now cross Congress, with its always growling traffic rushing away from or toward the lake, and turn left, walking west toward a large sign reading "Auditorium." Enter the foyer and look above the lobby doorways to the six stained glass windows there, one of the earliest public works of Frank Lloyd Wright. You can peek through the windows into the lobby, but the warmth of the Auditorium itself will escape you. Unless you are part of a group of 10 or more and arrange a tour, the only way to see the Auditorium is to buy a ticket for an event there.

The Auditorium Theater was first opened to great fanfare on December 9, 1889. At the time, it cost 25 cents to take an elevator to the top of its 270-foot tower, then the highest point in Chicago.

Before the Auditorium Theater was completed, the Republicans held their national convention here in 1888 and, under a temporary roof, nominated Benjamin Harrison.

Remember, you are standing in and near a tribute to the indomitable wills of at least three people—the 1889 architects Louis Sullivan and Dankmar Adler (with an assist from Wright, earning $25 a week), and Mrs. Bea Spachner, who helped raise the money to restore what Frank Lloyd Wright called "the greatest room for music and opera in the world—bar none."

On November 25, 1910, Mary Garden performed *Salome* there, and the chief of police almost closed the show, saying, "Miss Garden wallowed around like a cat in a bed of catnip. . . ." Billy Sunday, the

Auditorium Theater: "The greatest room for music in the world"

preacher famed for attempting to close Chicago down, condemned Miss Garden on Monday and took her out for an ice-cream soda on Tuesday.

For true nutty behavior by an opera performer, we must pause to remember P. Brignoli, a Chicago favorite who flourished just before the

Auditorium opened. Brignoli never allowed prima donnas to touch him, never did anything on Fridays, was frightened of the number 13, and carried an old stuffed deer's head with him as a child would a teddy bear. After talking and singing to it, he would place it on his window sill and order it to bring good weather. If the weather the next day turned out well, Brignoli would pet his deer. On lousy days, he would box its ears and refuse to speak to it. By all accounts he was a good singer, so no one cared what he did off stage to his mangy deer's head.

The Auditorium has featured the performances of Rosa Raisa, Marian Anderson, and Adelina Patti. On November 18, 1919, Amelita Galli-Curci premiered in *Rigoletto*. The audience made her famous overnight because it "rose up, shouted, screamed, stamped, stood on its figurative head and otherwise demeaned itself as no staid, sophisticated Saturday afternoon audience ever (had) acted before or since," one reviewer noted.

Then came World War II, and Adler and Sullivan's acoustically perfect hall was painted red and turned into a home for miniature golf and bowling. After more than a million men and women in uniform were entertained there from 1942 to 1945, the wrecking crews waited in the wings. They were defeated by Mrs. John V. (Bea) Spachner, a short lady blessed with unyielding determination. With architect Harry Weese cutting corners and paring budgets, Mrs. Spachner and others raised $3 million, restored the Auditorium, and reopened it on October 31, 1967, with a performance by the New York City Ballet.

The modernizations have continued. Before *Les Miserables* brought in the French Revolution, $500,000 was spent refurbishing the seats. Before *Phantom* floated on a candle-lit lake, more than $1.2 million went to upgrading the backstage area. Before *Miss Saigon* took us back to Vietnam, $600,000 was spent on the front entrance so that it now resembles how it looked in 1889.

Roosevelt University

Now retrace your steps, returning to Michigan Avenue, turn left, and enter Roosevelt University. Try to ignore the modern-looking chandeliers in the lobby and imagine what that grand staircase before you must have looked like in 1889!

In 1945, just as the troops were coming home from World War II, Roosevelt University was founded as a school devoted to providing equal educational opportunities. It was a time when that was difficult to find.

This fine, urban school has remained steadfast in that goal. Today, more than 35 percent of the students are black, Hispanic, or Asian, and the average age of the students, most of whom receive financial aid, is 29 years old.

The 40,000 alumni include the late Harold Washington, the first black mayor of Chicago; Herbie Hancock and Ramsey Lewis, two incredible jazz musicians; Matt Rodriguez and Fred Rice, two of Chicago's chiefs of police; plus the presidents of the Coldwell Banker Residential group, Macy's, and the Massachusetts Institute of Technology; and the chairman of the Board of Trade.

When I taught journalism and free-lance writing there, each class was an adventure because the students came from so many different cultures and generations.

However, no matter how fine the instructors or students, if you go to the beautifully restored Fainman Lounge on the mezzanine atop the staircase, you may notice that the television sets are tuned to the soap operas. It only means that, in some respects, Roosevelt is not unique among college campuses.

Fine Arts Building

Return to Michigan Avenue, walk north (to your left again; the building numbers should be going down as you walk) to 410 South Michigan and enter the Fine Arts Building, which proclaims above its inner doorway, "All passes—Art alone endures."

Walk inside through the sets of doors. Around the corner on your left, read the list of tenants, which should include ballet and opera companies; a chorus or two; a modern dance studio; teachers of piano, voice, guitar, cello, and art; churches; architects; hypnotists; yoga practitioners; the Fine Arts Denture Clinic; a cartoonist; and assorted kooks. The Fine Arts Theater (formerly the Studebaker) lives up to the name by presenting the finest artistic films around, some with subtitles and some with impossible English accents that often need subtitles! It also offers American films for special audiences. For instance, this movie theater is a favorite with my youngest son, Joel, because it was the first Chicago theater to offer *Spinal Tap*—Rob Reiner's spoof of the rock-and-roll life.

Opened in 1893, the Fine Arts Building was once the center of Chicago culture. Frank Baum and W. D. Denslow created the *Wizard of Oz* here. *The Little Review* was published here by Margaret Anderson.

Despite four orders from the U.S. Post Office that the magazine be burned, Ms. Anderson continued printing sections of James Joyce's *Ulysses*, and the censorship battle, which began in 1918, continued for three years.

The Little Theater movement in America was founded here in a 91-seat Grecian Temple, where Chicagoans got their first views of works by Shaw and Strindberg. And there are still art studios on the 10th floor, where sculptor Lorado Taft once worked.

Outside, George Mitchell's Artists Snack Shop has a sidewalk cafe with astroturf and white tables and chairs—a nice place to sit and observe Michigan Avenue or listen to opera singers practicing in the Fine Arts. When *Phantom of the Opera* was being performed in the Auditorium Theater, the Artists Snack Shop constantly played the CD.

Now continue to walk north on Michigan one block.

Railway Exchange Building

As you stand at Jackson and Michigan, look to the west to the Railway Exchange Building, the 17-story structure at 80 East Jackson. Notice that this once-dusty building is now clean, handsome, and grand. Walk past the frescoes honoring "civilization" and "progress" and notice the gleaming white marble lobby floor and the soft skylight. Thank you, restorers.

This building is now the home of the Chicago Architecture Foundation, which offers more than 50 architectural tours of Chicago costing from $5 to $20 plus lunchtime lectures on Wednesday at 12:15 p.m. for a $2 donation. For recorded information call 312-922-TOUR.

In 1904, architect Daniel Burnham's workroom was located on the top floor of this building and, in 1909, Burnham and Edward H. Bennett released "The Plan of Chicago," which attempted to mold the future of the city. Burnham, as fine a salesman as he was a city planner, said, "Make no little plans. They have no magic to stir men's blood."

Burnham's plan envisioned the lakefront as a playground for Chicagoans with manmade islands there for recreation. He saw a modern highway system, railroad tracks coming into the city in an orderly manner, and so on. Eventually, before the Depression, World War II, and greed stopped things, about half his vision became reality. Because of Burnham, Michigan Avenue was widened, new bridges were thrown over the Chicago River, railroad tracks were sunk below ground level, the shoreline was changed, and new park lands were bought. The shorelines of almost every other major city on the globe are either devoted to shipping, industry, or private ownership. Most of Chicago's lakefront is parks because of the foresight of Daniel Burnham.

Burnham wrote, "The lakefront by right belongs to the people. It affords their one great unobstructed view, stretching away to the horizon, where water and clouds seem to meet. No mountains or high hills enable us to look over broad expanses of the earth's surface; and perforce we must come even to the margin of the lake for such a survey of nature. These views calm thoughts and feelings, and afford escape from the petty things of life . . . Not a foot of its shores should be appropriated by individuals to the exclusion of the people." Alas, his words are too often forgotten.

Before we get to Orchestra Hall, we pass Sherry-Brenner Ltd. at 226 South Michigan. It is a famous stringed instrument store specializing in imported classical guitars and violins. Their violins are priced from $200 to $200,000, although they do own a $1.5 million Stradivarius. They also do much of the repair and restoration for the Chicago Symphony's instruments. Jim Sherry, the owner, doesn't remember every famous person he's sold a guitar to since he doesn't keep up on rock music, but he does know that Andres Segovia, Roy Orbison, Robert Plant, and Chet Atkins play his instruments. If you talk to him, he probably won't drop many more names than that.

Orchestra Hall

Continuing up Michigan Avenue, we arrive at Orchestra Hall, at 220 South Michigan, home of the world-renowned Chicago Symphony Orchestra, with the names of Bach, Mozart, Beethoven, Schubert, and Wagner over the entrance. This has not always been a peaceful place. Desire DeFauw, conductor from 1943 to 1947, was driven out of town by criticism of his programs, conducting, musicianship, and clothes. Chicagoans take their music seriously!

These days, the Chicago Symphony ranks among the very best in the world.

Back in 1971, when the Symphony returned from its first European tour, the city decided to embrace its national treasure in a most enthusiastic way. City workers turned out for a parade to welcome home the "World Champion of Orchestras." And the Chicago Press Club, unable to agree on a worthy individual, named the symphony the club's Person of the Year.

Since then, it has been recognized for its excellence. For instance, a good trivia question is: Who has more Grammys, the recording industry's award for outstanding achievement, than any other performer? As of 1990, Sir Georg Solti, the former conductor of the Chicago Symphony, had been awarded 28 Grammys, three times as many as Frank Sinatra or Barbra Streisand. Michael Jackson has a mere dozen. Sir Georg's nearest pop music competitor, Henry Mancini, has 20 Grammys.

The Art Institute

You'll see the Art Institute across the street. It's guarded by two lions designed in 1894 by Edward L. Kemeys, who discovered that he was a sculptor while chopping down trees in Central Park in New York. He happened to see an artist modeling animal heads at the zoo, decided he could do as well, and eventually succeeded.

The lions may look identical, but they are not. One is supposed to be on the prowl, the other stands in an attitude of defiance. Do not believe any Chicagoan who claims they only roar when a virgin walks by.

Art Institute: The steps to a treasure of art

The Art Institute is also the place where a six-year-old visitor created one of the finest Chicago trivia questions: What is the only Chicago building with the names of the Ninja Turtles cartoon characters incised above its doorway? If you look above the lions, you'll see Leonardo (da Vinci), Michael Angelo (which appears as two words on the lintel), Donatello, and Rafael. Actually, our young visitor tugged on his father's hand and shouted, "Look, Ninjas!"

The School of the Art Institute was raided in 1988 by aldermen and police when a picture of the recently deceased Mayor Harold Washington was displayed showing him wearing white lingerie, including a bra, bikini panties, garter belt, and hose. The bachelor mayor had been the subject of vicious rumors while he was in office, and his political cronies were trying to save his reputation by attacking the First Amendment.

Three local aldermen damaged the painting while detaining it. In 1992, a federal judge ruled that the aldermen and the former police superintendent had violated the 1st, 4th, and 14th Amendment rights of the artist, David K. Nelson, Jr. The aldermen claimed they were trying to prevent public disorder, but they were actually embarrassing the city with their lack of knowledge of the constitution.

In 1989, this entranceway was the site of large, angry demonstrations against a student art exhibit. "Dread" Scott Tyler asked for opinions about the proper way to display the flag. But to enter your views in the book provided there, you'd have to stand on an American flag. Politicians and veterans were outraged, and a drive began to have a constitutional amendment prohibiting flag desecration.

In another incident, the embarrassed Art Institute finally admitted in 1990 that Georgia O'Keeffe's *East River from the Shelton*, worth up to $500,000, had been "lost" since 1970. They did not want to use the word "stolen."

You may be getting tired by now and should probably save an Art Institute tour for another day. However, if you're feeling energetic, the riches of the Art Institute are available to you through a free pamphlet titled "Not to Be Missed" at the information desk.

The maps in the pamphlet will guide you to Grant Wood's *American Gothic*, and paintings by El Greco, Rembrandt, Renoir, and others. But the maps are terrible, which is an advantage; because of the confusion they cause, you will see many more paintings than you expected.

Refreshments are straight ahead, through Gunsaulus Hall and down the stairs. When you've found Louise Nevelson's *American Dream*, you will be in front of the delightful Garden Restaurant and McKinlock court, with its *Fountain of the Titans* by Carl Milles. This outdoor dining area is open May 23 through Labor Day, with the typical Chicago provision "weather permitting." There is also The Promenade restaurant near the transplanted Stock Exchange room.

The Art Institute is justly famous for its riches. There are rooms with walls overfilled with paintings by Manet, Degas, Corot, Renoir, Cezanne, Monet, Gauguin, Seurat, Matisse, and others. Many of these paintings were collected with typical Chicago hustle. Rich Chicagoans saw no reason to collect masterpieces any differently than the way they bought hogs. One trustee, using techniques perfected by Gustavus Swift in the stockyards, bought four works of art before breakfast and before an agent from the Louvre could get to them.

In 1890, some Chicago collectors confessed to a New York newspaper that they weren't sure what they bought (the paintings they brought back included works by Rembrandt, Franz Hals, and Meindert Hobbema). The paper concluded that the paintings probably cost "$1,000 a foot" and that Chicago would greet them "in huge floats, drawn by a team of milk-white Berkshire hogs. . . ."

By all means seek out a Chicago icon—Georges Seurat's *A Sunday on La Grande Jatte—1884.* Completed in 1886, this painting, created by applying thousands of tiny dots to a huge canvas, was the subject of a Broadway musical titled *Sundays in the Park with George.* Since Chicagoans love to beat New York out of anything and everything, we proudly remember that the New York Metropolitan Museum of Art could have owned it, but passed on the opportunity. Chicago collector Charles Bartlett bought it for $20,000 in 1924 and gave it to the museum two years later. It has become so valuable that the Art Institute trustees have stipulated it can never be loaned to any other museum. If you're going to see it, you've got to see it here.

What I like about the Art Institute is that it is constantly reinventing itself by adding wings, refurbishing and rehanging collections, and so on. It is never a static, staid museum.

The newest addition is the $2.3 million renovation of the Junior Museum. Now known as the Kraft General Foods Education Center, it displays a dozen works of art, videos, computer games, and puzzles. There are storytelling areas with more than 1,000 books, artist demonstrations, and a family room where children suffering from "museum fatigue" can go with their relatives. The center is free with regular museum admission.

Suggested admission is $6.00 for adults, $3.00 for students, children, and senior citizens, but Tuesday is always free. It is one of the top five most-visited American museums.

The Art Institute is open weekdays, 10:30 a.m. to 4:30 p.m.; on Tuesdays it remains open until 8 p.m.; Saturdays, 10:00 a.m. to 5:00 p.m.; Sundays and holidays, noon to 5:00 p.m.

A Magnificent Ghost,
a Genius Architect

Continue north on Michigan Avenue and you'll pass the Chicagoland Chamber of Commerce offices at 130 South Michigan, where polite folks will answer questions about hotels.

Walking north, you will pass the former Charlie Center at 112 South Michigan. This 18-story building was developed in 1907, renovated for $25 million, and reopened as an athletic club in 1986 before being sold to the Art Institute in 1992 for use as a student dormitory.

If you continue north, you will shortly be at Monroe and Michigan. If you look to the northwest, you'll see the 14-story, Tudor Gothic building known as the University Club, built in 1909. Frank Lloyd Wright called this structure "an effete gray ghost."

The facade of the Gage Building, at 18 South Michigan, was designed by Louis Sullivan, who said "form follows function," meaning what's going on inside the building should be reflected on the outside. Sullivan was a master at intricate adornment of buildings. He was also egotistical, arrogant, tactless, and died in a South Side flophouse in 1925 convinced he was a failure.

History: Ward Defends
the Lakefront

Crossing Madison Street, we come to the rather dingy facade of the Tower Building, at 6 North Michigan. And it is here that we should remember A. Montgomery Ward, another individual who stood against nearly everyone in his time to win something valuable for generations to come.

In 1890, Ward looked down on Michigan Avenue from his offices in the Tower Building and saw, to the east, shacks, garbage, circus litter, rotting freight cars, and an armory used for masquerade balls thrown by Chicago aldermen and featuring fallen women (or, rather, ones then in the midst of falling). Ward is supposed to have shouted to his lawyer, "Merrick, this is a damned shame! Go and do something about it." They found a notation on an ancient map, scribbled by the commissioners who created the Illinois and Michigan Canal. The ground between Michigan Avenue and the lake from Madison Street to 12th Street had the notation, "Public Ground—A Common to Remain Forever Open, Clear, and Free of Any Buildings, or Other Obstruction Whatsoever."

To make that come true, Ward spent $50,000 and 20 years of his life. He repeatedly went to court and he eventually won. The Illinois Supreme Court ruled that no building could be built east of Michigan Avenue unless all property owners along the avenue agreed to its construction.

The Art Institute was allowed to remain east of Michigan Avenue only after the signature of Mrs. Sarah Daggett, the one owner who refused to agree to its being there, was forged by her husband. The courts of the 1890s upheld a husband's right to do this! Such events did occur in the days before women's liberation.

Ward hated publicity and didn't particularly like it when the *Chicago Tribune* called him a "human icicle." In 1909, when the issue was finally decided, Ward gave out a single interview. He said, "I fought for the poor people of Chicago, not the millionaires . . . Here is park frontage on the lake, comparing favorably with the Bay of Naples, which city officials would crowd with buildings, transforming the breathing spot for the poor into a showground of the educated rich. I do not think it is right." He then added, perhaps wistfully, "Perhaps I may yet see the public appreciate my efforts. But I doubt it."

Chicago Public Library Cultural Center

From here it is a short walk to the Chicago Cultural Center, at 78 East Washington, which ends this tour.

Today, the Cultural Center, built in 1897, is a joy to behold. This wasn't always so. When Nobel Prize-winning author Saul Bellow studied there in the '30s and '40s, the inside of what was the Chicago Public Library Main Building was overheated, painted an ugly green, and dirty—a depressing place.

Carrara marble stairway in the Cultural Center

That began to change in 1973, when the library announced plans to move its books. Later, after years of controversy and discussion, after thousands of frustrated scholars complained that they could barely find the temporary central library let alone the books, a new building was finally created—the Harold Washington Public Library, which is part of the State Street Walk.

The old central library building stands on historical turf. Dearborn Park, where Abraham Lincoln spoke in favor of the new Republican Party and against slavery in 1856, was on this property until 1892.

There was once a grandstand across Michigan Avenue and a baseball field for the Chicago White Stockings, who became Anson's Colts, and eventually, because they were so young, the Chicago Cubs. Thus, the White Stockings are ancestors of the Cubs and not the Chicago White Sox.

Over 100,000 people cheered the White Stockings when the team came home after beating Memphis 157 to 1 in the 1880s. In 1876, with the help of a player named Billy Sunday, the team won the National League championship.

Enter the Cultural Center by walking to your left (west) on the north side of Washington. This entrance resembles a Roman temple. The

Randolph Street entrance is more Grecian. Ideas for bits and pieces of the entire building were taken from famous buildings elsewhere—it was the style of the day.

Just inside the door, above you, the stairway forms a Venetian Bridge. The Carrara marble is decorated with rare, dark green marble from Connemara, Ireland, with designs by the House of Louis Tiffany. Once a dark, grimy entrance, today, after a soap-and-water bath, the place sparkles. Notice the mosaics under the landings and the sea green lights if you walk to the far right or left before going up the stairs.

Walk slowly up to the third floor and then just look at that huge Tiffany dome, magnificent, overdone, a little ugly, but utterly original and backlit after being covered over for decades. Sit down in a comfortable chair in Preston Bradley Hall (named after a local minister who served on the library board for more than 50 somnolent years). Rest, contemplate an old building saved from destruction, and perhaps enjoy one of the many programs that take place almost daily in the hall. Every Wednesday at 12:15 p.m. the Dame Myra Hess Memorial Concerts here are broadcast live on WFMT–98.7.

Dance and theater companies are in residence in the center, which is also host to the Lyric Opera lectures, big band and classical music concerts, book signings, art shows, the Savvy Traveler seminars, special events for people over age 55, lectures, forums, and other events.

For instance, during Hispanic Heritage month, there were Puerto Rican, Panamanian, Mexican, and Colombian dancers; Bolivian, Colombian, Argentinean, and Cuban films; Andean folk music; Spanish opera; Latino theater and poetry readings; Mexican puppets; and lectures on Mexican murals.

If you call (312)346-3478, you can enjoy the arts even when the Cultural Center is closed. That's the Dial-a-Poem line, which offers round-the-clock readings.

Take the elevator to the fourth floor, ponder the $12 million spent by the Public Buildings Commission to bring this building into the twentieth century (thank you, Commission, for the air-conditioning), walk by the iron fourth floor landing, modeled after the Bridge of Sighs in Venice, and walk to the south end of the building.

The doors you walk through, we are told, are very like those in the Erechtheum at Athens. The second room you'll pass through is modeled after an assembly hall in the Doge's Palace in Venice. If you look closely at the "pillars" in the center of the wall facing the windows, you'll see an almost indiscernible line about 12 feet above the floor. When the old wall radiators were taken down because modern heating was installed, it was discovered that the false pillars on the walls did not extend below the radiators. New "ancient" pillars were built to approximately match the old ones, and the line indicates where they were joined.

Now walk down to the second floor and the location of the old GAR Museum, where you'll see a second Tiffany Dome, with more yellow in it and with more of a spidery design. Walk on down and out door to Randolph St., having seen a nineteenth-century building gloriously entering the twentieth century. The floor here is lit from below with various colored glass bricks.

The Cultural Center is open Monday through Thursday, 9 a.m. to 7 p.m.; Friday, 9 a.m. to 6 p.m.; Saturday, 9 a.m. to 5 p.m.; Sunday, noon to 5 p.m.

This ends your South Michigan Avenue tour.

Rest. Your feet deserve it!

2 MID–MICHIGAN AVENUE WALK

Randolph to Ontario: Historic flophouses to flipping bridges

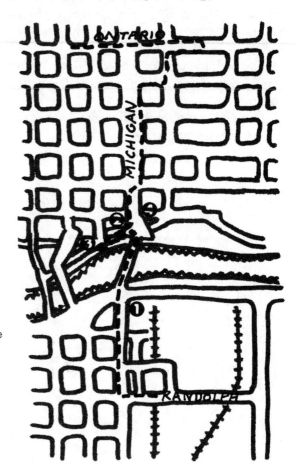

1. Fort Dearborn Massacre Site
2. Wrigley Building
3. *Sun-Times*
4. Tribune Tower

Time: About 2 hours, more if you find a restaurant you enjoy.

To get there: Many CTA buses go by Michigan and Randolph, where this walk begins, including the #1, #2, #3, #16, #58, #131, and #157. In addition, the Illinois Central Railroad stops there, and the CTA subway stops at Randolph and State just two blocks west of Michigan. There are also city parking lots with entrances just off Michigan.

Prudential and
Standard Oil Buildings

This walk begins with huge buildings and ends with fine restaurants. It is a stroll up an avenue built for walkers who look smart, carefree, and sassy.

The Prudential Building looms before you as you stand at Michigan and Randolph, with Prudential's trademark, a 65-ton sculpture of the Rock of Gibraltar, as part of this building.

Beaubien Court, the one-block street just west of the Prudential Building, and next to the Chicago Bar and Grill, is named after a wildly irresponsible, but charming, early Chicagoan, Mark Beaubien, who had 23 children by three wives. When he was supposed to be running the ferry across the Chicago river, he was off racing horses. When he opened the town's first hotel, which was in existence when Chicago incorporated in 1833, he let the kitchen run itself, often sang an endless ballad about the fall of Detroit, and said, "I play the fiddle like the devil and keep the hotel like hell." His beds consisted of a blanket, which he'd give to new guests, only to steal it back from them as soon as they went to sleep, so as to have it available for the next guest. Mark never ran out of beds. Sounds like the kind of guy who only deserves a one-block street.

The Standard Oil Building, behind (to the east of) the Prudential Building, was once the world's tallest marble-clad structure, with 8,000 tons of Carrara marble covering this structure. A strike of marble cutters in Italy in 1974 stopped construction of this building, and it stood half nude for several months.

Twenty years later, the seldom balmy Chicago climate had warped the marble. All 43,000 white Carrara marble panels had to be replaced by North Carolina granite before the marble fell off the building and someone was squashed on ground level. As you walk nearby, you will be forgiven for not strolling directly under the walls although the current slabs are firmly in place.

As if that wasn't bad enough luck, after donating 1,000 tons of marble chips to Governors State University, Standard Oil was accused of killing hundreds of carp, crappie, and bluegill in a nearby pond. One theory was that an adhesive on the marble leached into the water. But a fish pathologist eventually cleared the marble and Standard Oil. Bacteria killed the fish.

The sculpture in the reflecting pool is a bunch of rods intended to combine the sculptor Harry Bertoia's memory of swaying wheat fields with the music "of a wind-strummed Aeolian harp." Bertoia's work is overshadowed by street noises, but it does make clanging noises when the wind blows.

History: Jake Lingle Shot

Return to Michigan Avenue and note the entrance to the Illinois Central Railroad platform off Randolph and think about crime.

Chicago Tribune crime reporter Jake Lingle was shot in this IC underpass by a tall, young, blond man on June 9, 1930. Chicago criminals had always been warned they would be in serious trouble if they killed a policeman or reporter, so Lingle's death was shocking. Then it was discovered that, on a salary of $5 a week, he had a suite in a downtown hotel, a West Side home, and a Wisconsin summer place. He wore tailor-made suits, English shoes, and had a $100,000 account with his stockbroker. Clearly, this young man knew how to save money.

It was later whispered that Lingle, a close pal of Al Capone, took $25,000 of the Syndicate's money and, instead of bribing a judge, lost it on the stock market. Lingle allegedly later told "the boys" that they "can't touch a newspaperman." It was a fatal mistake.

Walk north on Michigan Avenue. Mills Audio/Video at 174 North Michigan has been in business for 52 years. It is the place to shop if you want to watch movies at home with the same quality you would find in theaters. This was an important consideration for two local movie critics. Both Roger Ebert and Gene Siskel have bought their home movie set-ups from the folks at Mills. It might be the one thing both agree on. Also at 174 North Michigan is the Joseph Outlet, a bargain shoe store where, according to *Chicago* magazine, you can "find Donna Karan mules two-thirds off retail, Anne Klein II flats, Escada pumps, Amalfi, Ferragamo, and other joys at 20 to 65 percent off."

The colorful object at Michigan and Lake in the Boulevard Towers Plaza is *Splash* by Jerry Peart. It is not a tribute to the Darryl Hannah movie of the same name. Dedicated in 1986, it is by an artist born in Arizona and a Chicagoan since the early 1970s. Peart says his works make people smile.

About two blocks north you'll arrive at Illinois Center. It's across the street to the east at 233 North Michigan, just up South Water Street. If it is raining, dash inside and explore the confusing passageways that connect this multibuilding development, allowing you to walk dry shod to the east toward the lake.

However, if the weather is good, stroll up Michigan Avenue, and notice the Beehive Shoeworks at 320 North Michigan, next door to the Me and Mrs. Lee Chinese Food establishment. At one time, Newbury Muffins, one of the earliest places to cash in on Chicago's recent muffin craze, was in this location. Alas, muffins may go, but shoes and Chinese food seem to be here to stay.

It's Natural, at 324 North Michigan, is a well-lit, friendly, clean health food store with employees who look riotously healthy. This is quite amazing since many people who work in such stores look as though they need a quick jolt of vitamin-everything.

The last time I visited this store, the clerk at the juice bar, a peppy woman who did not appear to be a day over 30 and who boasted she was a grandmother, convinced me to have a shot of wheat grass extract for "a quick energy kick." It looked and tasted green and I will not report on its alleged "cleansing" qualities.

The juice bar has a happy hour from 4 p.m. until closing when all drinks are only $1. I recommend the energy shake, although the carrot/apple juice was quite tasty.

The store has vitamins that are taken off the shelf if not sold in 90 days, wondrous massage oil, sandwiches, fruit, and sinful chocolate-looking bars. The buyer, Kathee Latour, says, "We simply do not accept the fact that we should be tired in the morning or have three colds a year." Then she tried to convince me to return for more wheat grass extract.

Continue north, cross the street, and stop in the 333 North Michigan Building to see the art moderne elevator doors by Edgar Miller (unless art moderne elevator doors bore you, in which case you can skip this particular thrill).

Fort Dearborn Massacre

Upon reaching Michigan and Wacker, look at your feet and you'll see the outlines of Fort Dearborn etched in the pavement. The fort was evacuated on August 15, 1812, and everyone who left was involved in the subsequent massacre.

The fort was surrounded by Pottawatomie Indians friendly to the British, and the troops weren't very happy about leaving. As they opened the gates at 9 a.m., they struck up the "Dead March." Famed Indian scout

Captain William Wells blackened his face, symbolic of the fact that he was already a dead man. It was not the happiest parade Michigan Avenue has ever seen.

About 500 Indians attacked at 18th Street and the Lake, killing 24 soldiers, 12 civilian men, two women, and a dozen children. The Indians lost only 15 braves and were still bragging about the victory 125 years later. The wife of the commander of the fort was eventually bought back from captivity for a mule and 10 bottles of whiskey, which sounds cheap unless it was good whiskey. Later the white man got his revenge on the Pottawatomie by gypping them out of everything but their loin cloths by 1835.

The 1928 sculptural relief panels on the bridge houses are very heroic, meaningful, and dull. Facing south, on the west side of the bridge, is the relief titled *Defense*, which pictures Fort Dearborn's inhabitants being led to safety by an Indian scout. The relief to the east is *Regeneration*, commemorating the Chicago Fire of 1871.

On the north side of the bridge and on the east side of Michigan Avenue is *The Discoverers*, portraying Louis Jolliet and Jacques Marquette who stopped in Chicago, and Rene Robert Cavalier-Sieur de LaSalle and Henri Tonti, who explored the Mississippi. The west side has *The Pioneers*, which depicts John Kinzie, a fur trader who bought a

Looking west on the Chicago River

log cabin in 1804 from Jean Baptiste Pointe Du Sable. These two reliefs were created by James Earle Fraser, who designed the buffalo nickel with an Indian head on the reverse side in 1913.

Cross the Michigan Avenue bridge. It is one of Chicago's 43 draw-bridges, which are raised and lowered about 30,000 times a year.

Look to the southeast side of this bridge and remember September 20, 1992. On that Sunday, while in the midst of a $31 million rehabilitation project on the bridge, one side of the 1,200-ton span flipped upward crushing a 40-ton crane. The crane's 285-pound wrecking ball was flipped off the bridge, bounced once on Wacker Drive, leaving a four-inch crater in the pavement, and landed on a blue Ford Escort owned by Jesus Lopez, a bridge maintenance worker. The ball tore through the rear window and came to rest in the back seat. Lopez lived. Six people were injured in the accident, none seriously.

The bridge, which normally takes 45 seconds to open (each span with the concrete decking weighs more than 6.5 million pounds), zipped to a perpendicular position in less than 5 seconds.

At the time, Bob Arzbaecher, a controller from Milwaukee, was on the river at the helm of his 30-foot boat, the *Onesimus*, named after a slave converted to Christianity by the Apostle Paul. It has a 35-foot mast, requiring the bridges to be raised. This time the bridge went up in record speed.

To bring down the bridge from its perpendicular position, a barge, which had been used as part of an oil rig platform in the Gulf of Mexico, was brought up the river and filled with 435,000 gallons of water to increase its weight from 1 million pounds to 4 million pounds. Cables were tied to steel brackets welded to the bridge, which was then pulled down to its normal position seven weeks after it flipped upward. In other words, this runaway bridge had to be lassoed into position.

In 1922, two years after this bridge opened, a safe cracker by the name of Vincent "Skimmer" Drucci swerved around the gates as the bridge was opening and tried to jump his car over the widening three-foot gap between sides of the bridge. He made it, with the cops jumping the bridge close on his tail, but his car crashed into the south end of the bridge.

Chicago bridges became so famous that when Paul Muni escaped in the movie *I Am a Fugitive From a Chain Gang*, he went to Chicago to work on the bridges. Also, bridges that don't work are another Chicago tradition. The first bridge, built at Dearborn Street in 1834, once got stuck for two days. Then, in 1849, a flood swept away every bridge in town. Most of the replacements were burned in the 1871 fire.

The north side of this bridge was the beginning of an Indian trail that once led to Green Bay, Wisconsin. Any trace of this trail has been obliterated.

Wrigley Building

Cross to the west side of Michigan and pass between the two Wrigley Building Towers, the approximate site of the home of Jean Baptiste Pointe Du Sable, a black, and Chicago's first settler. Some historians say that Jean Baptiste Guillory (or Guyari or Guary or Gary) was here first, but he didn't stay long and no one knows too much about him, so First Settler Award usually goes to Du Sable. Du Sable's cabin was 40 feet long, and he owned 44 hens, 38 hogs, 30 cattle, two calves, and two mules—Chicago's first tycoon.

The Wrigley Building, once the home of such radio shows as "The WBBM Air Theater," "Ma Perkins," and "The Guiding Light," is the corporate headquarters of the world's largest chewing gum manufacturer. At one time, the 16th-floor boardroom of the William Wrigley, Jr. Chewing Gum Co. also housed the world's finest chewing gum wrapper museum. It was a secret collection, not open to the public, and the result of salesmen around the world sending sample wrappers back to the home office.

William Wrigley, Jr., founder of the chewing gum empire, began as a soap salesman who gave away baking soda as a premium. Folks loved the baking soda so much that he began selling the stuff, and gave away gum as a premium. When that got popular, Wrigley began an empire, and the world lost a soap and baking soda salesman.

Wrigley taught the world to chew gum. He died in 1932, a man who was expelled from eighth grade, who began business life with $35 in his pocket, and who left a $200 million estate and lots of people with gum on their shoes.

His Wrigley Building, patterned after Seville Cathedral's Giralda Tower in Spain, has been described as "a luscious birthday cake down whose sides someone had drawn his fingers." It was the first large office building north of the river. When excavation for the building began in January 1920, the Michigan Avenue Bridge was under construction and the street in front of the building was known as Pine Street.

To answer a curiosity before it is asked: The hour hands on the four clock dials atop the tower are 6-feet, 4-inches long, while the minute hands are 9-feet, 2-inches long.

The building is floodlit at night by 1,000-watt metal halide lamps, creating my favorite nighttime corner in the city—the Michigan Avenue bridge over the Chicago River reflecting the lights on the Wrigley Building.

Chicago Sun-Times

Now proceed between the two towers, turn left, and stroll into the little plaza in front of the *Chicago Sun-Times* (and the former *Chicago Daily News*) Building. The area I'm writing about is near a McDonald's. Isn't this a most relaxing spot in the bustling city?

Next enter the *Sun-Times* Building. There is a long corridor before you, where you can see the huge presses to your left and an exhibit of photos or posters to your right.

Mike Royko, Sidney J. Harris, Ann Landers, John Fischetti, Irv Kupcinet, and others have worked in this building, which, because it once housed the *Chicago Daily News*, has inherited a 100-year-old tradition of fine journalism produced by quirky employees.

In 1876, the *Daily News* editorially supported the Indians in their massacre of Custer, and the *News* almost went under. In the 1920s, a foreign correspondent was not recognized by a guard, who didn't let him in the *News'* building. So he went around the corner and filed a 12,000 word story by telegraph—collect.

When Richard Loeb, who with Nathan Leopold committed the Crime of the Century by killing Bobby Franks, was stabbed in Stateville Prison during an alleged homosexual quarrel, *Daily News* reporter Robert J. Casey wrote, "Richard Loeb, who graduated from college with honors at the age of 15 and who was a master of the English language, today ended his sentence with a proposition."

On March 4, 1978, the *Chicago Daily News* ceased publication after 102 years, two months, and nine days.

Retrace your steps back through the plaza.

Riccardo's: Watering Hole for Writers

The Wrigley Building is before you with the 410 Club on 20,000 square feet and two levels. They can help you entertain up to 300 clients at a time. It's private, but you can enter if you are affiliated with any group that is also a member of the Club Corporation of America.

Down below the plaza is Riccardo's, formerly a watering hole for local journalists. Recently, it has changed owners several times, and, as this is being written, local newsmen aren't sure where they will gather to drink and tell lies.

If you enter Riccardo's, walk in the dining room, the second room to your left. There you will see three of the seven murals commissioned in 1935 by the original Ric Riccardo. They originally were displayed behind the bar, which recently has been refurbished in a most satisfying way.

By all means walk downstairs and observe the distinctive men's washroom, where the curved screens around the urinals do impart a certain continental elan.

When journalists gathered at Ric's on cold Friday evenings in the past, an accordionist would play, and sometimes a man and a woman would begin singing "Indian Love Call" from opposite ends of the bar. Alas, I do not know if that odd tradition will continue.

History: Indian War Dance

The last great Indian war dance in Chicago history began very near the corner where Riccardo's stands. The Indians had given up all their claims to land in and around Chicago, and, on August 18, 1835, had to leave town.

About 800 loincloth-clad braves gathered near here, their faces streaked with war paint, their hair adorned with hawks' and eagles' feathers. They made their way into the city, leaping, crouching, creeping, yelling, howling, and stopping at every home to scare the daylights out of the residents. Some local newsmen, when leaving Riccardo's, do the same thing today.

One witness, Judge Dean Caton, wrote, "Their countenances had assumed an expression of all the worst passions . . . fierce anger, terrible hate, dire revenge, remorseless cruelty . . . Their muscles stood out in great hard knots . . . Their tomahawks and clubs were thrown and brandished in every direction . . . and with every step and every gesture they utter the most frightful yells in every imaginable key and note, though generally the highest and shrillest possible . . . this raging savagery glistening in the sun, reeking with steamy sweat, fairly frothing at the mouths as with unaffected rage. . . ." The city was not to see a parade of its like until the Shriners began coming to town in the twentieth century.

In 1962 an anthropologist noticed a Pottawatomie reservation near Topeka, Kansas. He learned that these were the descendants of the original braves who attacked the Fort Dearborn inhabitants. They still had some handcrafted silver made by a local pioneer, John Kinzie, and they remembered stories about their wonderful victory in 1812.

Billy Goat Tavern

Walk down the steps to Rush Street and take a right on Hubbard, which is in front of Riccardo's. Yes, this is a dark, dank, slightly frightening area but it will take you to a dark, dank, delightful bar called the Billy Goat Tavern, which was either "est." or "born" (depending on which sign you read) in 1934.

Here reporters, printers, and all who can find the place come for "Cheezborger, cheezborger, no Pepsi, Coke," a phrase heard here years before the late John Belushi said it on "Saturday Night Live."

Read the many stories written about the Billy Goat, all lovingly preserved on the walls, including novelist Bill Granger's tribute calling it the "best tavern" in Chicago and Mike Royko's hilarious account of the determined streaker in the tavern at 1:30 a.m. one night.

But take special note of the stories about an important event in 1945, a day that darkened Chicago history for four decades. Sam "Billy Goat" Sianis tried to take Savonia, his goat, to the Cubs' World Series game. Despite having box seat tickets, the goat was tossed out of the game, leaving an angry Sam to pronounce a curse on the Cubs: They would not again appear in any World Series until his goat was allowed back in the game.

Later, when the Cubs lost that 1945 World Series, Sam sent a telegram to the team owner, Phil K. Wrigley, asking, "Who smells now?"

The curse was quite effective. The poor Cubs not only remained out of the World Series, they generally stayed in last place until 1982, when a goat was invited back to a Cubs game. The Cubs have been doing somewhat better since then, but they have yet to be in a World Series. As far as winning a World Series, don't mention that in the Goat. You will instantly be identified as a benighted tourist, and you may be teased about your apparent beliefs in fairies and leprechauns.

Reflect on the power of the curse, enjoy a dark, cold draft of beer, eat lots of fresh pickles with a "cheezborger, cheezborger," note that the washrooms are labeled Nanny or Billy, and then continue our trek by going east (left) on Hubbard to the corner, taking another left, and going up the newly-repaired concrete stairs. You'll emerge on Michigan Avenue, where you will proceed north (left).

Tribune Tower

When you reach the east side of Michigan Avenue, you will be standing before the Tribune Tower.

Consider the Tribune Tower. The *Tribune* held a competition in 1923 and the design you see won $100,000 for Howells and Hood, although many preferred the second-place submission designed by Eero Saarinen of Finland. Louis Sullivan said of the Gothic flying buttresses at the top of the building (which hold up nothing in particular), that they look as if the designers crowned the tower with a monstrous, eight-legged spider. The *Tribune* called its building "a symphony in stone," but Sullivan said it was "an imaginary structure . . . starting with false premises it was doomed to a false conclusion."

After the *Tribune* was bought by Joseph Medill in 1855, it helped found the Republican party and to elect Abraham Lincoln as president. In return for that favor for Lincoln, the *Tribune* got the right to name the postmaster of Chicago in 1861 so as to "extend the influence of the *Tribune.*"

Medill believed America belonged to the Anglo-Saxon race. The *Tribune* editorially supported lynchings of communists and strychnine or arsenic for tramps. Prior to World War II, the paper gave space to Chicago's Nazi vice-consul, and later saw one of its foreign correspondences broadcasting messages for the Third Reich.

On New Year's Day 1977, without explanation, the *Tribune* removed the motto "World's Greatest Newspaper." In reality, it is among the world's best newspapers. Well, it was embarrassed in 1989 when it announced the death of Alderman Vito Marzullo, then age 91. He was alive at the time. Today, in the main, the paper is modern, fresh, and just about young enough.

Tribune Tower: Attacked by an eight-legged spider?

If you walk into Tribune Tower, you'll see many inscriptions about newspapers and the First Amendment. If you look behind you, over the revolving doors, you'll see a magnificent stone screen with such oddly discordant figures as Robin Hood, the *Tribune* editors during World

War I, Zeus, a parrot, and a porcupine. It's all highly symbolic. True to its Gothic traditions, the building also has gargoyles, notably to the right and left of the entrance arch.

For years the *Tribune* printed "Injun Summer," a cartoon about that last Pottawatomie war dance by John T. McCutcheon, and Chester Gould came down on Mondays to work on his cartoon "Dick Tracy." Dick Locher, who doubles as a Pulitzer-prize winning editorial cartoonist, draws Mr. Tracy today in an office in the tower. When Warren Beatty wanted advice on how to make his *Dick Tracy* movie better, he had to ask Locher.

Harold Gray's "L'il Orphan Annie," Frank King's "Gasoline Alley," and Milt Caniff's "Terry and the Pirates" were all created at the *Trib*. Ring Lardner worked here in the '20s, and Claudia Cassidy, once the most feared critic in America, issued her barbs from this building.

Floyd P. Gibbons set off on a *Tribune* assignment of his own making in 1917—to find a ship being sunk by the Germans. And he was, perhaps, too successful in his quest. His luggage included a life preserver, fresh water, a flashlight, and a flask of brandy. He needed all that when he went down with the *Laconia* on February 26, 1917, and gave the world an unforgettable story.

Walk a few feet north and you'll see Nathan Hale Court, with a statue to that American patriot. At one time the building behind Hale was the home of the *Chicago American*, a newspaper that died September 14, 1974, after giving Wrong Way Corrigan his name and creating a tradition of slam-bang, big headline, find-the-scandal journalism. Ponder, for a moment, the death of big city afternoon daily newspapers, and continue on your way.

If you walk around to the rear of either side of the Tower, notice the stones of famous buildings embedded in the walls, allegedly including bits of the original Lincoln tomb, the Alamo, the Great Pyramid, Notre Dame, the Parthenon, Pompeii Baths, the Colosseum, St. Peter's, Hamlet's castle, the Great Wall of China, and Westminster Abbey.

At one time, along the south side of the building, you could see 18 famous *Chicago Tribune* front pages, from Lee surrendering at Appomattox to "Assassin Kills Kennedy." The *Trib*'s most famous front page, the one saying that Thomas Dewey had been elected President, wasn't there. And now the front pages are gone as well, replaced by the windows of WGN-AM Radio 720.

Hotel Inter-Continental

If you walk north, crossing the street named Cityfront Plaza/Illinois Street to 505 North Michigan, you'll see the Hotel Inter-Continental, which began life in 1929 as the Medinah Athletic Club and which still has a 25-yard swimming pool in its 16th story. There aren't many hotels with a swimming pool decorated in a Moorish, Hawaiian theme and now called a "natatorium."

Walk into the first entrance you find, and look at the ceiling. Or walk up the stairs, go past the elevators, walk up a few more stairs to the right, and look at the ceiling and ornamentation of the Cabaret Continental.

Possibly the most hilarious moment for this grand old hotel occurred in 1946, when the National Pickle Packers convened in the then Sheraton-Chicago. They hired World War II bombardiers to throw pickles from the 42nd floor into a barrel on the sidewalk. There were a number of direct hits.

Next, leave the Inter-Continental and return to the small street between the Tribune and the hotel. Take a left. You can look at the ancient stones embedded in Tribune Tower as you walk to the east.

NBC Tower

Cross the plaza behind the Tribune, walk to your right a few feet and enter the 40-story NBC Tower. Notice the way the marble and trim make the building look both modern and slightly classic as if it is an updated version of NBC Headquarters at 30 Rockefeller Center in New York. That's exactly the feeling the designer, Chicagoan Adrian Smith, wanted.

This 850,000-square-foot building opened on October 20, 1989, with a spectacular party for 1,300 people including music by Doc Severinsen and Paul Shaffer, shrimp and lobster, and 30 different NBC stars. Network anchorman Tom Brokaw was pulled from San Francisco earthquake coverage to serve as the master of ceremonies. WMAQ-TV had moved from the Merchandise Mart, which had been the station's home since 1930, to the first five floors of NBC Tower.

The building is very impressive. When it opened, the *Chicago Tribune's* Pulitzer-prizewinning architecture critic, Paul Gapp, called it, "the best-looking masonry-clad skyscraper constructed in Chicago since the 1930s. Its crisp, shimmering, almost mesmerizing presence on the skyline is a

Proud as a peacock off Michigan Avenue

triumph of good taste, skillful detailing and a mature respect for architectural history." He also wrote "the crisply delivered perfection of the NBC building will always be counted on as one of Chicago's strongest late-twentieth-century design performances."

If you take an immediate right after you enter the lobby, you might find the almost hidden Tower Grill (if you are lost, ask the security people, who are among the most polite in town). This very tiny bar features jazz most nights, a cabaret review on Saturdays, and delicious free snacks.

If you walk down the marble corridor toward the east entrance and then take a left, you can ask the guard what TV shows are currently taping in the building. You might be able to get tickets to see one of the talk shows coming out of Chicago. If you do, you will probably sit in one of the largest television studios anywhere in America, the 11,600-square-foot Studio A.

An NBC souvenir shop is near the entrance to the TV station, and you can buy "Saturday Night Live" T-shirts there. A building tour costs $5 for adults, $4 for students and senior citizens.

Leave by the east exit. The Sheraton Hotel is the large 34-story, 1,215-room, $180 million structure across the street. It is an uncommonly beautiful building that began life with some unfortunate headlines. On January 15, 1992, when applications were accepted for jobs in the new hotel, over 3,000 people stood in freezing, snowy weather hoping for employment. At the time, it was widely seen as an example of America's economic troubles. Officials at WMAQ-TV hurriedly organized a coffee brigade to help warm the chilly job seekers, many of whom were suffering because the Illinois unemployment rate was then over 9 percent. There were single parents, people in suits and ties carrying brief cases, and people with degrees in diagnostic radiology looking for one of the 1,000 jobs paying from $6 to $10 an hour.

You are now in the midst of Cityfront Center, which, if the economy is nice to builders, will become $3 billion worth of office towers, hotels, apartment buildings, and shops by 2020. The 13.5 million square feet of planned office space would be about equal to 3½ Sears Towers. The 4,000 hotel rooms would fill the Drake Hotel 7½ times.

Take a left, walk down a slight hill to Illinois and take a right, heading east toward the lake. You will shortly pass the Market Place, a tasty but expensive deli.

North Pier

If you continue walking east, you will see North Pier, 435 East Illinois, an 85-year-old warehouse that was recently turned into a mall. It redefines the word eclectic.

The Baja Beach Club, where I have never had a good time, is an overwhelmingly huge dance hall with games and many bars. I prefer Dick's Last Resort, which is at the west end of North Pier. This restaurant overlooks a small channel called the Ogden Slip, and you can watch the boats go by while eating a fairly good meal or having a drink.

Inside North Pier, you'll find the City of Chicago Store, with traffic signs, voting machines, Chicago books, maps, and mugs. Also in North Pier, you can buy nautical T-shirts, flags, muffins, children's clothing, candy, fake jewelry, kites, knits, men's ties, CDs, flowers, pizza, toys, play miniature golf, or make a music video.

The Chicago Children's Museum ($2 for a child, $3 for an adult) is also in the building. Recommended for preschoolers through age 10, it offers hands-on experiences blowing bubbles, driving an ambulance, cooking, and crawling through multitextured tunnels.

Leaving North Pier, if you want to learn about Lake Michigan cruises, take a right and walk east under Lake Shore Drive toward Navy Pier.

Ships like the *Spirit of Chicago* and the *Odyssey* will take you on luncheon or dinner cruises that are romantic because the skyline is so spectacular.

Navy Pier is also the home of the Lakeside Group's many art shows including the world famous Chicago International Art Expo, a five-day annual event in mid-May. In 1992, the 13th annual Expo brought in 176 of the world's most prestigious galleries from 19 countries and 40,000 collectors. By 1993, the Art Expo had two competitors, and Chicago had three simultaneous international art expositions.

If cruises aren't what you're looking for, take a left on Peshtigo, a one-block street named after a Wisconsin city that burned the same day Chicago did in 1871. About 800 people were killed in Peshtigo, but Chicago had the telegraph wires, so the Chicago fire got the newspaper coverage, plus a place in the history books. Few people today remember the Peshtigo fire. Even disaster sometimes needs a good press agent.

Take a left at the end of the street and head back toward Michigan Avenue. Climb the stairs, take a right, and walk north.

If you enter the corridor at 535 North Michigan, you will be in the House of Hunan. In 1977, this became the first Chinese restaurant on North Michigan Avenue. The owner, George Kuan, who met his former partner Austin Koo while in boarding school in Taipei, has a degree in computer science.

Continue north to Ohio. You will see the Szechwan House across the street. The owner, Austin Koo, adopted his American name after visiting Austin, Texas. Koo, a lawyer from Taiwan who came to America with a wife, two children, and $2,000, celebrated his 20th year in America, the restaurant business, and the opening of his 20th restaurant in 1992.

The bestselling entree here is General Tso's or Governor's Chicken, which is chicken sauteed in bell peppers, minced ginger, and garlic. Tennis star Michael Chang ordered a delivery of beef with broccoli before winning a match; movie director Penny Marshall had hors d'oeuvres and Chinese beer delivered to her editing sessions for *A League of Their Own*; various basketball stars dine here; as does football an- nouncer John Madden, who has never gotten angry while eating here.

The story of the partnership between Koo and Kuan, who do not like each other very much these days, is complicated. Austin Koo opened one of the first Szechwan restaurants in Chicago and Kuan joined him as a partner. Later, one partner bought the other out, each opened restaurants on his own, with the help of bankers or the ever-personable Alfred Hsu, and they now separately control the best Oriental restaurants in town.

Turn right (east) on Ohio. You will pass the Sayat Nova, at 157 East Ohio, run by Leon and Arsen Demerdjian, and a favorite restaurant of local media types. Try the raw kibbie, which resembles steak tartare and which is only made when the meat is absolutely fresh. Or try the beoreg (cheese pastry), a taboule (cracked wheat salad), the sautéed lamb, or the fresh trout any day it is on the menu. This is a family-run, downtown restaurant with a reputation for great food.

This ends the mid-Michigan Avenue walk. Perhaps it is time to reflect on art, newspapers, and buildings topped with spiders.

3 NORTH MICHIGAN AVENUE WALK

Huron to Oak Street: Water Tower and beyond

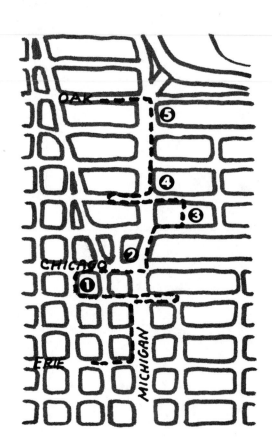

1. Holy Name Cathedral
2. The Water Tower
3. Ritz Carleton Hotel and Water Tower Place
4. John Hancock Center
5. The Drake

Time: Less than 2 hours.

To get there: Buses plying North Michigan Avenue and stopping at Huron and Michigan include #11, #45, #125, #145, #146, #147, #151, and #153. Parking is almost impossible in this area, although there are lots just west of Huron and Michigan on Rush Street.

Beginning the Magnificent Mile

This is the Magnificent Mile, containing men's and women's shops, little boutiques, and some of the world's best and most expensive stores.

It is a place to go with your credit cards locked somewhere else. You are entering one of the most concentrated retail strips anywhere in the country, an area that competes with Madison Avenue in New York and Rodeo Drive in Los Angeles. According to the Greater Michigan Avenue Association, sales here were nearly a billion dollars in 1991.

We start at Michigan and Erie, at the first Sony Corp. of America Gallery of Consumer Electronics. This 3-story, 10,000-square-foot showroom, which opened on December 11, 1991, is designed to educate the public and, by the way, to sell electronic products. The first floor has displays of home theaters and a wall that shows off new technologies. The last time I was there, I saw a video walkman the size of a paperback book with a 4-inch screen for $1,197, a little expensive for the privilege of being able to see "Wheel of Fortune" while strolling through town.

The second floor has a theater for patrons to test equipment designed for automobiles and a sports center featuring mannequins showing how waterproof Sony products can be.

You'll find Nike Town next door. When it opened on July 2, 1992, comic and TV star Jerry Seinfeld said, "Let's face it. This is a shoe store." Yes, and this is a 68,000 square-foot shoe store with a second-floor basketball half-court so the prospective buyer can test the shoes to see if they help his slam dunk.

Throughout the store there are shoe-oriented museum displays including Michael Jordan's autographed Olympic shoes, sculptures of Scottie Pippen, the bat boots from *Batman Returns*, continuous video presentations of Nike commercials, a 22-foot-long aquarium with fish swimming around gym shoes, and pavilions dedicated to women, kids, and running. It is quite a shoe store!

The Terra Museum

Next, cross to the west side of Michigan Avenue, make a right turn and walk a few feet north. The modern-looking building with the white marble facade, at 664 North Michigan, is the Terra Museum—dedicated to preserving and sharing American art through education. It was founded by Daniel J. Terra, a chemical engineer who discovered the fast-drying ink used in *Life* magazine. That made him enormously wealthy. He was President Ronald Reagan's ambassador-at-large of culture. By the time you read this, he will have opened a similar museum for American art in Giverny, France, directly next door to the Monet Museum.

In 1992, Daniel Terra asked the U. S. Tax Court to overturn $7 million in taxes and penalties that the IRS said he owed, plus $4 million owed by the Terra Foundation, and $500,000 owed by his wife, Judith. The issue was whether this museum and the one in Giverny were used to avoid taxes. The IRS became interested in the museums and Terra after learning that the museum invested in First Illinois Corp. of Evanston stock, a bank that Terra ultimately controlled. In other words, was Terra self-dealing? Terra also wanted the IRS to drop its bill to him for use of 22 paintings that the agency said belonged to the foundation but were used in Terra's personal Washington residence.

This comfortable and quiet museum, which specializes in American artists, is open Wednesday through Saturday, 10 a.m. to 5 p.m.; Tuesday, noon to 8 p.m.; and Sunday, noon to 5 p.m. Admission is $4 for adults, $2.50 for seniors, and $1 for students. The first Sunday of every month is free.

Stuart Brent's Bookstore

Just two doors to the south you will see Stuart Brent's Bookstore, a must stop because Brent knows books and people. Brent has been described as a "battler with a hint of Norman Mailer in his face."

Brent grew up on Chicago's tough West Side, taught school, came back from World War II to open a bookstore called The Seven Stairs (it had eight, actually), and started his life's work. He told Nelson Algren to name his book *The Man with the Golden Arm*. He showed Ernest Hemingway the joys of Rush Street, had tea with Noel Coward in Woolworth's, toured Chicago with Ben Hecht, and allowed Algren and Simone de Beauvoir to tryst in his store.

Brent is an irascible original, who resolutely believes that books can change your life and proudly states, "After all, I am the single most successful personal bookseller in all America." And he does mean personal. He has been known to throw seekers after trash out of his store. Until recently he refused to sell many books including *The Joy of Sex*, which he now stocks, saying that he has "since discovered the delights of sex."

Brent has summed up his life by telling the *Sun-Times*, "So I sell books. When you buy a book, a corner of your heart will grow a little larger. It's what makes you alive, kid."

Following the 1992 Chicago Bulls championship, rioters looted Brent's store. At first this was the subject of civic pride: At least our rioters want to read fine literature and good books. Later, it became known that the "looters" were just breaking windows on the way to the clothing store named The Gap. They grabbed a beautiful picture book of the Sistine Chapel from Brent's window and threw it to the ground.

But do not despair. Stuart Brent's remains a store in which every clerk is a book lover. Enter if you want to become involved in the excitement of reading.

Next to Stuart Brent's, and around the corner from Express, is the Hyatt Regency Suites hotel at 676 North Michigan. Built in 1990 in an art deco design, it features architectural suites. These three special suites were designed to look like the work of Frank Lloyd Wright, Mies Van Der Rohe, and McIntosh. The speciality suites go from $260 a night, possibly a small price to pay if you wish to sleep in a room very much like the bedroom that your favorite architect might have designed.

The Allerton Hotel

When you arrive at Erie and Michigan, notice the Allerton Hotel sign toward the east. For seven years, until the program ended in 1968, "The Breakfast Club" was broadcast atop the Allerton. The actual place where the broadcast originated has since become meeting rooms. Back then, audience members marched around the breakfast table and sang, "Good morning breakfast clubbers, good morning to ya, we got up bright and early, just to how-dee-doo yah." Sam Cowling presented "Fiction and Fact from Sam's Almanac," Fran Allison was Aunt Fanny, and Don McNeill, the host, said, "Be good to yourself." McNeill recalled that "The Breakfast Club" was previously broadcast from two other Chicago hotels, the Sherman and the Morrison. Both are no more. "If you want your hotel knocked down, just invite the Breakfast Club," he said.

It is said that, in 1946, Mel Torme came to the Allerton to write the "Christmas Song" with the lyrics "chestnuts roasting on an open fire." If you are near this hotel, you are standing close to where an American song classic was composed. Do not let Jack Frost nip at your nose!

Today, the Allerton has the L'Escargot Restaurant, which warms its patrons both with its wood paneling and its French food. The Penthouse Suite was once the home of the late Byron Wrigley, a member of the chewing gum family who was also a painter. Today it is a meeting room not available to the public.

Expensive Shopping

Now let's walk north, on the east side of the street, plunging onward into deepest credit card land.

Across the street we see Ann Taylor, and Brooks Brothers. You only need walk a few feet inside to know that you are far from the home of the blue light specials. Walk into Tiffany's and admire the marbled walls and the gigantic peach vases.

At 700 North Michigan is Chicago Place, a shopping mall centered around Saks Fifth Avenue with Talbot's and Luis Vuitton luggage on Michigan Avenue. It opened in 1990 just as the country—and many shoppers with lots of money—went into a recession.

It has eight levels, 320,000 square feet (Saks has nearly half the mall and is on seven levels), and 50 stores. Walk in, look up, and notice the modern lobby, which looks like a grand survivor of the '40s.

By all means, find the Nancy Drew Store on the seventh floor. It features the delightfully different art, furniture, and clothes painted on and designed by this world-famous Chicago/St. Joseph, Michigan, artist.

Other stores in the mall include Bockwinkel's, which has the distinction of being the only grocer on Michigan Avenue; Casablanca coffees; Enchanted Kingdom, which sells collectible dolls; the Great Steak & Fry Co., which specializes in Philadelphia cheese steak sandwiches; Joy of Ireland, Michigan Avenue's only Irish import store; Rigorno, which stocks more than 3,000 sunglasses; Words in Motion, the first store to specialize in books on tape; plus a Taco Bell and a Wendy's.

Walking north you will actually see a McDonald's on Michigan Avenue. This had to be rather upscale so as not to ruffle those who would protect the character of Michigan Avenue. I don't think the strange, cheap-looking, stained-glass dome or the bad elevator music overcome all the objections. It received some bad publicity when *Tribune* columnist Mike Royko wrote about a concentration camp survivor's efforts to feed the homeless. He was criticizing McDonald's because it had thrown the people he was feeding out of the restaurant.

The Neiman Marcus, at 737 North Michigan, has a grand archway and the fancy goods we have come to expect of this store.

At Superior and Michigan, just beyond Neiman Marcus, you can see the sign proclaiming that Gino's East, at 160 East Superior, has the "world's most celebrated pizza." This restaurant was opened years ago by two cab drivers, and it once had the second-best thick-crust pizza in Chicago according to *Chicago* magazine. The best, at the time, was Giordano's, at 6253 South California, which was called "the Cecil B. DeMille of pizza."

Holy Name Cathedral

What follows is an optional but fascinating side trip. If you wish to continue shopping and browsing, walk north on Michigan Avenue to the Water Tower and turn now to that entry in this walk.

However, if you're in the mood to see how religion and gangsterism coexisted, walk west on Superior for two blocks to State Street and Holy Name Cathedral. Its 1,200-pound doors look like the gnarled roots of an ancient tree, and its interior features a statue of Christ suspended in mid-air.

Historians record that this ground was given to the Catholic Church as a political payoff. William B. Ogden and Walter L. Newberry owned a lot of North Side property and they wanted a bridge over the river at Clark Street so folks could get to their land. They gave the block on which Holy Name now stands to the Catholic Church so as to get the Catholic vote for the bridge. It worked. Catholics got a church. Chicago got a bridge. And perhaps even heaven profited.

This area also has a bloody history. Dion O'Banion, who was arranging flowers in his shop for the funeral of murdered Mike Merlo, first president of the Unione Siciliane, was killed at 738 North State on November 10, 1924. O'Banion, who allegedly knowingly let Johnny Torio get caught with 13 truckloads of beer in a federal raid, was busy creating Torio's $10,000 floral piece for Merlo, plus Capone's $8,000 worth of flowers. Three men entered his shop, located across the street from where you are standing, and pumped five bullets into him.

After that, local newspapers called O'Banion an "artist in crime who mixed bootlegging with roses, murder and funeral wreaths" and who died

Holy Name Cathedral without bullet holes

"crashing back . . . into a showcase full of chrysanthemums and roses."
Thus the Chicago artistic community lost a contributor to fairs and balls.
O'Banion's flower shop was razed in 1960.

Two years after O'Banion's death, again within sight of where you are standing, Hymie Weiss (formerly Wajciechowski), who took over O'Banion's gang, was gunned down while he was with attorney W. W. O'Brien. The cornerstone of Holy Name Cathedral was chipped in the attack, but has since been repaired.

After considering the odd way religion and violence have occupied this area, visit Holy Name, which is open to the public daily from 6 a.m. to 6 p.m. As you enter, the room is bathed in ever more light the closer you get to the alter. No matter what your religious affiliation, this is an awe-inspiring edifice.

Notice the hats of three Chicago cardinals hanging from the ceiling. They will remain where they are until they disintegrate.

Next, walk north to Chicago Avenue (to your right as you leave the front doors of the church), then take a right, and go east.

Park Hyatt Hotel

Be sure to notice the doorman in front of the Park Hyatt Hotel, at Rush and Chicago. He may be the best-dressed doorman in Chicago. If the weather is cold, he will be wearing a $10,000 custom-made, black diamond, full-length mink coat, cape, and hat. At one time, Fred, one of the doormen, shared the coat with his brother, Dave, another doorman. Fred says the coat is a little long on him and a little short on Dave, but things work out well enough for both of them.

The Penthouse Suite, which goes for $2,500 a night weekdays and $1,600 a night on weekends, has been the home away from home for Elizabeth Taylor, Yul Brynner (who couldn't bring his dog), Mitzi Gaynor, Red Buttons, Phyllis Diller, Eddie Murphy, Paul Anka, Dudley Moore, and Barry Manilow. The $2,500 includes champagne (Dom Perignon), caviar (Beluga), and rooms furnished with an 1898 Steinway grand piano, a Louis XV writing desk, antique Oriental silk cushions, a Chinese temple statue in the master bedroom, three baths, and a fine view of Michigan Avenue and the lake.

The Park Hyatt's La Tour Restaurant is the subject of much critical praise (four stars according to more than one discerning diner), and it offers a relaxed view of the Water Tower park.

High tea in the lobby of the hotel includes finger sandwiches, pasties or cake, scones, and the tea of your choice. I am also told that the ladies' room in this hotel is one of the nicest in town, with each stall being complete and private. You must explore this one on your own. I did not personally check this out.

Water Tower Survives the Chicago Fire

Leaving the Park Hyatt, we next walk across the street and through the park in front of the Water Tower, the most artistically beautiful stand-pipe ever created. This structure survived the Chicago Fire of 1871 and Chicagoans love it. It also survived intense controversy: Oscar Wilde called it "a castellated monstrosity with pepper boxes stuck all over it."

The fire, which spared the Water Tower and made it a symbol of survival, began south and west of here, in Patrick O'Leary's barn at 137 DeKoven, now the site of the Chicago Fire Academy (see South Side Drive). One of the O'Learys was Big Jim, who later became an important gambler and politician, proving that tragedy need not prevent someone from being a success.

There were only five inches of rain in Chicago that entire summer, and the city was almost entirely built of wood—streets, sidewalks, and homes. No one knows for sure what happened in that barn on the evening of October 8, 1871. People blamed tramps, neighborhood boys who were smoking, the carelessness of a neighbor, and even the combustibility of the entire Midwest due to a comet depositing flammable elements in our soil years ago. But almost everyone believes Mrs. O'Leary's cow did it by kicking over a kerosene lantern, and since the cow never said that it didn't, that's the story most people accept.

When the fire started, citizens called the fire department. So did a watchman in City Hall, who gave the wrong address for the blaze. The fire units rushed to an area a mile away from the O'Learys's. By the time the firemen found the right barn, the fire had spread and was uncontrollable.

And the city burned. Three hundred people died. A third of the city was left homeless. The fire generated heat of more than 3,000°F, which created a firestorm that shot burning timber through the air over the Chicago River, causing the fire to spread.

Thousands of rats ran along the gutters. Horses stampeded. Hoodlums sacked stores and attacked citizens. A woman knelt at Wabash and Adams, holding a crucifix as her skirt burned.

Water Tower or "Castellated monstrosity?"

They say that the first structures to be constructed after the fire were gambling dens and brothels. Maybe so. With the infusion of money from insurance companies, Chicago rebuilt. The fire, which was a disaster, actually helped the city by destroying aging structures and allowing for the greatest building boom with the most creative architecture any city had ever seen.

Horse-Drawn Carriages

If you look across the street, you'll see Bistro 110 at 110 East Superior, which has an outdoor cafe when the weather is nice. This has quickly become one of Chicago's "in" restaurants. They report that 25 percent of all their diners will order the wood burning oven-roasted chicken. I also recommend the baked artichoke appetizer for a delicious dish you can't get elsewhere.

Dennis Quaid, Meg Ryan, Alec Baldwin, and Michelle Pfeiffer have dined here.

Filene's Basement, at 830 North Michigan Avenue, is the former site of I. Magnin's, a furrier of some renown. R. H. Macy & Co. bought I. Magnin, then closed it in June 1992, when Macy's was operating under Chapter 11 bankruptcy protection. Filene's got the lease through 1997 for $2.15 million.

No one knows what effect Filene's, which sells clothing and accessories at 20 to 60 percent less than traditional department stores, will have on the upscale Michigan Avenue.

You can, if you wish, hire a horse-drawn carriage at the corner of Pearson and Michigan, just north of the Water Tower, for a romantic ride through the city for under $40 for a half-hour. Yes, the horses wear a diaper, which, according to experts, captures more than 90 percent of what the horse drops.

On September 1, 1983, a taxi somehow got its rear bumper entangled with the right hoof of Elwood, a four-year-old carriage horse, who was dragged 80 feet along Michigan Avenue. The horse screamed, the two passengers (a man, age 42, and a woman, age 28) were shocked, and the never-ending battle between the City Council and the horse carriage operators got hotter. As a result of Elwood's mishap (and no one knows if the horse bumped the taxi or the taxi backed into the horse), the carriages were banned during evening rush hours from 4 to 6 p.m.

The double-decker, British-style bus tours also depart from this area.

If you do not take a carriage ride, cross the street to the pumping station east of the Water Tower where WGN radio and TV present Here's Chicago!, a multimedia promotional view of the city costing

$5.75. There is also a gift shop inside where all the souvenirs you have ever wanted are available.

Water Tower Place
and the Ritz-Carlton

Next, continue north on Michigan, to FAO Schwarz at 840 North Michigan. This 3-story, 32,000-square-foot toyland, which opened on September 16, 1992, features a 22-foot clock tower with red, sequined high heels that tap to music, plus a 16-foot replica of the John Hancock Building made from Erector set pieces, and the Water Tower made with Legos. There is also a Barbie department, a xylophone bridge that plays music as you cross over it, and the 65-foot-high Great Swoop Gravity Loop with 25 balls zipping along a track at 280 feet per second.

Crossing the street, enter Water Tower Place, the tenth tallest building in the United States, costing $195 million to build. What we have here is shoppers' heaven, with 125 stores in the Atrium Shopping Mall, 10 restaurants, 2 banks, and 7 movie screens. This is, according to *The New York Times*, "the second-highest revenue-producing mall in America." Seems worth visiting.

In addition to Lord & Taylor and Marshall Field's, you will find Banana Republic, with its perpetual safari look; Bigsby & Kruthers, for men's suits; Eddie Bauer, for the camper who doesn't have everything; M. Hyman & Son, for big and tall men; Laura Ashley, for the women who love paisley; and a McDonald's with a tiny fountain all its own.

There are also Godiva Chocolates and Mrs. Fields Cookies, and the bookstores Kroch's & Brentano's on the fourth floor and Rizzoli International on the third floor. If you're looking for a bargain hair-do, Vidal Sassoon also on the third floor has apprentice workshops during which it is possible to get a cut for $12, and a permanent or color job for $15. It's by appointment; just call (312) 337-9497 and ask for someone in staff training.

If you make it to the seventh floor, you'll find D. B. Kaplan's Delicatessen, a place with a menu devoted to puns. One ice-cream concoction is called the Princess Di-et and others are called John's Candy and Oral Hersheyheiser. A vegetable platter is a Garden of Eatin'. There're sandwiches named Bruce Springstongue, Studs Turkey, Jack Pumpernickleson, Bryant Gobble, Barbara Spiceand, Sylvester Stalami, David Liverman, and Roseanne Barr-B-Que.

Next, somehow wander out of Water Tower Place (not easy to do), and go east on Pearson to the Ritz-Carlton. The rock group U2 stayed here.

Enter the elevator and go to the main lobby on the 12th floor (the elevators stop at one, two, and twelve). Notice there are chandeliers in the elevators. That's class.

Get out of the elevator, walk straight ahead to an area known as the Green House, which is just beyond a fountain with a sculpture showing three birds standing on top of each other. If you have the money, sit in a wicker chair, look at the plants, and order a drink. Warning: It will be expensive. But you are now in the lap of luxury.

Tea is served from 3 to 5 p.m. seven days a week in the Green House or on the Terrace, which is, as you face the elevators, around and to your right just beyond an indoor waterfall with real trees.

In this hotel, it is possible to rent the State Suite for $2,500 a night, which has five baths, a kitchen, library, Italian silk sheets costing $600 a set in the four bedrooms, hangers padded with silk in the closets, and 22-foot-high living room ceilings. It is rumored that Michael Jackson, Roger Moore, Mick Jagger, Lionel Richie, and Tina Turner came here to enjoy the comforts away from home.

The Ritz-Carlton also features one of Chicago's fanciest Sunday brunches in an elegant setting, for $28 per person.

John Hancock Center

Next, return to ground level and exit on Pearson, going west to Michigan Avenue, taking a right and going north to the John Hancock Center.

Toward the left (north) and down the steps to the plaza is the Chicago Athenium, a national museum of architecture and design, dedicated to "the advancement of design in cities with the idea of promoting design excellence in the human environment." The museum opened this site in 1991 and has a $2 suggested donation. It's open weekdays, 11 a.m. to 6 p.m. and on Saturday, 10 a.m. to 5 p.m.

Cross its plaza and go down the stairs and toward the back (east) to take the tower elevators to the observation deck. The trip costs $3.65 for adults and $2.35 for children and seniors and, on a clear day, it is well worth the price. As you zip upward, you are speeding along at 1,800 feet per minute. You will soon be 1,030 feet above the ground. On a clear day you can see four states.

Looking up from the courtyard of the Fourth Presbyterian Church
to the John Hancock Center

There is another way to see the same thing. Walk toward the Chestnut
side of the Hancock Center, enter the doors saying "The Ninety-Fifth",
and take the elevators there. The Ninety-Fifth is a restaurant, but there
is also a bar called Images directly up the stairs on the 96th floor, where

domestic beer is $4.50 and fancy mixed drinks are $6.00. In other words, for 85 cents more than the $3.65 you'd spend to go to the observation deck, you can get the same view and a beer. The best time to go to the Ninety-Fifth is at sunset or during lightning storms, when the clouds are often below the 95th floor of the Hancock. You should get there early, however, because they do not take reservations for window seats. And the best view, I am told, is from the ladies' room!

The Ninety-Fifth, with its harpist entertaining nightly, is one of Chicago's most expensive restaurants, with entrées ranging from $22.00 to $35.00. Everything is à la carte. But the view is unsurpassed.

As you return to the main floor, note that you are passing 47 floors of apartments, from floors 45 to 92, above a swimming pool on the 44th floor. A four-bedroom condominium in the John Hancock Center might sell for as much as $1.5 million.

When a man wearing a Spiderman costume attempted to climb the Hancock in November 1981, fire commissioner William Blair ordered his men to spray him with high-powered hoses when he reached the 37th floor. Although spiders can be pesty things, at the time it was seen as a rather severe penalty for a human climber, who eventually returned to ground level unhurt.

Streeterville Plaza
Named for Cap Streeter

When you return to the ground floor, you are in Streeterville Plaza, named for one of the most colorful characters in Chicago history. On July 11, 1886, Captain George Wellington Streeter stranded his steamboat on a sandbar here as he was bound for Honduras where he hoped to sell guns to South American outlaws. Within a few days the sandbar built up around the boat, and soon Cap and his wife, Ma, were on dry land. "Found land," he called it.

Cap invited local contractors, who were building homes for the rich on Chicago's North Side, to dump whatever they wanted on his land. Within a few months, Cap could lay claim to 186 acres. He stood on his rights. It was his land. He did not recognize the sovereignty of the City of Chicago or the State of Illinois for his "District of Lake Michigan."

Ordinary folks called the area Streeterville, but rich people didn't like squatters dirtying up their front yards, and so began a 30-year war between Cap and the Chicago establishment. Most of the time, Cap won.

Ma, using her ax, clipped off the heel of one rich dude who tried to throw Cap off his property. When sheriff's deputies invaded Cap's property in 1894, Ma poured boiling water on them. During another raid, Ma's ax almost severed the arm of one policeman and nine of the city's finest were wounded by Cap's birdshot. During yet another raid, one policeman was killed, but Cap was acquitted of murder when he proved that he only used birdshot, never bullets, and the man died of a bullet wound. One of Cap's friends stabbed another cop with a pitchfork, killing him, and was acquitted on a plea of self-defense.

Then 100 hired gunmen (or maybe it was 50—accounts differ and grow with each passing year) invaded Streeterville. Cap and Ma looked done for, until the gunmen found Cap's liquor supply. They got drunk, Cap rounded up his friends and, during a brisk one-sided half-hour's battle, wounded 33 members of the invading army. Cap then loaded the still living into his wagon, drove them to the Chicago Avenue police station, and demanded that they be charged with trespassing, assault, and battery. Cap was eventually captured by police, who couldn't hold him because shooting *at* a Chicago police officer wasn't considered a crime then. You had to actually wound a cop before you could be charged with a crime. They changed that after Cap discovered the loophole.

Finally, a frontier gunfighter named John Kirk was mysteriously murdered and Cap was found guilty of the crime. Nine months later, Cap was ordered pardoned, but things became more difficult in Streeterville. Ma died and was replaced by Alma, Cap lost an eye in yet another gun battle, during which he shot a police captain.

The courts and Cap's desire to do a sinful thing—sell beer on Sunday—finally ended his stay in Streeterville. On December 10, 1918, Cap was thrown off his property. Cap retired and operated a hot dog stand on Navy Pier until his death on January 21, 1921, at age 84, an honored citizen who fought the establishment and lost. His land was the subject of continuing court battles until 1940, when the last of his heirs and those he sold property to for as little as $1 had their suits dismissed in federal court.

Cap Streeter's land is conservatively worth more than $1 billion today. And all he wanted to do on it was serve beer on Sundays and squat.

More Ramblings on Michigan Avenue

Walk west on Chestnut, cross Michigan and notice the building at 840 North Michigan. In 1990, they announced that it would have 28 stories, 400,000 square feet with four stories of retail space topped by a 288-room Park Hyatt Hotel. That was before Japanese financing evaporated in the face of the recession and Chicago hotels were being overbuilt and under-occupied. You will note that 24 stories have evaporated.

Eventually, a scaled-down sensible building of four stories and 90,000 square feet was built with money from banks in England and Germany.

There is a theory that two kinds of shoppers stroll North Michigan Avenue: Those who mainly shop in vertical malls, like the Water Tower, and those who stay on the street to shop the storefronts.

That's why The Gap, Banana Republic, and FAO Schwarz all have stores on Michigan Avenue and in the Water Tower. The 840 North Michigan building's tenants include FAO Schwarz, the German-owned Escada women's clothing stores, and Waterstone's Booksellers.

Next, walk west crossing Michigan Avenue. By all means browse through Waterstone's Booksellers, which opened November 7, 1992. There are more than 110,000 titles in this 3-story, 21,000-square-foot temple to reading. Notice what isn't there: No greeting cards, no calendars, no magazines. Just books. The background music is classical, and according to assistant manager Maria O'Neill, "All of our booksellers are also book buyers and book readers." Sounds like the sort of people who might have good recommendations.

Continue west along Chestnut; you will shortly arrive at 103 East Chestnut, the Quigley Preparatory Seminary North, a school for young men interested in the priesthood. If you ring the bell between 8 a.m. and 4 p.m., someone will answer the door. Ask to see the chapel, which is at the end of the hall to the right on the second floor. If it is afternoon, the rays of the setting sun will be the only illumination through the deep reds and blues of the stained-glass window. There is an awe-inspiring silence—a moment to contemplate and escape the city.

Now return to Michigan Avenue. Walk on the west side of the street past the Fourth Presbyterian Church, which was built in 1912. Movie critic Roger Ebert was married there in 1992, and the emotional ceremony never once included a direct mention of any movie. When Gene Siskel danced with the new Mrs. Ebert, someone who knew of their sometimes contentious relationship observed, "This is the first time Siskel danced with Ebert." When Ebert said, "I will," it was his shortest recorded answer to a direct question.

Across Michigan at Delaware, you'll see the Westin Hotel, which one restaurateur said has the best food service of any hotel in the country.

If you look to the west on Delaware, you'll see the entrance to the Four Seasons Hotel. When Madonna was in Chicago in 1991 to film *A League of Their Own*, WMAQ-TV assigned me to search for—but not necessarily to find—Madonna after there had been many sightings of her all over town. It was later learned that a Madonna impostor was also out teasing the star-struck locals with false sightings. Many people, including one policeman and a man who wanted to give her a bustiere, indicated she was staying at the Four Seasons.

The Four Seasons, with a spectacular but somewhat low-ceilinged lobby, occasionally displays the life-like sculptures of J. Sewart Johnson, Jr. If you see an unmoving man with an umbrella hailing a cab at curbside, you'll know the figures are on display as they were during the 1992 holiday season. It has been said that Johnson's figures are so realistic that a sculpture of a man eating a hamburger once got the interest of a small dog who went into a barking fit after sniffing the bronze pant legs.

Johnson is the grandson of one of the founding brothers of the medical supplies firm Johnson & Johnson. When told that other artists have criticized his works for resembling Norman Rockwell's paintings, Johnson, who certainly doesn't need the money he earns from his art, answered, "I do what people show an interest in." His 70-foot giant, titled *The Awakening*, is on display in Washington, D.C.; a lifescale sculpture of Abraham Lincoln was unveiled in Gettysburg, Pennsylvania, in 1991, and his works are in public and private collections in Canada, Paris, London, Osaka, Bonn, Istanbul, Zurich, Sydney, and Hong Kong.

Knickerbocker Hotel

Continue to walk north on Michigan Avenue; take a right at Walton. The entrance to the Knickerbocker Hotel is at 163 East Walton. It began in 1927 as the Davis Hotel, became the Knickerbocker in 1931, changed to the Playboy Towers in 1970, and returned to the Knickerbocker after 1979, when $5 million was spent to remodel the place.

It still has the lighted dance floor in the grand ballroom, with 760 fluorescent lamps under the feet of those dancing the light fantastic.

We are told that the 14th floor of the Knickerbocker was once a speakeasy during the sinful days of Prohibition. There is a hidden staircase from the 12th to the 14th floors. It's now a service entrance, but when the hotel was originally built, by gentlemen who were fronting for the Purple Mob of Detroit, the 14th floor had two casinos. Only one elevator serviced the 14th floor. In case of a raid, gamblers and drinkers could dash down the secret staircase to the 12th floor and get a different elevator out of the building.

Drake Hotel

Exit the Knickerbocker and cross the street to get to the Drake, a hotel that prides itself on its dignity. Its list of celebrity guests is four single-spaced pages. It includes Bing Crosby, Amelia Earhart, Princess Grace of Monaco, Sophia Loren, Dustin Hoffman, Bill Murray, Jack Nicholson, Winston Churchill, Queen Elizabeth, Prince Phillip, King Hussein of Jordan, Nehru of India, Herbert Hoover, Dwight Eisenhower, Gerald Ford, Ronald Reagan, Charles Lindbergh, Walt Disney, Charleton Heston, and Edith Rockefeller McCormick, who died in her Drake Hotel suite in 1932, still hoping her husband, Harold, might return. Harold's name had been linked with Ganna Walska, Betty Noble, Pola Negri, and Baroness Violet Beatrice von Wenner, who accompanied him during his whistling concerts.

The Drake opened in 1920, having been designed by Ben Marshall, who also designed the Blackstone Hotel on south Michigan Avenue. He was remembered for his tailoring, his white Packard automobiles, and the many young ladies he escorted about town. The Drake has windows that can open and shut, a rarity in hotels these days.

A Presidential Suite on the fifth floor is in the former quarters of the widow of Maurice L. Rothschild, who occupied this area for 58 years until her death in 1980 at age 102. Since the suite was re-opened in 1982, it has been the temporary home to the prime ministers of Australia and Tunisia, the queens of Thailand and the Netherlands, the president of Italy, and Nancy Reagan.

A $20 million restoration was completed in 1986, and the hotel is beautiful today.

As you enter the Drake, walk to your left through the arcade and into the Cape Cod Room, where you ought to taste the Bookbinder red snapper soup with sherry on the side in a room famous for its fish dishes. The restaurant has been a *Holiday* magazine award winner for 36 years.

Also in the arcade, before you get to the Cape Cod Room, is the Coq D'Or. It is here that the second drink was served in Chicago after prohibition was repealed. It was a straight whiskey because there were so many people waiting for a legal drink that the bartender only had time to pour whiskey at 40 cents a glass. That was at 8:30 p.m., on Wednesday, December 6, 1933. The Palmer House, which can be found on the State Street Walk, had allegedly served the first drink at 8:26 p.m., beating the Coq D'Or by a mere four minutes and starting a celebration lasting until dawn, during which more than 200,000 gallons of whiskey were served in Chicago alone. It was quite a party!

Next walk upstairs to the lobby, with its open fireplace, comfy chairs, and expansive feeling. A harpist accompanies English afternoon tea in the Palm Court here, with a pianist for cocktails and jazz trios Friday and Saturday nights. This is a great hotel in the old style.

Return to Michigan Avenue and continue walking north to the 900 North Michigan building. When this structure opened in September 1988, Bloomingdale's did $1.37 million worth of business beating the single-day sales record of the Bloomingdale's in New York.

Fans have been known to follow Oprah Winfrey as she shops here and make comments on how good the colors she chooses would look on her.

The Oak Tree restaurant, on the sixth floor, is a survivor, one of the rarities that disappeared and then was reborn. It formerly existed around the corner and a block away, at Oak and Rush, where a Barney's store now stands. And it rents a space that housed two short-lived eateries, CityScape and the Carnegie Deli. According to one reviewer, it features hearty, home-cooked food and is "a pleasant way to start the day."

Across the street, in the 919 North Michigan building, is the Carol and Irwin Ware Fur salon. Irwin graduated from the University of Illinois with a degree in accounting at the end of the Depression and no job. So he went to work for a retail furrier who liked to bet on horses. The boss's absences while at the track allowed Irwin to quickly learn the business.

In 1955, when Ware was a widower with four children, he met Carol Morris, who had modeled petite fashions and shoes. They married in 1957 and later went into business together. Mrs. Carol Ware said, "We have sold furs to Jill St. John, Oprah, Mrs. Bob Hope, Yul Brynner, all the Gabors, and anybody who can walk. I've flown to San Francisco to show our furs to Danielle Steele. Our motto: Have fur, will travel."

When asked about today's more independent woman, who might not wait for a Sugar Daddy to give her a fur, the irrepressible Mrs. Ware said, "First she buys her condo, then her car, and then she buys her coat. I've often said that they come to me before the face lift. If they're having problems in their lives and they want to feel more glamorous, sometimes a fur can change their image faster than a face lift."

The Wares are even appearing in literature. In Sidney Sheldon's novel *The Stars Shine Down*, Lara Cameron, the "young and beautiful" character who was creating a business empire, arrived in Chicago and "went into action. She visited Kane's and Ultimo for designer dresses, Joseph's for shoes, Saks Fifth Avenue and Marshall Field's for lingerie, Trabert and Hoeffer for jewelry, and Ware for a mink coat. And every time she bought something, she heard her father's voice saying, 'I'm nae made of money. Get yourself something frae the Salvation Army Citidel.'"

Continue north to Oak Street, and notice that traffic heading toward Lake Shore Drive descends into an underpass. In 1962 Chicagoans successfully prevented an elevated highway interchange from being built here. It would have ruined the view of the lake.

This ends your north Michigan Avenue walk. If you wish to continue shopping, turn to the next stroll, the Oak Street walk, which features many designer boutiques.

4 OAK STREET WALK

The shoppers' paradise

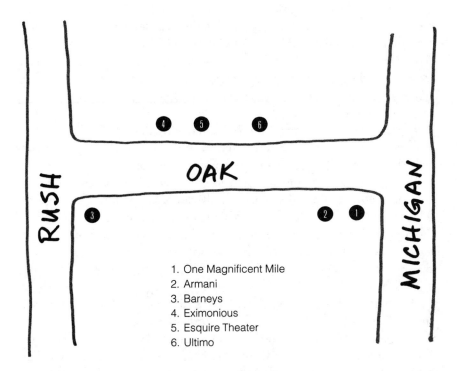

1. One Magnificent Mile
2. Armani
3. Barneys
4. Eximonious
5. Esquire Theater
6. Ultimo

Time: 2 hours or more, depending on how intensely you want to shop.
To get there: The #145, #146, #147, and #151 CTA buses stop at
Walton and Michigan, one block south of the beginning of the walk.
However, since we're going to look at expensive, designer clothing,
perhaps a cab ride is more fitting, especially since it should cost less than
$4 to get to Oak and Michigan from State and Madison or many other
Loop locations.

Start at One Magnificent Mile

Oak Street, from Michigan to Rush, is the mecca for shoppers who enjoy spending money and who must be seen in the latest styles from Italy and France. This is the walk for the fashion-conscious, and, even if you are here to browse rather than to buy, it is fun to see what the rest of the world considers to be the ultimate style.

Like so many areas of Chicago, Oak Street is in transition. Today, the street still has a neighborhood feel, with the various shop owners tending to know and like one another. But that may not last for long. Rents have been soaring on this street, many of the smaller shops have moved elsewhere, and there is a danger of Oak Street becoming an extension of Michigan Avenue, with its huge, powerful, fashionable stores. In fact, even today the number of independent shops on the street is dwindling. Many of the stores belong to small chains of boutiques or are owned by large corporations.

If some of the boutiques mentioned here have disappeared by the time you take the walk, do take a moment to mourn their passing. It means that the street is changing, and perhaps not for the better.

Putting aside such melancholy thoughts, let us begin this walk cele- brating the many ways the human body can be draped by entering One Magnificent Mile, 980 North Michigan, at the corner of Oak and Michigan. Take the escalator to the second floor and enter Spiaggia, an elegant 140-seat restaurant with glass doors with huge marble handles. Spiaggia also offers a wonderful view of Michigan Avenue and the park at Oak Street.

Ask what celebrities have dined here and the list will seem endless. It includes Dustin Hoffman, Dolly Parton, Harry Connick, Jr., Robert Duvall, Joe Pesci, Burt Reynolds and Lonni Anderson, Robert De Niro, Steven Spielberg and Kate Capshaw, Peter Ustinov, Walter Matthau, and Madonna, when she was in town filming *A League of Their Own*.

Chef Paul Bartolotta has made this the cutting edge of Italian restau- rants. He was enticed from Italy to New York, and then in 1991 to Chicago reportedly at great expense. His specialty is "red snapper in crazy water," or dentice in acqua pazza, a $26.95 dish from the Gulf of Naples. In 1992, the *Chicago Tribune* called Spiaggia "probably the city's best Italian restaurant."

It should be noted that the average dinner check is $55 and nearly half the 100 wines listed here cost more than $50 a bottle. It is not a restaurant to visit *after* bankruptcy. However, Cafe Spiaggia, an oddly shaped room near the older Spiaggia restaurant, has both the chef's touch and less expensive meals.

The South Side of the Street

Once you have resisted the temptation to begin a shoppers' walk by sitting and drinking or eating, retrace your steps, exit One Mag Mile and walk west on Oak Street on the south side of the street. This simple walk will consist of strolling up one side of Oak Street for one block, crossing the street, and then coming back on the other side.

Benetton's, at 121 East Oak, is part of a chain of Italian-made knitwear stores. The franchise, named after Luciano Benetton, offers mohair, angora, and cashmere sweaters for around $65 and up. It is the winter place to go, especially if you have begun the walk feeling a little chilly.

At 113 East Oak is Giorgio Armani, a store that was designed by Armani and an Italian architect. The muted, gray background of the boutique makes the clothes appear as if they were on a stage. Armani and two other boutiques are owned by Joan Weinstein, who we will meet later in this walk.

Continue walking west. At the nearby Water Mark, 109 East Oak, mother and daughter Cristi and Nancy Gross sell handmade papers, thank-you notes, wedding invitations, Christmas cards, bar and bat mitzvah announcements, and Miss Grace's Lemon Cakes from Beverly Hills.

Bottega Veneta, at 107 East Oak, imports Italian leather goods from Vecenzia, which is near Venice. The shop is known for its woven leather bags (just feel how soft they are), luggage, billfolds, $1,300 handbags, $1,200 attache cases, and distinctive silk ties. Sales here are in January and June with as much as 50 percent off.

If you are a career woman and need that certain power suit, visit Ann Taylor at 103 East Oak.

Or take a look at the perpetual video fashion show on the TV screen to the rear of Gianni Versace, at 101 East Oak. The Versace shop, the largest in the world devoted to that Italian designer, was introduced to Chicago with a grand kick-off fashion show on March 26, 1986, at the Field Museum. Iman, one of the highest-priced models in the world, paraded under the watchful eyes of Versace, as well as under two stuffed, charging elephants and assorted dinosaur bones.

When Don Johnson started wearing Versace on "Miami Vice," the designer became famous in America. Rod Stewart, Eric Clapton, Harry Hamlin, and Robin Givens have shopped in this store. Elton John and Luther Vandross buy much of their wardrobe here. The manager/buyer, Joy Sander, once had to rush out to buy a suitcase for Elton John to hold all his purchases. And Vandross once entered the store just as one of his songs was being played, a happy coincidence.

Men's suits start at $1,800, women's dresses at $1,000 and up, and women's suits at $2,300 and up. A Versace evening gown starts at $2,500, but could easily reach $8,000. Thirty to 40 percent off the previous season's apparel sales are in January and June.

After looking around the Versace shop and noting that the three-story building was turned into a two-level store to give higher ceilings, continue walking west to 67 East Oak where you will see Rag Trade a few steps below street level. The owner, Timothy Robert, guarantees that "for sure" Rag Trade features the best buys on Oak Street, including very inexpensive used designer clothing. It is a vintage and resale shop where my son bought a cool pair of pants from the '50s for $10. It also had wooden angels from Bali hanging from the ceiling and none of them were pornographic. In Bali, variations of such carvings could not be viewed in polite company.

The store has been in this spot since 1964, but it is often overlooked since it is in what should be termed the garden level. It's a very different shopping experience from the rest of the street and a real find.

As the walk continues, you arrive at Pompian, 57 East Oak, a place where women such as Mrs. Juanita (Michael) Jordan are known to shop for clothes. Doris Lavin, the owner, has been in the business for 40 years. The secret of her longevity: "Forget the past and have a good view of the present." She also advises that "daytime dresses are dead." Her sportswear can be priced as high as $2,000 a suit.

At 55 East Oak is Sulka, a three-story boutique. The second floor is decorated with wild boar hide tile. In 1992, the custom suits started at around $3,000. The store also features $95 socks and $600 silk robes made by an 80-year-old master robemaker. The fitting rooms have silk paisley on the walls and the whole store is wheelchair-accessible.

When you visit Jeraz, at 51 East Oak, be sure to ask for Jerry Frishman, who says, "My wife's the owner. I work for her." His youthful, pretty wife, Loren, readily agrees, "He does work for me . . . every day."

Jerry Frishman is a delightful man with a quick wit, an easy manner, and extensive knowledge of his Italian suits designed by Verri, Lucian,

Soprani, and Basale. Most of the suits here come from Milan, in northern Italy because, Frishman observes, "In southern Italy, all they do is fish, sit outside, drink coffee, and watch the broads go by." Frishman has five tailors, suits by the best Italian designers from $1,000, and a way of cutting through fashion nonsense to make sure that his customers get what they want.

Frishman, who hires only the best tailors he can find, believes that tailoring is an often overlooked aspect of this business. He also only carries designers exclusive to Chicago. Since all of these suits are hand-made, they are limited in quantity. A designer may only make 12 suits a year of each style, so Jeraz would get four.

Note the youthful-looking first floor and the designer-oriented second floor, each redecorated in 1992.

Ilona of Hungary, at 45 East Oak, is a skin care institute where the staff provides very private $55 facials, $35 herbal wraps during which hot towels dipped in herbal tea are wrapped around you, $15 manicures, $30 pedicures, and massages—$50 for women, $55 for men because the males generally have more body to massage. Owned by Ilona Mezzaros, the clinic also has outlets in New York, Denver, Houston, Costa Mesa, and Palm Springs.

The manager of Ilona of Hungary is Teresa Gold of Poland, who says that more than 40 percent of the customers are men because "men are so into skin care that they are now the leaders of women when it comes to beauty."

Among the celebrities who have availed themselves of Ilona's services include Kelly McGillis when she was in Chicago filming *The Babe*, Robin Givens, and James Earl Jones.

A few steps below street level at 43 East Oak is Bravco—a store specializing in the same hair and beauty products sold at Oak Street's 22 hair and beauty salons but at much lower prices.

At the corner is Barneys New York, a 3-story, 50,000-square-foot men's and women's clothing store that opened September 8, 1992, replacing the Oak Tree, a restaurant. About 40 percent of the clothing in the store carries Barneys own label, with designers like Calvin Klein and Donna Karan getting boutiques within the store.

Barneys was founded by the late Barney Pressman in 1923 as a discount men's store in New York. It began to go upscale in the 1960s and formed a joint-venture with a Japanese retailer in 1989.

This 10-store chain is a $200 million a year operation, but it remains a family-run business with eight members of the Pressman clan involved in store operations, including Barney's son, Fred, who is president.

The store posed several questions for Chicagoans: Will shoppers accustomed to seeing similar stores on Michigan Avenue travel the block up Oak Street to buy? And, despite a good reputation in New York, what does the name Barneys mean to Midwesterners?

Cross the street and head back east, making a U-turn at Rush Street.

The North Side of the Street

At 32 East Oak is Sacha of London. This is a shoestore specializing in trendy, cool black shoes and cowboy boots that will probably see neither horse nor cow in their lifetime. The staff seems very friendly.

Sugar Magnolia has moved to 34 East Oak and has changed more than its address. It used to be the spot for Gold Coast junior high school girls, but now is an upscale women's boutique for every age. They still carry their rhinestone studded T-shirt with the sheet music from the Grateful Dead's song "Sugar Magnolia." If you've named the store after the song, you've got to stock the T-shirt.

My Sister's Circus or Isis (the store has both names), at 38 East Oak, began as the Bikini Zoo in another location. Later, the two sisters changed the Bikini Zoo to My Sister's Circus and sold one-of-a-kind dresses for 14 years. When they amicably parted, one sister, Suzanne Fey Gantz, opened Isis, named after the Egyptian goddess of womanly goods, adding that name to the previous Circus name. Isis features fun sportswear.

Be sure to ask Micki Fullett to show you the washroom, which is a shrine to the contemporary celebrities and rock stars who have visited the store. Van Halen, Chynna Phillips, Joe Pesci, the guys from Aerosmith, Sammy Hagar, and others have all signed the walls. Cher did not sign. Ms. Fullett proudly recalled the time Delta Burke literally bought the jacket off the clerk's back. "I later saw her wearing it in a picture in the *Enquirer*," Ms. Fullett said.

According to another employee, Dawn Marotta, the single most incredible weekend was July 4, 1992, when the entire store was remodeled in just three nights as the staff chanted "We can do it, we can do it." A sign in the window proclaimed, "There's nothing wrong with a little plastic surgery."

When I interviewed Sela Ward, the star of NBC's "Sisters," in My Sister's Circus ("Sisters" in Sister's Circus, get it?), she revealed for the first time how her husband-to-be proposed to her. He gave her three rings, saying, "I give you this one because I love you . . . This because we should be together always . . . And this because I want to marry you." Then in retelling the story, Ms. Ward's eyes again filled with tears as she recalled, "I went 'Oh my God' because he caught me completely off guard because I was expecting who knows what. I didn't answer him. I reached in my purse. Now he's very confused because traditionally women are supposed to say 'YES!' or go 'OH, GOD!' and be in tears. I took a box out of my purse and handed it to him. He's looking at me as if to say 'I don't get it.' He opens the box and he pulls out a watch. I say 'Turn it over,' and on the back I had engraved 'Yes.'"

In the basement at 46 East Oak is TJ's, the only bar on Oak Street. Formerly called Scalawags and the Loading Zone, TJ's is decidedly and quietly homosexual in orientation. As Laird Brandon, a former manager said, "We've been hiding out here in the basement where we mind our own business for nine million years." The comedienne Pudgy had a drink here and stayed to do her act.

At 50 East Oak on the second floor is the Boutique of Hino and Malee, one of the most successful international designers based in Chicago. They met in Chicago after leaving Japan and Thailand respectively, and started designing and making clothes. Their clothes are usually loose-fitting and flowing, and are generally in basic colors—black, white, tan, and so on.

When you get to Eximonious of London, Winnetka, and Chicago, at 52 East Oak, pause and consider what is not there. At one time, the Oak Street Bookshop was at 52 East Oak and its owner, Carol Stoll, was a self-identified "living legend." In 1985, director Bryan Forbes wrote in the *London Times* about the "culture in an ill-read neighborhood." He added, "Every community should have its Oak Street Bookshop, presided over by someone who cares to keep the flame alight. Carol Stoll loves books, and with her love of books comes a rare hope for us all in a world where the real quality of life is under constant attack from the yahoos." Now that Carol's bookstore has departed this street, it may be an "ill-read neighborhood."

Moving east, walk by the Loew's Esquire Theater, which was once one large theater, and now has six screens. If you go to a movie here, and the choices are often excellent, take the elevator to the third and fourth floors and try the Australian Walkabout designer water. Why not?

At 72 East Oak is Betsey Johnson, which is part of a chain based in New York featuring clothes for women. Betsey Johnson has only been in Chicago since 1989, yet the store always manages to be both cutting edge and accessible. Also, the clothes are often between $10 and $100.

At Stuart Chicago, 102 East Oak, owner Stuart Goldin is proud of his collection of men's Italian suits, ties, and shirts. He quickly took a German suit coat off the rack and put it on me to illustrate the latest trend in men's styling. "Guys have been working out so much and their chests have gotten so much larger that now the suits are being specially tailored for the in-shape male," Goldin said.

Goldin is proudest of his Palzileri line, an Italian designer of shirts and pants, who Stuart says will become "number one in this country." He has fitted the weight-lifting weatherman for the local ABC station and former Bear Walter Payton.

The store at 104 East Oak, Marina Yachting, is owned by Steve Timmer and Tony Weege, both under 30 as of this writing. On this street that makes them whippersnappers and the subject of conversation by other store owners. The store carries sailing clothes, including water-proof cotton sweaters for $200. Handy place to visit on a rainy day. Also at 104 East Oak is Great Lakes Jewelry, which was listed as a place for bargains by *Chicago* magazine in 1992. The magazine found $15 sterling silver earrings, necklaces from $60 to $200, and other items manufac-tured by Great Lakes, which accounts for about 65 percent of the merchandise.

At Contessa Bottega, at 106 East Oak, good customers may be picked up in a Rolls Royce and refreshed with champagne during the arduous trip to this lively shop. By all means visit Contessa Helena Kontos, the owner and life force. She is a contessa because her maternal grandfather was a count in Rome. Whitney Houston, Ann Jillian, Jane Seymour, Natalie Cole, and others wear clothes designed by the Contessa. Her Contessa Helena Eau de Parfum ranks among the top five in sales at Marshall Field's stores, possibly because Natalie Cole "bathes in it," according to Helena.

And Petros Kogiones, the owner of Dianna's Opaa in Greektown, has been her husband-to-be for several years now. If you look in the Greek-town section of this book, you will see that for many years Petros has been attempting to set a world record for kissing women. When I asked Helena what she thought of that, she said, "Let him practice with others. He comes to me when he is ready!"

Contessa Helena Kontos, life force of Contessa Bottega

Upstairs there is the Ultimate Bride. The Sonia Rykiel designer dress shop is on the ground floor. It is owned by Joan Weinstein, who also owns Ultimo and Armani, and whose story will be told when you arrive at Ultimo in a few minutes.

Charles Ifergan, a hairdressing salon, is also at 106 East Oak. Bargain nights are Tuesdays and Wednesdays when apprentice workshops are held under the supervision of Ifergan and style director Michel Botbol. Haircuts and blow-dries are free, according to *Chicago* magazine, and coloring is only $5 to cover the cost of the chemicals.

At 112 East Oak is Marilyn Miglin, a famous hair and beauty salon. Marilyn Miglin also has her own line of cosmetics, including the most expensive perfume in the world—the $400-an-ounce Marilyn's Pheromone, with 179 ingredients including some impossible-to-get fragrances from ancient Egypt.

According to a pamphlet on the perfume, traces of fragrance were found in 5,000-year-old Egyptian tombs. "At last, Marilyn Miglin's requisite for a perfume's lasting qualities was about to be answered." In other words, you better like Pheromone because it's going to stay around for a long time.

After research at the University of Chicago, Miglin "got lost in the desert on a camel. I crawled on my stomach through many, many tombs," she said. But finally she found the formulas carved in temple reliefs and ancient hieroglyphics. They were then translated by an Egyptologist and mixed by an Italian perfumer. The result contains oils from Italy, Belgium, Madagascar, and Portugal, plus tonka extract from Venezuela, "Lotus blossoms from Marrakesh, wild Narcissus from France, the sacred Egyptian Kyphi, the provocative Cyprinium and mysterious Mendesium," and "Ylang-Ylang, Fo-ti-tieng, Aegyptuim, Penny Royal, Iris, Rosemary, Sandlewood, Attar of Rose, Patchouli, Lotus Palm, and Oak Moss." It is not to be worn just to freshen up after a hard work-out.

Miglin's clients include Raquel Welch, Diana Ross, Nancy Reagan, Barbara Bush, Marilu Henner (John Travolta bought Pheromone for her), Carol Channing, and Maria Shriver.

Miglin, herself, is quite a story: A teenage ballerina, a former Chez Paree Adorable (the memorable chorus line in what was then the grandest nightclub in Chicago), a dancer with Jimmy Durante and on Ford TV commercials, then a model, and finally the owner of a cosmetics boutique that has grown from a staff of one in 1963 to a staff of more than 80. It was, according to *Crain's Chicago Business*, the eighth largest woman-owned firm in 1988.

In her store, you can buy one of her dozens of products or get a two-hour professional beauty consultation or a professional makeup application for $50 each.

Next stop: Ultimo, at 114 East Oak, where they keep Chicago ahead of New York. The owner Joan Weinstein has 15 people in the alterations department, meaning that they can totally remake blouses or cut suits down three sizes, if need be.

Ultimo carries the latest and the best. If you open a Vogue or Elle and like something you see, often the only place to get it in Chicago is Ultimo.

As you enter Ultimo, you see no clothes. Instead you feel as though you have walked into the vestibule of a rajah's palace, with opulent fabrics, carpets, and flowers greeting you.

Ultimo originally opened as a men's store in 1969, when the height of fashion was jeans, sandals, and dashikis. The late Jerry Weinstein suggested that his wife, Joan, "do something upstairs." Thus, the famed women's department was born. Here, dresses are bought in small quantities so that, heaven forfend, two women will not show up at a society benefit wearing the same $3,000 dress.

Jerry died of a heart attack at age 46 in 1972, while Joan was in Milan on a buying trip. Joan said, "I thought of many things." Then she paused and her eyes showed undiminished pain, which was quickly replaced by determination, "But I thought I must keep my mind busy."

Thus, the most active retailer on Oak Street was created. When the Armani line became very popular at Ultimo, Mrs. Weinstein opened a

Joan Weinstein of Ultimo, Sonia Rykiel, and Armani

separate store across the street in 1987. The same process happened for Sonia Rykiel in 1988. And, when talking to this unbelievably energetic and forthright woman, one gets the feeling that it may very well happen again and again.

"Oak Street is the best mall street in Chicago," she declares. "If you're too small for Michigan Avenue, the next best choice is Oak Street where a small store will be more noticeable."

When asked about her success, Mrs. Weinstein answered, "Chicago is an understated classic city. Ultimo, Armani, and Rykiel are successful because they sell to people who do care."

Ultimo has been renovated many times since it opened in 1969, but always with the same decor, originally designed by photographer Victor Skrebneski. The sensual feel of the place is enhanced by the hundreds of yards of fabric. It's like a harem in waiting.

In 1992, men's suits at Ultimo were priced as high as $3,000 and women's designer dresses were from $200 to $4,000.

Ultimo expanded in the past by buying out Acorn, a restaurant which formerly adjoined the clothing store. In 1986, *Time* magazine said that the hamburgers at the Acorn on Oak ranked among the four best in America. I guess now there are only three best.

Shoppers at Ultimo have included playwrite David Mamet, rocker Eric Clapton, actor John Malkovich, and TV talker Oprah Winfrey, who bought dresses for her staff to wear to the daytime Emmy Awards. There are sales here in January and June.

This ends your Oak Street walk. You have visited many stores with the designs that are the height of style. It is estimated that this one block takes in more than $100 million worth of business a year. And that is a lot of Italian suits and dresses.

5 STATE STREET AND THE LOOP WALK

From the new library to the old river

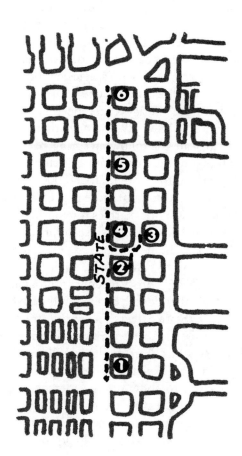

1. Sears Roebuck Store
2. Palmer House
3. Kroch's and Brentano's
4. Carson Pirie Scott & Co.
5. Marshall Field & Co.
6. United of America Building

Time: 2 hours, less if you're not in the mood to look at clothing stores.
To get there: Nearly every form of public transportation known to man stops along or near State Street. The corner of State and Congress, where the walk begins, is a stop for the #2, #6, #11, #15, #29, #36, #44, #62, #99, #145, #146, #162, and #164 buses. The subway stops at Jackson, Harrison, and State Street, and there is parking for cars in city lots south of Congress on State Street.

From Trail to Mall

Everyone knows State Street is "that great street." Well, it wasn't—at least not for many years. Then in 1979, the new State Street Mall opened, but it never quite got the attention desired by the planners.

As it is today, State Street is a sometimes vital merchandising area, bustling with people, slightly tacky in spots, needing to be revitalized yet again, changing almost daily, and often an exciting place to visit.

State Street was originally a trail laid out by the legendary Gurdon Hubbard, a trapper and trader nicknamed "Swift Walker" because he could cover 75 miles in a single day and out-walk and out-run any Indian. He was the husband of a 14-year-old Indian lass named Watseka. He also became Chicago's first meat packer when he collected hogs during the winter of 1828–29, and piled them on the riverfront where they froze, awaiting sale the following spring.

Hubbard was an uncanny investor, buying lots for $66.33 in 1829 and selling them for more than $80,000 seven years later. He did it again in 1835, when he bought more property for $5,000 and sold it four months later to New York sharpies for another $80,000. History records that he eventually "cast aside" Watseka for someone called a "legal helpmate."

Hubbard Trail became State Road in 1834, when road commissioners marked Swift Walker's old, straight path with milestones. State Road originally ran from Vincennes, Indiana, to Chicago. Eventually, State Road was abandoned, except for its path through Chicago, which became known as State Street. The entire street was then worth about $60.

As you stand at Congress and State, you are in front of the former Sears Roebuck Store, built by William LeBaron Jenney in 1891. Jenney's use of a steel skeleton allowed him to create huge windows that let in more light to show off the merchandise in the building. If you look closely, you'll see the name "L. Z. Leiter" carved into the parapet. Levi Leiter, who commissioned this building for $1.5 million, formed a partnership with Marshall Field to create the famous department store before branching out on his own. This building, also called the Second Leiter Building in architectural guidebooks, is known for its simple design.

It was renovated in 1984, with no changes to the exterior because it is a national landmark and has now emerged as One Congress Center. Chicagoans can pay their gas bills on the first floor. The Illinois Department of Employment Security, on the second through sixth floors, mails out unemployment checks from this building. Student loans are handled by the U. S. Department of Education on the seventh floor, and Social Security administrators are trained on the eighth floor.

The Harold Washington Library Center

The Harold Washington Library Center is across the street. First, look at the building. The hybrid neoclassic design was a contest winner. I think the critics have been very kind to this structure, which bears the name of the first African-American mayor of Chicago, a man who lived in controversy during his first term and who became almost universally respected (if not loved) by the time of his death. I think the building named after Harold Washington looks rather ridiculous, with a Greek temple pasted on what appears to be an imitation of the Monadnock Building (see LaSalle Street walk).

The building is topped with $3 million worth of sculptures, including a green-painted leafy ornament 36 feet high and 70 feet wide, designed by Kent Bloomer, a Yale University professor. There are also five, two-ton owls sculpted by Raymond Kaskey.

Once inside, there are problems: You can't get there from here. Only staff and the disabled have elevator service from the main floor to the rest of the building. Most patrons must use the slow-moving escalators.

Once you get there, it's not easy finding what you want. As Elaine Markoutsas wrote in *Crain's Chicago Business*, "the new library isn't always user friendly." In fact, the computerized card catalog has been under severe criticism because it is difficult—some say well-nigh impossible—to find the book you're looking for.

And once you've found it in the catalog, it may not be on the shelves or it may not be what you want. As *Chicago* magazine asked, "Why build a $145 million library to house a book collection that is second-rate?"

The library has 2 million books, 8,500 periodicals, 860,000 government documents, and more than 3 million microforms, plus a staff of 600. The pluses include the helpful, usually friendly staff; handsome maple furnishings; the university-style carrels for quiet reading and study; and the light, airy feel to this spanking new structure.

After exploring the library, walk north on State Street toward the ugly elevated structure over Van Buren. Incidentally, in the 1983 movie *Risky Business,* Rebecca DeMornay and Tom Cruise made love in a late-night elevated car while Tangerine Dream played "Love on a Real Train." This structure may look ugly to you, but it was the height of romantic lust to a Hollywood writer!

The peak of popularity for the elevated system was reached in 1926 when the el had 228,812,676 riders. With more people driving automobiles and fare increases, ridership has declined. In 1991, the CTA rapid transit lines served 134,925,152 riders.

The Old Vice District

There is a park on the west side of the street with a fascinating past. Pritzker Park is located on what was once one of the most disreputable and seediest places in town. It now has a sandbox, a "grand meadow," which is actually too small to be described either as a "meadow" or "grand," and a black granite wall which re-creates a wall seen in Rene Magritte's painting *The Banquet*. It's all explained on a handy plaque on the site.

In 1896, Mickey Finn, an ex-pickpocket, opened the Lone Star Saloon here and later invented a knockout mixture that subsequently made his name famous. The area was then known as Whiskey Row and in the early 1900s one Johnny Rafferty planned his confidence games here. If you saw the movie *The Sting*, you saw an approximation of some of the stunts pulled on gullibles from Terre Haute or Galena. In the 1870s, State and Van Buren was the beginning of "Satan's Mile," a vile vice district. One turn-of-the-century reformer described the goings-on as "only conceivable in Sodom and Gomorrah."

Continue along the east side of State. After crossing Van Buren, you will be passing by the Goldblatt Store, a landmark built in 1912, originally known as Rothschild's (1912–1923), later the Davis Store (part of Marshall Field & Co., 1923–1936), and once part of a Chicago-based chain of department stores.

This store was supposed to be converted into Chicago's new public library. The city bought the store, but then the controversy and the arguments became heated in the wake of media investigations. It was said that the fire sprinklers didn't work and that the floor couldn't hold the load of all those books.

Finally, and happily, DePaul University bought the 222,000 square feet of space on the 11 floors. Over $70 million will be spent to turn it into DePaul Center, with the city of Chicago renting floors two through five, retail spaces opening up on street level, and DePaul occupying floors six through 11 with skybridges linking this building with the adjoining DePaul property to the east. Goldblatt's 38 elevators will be replaced, the terra-cotta facades and cornices will be rehabilitated, and a park will be created at State and Jackson.

If you look to the west, across State Street, between Jackson and Adams, there is a cul-de-sac that has the Everett McKinley Dirksen Federal Building blocking its west end. Here you will find McDonald's and Wendy's Hamburgers, Aurelio's Pizza, and Popeye's Famous Fried Chicken vying for your attention. Think of that. An entire mews devoted to fast food. And who says that State Street isn't that Great Street?

The Palmer House

Continue strolling north on State Street. In slightly less than half a block you'll reach the entrance to the Palmer House, the oldest continually operating hotel in the country. It is safe to say that State Street wouldn't be here if it were not for Potter Palmer, builder of the original Palmer House and the man who invested $7 million in the street in 1866. He widened it, leased a store to Marshall Field and Levi Z. Leiter, founders of Marshall Field & Co., and built a fine hotel which opened on September 26, 1871.

That was not the most auspicious date to open a 225-room hotel costing $300,000. It burned to the ground in the Great Chicago Fire just 13 days later.

A second, allegedly fireproof, hotel was built in 1873, and Palmer invited his competitors to "build a fire in the center of any chamber or room of the Palmer House proper." Palmer bet that, after the room was closed for one hour, the fire would not extend beyond that single room. No one ever took him up on his challenge.

The current hotel was rebuilt in sections from 1925–1927, completely replacing the old Palmer House, where John Coughlin got a job as a rubber in the baths as a youth and became "Bathhouse John," a memorable crooked Chicago alderman. It is also the place where the first drink was served after the repeal of Prohibition.

Today's hotel is part of the Hilton chain. In 1975, President Gerald Ford stayed in the Presidential Suite. In 1976, candidate Jimmy Carter stayed in a regular room and carried his own luggage.

Walk into the Palmer House, go about halfway through the arcade, and take the escalator to the lobby. Look up and be dazzled by the painting on the ceiling featuring three panels of nudes looking graceful and bashful.

If you walk toward the stairway at the rear of the lobby, you'll approach the Empire Room, once the finest big-name entertainment spot in Chicago, and now a restaurant. Veloz and Yolanda, a dance team, worked there for 34 weeks in 1935, and the room saw the talents of Eddie Duchin, Ted Weems, Sophie Tucker, Hildegarde and Maurice Chevalier.

Walk up the stairs toward the Empire Room, do not be taken aback by the maître d', and look inside the Empire Room, with its black-and-gold trim and its huge mirrors behind pillars at either end of the room. Like thousands of others, I took the most beautiful girl in my high school class here for our senior prom. Over the years, the Empire Room may have seen more strapless evening gowns and unforgettable nights than any other spot in Chicago.

Return to the escalator, go down, take a left, and exit on Wabash Avenue, so-named because Indiana teamsters from the banks of the Wabash River would stop there. It was once paved with stove lids because it was so muddy.

The Mid-Continental Plaza Building is in front of you, but you can't see all of it because of the el train structure, which no one likes, which everyone would like to see replaced, and which occasionally is the scene of an accident. But that doesn't happen often enough to be worried about it.

Kroch's and Brentano's

Go left and walk north to Monroe Street, crossing to the east and entering Kroch's and Brentano's Bookstore, the largest in the city. They have an uncountable number of paperbacks in the basement, perhaps as many as 30,000 titles. According to the publishers, Kroch's windows are the most fought-after pieces of real estate in the city. In fact, if this book is not in the windows, please feel free to stop this walk for a few moments, enter Kroch's and complain about their oversight. Thank you.

This store has always fought the good battle for publicity for books. Roseanne Barr, before she was Roseanne Arnold, signed her book here, as did Joan Rivers, and Vanna White of Wheel of Fortune. Vanna did not turn a single letter when she visited.

One fan, while waiting for Kirk Douglas to autograph his book, said, "This isn't about a can of soup and a pound of beef; I'm going to meet Spartacus."

Others who have autographed books here include: former President Jimmy Carter, Jimmy Stewart, Bob Hope, Kareem Abdul Jabbar, Sidney Sheldon, Amy Tan, Stephen King, Erma Bombeck, Chicagoans Eugene Izzi and Sara Paretsky, Elmore Leonard, Kurt Vonnegut, Jr., and Leo Buscaglia, who also hugged every fan—the signing took seven hours!

A little farther north, at 19 South Wabash, in a 95-year-old building, is Iwan Reis & Co. tobacconists, the city's oldest company continuously owned and operated by the same family. The store always has that distinctive fresh tobacco scent and boasts a fine collection of antique pipes. Since 1857—that's a lot of puffing!

Carson Pirie Scott

Now return to State Street by walking west on Monroe. When you arrive at State and Monroe, you are in front of Carson Pirie Scott & Co., another architectural landmark. Walk to the State and Madison entrance, one block north (to your right), noticing both the plaque explaining the building's historical interest and the way architects Louis Sullivan (1899, 1904), Daniel H. Burnham (1906), and Holabird and Root (1960) designed and redecorated this store. Sullivan's ornamentation of this building is both delicate and unsurpassed.

The store's roots go back to Samuel Carson and John T. Pirie, who sailed for America from Northern Ireland on August 26, 1854, but were shipwrecked off Newfoundland. They later worked for family friends in small Illinois towns and earned enough money within two years for Carson to bring his bride, Elizabeth Pirie, his partner's sister, back from Belfast. Later, Mr. Pirie married Mr. Carson's sister to keep everything in the family.

Carson and Pirie, to be joined by John E. Scott in 1890, opened their first Chicago store in 1864, and were burned out in the 1871 fire. But Andrew MacLeish, general manager, stood in the store as the flames approached and offered fleeing Chicagoans "fifty silver dollars for every wagonload of merchandise you save out of this building." About 40 percent of the inventory was saved.

Carson's is now owned by P. A. Bergner & Co., of Milwaukee. In October 1990, it became the official retail headquarters of the Chicago

Bulls, which is why you can buy Bulls' team memorabilia on the first floor. Carson's Christmas windows have been a special treat for decades.

Enter the store through the State and Madison doors. You'll find a department store that is constantly updating itself. In the basement, the Corporate Level has everything for the executive man and woman, including fashions, a bank, and a post office. On the second floor is Metropolis, an in-store shopping mall with the largest Liz Claiborne shop in America, plus fashions from Esprit, Anne Klein, and others.

Crowds and History at State and Madison

Return to State and Madison and consider several more facts while standing at allegedly "the world's busiest corner."

At one time, because of the hill on which Fort Dearborn stood, the Chicago river entered the lake near here.

A little later, in the 1830s, you could buy lots on this corner, now valued at "beyond expectations," for $6.72 an acre. Still later, in the McVicker's Theater near this corner, Chicagoans saw the acting of Joseph Jefferson, Edmund Keane, Edwin Forrest, and, in 1862 in Shakespeare's *Richard III*, John Wilkes Booth, the man who later shot President Abraham Lincoln.

On November 11, 1924, after the assassination of the beloved Dion O'Banion, local flower arranger, bootlegger, and patron of culture, Louis Alterie told reporters he wanted a shoot-out at the corner of State and Madison with the guys who killed O'Banion, specifically with certain members of the Capone gang. Alterie was always loyal to his pals, although that shoot-out never occurred. According to *Chicago* magazine, when his buddy "Nails" Morton died after a fall from his horse, Alterie rented the nag, shot it through the head, and called the stable owner, telling him, "We taught that god-damn horse of yours a lesson. If you want the saddle, go and get it." It is reported that the horse never threw a rider again.

Toys 'R' Us has announced that it will open a 45,000-square-foot store plus a 15,000-square-foot Kids 'R' Us adjoining store on this corner by Christmas 1993. Toys 'R' Us, with 497 stores nationwide and 29 in the Chicago area, does about $6 billion in sales a year.

The odd, huge box at the corner of State and Madison is *Human Nature/Life Death*, a neon sculpture by Bruce Nauman, who began doing these things after observing old beer signs. His six-foot circular sculpture, which was installed in 1985, pairs the words "life/death, love/hate, pleasure/pain, and human nature/animal nature."

Cross Madison, walk a few feet to the south, and stop at the Hot Tix Booth, 24 South State, to learn about half-priced tickets to many Chicago theaters. What a great idea—you can get these tickets only on the day of performance, but you save money and the theaters fill the empty seats.

Reverse your steps, walk north, and you'll be across the street from the Wieboldt's Building at 1 North State Street, now occupied by Filene's Basement and T. J. Maxx. By this time, you should have passed several fruit, flower, and popcorn vendors, perhaps a few street musicians and, in the winter, even someone selling hot chestnuts. When Richard Daley was mayor, such entrepreneurs were energetically frowned upon. Now they are legal, and Chicago enjoys their presence even though the hot chestnuts seemed like a New York idea.

The Decrepit Masterpiece

There is a masterpiece in a state of decline on the west side of State Street at Washington, a half block north. The 32 North State Street Building, formerly the Reliance Building, is dirty and, from the outside, looks decrepit. Yet, if you walk toward the entrance near the Charles Shops Exotic Lingerie Store window, which is usually filled with undies with holes in them, you'll see a plaque put up in 1957 by the Chicago Dynamic Committee. The plaque lavishly praises this building, designed in 1890 by Daniel H. Burnham, and calls it "a glass tower . . . witness to the best architectural spirit of the nineteenth century . . ." Today it is grimy, and you have to look hard to imagine that it was once glorious.

Across the street, in an empty lot, Gallery 37 has operated since 1991 while builders decide what to do with the property. High school students are paid to work as printmakers, silkscreeners, quilters, ceramicists, maskmakers, or in other arts during six weeks each summer, often offering an alternative to gang involvement or decorating buses and underpasses with graffiti. It's a highly successful program, involving 450 students, 100 professional artists, 40 corporations, and 14 city departments. It began in 1989 when the late artist Keith Haring created a 500-foot-long mural with the help of local students. Proceeds from sales benefit the entire project, and some organizers have even dreamed of making the project self-sustaining.

At the moment, it is also the site of a lost dream. Architect Helmut Jahn had designed a two-tower project for this site, with a retail section along State Street across from the Field's store. But the 1.2 million-square-foot project depended on the construction of the first office tower, which never attracted the tenants it needed. As of 1992, the lot remained empty, and some folks were saying that Gallery 37 was so successful that perhaps the block should be taken by the city to create a permanent open space.

Crosby's Opera House

On the north side of Washington, just west of State Street, stood Crosby's Opera House, where, in 1868, the Republicans nominated General Ulysses S. Grant for president. But that is not why Crosby's Opera House is famous.

On January 21, 1867, it was the scene of the greatest lottery—and possibly the most skillful swindle—in Chicago history.

The opera house's opening night, in 1865, was delayed several days because of the assassination of Lincoln. Financial difficulties continued to beset the theater, and finally Crosby had to sacrifice it. He chose to do so by actually giving it away, by lottery.

Chicagoans loved the idea. Thousands bought the $5 lottery chances, which came with a book of engravings, suitable for framing and display-ing. When January 21 arrived, "the city was taken by storm," according to one newspaper. Thousands of strangers arrived, filling the hotels, the armory, and saloons. They looked over the opera house with a smug, proprietary air. Courts, businesses, and even the Board of Trade closed when the drawing was scheduled.

The 210,000 chances, plus the 25,593 held by Crosby, were put into a giant wheel. Another, smaller wheel held 302 prizes ranging from the opera house to worthless decorations. It took 113 spins of both wheels before the opera house was awarded to ticket number 58,600. But no one stepped forward to claim that number.

The mystery of who was the owner lasted for three days, until a letter appeared in a St. Louis newspaper from a Colonel Abraham Hagerman Lee of Prairie du Rocher, Illinois. Lee, a person no one in Prairie du Rocher knew, claimed he was very excited by the news, but that he couldn't leave his sick wife. On January 26, another letter from A. H. Lee appeared in the *Chicago Republican* newspaper. That letter claimed that Lee's wife was better, thank you, and that Lee had come to Chicago in secret—and he had accepted Crosby's offer to buy back the opera house for $200,000.

Oh, the suspicious minds! People said that Crosby drew all the best stuff anyway—two paintings and a bust of Lincoln. Furthermore, Crosby sold $900,000 worth of chances. Even if Lee existed and he was paid $200,000, Crosby was doing pretty well.

Things got so hot for Crosby that he had to leave town. His uncle, Albert, was managing the opera house when Grant was nominated there.

However, Crosby fared better than Chicago's first season of opera in 1853. Rice's Theater, on the south side of Randolph, was presenting Bellini's *La Sonnambula*, when the theater burned to the ground. One drunken opera lover sat in his seat applauding what he thought was a fake fire until he was dragged to safety. Total time for the first season of Chicago opera: One hour.

On the northwest corner of Washington and State is an odd-shaped object that looks like half a handcuff for a giant. *Being Born* is the 1983 creation by Virginio Ferarri, an artist-in-residence at the University of Chicago until he opened his own studio in Chicago in 1976. The work is a tribute to art and technology. Ferrari has explained, "The two stainless steel elements fit exactly into each other, symbolizing the process of die making." I'm not sure if it helps to know that.

Marshall Field & Co.

Once you reach Randolph and State Street one block north, you are standing under the 7¾-ton, cast-bronze, Marshall Field's clock, one of the most famous meeting spots in Chicago. Even though there is an identical clock on the Washington Street side of the store, saying, "I'll meet you under the Field's clock" means the one on the Randolph Street side every time.

This clock was stuck at 7:12 a.m., April 13, 1992, when the Chicago River sprung a leak, and it was not reset for almost five months.

Enter Field's through the door nearest Randolph Street, walk to the center of the store and look up through the skylight. Each Christmas this open area becomes everyone's vision of what a downtown Christmas should be, with a huge tree and many traditional decorations.

The clock: Nothing more needs to be said

This 2 million-square-foot store (second in size to Macy's in New York) was the subject of a $155 million, five-year renovation project that was completed on November 7, 1992. A dark, often cold, forbidding alley that once existed between the State Street and Wabash stores was replaced by a 165-foot atrium. The 6-ton, cast-iron fountain here was in the original plans for the store, but was never built.

Blair Kamin, the architectural critic writing in the *Chicago Tribune*, noted that "the dowager queen of Chicago's Big Stores looks more regal than ever . . . some Field's customers have been heard to exclaim that the renovated store looks just like the original. It doesn't; it looks better. And it works better. . . ." But he asked, "Will that help bring suburbanites back to the Loop to shop? Will it resuscitate the heart of State Street?" By the way, Kamin didn't like the 11-story, 165-foot atrium with the new/old fountain in it, writing that it "has the synthetic feel of a Houston shopping mall." You be the judge.

Much of the money for the restoration of the store was spent on hiding state-of-the-art air-conditioning in the basement and replacing the slurry of cement and cinders that was poured in 1902 under the wooden floorboards. During the last nine decades, the cinders began breaking up, creating movement in the wooden floors.

One significant improvement: There are no longer screens on the upper floors of the atrium. There were rumors that the screens were installed after a man leaped to his death there in the wake of the 1929 Stock Market Crash, on the way down breaking the collarbone of a Field's floorwalker. Perhaps this is an indication of lessening fears of a future severe economic reversal.

Walk straight ahead, escalate to the third floor, and take a left to the Crystal Palace, an old-fashioned ice-cream parlor, whose ice cream took fourth place in a recent local judging. The Crystal Palace is a symphony of olde-tyme furnishings, pink hue covers counters and chairs, and stained glass fills its arches.

Now that you're in Field's, who can resist buying a Frango Mint? Field's sells more than a million pounds of the mints yearly. I have friends in foreign lands like San Francisco who keep frozen Frangos just to have a true taste of Chicago around the house.

The Minneapolis-based Dayton-Hudson Corp. bought Field's in 1990 for $1.04 billion. Therefore, it owns the right to make Frango Mints, and promises to offer more than the nine flavors and to have more places where you can buy them, including airports.

The original mint was created by Frederick & Nelson Co. in Seattle. When Field's bought that store in 1929, it acquired the right to make "Francos," short for Frederick and Nelson Company. When the dictator Francisco Franco came to power in Spain, the name was changed to Frangos.

Return to Randolph and State, and think about history.

History at Randolph and State

In 1847, Long John Wentworth, the six-foot-six-inch mayor of Chicago, got angry at the signs overhanging this area, so he ordered the police to take them all down and pile them in the center of Randolph near State. During his second term as Chicago's first Republican mayor, Long John fired the entire police force on March 26, 1861, because the new police board might take over some of his powers. A captain, six lieutenants, and 50 patrolmen were fired at 1:40 a.m. By 10 a.m. the next morning the police board hired back most of them, despite the fact that there were 1,500 applicants for their jobs.

Wentworth, who was an energetic mayor, also charged into the Sands, a vice district near Chicago Avenue and State, with axes, crowbars, and teams of horses with hooks and chains. All the shanties were pulled down or burned while their owners were away enjoying a dog fight. Imagine handling a vice problem by pulling down the entire neighborhood!

Randolph and State was the center of gambling in Chicago in the 1870s and 1880s. To the west, the area between State and Dearborn along Randolph was known as "Hairtrigger Block" because of the many gun battles there.

It was also in this general vicinity that Gentle Annie, known as the fattest madame in town, fell in love with Cap Hyman, a gambler. Refusing to take no for an answer, Gentle Annie stormed into Cap Hyman's gambling house on September 23, 1866, dragged him from the sofa, knocked him down the stairs, and chased him up the street with a whip. The couple was married only a few weeks later, proving that love will have its way.

Vaudeville and Movie Palaces

If you look to the west, just beyond Randolph and State, you'll see the grimy flat facade of the Oriental Theater, once one of Chicago's grand movie palaces. It's just west of Ronny's Steak Palace. Here, on December 20, 1903, at about 3:30 p.m., Eddie Foy was appearing in the Iroquois Theater in *Mr. Bluebeard*. Almost 1,700 people, including many children, attended this special performance in what was then a marble palace. In the midst of a number titled "In the Pale Moonlight," an overloaded electric circuit flashed and the flame caught some flimsy drapery on the side of the stage.

Foy made sure his eldest son, Bryan, got out the stage door and then he urged the orchestra, "Play, play anything, but for God's sake don't stop, play on!" It didn't work. There was a panic. People piled up at the exits, jamming the doors shut.

Estimates vary, but between 571 and 603 people died that day, including 212 children. It was a scene of horror as scores were smothered, untouched by the flames. Over 200 bodies were found in a single narrow passageway. It was the second greatest fire death toll in American history—only exceeded by the 800 people killed in the Peshtigo, Wisconsin, fire.

Investigations and indictments followed, but there was no legal punishment for what happened. Today Chicago's fire code demands that all theater doors be made so as to open outward. The "panic bars" you see on theater doors are a tribute to the Iroquois Theater fire victims.

Also just west of where you now stand, at 64 West Randolph, a Chicago Tin Pan Alley flourished after the turn of the century. Most people do not know that such songs as "Let Me Call You Sweetheart," "Down by the Old Mill Stream," "Memories," "Sweet Sue," "I'll See You in My Dreams," "My Buddy," and "My Blue Heaven" were written in Chicago.

As you walk north on State Street, you'll pass the former Loop Theater, now housing an electronics store. Russ Meyer's *The Vixen* played here in the late 1960s, becoming the first adults-only film on State Street, and paving the way for other, sleazier movies and, some say, helping to hasten the decline of the Loop. Incidentally, most people believe that the Loop is so called because of the elevated trains that "loop" around the business district. Actually, it's named the Loop because of the cable car routes that looped through downtown in the 1880s.

Across the street, you'll see the white building with the words "State-Lake" on the arch. The old State Lake Theater, another former popcorn palace, was built here in 1917 as part of the Orpheum Circuit.

If it ever becomes time to write an epitaph for such grand theaters, perhaps the most fitting was found by author Ben Hall in the Paradise Theater in Faribault, Minnesota. A sign there read: "Please do not turn on the clouds until the show starts. Be sure the stars are turned off when leaving."

As long as the nostalgic mood is upon us, the Chicago School of Television, which pioneered minimal sets and using real people as hosts, had one of its finest practitioners at 190 North State. Burr Tillstrom's "Kukla, Fran and Ollie" was once broadcast from this address. How many of you can remember three other KFO characters and hum their theme song?

WLS-TV is now located here—it's the station that gave a big break to Oprah Winfrey, when she took over a 9 a.m. local TV talk show. Today, she is one of the richest women in show business, and she broadcasts from her own studio west of the Loop.

This was also the site of one of the most bizarre building guard demands of all time. In the 1960s, WLS-TV was the scene of an early morning fire just days after a new guard service took over. When the members of the fire department arrived, carrying huge hoses, extinguishers, and wearing helmets and big boots, the guard requested that they sign in before going up to the blazing studios. The lieutenant offered to sign in on behalf of all his men, but the guard demanded that each man sign in individually and list his identification number. The guard service was terminated that day.

Chicago Theater

If you continue a few feet north, you will be standing under the marquee of the Chicago Theater. Here, at last, we have a movie palace story with a somewhat happy ending.

Built in 1921, the Chicago Theater was the flagship of the Balaban and Katz theater chain. It was supposed to be awe inspiring, and it was.

Every important performer appeared there for four decades, often earning astronomical salaries even by today's standards. For instance, in 1935, Rudy Vallee earned $13,125 for a week's work, while the next week Sally Rand did her fan dance for $4,375. Jack Benny got $10,900 in 1940, the same year the Marx Brothers and Bob Hope earned more than $13,000 per week.

By 1942, the Andrews Sisters got $8,250; Tommy Dorsey and his band, $10,500. In 1946, Frank Sinatra earned $26,250 (out of which he had to pay Skitch Henderson and the Pied Pipers).

Dean Martin and Jerry Lewis earned $21,000 for the week of November 23, 1950. Nine months later, after becoming national hits in comedy and singing, they earned a record $62,201.25. To compare, that same year, Red Skelton earned $26,250 a week; the Mills Brothers, $7,551.25; Billy Eckstine, $14,152.50; Dinah Shore, $21,000 (she had the Will

Mastin Trio with her); and Peggy Lee, $7,469.87. The last live act there, Eydie Gorme, played the Chicago Theater the week of August 29, 1957, and earned $13,355.

For years after that, the Chicago Theater was slowly declining, until 1982, when a demolition permit was requested. There was an immediate uproar because the theater had been placed on the National Register of Historic Places.

Then a $26 million package was put together. This included the purchase of the Page Bros. Building just to the north. The interior of the building was completely gutted and rebuilt. In other words, the outer brick structure of the Page Building was used as a facade to hide a new wooden office building inside.

Over $4 million was spent to clean the old movie palace. Three inches of filth were vacuumed from some areas. The gold leaf was oiled and brought back to life. Chandeliers were found from other now-dead movie palaces and brought here. The organ was restored, and all the ropes used to fly curtains and scenery were replaced.

Then, on September 10, 1986, Frank Sinatra stepped on stage. He was backed by the Count Basie Orchestra, augmented by a dozen strings. He sang "My Kinda Town" (rather off key and unconvincingly, I thought—Sinatra took at least an hour to warm up), and the Chicago Theater was officially back to life.

A few years later, the Chicago Theater was again in financial difficulties and at this writing it is an on-again, off-again showcase.

If it is open, do step inside and look around. Notice the B & K emblem on the huge stained-glass window facing State Street and the balcony below it overlooking the lobby. Here pianists and other performers would entertain the throngs waiting to enter the theater. It is rumored that Frank Sinatra was once hired as a lobby singer here.

The Corner of State and Lake

Walk out of the theater, pass the Winners Circle—yes, it is possible to legally place a horse bet in the Loop—and go to State and Lake, under the elevated tracks. This corner is historically interesting because here Long John Wentworth picked a fight with a Scottish roughneck named Allan Pinkerton, Chicago's first detective. Wentworth was bigger, but drunker, than Pinkerton, who destroyed him with punches to the belly. Pinkerton quit his job and later went on to fame and fortune as protector of President Abraham Lincoln and the person in charge of Union spies during the Civil War.

In 1849, Lake Street was excavated down to lake level and planked in the hopes that sewage would run off under the street. That didn't work, the water and refuse gathered under the planks and the street smelled.

Engineers then advised that the only way to get Chicago out of the mud, which was sometimes posted with warning signs saying "Bottomless," was to jack up the entire town 10 or 12 feet. Chicago was built on a gigantic mud lake.

Work began in 1855. George M. Pullman, who later built railroad sleeping cars, once lifted an entire block, using 600 men and 6,000 jack screws. Nothing was disturbed in the block as each man turned his 10 screws a quarter turn to gently raise the building, after which a new stone foundation was inserted under it.

Meanwhile, people moved their homes (as long as they were going to be jacked up anyway) hither and yon. Accounts of the time tell of people watching a jail with prisoners inside moving down the street.

The State Street walk ends at Wacker and State, where pioneers in prairie schooners got supplies before moving west in the 1830s.

The new Stouffer Riviere Hotel is there with 27 stories, 565 rooms, and 375 tons of marble throughout the structure. It offers complimentary coffee and newspaper with a wake-up call, a 25-minute guaranteed room service delivery 24 hours a day, complimentary shoe shine, and an indoor swimming pool.

To make sure that any piece of paper on the floors of the public areas is quickly cleaned up, management will often hide $5 in it to reward employees who quickly do the right thing. When 25 travel writers were welcomed to the hotel in 1992, they each received a poster of the view from room 2720. Sounds like the place to stay if you enjoy that sort of thing.

Heald Square, with a statue of George Washington, Robert Morris, and Haym Salomon, is just around the corner, to your right. Morris and Salomon were the financiers of the Revolutionary War and both died broke. The statue was dedicated on December 15, 1941, the 150th anniversary of the ratification of the Bill of Rights. Chicago's Mayor Edward J. Kelly praised our rights and then, because it was just eight days after Pearl Harbor, declared that our rights were in danger from "blood-mad gangsters, hordes of yellow enemies."

Lorado Taft, whose ancestors fought in the Revolutionary War, designed the statue, the final monument he created before his death. And

Heald Square is named after Nathan Heald, the commander of Fort Dearborn.

Parts of State Street aren't that Great Street—yet, but I have hopes for its future.

6 LASALLE AND DEARBORN STREETS WALK

An amazing outdoor sculpture walk

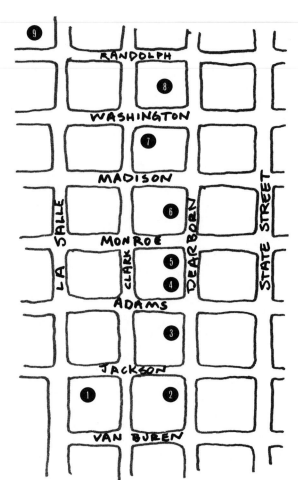

1. Board of Trade
2. Monadnock Building
3. Calder
4. Marquette Building
5. Xerox Building
6. Chagall
7. Miró
8. Picasso
9. State of Illinois Dubuffet

Time: 2 hours or less.

To get there: The #156 LaSalle bus will let you off at Quincy and LaSalle, one-half block from the Board of Trade. Otherwise, State Street buses will drop you at Jackson and you can walk west.

Chicago Board of Trade

Without really planning it or announcing it in advance as a glorious civic intention, Chicagoans have created one of the great modern, outdoor sculpture walks. Within three blocks along Dearborn Street, anyone can see major works by Calder, Chagall, Miró, and Picasso, plus architectural landmark buildings.

Let's begin two blocks west of Dearborn, at LaSalle and Jackson, where we can begin to understand the powerful commercial interests in Chicago. The building blocking LaSalle Street is the Chicago Board of Trade, 141 West Jackson.

The Chicago Board of Trade visitors' center, on the fifth floor, is open from 9:15 a.m. to 1:15 p.m. weekdays. Polite guides there will tell you why all the men in blue, green, and red jackets are yelling so frantically about wheat, soybeans, corn, oats, silver, gold, plywood, and mortgage-backed certificates.

The Chicago Board of Trade was founded in 1848. Today, it is said that fewer than 500,000 Americans have ever traded a futures contract. Some of them are smiling and living in Palm Springs. Some aren't.

The Chicago Board of Trade is in the big league—fortunes can be made or lost. It is said that once upon a time Philip D. Armour, the packer, decided to drive the price of wheat to a new low. He called an old pal of his, George Seaverns, locked the door to his office, swore Seaverns to secrecy, and tipped him off that wheat was "bound to rise." Seaverns put everything he had into wheat, mortgaging his house and bringing several of his friends into the deal. Then the market collapsed. Armour called his friend and is supposed to have said, "George, I knew you'd tell." Then he made out a check to cover Seaverns' losses.

As of today, the Board of Trade Building is partly a landmark and partly not. The Chicago City Council Cultural and Economic Development Committee decided, in 1977, that the art deco lobby and a few other sections of the building were landmarks. The rest could be remodeled at will, which is just the victory the Board of Trade lawyers wanted.

By the way, almost no one sees the 30-foot cast aluminum statue of Ceres, Roman goddess of agriculture, which is at the top of the building, 309 feet above the street. The statue was completed in 1930 by John Storrs, a native Chicagoan, who went to France and became a student of Auguste Rodin.

Continental Bank

Walk north on LaSalle past the solid columns of the Continental Illinois Bank and Trust Company of Chicago, and remember a time when they were not so solid, indeed.

In fact, in July 1984 this, the largest bank in Chicago and the seventh largest in America, was the subject of the biggest government takeover of a bank—$4.5 billion. With new management and almost $12 billion in guarantees from a safety net of other banks, the Continental began to come back to life. In 1986, the Federal Deposit Insurance Corporation announced that it would begin to sell its shares of the Continental in an attempt to recoup its losses because of the rescue. The government estimated that it would lose close to $1 billion to save this bank.

In 1993, a $10 million renovation of the second-floor grand banking hall was completed, a symbol of this bank's recovery. Currently, it is Chicago's 44th largest business, and its chief executive earns $1.5 million a year.

The Rookery

Remembering to change your mind about banking being a dull profession, continue walking north to the Rookery, at 209 South LaSalle Street, which was designed by Burnham and Root in 1886, with the lobby remodeled by Frank Lloyd Wright in 1905. It is, according to a plaque in the lobby, Chicago's oldest skyscraper and was once the largest office building in the world.

It's named The Rookery because a temporary city hall, located here from 1872 (after The Chicago Fire) to 1884, attracted a lot of pigeons. The old Rookery was built around an iron water tank, which survived the fire and which housed Chicago's first public library.

In 1992, the Rookery was the subject of a $92 million restoration job. According to the *Chicago Tribune*, "the Rookery is the first Loop historic structure to be restored as a modern office building with state-of-the-art heating, air-conditioning, elevator, security and telecommunications systems." It's wonderful to report that some folks are willing to rejuvenate the old rather than instantly apply the wrecking ball.

After looking and marveling at the decorations in the lobby, notice the stairway starting above the second floor landing. A semicircular tower, jutting into the court, encloses this stairway, making it useful as an indoor fire escape. By all means, look up at the 5,000 pieces of freshly-cleaned glass in the ceiling (it was covered with tar paper in the 1940s) and the white Carrara marble in the lobby.

The Rookery was once the scene of John W. "Bet-a-Million" Gates' whist and bridge games. The card games would begin on Saturday nights, and $100,000 would change hands before Monday morning.

A man who once ran errands for Gates told me that Gates was instrumental in creating the Steel Wire Trust, which evolved into U. S. Steel. But Gates was cut out of the final deal. He angrily demanded to know why, saying, "Is it merely because I do in public what you men do behind closed doors?" To which J. P. Morgan is alleged to have replied, "Young man, that's what doors are for."

Next, walk north to Adams. You are at LaSalle and Adams, where the last wild bear was shot in the corporate limits of Chicago on October 6, 1834, by Sam George, a man not even trivia buffs will remember.

Take a right and walk to Clark and Adams.

A Modern Jail

Look to your right at 71 West Van Buren and you will see, peaking from behind a modern steel-and-glass structure, a strangely beautiful mono-lith—the Chicago Metropolitan Correctional Center. It is a triangular building that looks like a huge, concrete computer punch card. Designed by Harry Weese and built in 1975, this jail holds about 400 federal prisoners awaiting trial or sentencing, or serving brief terms. Rob Cuscaden, an architectural critic, called it the best designed building of 1975.

The idea that this was to be a prison without outside bars created that computer punch card appearance. The windows are 7½ feet tall, but only 5 inches wide, to prevent escapes.

A Bit of History

Turn right on Clark, and walk one block south to Jackson. As you pass Clark and Jackson, notice Nita K. Sonderland's *Ruins III* (1978) almost hidden in the southwest corner of the Federal Building Plaza. It looks really strange, like two chess pieces overseeing some columns. In 1841, a child was lost here in a field of tall grass. A horseback rider saved the child from certain death only because he saw the grass waving a bit as the boy walked through it. And that was less than 150 years ago!

Take a left on Jackson and walk one block to Dearborn.

Dearborn, the street and the old Chicago Fort, were named after Henry Dearborn, a Secretary of the Army. One historian wrote that Dearborn "was one of the most ineffective leaders the nation has ever had to put up with." During the War of 1812, Dearborn organized an expedition to capture Montreal, but did not get across the border. Some say he had trouble finding Canada! His later efforts were even more feeble and indecisive, and he was finally fired in 1813.

Monadnock, Manhattan, and Fisher Buildings

Before you, at 53 West Jackson, is the Monadnock Building, with walls said to be 72 inches thick at the base. Designed by Burnham and Root, and built in 1891, it is the tallest building ever created of masonry construction.

Owen F. Aldis, the client for whom the building was created, often rejected Root's sketches as being too ornate, which is why the gently rippling front of Monadnock looks so spare and modern today. Architecture writer Ira Bach mentions a test of the building when there were doubts that its walls could stand Chicago's gusty winds. When winds of 88 miles an hour hit the city, engineers rushed to the Monadnock and measured the structure's vibrations. They were not more than $5/8$ of an inch. For comparison, the John Hancock Center moves three to four inches.

As you stand at Dearborn and Jackson, if you look to your right (to the south), you can see the Manhattan Building at 431 South Dearborn, the first 16-story structure in the world. The Fisher Building, an architectural landmark designed by Daniel H. Burnham, is a little closer to you at 343 South Dearborn.

Calder Stabile in the Federal Center Plaza

Begin to walk resolutely north, which should be to your left, until you approach the glass-and-steel Federal Government Center at 219 South

Dearborn. It was designed by that great twentieth-century architect, Mies Van Der Rohe, and opened in 1964.

You can't miss the Alexander Calder stabile, titled *Flamingo*, in the Federal Center Plaza to your left (west). Both the Sears' lobby and the Federal Center Plaza Calder structures were dedicated on the same day, October 25, 1974. Calder had a great time, riding down State Street in an orange-and-gold circus bandwagon, accompanied by calliopes.

Calder's 53-foot *Flamingo* reminds me of a giant praying mantis. In spring, when it is time to pay income tax, that isn't a bad symbol for government, especially if we misspell "praying" and make it "preying." Calder titled it *Flamingo* because "it was sort of pink and has a long neck."

Indians, Hoodlums, and Chicago's Last Cowpath

Continue north on the west side of Dearborn and enter the Marquette Building, at 140 South Dearborn. The mezzanine balcony is decorated with tile mosaics of Chicago history showing Indians extending a friendly greeting to Father Marquette, who discovered Chicago in 1673, preached here, and died nearby in 1675. There is a poignant note above one doorway to the building, "In vain I showed the Calumet to explain that we had not come as enemies." The Indian tribe is spelled "Calvmet" on the doorway.

You will soon reach the corner of Dearborn and Monroe. Roger Plant's notorious "Under the Willows" brothel was located only two blocks west of here in the 1860s. Plant, an early believer in the power of advertising, painted in gold letters on every blue shade in every window of his building the tantalizing question, "Why Not?" After the Civil War, Plant retired as a successful panderer, bought land, farmed it, and was a respectable patron of fashionable racetracks in town. Chicago has always respected money.

The offices of Mike McDonald, the hoodlum of the 1880s who first said, "You can't cheat an honest man," were only a block west of you. McDonald, adept at saying memorable things, also said, "Never give a sucker an even break."

The Chicago Loop's last cowpath is also about a block west of you. Farmer Willard Jones deeded the property in 1844, but reserved the right in perpetuity to take his cows to and from the barn along a path between Monroe and Madison. Just west of a number "100" in the sidewalk, at

100 West Monroe you'll see some steel doors. The path is behind them (air-conditioning equipment blocks part of it). No cows have used it for decades, although it is always available to them. It's not much to see. Take my word for it.

Three Italian Restaurants

Having decided not to look for the blocked cow path, why not check out the Sharper Image store in the Xerox Building at Dearborn and Monroe? The merchandise changes all the time. On my last visit, I could have bought (and didn't) gold-plated barbells, a $2,000 massage table, or a three-piece suit of armor marked down from $4,200 to $3,495. Since that wasn't anywhere near what I could afford, I didn't ask if they had one in my size.

Let's cross Monroe, where three fine restaurants are just to the west of you at 71 West Monroe. Walk to the Italian Village on the second floor, where the Christmas lights never dim. Of the three restaurants here, this is my favorite. The booths have names like Casa Realle (the King's Palace), La Pergula (the Gazebo), and La Posta (the Post Office). Opera stars Luciano Pavoratti and Placido Domingo have dined here and, of the 200 dishes created by Chef Mario Gianonni, the signature is veal alla Bartoletti, which is veal sautéed in sherry with pine nuts, mushrooms, and a touch of tomato.

The Italian Village has been owned by the Capitanini family since 1927 when Alfredo created his dynasty. Today, three third-generation Capitaninis run the business, while the second generation keeps a firm hand in all matters. It is one of the Loop's most memorable restaurants, and it never fails to provide a fine meal, great service, and impossible to duplicate atmosphere.

The lower level Cantina, meaning wine cellar, has a Vista del Mare room with aquariums lining the walls. This room opened in 1955 and is famous for chicken Vesuvio, spaghetti mari e monti, and stuffed veal chop à la Cantina.

The main floor Vivere opened in 1990 and was named as one of the best new restaurants of 1991 by *Esquire* magazine, which wrote that it was "amazing," with "one of the country's great wine cellars." *Esquire* praised the wild mushroom soufflé with cream and onion, and the sea scallops with arugula, and concluded, "if you have time for only one meal in Chicago this year, make it amid the quirky splendor of Vivere."

Next enter the First National Bank Building Plaza. The building, 60 stories tall, sweeps upward, in a slightly curving shape, and resembles an elegantly scripted "A."

Chagall Mosaic

In the plaza, by the fountain, is the Chagall. It is a 70-foot-long mosaic called *Les Quatre Saisons*, unveiled on September 27, 1974, on a day when Chicago fell in love with Chagall and vice versa.

Norman Ross, veteran Chicago radio personality and vice president of the First National, remembered that when Chagall arrived he discovered that Chicago was stronger and more exciting than he had remembered. So he added darkness and strength to the mosaic, inserting bits of Chicago brick, making some buildings taller, tinkering with it until he almost had to be pulled from his work for fear the unveiling would have to be postponed. Then, Ross recalls, Chagall stepped back, had tears in his eyes, gave Ross a friendly touch on the shoulder and said, "Pas mal" (not bad).

The next day, during the unveiling, Chagall actually kissed the late Mayor Daley on the cheek. Daley did not return the affection.

To answer the most-asked question: The mosaic represents the four seasons. On the side facing Dearborn and the Inland Steel Building, the north half is autumn and the south half, the one nearest Monroe, is winter. On the side facing Clark Street to the west, spring is on the south and summer is on the northern section.

Chicago Daily News art critic Franz Schulze called the mosaic "the late work of a great artist. It is not a masterpiece, and it is not likely to change the course of art. At the same time, it contains passages of loveliness that could not have been conceived by anyone other than an immensely gifted man."

Throughout the late spring and summer there are free noon concerts here, making this plaza the perfect place for a bag lunch.

Loop Synagogue

Cross the plaza and exit on Clark Street; walk north to the Chicago Loop Synagogue, at 16 South Clark, next to the Wendy's. There is a metal sculpture above the entrance titled *The Hands of Peace*, by Israeli sculptor Henri Azaz. The letters behind the priestly hands say, "The Lord bless thee and keep thee, the Lord make His face to shine upon thee and be gracious to thee; the Lord lift up His countenance upon thee and give thee peace."

Christ of the Loop

At Madison and Clark, look to the west, at St. Peter's Church and Friary, 110 West Madison. The gigantic *Christ of the Loop*, an 18-foot-high, 26-ton figure of Christ, is the work of Latvian sculptor Arvid Strauss.

If you look to the east one block, you'll see Madison and Dearborn. Here, on September 7, 1927, Tony Lombardo, a sidekick of Al Capone, was watching an airplane being hoisted up the side of a building. We do not know why the airplane was so engaged and neither are we sure why two bullets suddenly entered Lombardo's head. If it makes any difference at this late date, police at the time suspected that Bugs Moran engineered this execution in revenge for Hymie Weiss' slaying (see Holy Name Cathedral entry on North Michigan Avenue walk).

Miró Sculpture

Continue north along Clark Street to Washington and enter the Chicago Temple Building, 77 West Washington, where the sounds of organ music softly push aside the angry Loop traffic noises. In the space of just a few feet, you have seen downtown structures dedicated to the Methodist, Jewish, and Catholic religions.

Leave the Chicago Temple Building, but notice the odd sculpture in the Brunswick Building Plaza just east of the Temple. It is *Chicago* by Joan Miró, dedicated on the artist's 88th birthday on April 20, 1980. Miró, the son of a jeweler and watchmaker, was born in Barcelona in 1893, became part of the surrealist movement in Paris in the 1920s, and died in 1983.

Some people believe Miró's *Chicago* represents an abstract woman with a Spanish comb in her hair. Others think it has "the mystical force of a great earth-mother." To create this work, a craftsman inserted ceramic tiles into wet cement-plaster after it was sprayed on wire mesh. A week and a half after it was unveiled, Crister Nyholm, a part-time art student, splashed it with red paint. He said, "I just don't like it." His art criticism cost him $17,000—the cleaning bill.

Looking from Miró to Picasso

Next, cross Washington and walk north on Clark Street along the Chicago Civic Center Plaza (now called Daley Center).

Picasso Sculpture

The County Building is directly west of you and, behind it, its twin, the Chicago City Hall. Historians love to note that these are virtually identical buildings, yet the County Building cost $1.5 million more to build than City Hall.

In 1973, according to *Chicago* magazine, a test revealed that the sound levels during debate in the City Council chambers were several decibels above the level permitted by the city's recently passed noise ordinance. But then, over the years, more than merely the sound has been illegal in that often less-than-august body.

Daley Center is directly to the north. It is made of Cor-Ten steel, which will resist corrosion, allegedly forever. For a long time after the building was completed in 1964, Chicago was blessed with a big, ugly, rusty Civic Center. Now it's oxidized to a nice dark brown and no one laughs at it.

People still sometimes laugh at the controversial, 162-ton, 50-foot Picasso sculpture, made of the same Cor-Ten steel and sitting in this plaza. Architect William F. Hartmann convinced Picasso to give the statue to Chicago after bringing gifts to the artist. Hartmann's souvenirs included a White Sox uniform, a Bears helmet, a fireman's hat, photos of Ernest Hemingway and Carl Sandburg, and a Sioux war bonnet.

No one really knows what the statue represents; Picasso never told us and its official name is *Untitled*, although everyone calls it "The Picasso." When it was unveiled to a crowd said to number 500,000 people on August 15, 1967, Mayor Richard J. Daley said, "We dedicate this celebrated work this morning with the belief that what is strange to us today will be familiar tomorrow." Mayor Daley said that it is justice as a woman or a phoenix rising from the ashes of Chicago's 1871 fire.

Sir Roland Penrose, Picasso's friend, said it was the head of a woman with "ample flowing hair"; while another Picasso buddy said it was really a portrait of Kaboul, the artist's pet Afghan hound. A local artist and advertising executive, Edward H. Weiss, thought it was a portrait of Jacqueline, Picasso's second wife. An art historian, William B. Chappell, wrote that it was both Kaboul and Jacqueline, and traced Picasso's crossing of the heads of a woman and a dog back to the 1940s.

A local columnist thought it looked like a baboon. A local underground newspaper believed it was obscene and proved this contention by printing pictures taken of it from behind. The alderman, who wanted it deported and replaced by a statue of Ernie Banks, then Mr. Cub, said it

The Picasso did not frighten the pigeons

was "a heroic monument to some dead dodo, a Barbary ape, or some sort of Trojan dove." Other Chicagoans have said it looked like a cow, a vulture, a platypus, a robot, and even the abominable snowman. A stripper named herself Miss Rusty Picasso in its honor.

Mayor Daley was right—Chicago has gotten almost too familiar with the statue. According to Henry Hanson of *Chicago* magazine, since then, this statue has "worn a sweatband, a party hat, and a Bears' helmet. It has been revered as an icon and denounced as a monster. Picketers with cleats on their boots have scaled it and scratched its nose. The homeless have been driven from beneath it at night by spotlights that illuminate it. Hundreds of orators have addressed crowds nearby, and children regularly slide on its sloping base."

John Belushi and Dan Aykroyd drove a police car across the sidewalk in front of the Picasso in *The Blues Brothers*.

These days, Chicagoans no longer yell about it or laugh at it. It has become the symbol of the city, imprinted on thousands of ash trays and shot glasses after a federal judge ruled that it wasn't completely the property of the city and that "uninhibited reproduction" of the statue would benefit society. In 1992, Paul Gapp, architecture critic for the *Chicago Tribune*, wrote, "Happy 26th birthday, O Great Enigma. Could it be that we wouldn't love you as much if we knew what you were?"

History at Clark and Randolph

Continue walking north on Clark to Randolph. The Senate, a gambling den, was located one block to the east of you, at Dearborn and Randolph, in the 1880s. The games were so "high toned" that, when police raided this establishment, Frank Connelly, the owner, took his customers to the police station in carriages, paid their fines, and brought them back to continue playing as though nothing had happened.

The Chippewa, Ottawa, and Pottawatomie Indians, including 76 of their chiefs, were paid off for their land in 1834 about three blocks west of this spot. Before they left town, local sharpies made sure that nearly everything the Indians received in payment was given to local entrepreneurs for liquor. It has happened to many a tourist since.

Lager Beer Riots

Now moving forward in time, this corner was the scene of one of the major confrontations of the Lager Beer Riots of 1855, an important moment in Chicago history. Chicago had elected a "Know Nothing" mayor, Levi D. Boone. The mayor belonged to a short-lived political party that hated all foreigners. Boone's first action was to raise liquor licenses 600 percent and to enforce a half-forgotten law closing saloons on Sundays. Boone applied the Sunday closing law only to bars selling beer. Those selling good old American whiskey were exempt.

This outraged Chicago's Sunday beer-drinking Germans, a group not to be tampered with lightly. Insult our baseball teams or even sneer at our wives' looks, but never, ever, take away a Chicagoan's beer.

A mob of more than 400 Germans, marching behind fifes and drums, came to Randolph and Clark on April 21, 1855, and told those who stood in the courthouse that if their decision went against the 200 German saloonkeepers arrested for selling beer on Sunday, Chicago would burn. There was a brief battle and the crowd retreated north over the Clark Street bridge, vowing to return with reinforcements.

At 3 p.m., more than 1,000 angry, beer-starved Germans, armed with shotguns, rifles, pistols, clubs, and knives, came back to face 200 police and deputies. The mayor ordered the Clark Street bridge opened when half the crowd was across temporarily splitting the mob. Then the gun battle began. After nearly an hour, 20 men were seriously injured, one German died, and one policeman lost his arm because of a shotgun blast.

The result: The Sunday closing law was no longer enforced, the voters defeated a state prohibition law a few months later, and the Know Nothings were eventually voted out of office.

If you look to the east, you'll see the Garrick Garage with its huge "Park" signs. This was once the site of the Garrick Building, which contained a fine theater. When it was demolished in 1961, according to a plaque on the garage's west wall, many museums and universities got plaster and terra-cotta decorations designed by Adler and Sullivan in 1893. One piece of terra-cotta was saved and used to create the design on the front of the garage, which is now a sad tribute to the past.

State of Illinois Center

Before you stands either an odd, blue spaceship or Darth Vader's extra helmet. The State of Illinois Center at 100 West Randolph was dedicated on May 6, 1985. Ever since, this building designed by Helmut Jahn has been the subject of controversy.

First, there is the overall design. There seems to be no middle ground on this one. People either love it or loathe it. You will either see it as grim, mysterious, and foreboding, or as "the first building of the twenty-

Dubuffet's sculpture and the bottom of the State of Illinois Center

first century," as Governor James R. Thompson said when he dedicated it. The building is now named for the former governor who so often defended it.

Then, there is the air-conditioning. The original plans seemed sound: At night, when electricity rates are lower, eight giant ice cubes were to be frozen. They were to stand in ice banks 40 feet long, 12 feet wide, and 14 feet tall in the building's sub-basement. Then, during the day, all that stored cold would be released to cool the building. For some reason, that doesn't really work. Perhaps the 24,600 glass panels on the outer walls conduct too much heat during the day, but in its early months it was a miserable place in which to work.

It is, however, one of those places in Chicago that people must visit, meaning that you will join about 2.5 million others who stop by each year.

The black-and-white, friendly, cloudlike sculpture in front of the building is *Monument with Standing Beast* by Jean Dubuffet. It is a fiberglass construction that the artist hoped was a "drawing which extends . . . into space."

In 1977, a law was passed mandating that one-half of one percent of anything spent on new state buildings must be used to buy art. They have bought well. On the 16th floor, there are paintings by Chicago artists Gladys Nilsson, Jim Nutt, and Karl Wirsum. Also be sure to visit the State Art Gallery on the second floor, which is devoted exclusively to Illinois artists.

A tour of the building should begin in the atrium, all 7.9 million cubic feet of it, one of the largest enclosed spaces in the world. It has already been featured in several movies and TV shows, including the big, final shoot-out scene in *Running Scared* with Gregory Hines and Billy Crystal. Remember the bad dope dealer machine-gunning the good guys as they went up and down the glass-enclosed elevators, while Hines scaled the outside of the building for no reason other than it was both the most difficult way to get inside and the most visually spectacular?

As you go through the building, notice what isn't there—light switches. They have been eliminated because computers control the lights, making them more energy efficient.

Next go to the 16th floor for a view of the building from the top. A guest book there can be fascinating. In addition to visitors from Istanbul, Korea, Sri Lanka, Finland, and Burbank, last time I went there three Momar Quadaffis were registered.

The Chicago Title and Trust Center is at 161 North Clark, across the street from the State of Illinois Building. When there was an opening night party for this $310 million project in November 1992—and the building was only 34 percent leased—party-goers called it the "last building of the decade," according to the *Chicago Tribune*. That was later amended to last building of the century and millenium. The 1.2 million-square-foot building was completed when Chicago had a glut of office space. One anonymous official said, "This building will look good for 100 years, and maybe it will take at least half that long to make any money."

History and Geography at Lake Street

Let us leave the State of Illinois Center, by walking to Clark Street and proceeding north to Lake Street where the City Saloon offered theatrical attractions as early as 1836. Before radio, television, and films, Chicago-ans were entertained by the Annual Entertainment by the Inmates of the Indiana Deaf and Dumb Asylum and the Druid Horn Players performing "fascinating numbers played on ox horns." In those days, it was better than staying home and watching the prairie grow.

The Tremont House, once Chicago's most famous hotel, opened one block east of here in the 1830s. Sportsmen and tenants would sit in the doorway of the Tremont and shoot ducks on State Street.

If the reader-walker is in a true historical mood, he will want to know he is standing on a former sand bar. Lake Michigan has only gradually receded to its present shoreline. Each time it retreated, it left behind a sand bar. According to *Daily News* reporter Lois Wille, all of suburban Oak Park is on a former sand bar left there more than 8,000 years ago. Western Avenue, another former sand bar, is 20 feet below Oak Park, and Clark Street, built on yet another sand bar, is 20 feet below Western Avenue.

Eastland Disaster

Walk another block north to the Chicago River and think about July 24, 1915. At 7:32 a.m., 2,500 employees of the Western Electric Co. were on board the steamship *Eastland* ready for an all-day lake excursion. Then the boat tipped on its side, drowning 812 people. One *Chicago Daily News* story said, "A little shoe floated on top of the water, thick with the flotsam and jetsam of the great tragedy . . . the little shoe pleaded with silent eloquence for recognition."

Many theories were advanced as to why the boat tipped over, but none satisfied every authority. Eventually the *Eastland* was righted, and became the *USS Wilmette*, a Naval training ship between World Wars I and II. In 1921, the *Wilmette* became the only American ship ever to sink an enemy submarine in the Great Lakes. It sent a German U-boat to the bottom in compliance with an arms limitation treaty. The *Wilmette* was sold for scrap in 1946 for $1,937.99.

Marina City

The two circular towers to the east belong to Marina City, at 300 North State Street, built in 1964. They are 65 stories high with 896 condominiums above 19 floors devoted to commercial areas. A stunt for *The Hunter*, starring Steve McQueen as a bounty hunter, was filmed at this building.

Marina City has been pictured on Chicago postcards and telephone book covers. It was a symbol of the design bravery of the city, but it had also become "a financial nightmare."

The first 19 floors of this structure (but not the condos above them, which could sell for $169,000 for a two-bedroom unit in 1992) were in deep money trouble. In 1992, the *Chicago Tribune* called Marina City "a seedy, crumbling wreck." A Cook County Circuit Court judge, Lester Foreman, said, "The way things are going, Marina City will fall into the river." He also angrily said, "I am totally disgusted and ashamed that an agency of the U. S. government would treat this building like this."

The Resolution Trust Corp., the federal thrift bailout agency, took over the property in 1990 and then abandoned it on December 31, 1991.

At that point, the commercial property had been entangled in a foreclosure action since 1987 when a Houston bank went into default on a $12.5 million mortgage. This and other legal difficulties got the property so tied up that necessary repairs could not be made.

By 1992, the vehicle ramps in the garage vibrated so much when a truck or car went over them that residents feared the ramps would collapse, concrete stairs had buckled, walkways had been closed off, supporting steel beams were so corroded that some had holes in them, and a concrete column holding up one beam under a ramp was so seriously cracked that reinforcing bars were exposed. The *Tribune* reported that money was so tight the property manager couldn't buy light bulbs or cleaning supplies without adding to the longstanding debts, which were more than $23 million.

A major creditor, the electric company, wanted payment of overdue bills and was threatening to cut off service.

Asbestos in an abandoned theater and in the office building also posed an environmental problem. The cost of paying back taxes, interest, and the environment cleanup would be between $10 and $12 million. In 1992, no one wanted to buy it and no one wanted to fix it.

Looking away from a money nightmare, do notice the building at 77 West Wacker, with its Portuguese royal white granite and glass outer walls and its clean white marble lobby. The lobby has a sculpture titled *Three Lawyers and a Judge* by Xavier Corbero and a wall painting by Antoni Tapies. This building is the first Chicago design by Ricardo Bofill of Barcelona, an architect ranked among the top 10 in the world by the Art Institute. If you can stand back far enough to see to the top, you may agree with me that Bofill appears to be attempting to humanize the glass and steel box, and the attempt seems to have worked. Blair Kamen, architecture critic for the *Chicago Tribune*, disagreed, calling 77 West Wacker Drive "a kind of paste-on Parthenon;" "a skyline dud;" and "pallid, not powerful." He wrote that this building paled in "comparison to the straightforward but elegantly curved trusses of the nearby Clark Street Bridge."

Three fascinating companies each occupy 11 floors, or a quarter of the building each. The largest printing company in the world, R. R. Donnelly, has its corporate headquarters here. They print *Time* magazine. Kemper Securities has another quarter of the building with Keck, Mahin, and Cate, Chicago's 10th largest law firm, occupying the top quarter of 77 West Wacker.

This ends the Dearborn sculpture walk. Think of it. Without paying a cent, you have just walked past works by Picasso, Chagall, Calder, Miró, and Dubuffet. There are times when, mostly inadvertently, man can create beauty in the midst of intense commerce.

7 WACKER DRIVE RIVER WALK

From the Sears Tower to a river that sprung a leak

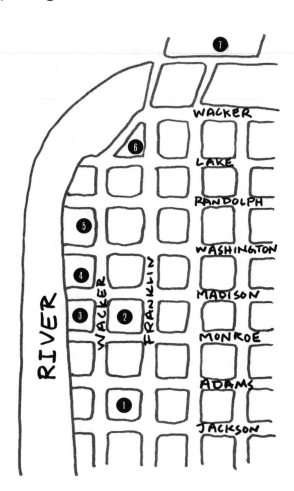

1. Sears Tower
2. 1 South Wacker
3. Mercantile Exchange
4. Opera House
5. Morton Thiokol
6. 333 Wacker
7. Merchandise Mart

Time: About 3 hours, less if you stride rather than stroll.

To get there: The Sears Tower, at the beginning of this walk, occupies the square block bounded by Franklin, Jackson, Wacker, and Adams in the southwest section of Chicago's downtown area. The #1, #7, #126, #151, and #156 CTA buses stop at Wacker and Adams.

An Area of Brand-New Buildings

You will be walking along the south branch of the Chicago River, which is just west of some of the newest office buildings in Chicago. Because Chicago is justly famous as an architectural museum and because several of these buildings are recent additions to the street, this is a chance to see the latest ideas in commercial construction.

If that doesn't sound very romantic, well, it depends on your definition of romance. A walk down this wide thoroughfare includes a stroll past the world's tallest building, an opera house with a past, and one source of the Kennedy wealth.

Sears Tower, World's Tallest Building

The walk begins at North Wacker and Adams, at the Sears Tower, the world's tallest building, with the world's fastest elevator. The Sears Tower is 110 stories tall, 1,454 feet to the top of its tower, and 1,707 feet to the very tippy top of its antennae. That elevator to the 103rd floor allegedly zips up to 1,353 feet in 55 seconds, achieving 20.45 miles per hour. It has never gone through the roof.

Sears' literature claims that the Sears Tower "has one of the most complete safety systems ever devised for a high-rise building," thus alleviating fears of the world's biggest *Towering Inferno*. This system includes smoke detectors on every floor that will alert a computer, which will then cut off the air flow to the affected area.

The Sears Tower, which cost more than $150 million and took three years to build, features in the Wacker Lobby an animated mural, modestly titled *Universe*, by Alexander Calder. The work includes three flowers, a spine, helix, sun, and pendulum, each driven by its own motor. With the spine moving at 4 rpm and the helix at 15 rpm, it looks rather happy.

Engineers have determined that during a so-called Maximum Storm, or one liable to occur in this area only once every 100 years or so, the building would actually sway six to ten inches in the wind. No need to take motion-sickness pills before going to the top—you can't really feel the sway. It is not true that toilets above the 100th floor have waves with whitecaps in them.

On Wacker Drive looking toward the Sears Tower

In May 1981, a man wearing a Spiderman suit, Dan Goodwin, climbed the Tower.

After considering the Sears and other towers, *Chicago Tribune* architectural critic Paul Gapp wrote, "There is romance and almost a bit of magic about all this (skyscraper building), but also a touch of madness. Many critics agree that urban gigantism has gone too far in recent years, wiping out any sense of human scale and disfiguring cityscapes . . . Perhaps it is time for a skyscraper embargo."

There's only one way to see if you agree with Gapp. Visit the Sears Tower and go to its Skydeck, where the admission fee is $3 for adults and $1.50 for children. On a clear day, the view is unsurpassed.

As of this writing, Sears has vacated the building in favor of a new headquarters in suburban Hoffman Estates. Among those replacing Sears is Ernst & Young, an accounting firm, which will occupy three floors. But many of the E&Y employees won't have assigned offices because they work at home or spend most of their time in clients' offices. When they want to visit downtown they'll call a concierge who will reserve office space for them. The company calls this approach hoteling—call ahead, get a reservation, have the phone lines and computers installed, and see your name on the door when you arrive.

Others leasing the huge spaces in this building include a Boston-based engineering firm, patent and trademark lawyers, and the stock brokerage firm of Shearson Lehman Bros.

South to the Mercantile Exchange

Leave the Sears Tower on the Wacker Drive side (but do notice the trees growing in the enclosed lobby) and walk south to the 311 South Wacker building, the tallest concrete building in the world at 971 feet. It is a 1.3 million-square-foot, 65-story building which opened in 1990. For those of you interested in what it takes to create a record-holding building, 110,000 cubic yards of concrete were used in the structure.

It has a spectacular lobby with bronze sculptures, a waterfall, 40-foot artificial palm trees, and Yvette's Wintergarden Restaurant, where good food, music, and fine service create a most pleasant atmosphere. This is the place to go for dinner and dancing, with live music Monday through Saturday and no cover charge. Do notice the 40-foot art deco mural on the back wall of the restaurant.

The maître d' was Arturo Petterino, who played himself in the movie *The Joker Is Wild*, the Joe E. Lewis biography. In 1992, after 35 years as a maître d' in New York (Copacabana), Chicago (Chez Paree), and Miami Beach (Eden Roc), he was considering retirement. If he's still on

Bronze sculpture and waterfall in 311 South Wacker lobby

the job, ask him about how he dealt with Frank Sinatra, and if he's finished writing his book, *This Way, Please*.

Leave this building, retracing your steps, heading north.

There have been peregrine falcons nesting on the 34th floor ledge of the 125 South Wacker building since 1987. You probably won't see one unless it's young and on its first flight. In 1992, two baby peregrines were found wandering on the sidewalks near Union Station and near 30 South Wacker. After being examined by the Lincoln Park Zoo, they were returned to their nests. A biologist said that young birds will often rest on the ground after their first flight, but there are too many concerned Chicagoans around to let them recover and fly off again.

The falcon nests are part of the Chicago Peregrine Release and Restoration Program, which is reintroducing the endangered species back into the wild after DDT contamination destroyed every peregrine falcon east of the Rocky Mountains. The Chicago Academy of Sciences (see the Lincoln Park walk) directs this program.

Walk past Oberweis Securities, the LaSalle National Bank, the Northern Trust Bank, and the very white United States Gypsum Building, which isn't square to the street. USG Corp. moved to its new corporate headquarters east of the Sears Tower at Franklin and Adams.

United States Gypsum perhaps participated too heartily in the go-go 1980s. It took on $2.5 billion in debt to ward off a corporate raider in 1988, was involved in many lawsuits after workers accused their bosses of harming their health during the manufacture of asbestos, suffered through the steep decline in the housing industry during the recession, entered bankruptcy court, and finally, changed its name to USG Corp. to show the world that it did more than handle gypsum.

Eventually, you will get to 1 South Wacker, a 40-story building designed by Helmut Jahn, who also created the State of Illinois Center (the Darth Vader helmet on the Dearborn Sculpture walk). AT&T is in 14 floors of this magnificent, dark-glass-and-steel structure, with a variety of bankers, investment houses, and magazines occupying the rest of the building. Notice the lobby with its marble and bars of light.

At Madison, look west toward Wells Street. The world's tallest building, the Miglin-Beitler Tower, isn't at 201 East Madison. Plans were announced in 1989 for a needlelike, $450 million, 125-story structure, 15 stories higher than the Sears Tower. But the Mellon Bank Corp. of Pittsburgh put the proposal on hold in 1992; financing was tough to find and two ground-breaking dates have come and gone. It remains a great might have been.

Next, cross Madison Avenue to the Chicago Mercantile Exchange Center, 10 South Wacker, to visit the world's largest financial futures market.

The visitors' gallery is open from 7:30 a.m. to 3:15 p.m. You will look down on a beehive of activity. They're trading futures on live hogs, pork bellies, live cattle, and feeder cattle to the left. In the far left corner, the future prices of Canadian dollars, deutsche marks, Swiss francs, Japanese yen, British pounds, and French francs are being determined. To the right, they're trading interest rate futures for Eurodollars, Certificates of Deposit, and Treasury Bills. And to the far right they're trading futures on stocks.

Notice the different jacket colors. Red is for exchange members; yellow for employees of clearing firms, which match purchases and sales; and light blue is for pit reporters, who give the trades to computer operators on the catwalk.

This center communicates with the world through 6,350 phone lines.

If you are hungry, try the Mama Mia Restaurant, which has an outdoor cafe to the west on the concrete banks of the Chicago River.

Civic Opera House

Otherwise proceed north to the Civic Opera House, which is the home of three theaters, including the Lyric Opera and the Civic Theater.

This structure was built by Samuel Insull, and it is here that we should reflect on how high human beings can rise and how far they can fall.

Insull learned Pittman Shorthand at age 14, and that allowed him to become the English representative for the Thomas A. Edison Co. Insull operated the first telephone switchboard in England, with George Bernard Shaw, who would become a famous playwright, as his battery boy.

Insull came to America in 1892, eventually coming to Chicago to buy and operate electrical companies. Later, he expanded by buying railroads.

By 1926, he could look at the city and know that every light in Chicago was shining because of the power he supplied. By 1929, he was the president of 15 corporations, chairman of 56, and board member of 81. The companies he headed were worth between $3 and $4 billion, while his personal fortune was about $150 million! He threatened to buy and sell entire political parties!

His empire had 600,000 stockholders; 500,000 bondholders; 4 million customers, and produced an eighth of all the gas and electricity consumed in America.

Limousines three-abreast on opening night

Because his actress-wife felt unhappy and unfulfilled, he built the Lyric Opera House, which was also supposed to gain a place for Insull in high society.

The man seemed to be sailing through the Depression with ease and, by 1931, banks were willing to lend money to Insull, but not to the City of Chicago.

But then came the day of reckoning. Even Insull's stocks were wilting with the Depression. Cyrus Eaton, a mogul, threatened to dump Insull's stocks on the market, further depressing their value, which had to be kept high because they were used as collateral on loans. Insull paid $40 million to Eaton to prevent the dumping, but he could not do that forever.

On July 5, 1932, after the value of his stocks crumbled, the New York bankers were able to force Insull out. When he left his companies, all he had was an $18,000 a year pension. In 1938, Insull collapsed in a French subway station. He had only 35 cents in his pockets. His estate was valued at $1,000; his debts at $14 million.

The Lyric Opera has become big enough and powerful enough that Luciano Pavarotti, one of the most famous tenors in the world, could be banished from it. That happened in 1989 after Pavarotti had canceled 26 of 41 scheduled performances there in the preceding five years.

Morton Building

Next, cross Washington to 110 North Wacker, the long, low, four-story Morton Building, and think about corporate histories.

The Morton in the title comes from the Morton Salt Company, with $370 million worth of salt sales a year and a company with a long and illustrious history beginning in 1848. Jay Morton got control of the company in 1886. His father, J. Sterling, was secretary of the Nebraska Territory at age 26 and the founder of Arbor Day. In 1914, the company put a little girl carrying an umbrella and spilling salt on their packages. Originally, the accompanying slogan said, "Even in rainy weather it flows freely," but that was changed to "When it rains, it pours," a phrase that achieved advertising immortality.

As a result of a variety of mergers, the company also made Janitor-in-a-Drum, Spray 'n Wash, Glass Plus, and No-Pest strips. Through the years, various Morton relatives have donated a wing to the Art Institute and created the Morton Arboretum in Lisle, Illinois.

In 1982, when Morton's sales were approaching a billion dollars a year, the company bought Thiokol Corp. "Thiokol" is from two Greek words meaning sulfur and glue and indicates that the origins of the company were in the discovery of synthetic rubber.

The only problem was that in the '30s and even the '40s no one wanted much synthetic rubber. Besides, the plants that made it smelled like rotten eggs.

Then it was discovered that a liquid polymer made by Thiokol was the best solid propellant fuel binder known to man, and Thiokol got in the business of making such rockets as the Pershing, Nike Zeus, Sidewinder, Maverick, and even motors for the space shuttle.

And that is how a salt company got involved in the Challenger Space Shuttle disaster, when one of their rockets exploded, killing seven astronauts on January 28, 1986. Some Thiokol engineers said that it was not safe to launch that day because of the cold weather; other executives pushed for the launch. Morton separated from Thiokol in 1989, spinning off a separate, publicly traded company. One analyst then suggested that the CEO of Morton, who was being paid $3.77 million in 1990, get a $2.62 million pay cut.

Both companies have done well. When Iraq invaded Kuwait, Thiokol's stock rose 60 percent because it was a supplier of solid fuel rockets to the military.

Recently, Morton International has been making lots of air bags for automobiles, becoming the sole supplier for Chrysler and picking up a Ford account. The air bags have been good news for this company with $2 billion in sales in 1992. Recent mild winters have resulted in lower salt sales and the recession has hit some of its other chemical businesses.

The Morton building, designed in 1961, was called "surely one of the ugliest buildings in the city," by *Chicago Tribune* architecture critic Paul Gapp. I do believe he has a point. There were plans to tear it down and build a one million-square-foot office tower there, but Japanese financing evaporated.

Continuing to walk north on Wacker toward the Chicago River, it should be remembered that The Wigwam, a rectangular wooden building, was also built near Lake and Wacker. In 1860, when Abraham Lincoln was nominated there as Republican candidate for president of the United States, one witness recalled "for 10 minutes nothing was heard but the roar of human voices."

Wolf Point

Continue north, cross the Chicago River on the Franklin-Orleans Bridge, and then look at the river. Both banks of the river at this point

Across the Chicago River, one of my favorite buildings—333 West Wacker Drive

have historic significance. In fact, the city of Chicago was founded both here and to the east at Michigan Avenue and the river, where Fort Dearborn stood. To the east, there are several suitable plaques indicating where the fort was. Nothing marks the history that began here, probably because most of it involved taverns and boozing.

Chicagoans say that Wolf Point is the spit of land pushing into the river just south and west of the Merchandise Mart, where there is a rudimentary park with a few trees, grass, a concrete parking lot, and the Apparel Mart. Historically, Wolf Point occasionally also referred to the bank of the river on the other side where the 333 Wacker Building stands. It is said that a wolf was killed trying to get into the meat supply of a tavern here, thus creating Wolf Tavern and appending a name to Wolf Point.

By the way, the 333 West Wacker Drive Building is simply magnificent. As you look at it, you can understand how architect William Pedersen solved the problem of having to build on an oddly shaped triangular lot. This building shimmers at sunset and looks even better when you're standing on the deck of a boat in the river.

Paul Gapp chose it as one of the top 10 most important post-World War II works of Chicago architecture. He wrote, "Pedersen never did another building quite like it because, somewhat like John Hancock Center, it is unrepeatable. But 333 will leave an enduring record of itself in design history because it is a building of uncommon beauty that happens to be precisely right for the site on which it stands. That is a rare quality, indeed."

But back to the point, Wolf Point, that is. There are stories that a trading post stood there in 1778 and that it was run by a fellow named Guarie.

Later, this area achieved historical significance because it was the site of Chicago's first tavern, which opened in 1828. Within a year, two more taverns were added to the settlement here and one writer observed, "as few as the inhabitants of Chicago were at that time, one of their principal avocations seems to have been that of keeping tavern."

By 1832, the original tavern, under new ownership, was given the name Rat Castle, because of the "regular boarders who infested its premises," and it was generally known as the place where men of character stopped.

The Sauganash Hotel stood on the south bank of the river and it was here that some 60 people gathered in that hotel in 1833 to vote to incorporate Chicago. Later that same year, it was the site of Chicago's first election. There were only 150 people in the village then. Four years later, the first census revealed that there were 4,170 people in Chicago, including Richard Harper, who listed his occupation as "loafer." Today, that man would be either a Chicago alderman or would be otherwise employed by the city.

Merchandise Mart

The large building to your right is the four million-square-foot Merchandise Mart, which, with the 25-story, two million-square-foot Apparel Center to the west of it, constitutes the largest wholesale buying complex in the world. (For reference purposes, Sears Tower also has 4 million-square-feet. The Pentagon is bigger than both of them, but it isn't involved in merchandising anything except defense contracts.)

The Merchandise Mart was built for $32 million by Marshall Field III in 1930 and received a $100 million, 10-year renovation begun in 1988.

Merchants Row at the Merchandise Mart

The Mart has been owned by the Joseph P. Kennedy family since 1946, and it is among the enterprises that allow the Kennedys to be jetsetters and to spend their money elsewhere in the world.

There is a hall of fame of American merchants in front of the Mart. Seven heads were unveiled in 1953 by Joseph P. Kennedy and his son, John, who later became President of the United States. One more was added in 1972, none since, a possible comment on merchandisers in the 1980s. Those honored include Marshall Field, Edward A. Filene, George Huntington Hartford (founder, Great Atlantic and Pacific Tea Co.), Julius Rosenwald (president/chairman, Sears), John P. Wanamaker, Aaron Montgomery Ward, Frank Winfield Woolworth, and General Robert E. Wood (president/chairman, Sears).

The Apparel Center, a nearly windowless building because that allegedly saves energy (while presumably driving those inside nuts), is not a hit with local critics. Donald M. Schwartz, writing in the *Chicago Sun-Times* in 1977, called it "a vast monotone of largely windowless concrete" with "all the charm of two gigantic cardboard boxes" which "repels your advance, your interest, even a casual glance." Can't win 'em all.

There is a Holiday Inn on the 14th floor and the rooms circle a huge atrium. Despite the cold concrete there, the staff is friendly. And the place has a great swimming pool.

On the lower level, I. B. Diffusion has its own line of casual wear from last season at about 30 to 50 percent discount, according to *Chicago* magazine. However, the magazine also warned that some items are priced at full retail. Also in the lower level, according to the magazine, Arbetman & Goldberg buys men's apparel overruns, bad credit leftovers, and midseason shipments below wholesale, and passes along the savings. But the magazine warned that amid the great buys like Yves St. Laurent sports coats for $150, there are knockoffs with strange labels like Bissoni instead of Missoni. A Burbank trenchcoat was priced at $125, one-tenth the price of a Burberry. Prices are negotiable.

For many years, WMAQ-AM-TV, NBC in Chicago, was on the 19th and 20th floors of this building and that area was also a center for radio broadcasts in the '30s (see Mid-Michigan Avenue walk for the present location of WMAQ-TV and NBC Tower). "The Quiz Kids" began there on June 28, 1940, with this question, "I want you to tell me what I would be carrying home if I brought an antimacassar, a dinghy, a sarong, and an apteryx." It went on to become both a popular and loathed show. Every kid in America was compared to Joel Kupperman, who was then the smartest boy in the world. "Curtain Time," "First Nighter," and "Club Matinee" were all broadcast from here, as was the early "Today Show," with Dave Garroway closing every broadcast by opening his right hand and saying "Peace."

There is one more must stop on this tour. Leave the Merchandise Mart through the east doors—they're the ones facing the elevated tracks. Turn left, or north, and walk one block to Kinzie, take another left and stroll west about two blocks to the Kinzie bridge over the Chicago river, where you will find the scene of a monumental blunder.

If you look in the water near the bridge supports, you'll see some famous pilings. These logs were driven into the river bed in 1991 to protect the bridge. On April 13, 1992, the city discovered that the logs had gone through the old railroad tunnels under the river. The ancient tunnel system, built for hauling cinders and garbage out of the Loop and recently used for telephone and other cables, flooded, causing more than $1 billion dollars worth of damage and business losses. It took weeks to pump out the millions of gallons of water.

But the situation had typical Chicago twists to it. The flood potential went undetected because city engineers never made a final inspection of the project because they couldn't find a convenient place to park near where you are standing.

A city engineering technician took photos of the dangerous condition of the freight tunnel, took them to an Osco Drug Store for developing, and left them there for days, despite the fact that City Hall has a photo lab that would have processed them in two hours. Maybe he just lost the receipt or was waiting to find a cents-off coupon.

And the *Chicago Sun-Times* reported that "construction crews briefly considered using zebra manure to plug the leak." A diver reported that the stuff was water-resistant, cohesive, and used in nuclear accidents. Alas, there was not a lot of it around Chicago then or since.

The city's first train left this site on October 15, 1848, because the first railroad station was built here also in 1848.

It has also been the scene of other screwups. A cabdriver was killed and two passengers were injured here in 1987 when a drunken bridge tender raised the bridge at the wrong time.

Let us not linger here for fear that the aura of bungling that infests this area will cling to us.

This ends the Wacker Drive walk. If you are hungry, I'd suggest walking another three or four blocks north on Wells Street—which is the street you found on the east side of the Merchandise Mart when you exited—to either Carson's for Ribs or Ed Debevics', both of which are mentioned in the Ontario Restaurant walk and offer good food at a reasonable price.

8 GOLD COAST WALK

Astor and State Parkway:
At play in the streets of the wealthy

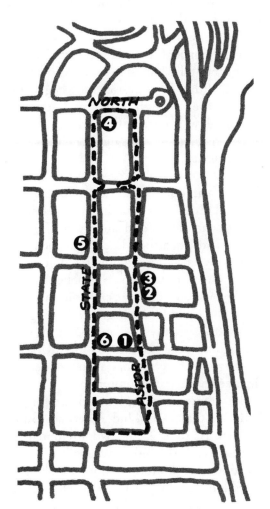

1. 1308–1312 Astor
2. Court of the Golden Hands
   (1349 Astor)
3. James Charnley House
   (1364 Astor)
4. Archbishop's Residence
5. Playboy Mansion
   (1340 North State Parkway)
6. Ambassador East Hotel

Time: Less than 2 hours.
To get there: The #36, #70, and #151 CTA buses all stop quite near State and Astor Streets. Ask the driver or almost any passenger for the directions to the corner where the walk begins.

The Lap of Luxury

Chicago's Gold Coast has been home to the city's richest citizens since the 1890s. Modern apartments with faceless lobbies have risen among the old mansions in the past two decades, but today that process has slowed nearly to a stop. That's fine because it preserves a beautiful neighborhood where the top strata of society lived life to the hilt before the stock market crash of 1929.

Early in Chicago's history, Astor Street was named after John Jacob Astor, a pioneer fur trader. The area languished until 1882, when Potter Palmer built the "mansion to end all mansions" at 1350–1360 Lake Shore Drive. Within 20 years, rich folks began forsaking the South Side to join Palmer, even though there was a servant problem. The old lakefront graveyards were nearby. Every time a foundation was dug new bones were discovered, and servants might quit because they thought the big houses were haunted.

By 1928, the Gold Coast was the Lap of Luxury. A real estate listing for that year described the apartments at nearby 1200 North Lake Shore Drive: This 13-story building devoted its first two floors to quarters for butlers, chauffeurs, and laundresses. The 13th floor had playrooms and extra maids' quarters. Each apartment, with 18 large rooms and six bathrooms, had four rooms for domestiques. The description almost makes one want to become a robber baron.

The 1929 stock market crash virtually ended home construction in the area. The Gold Coast began to be ringed by modern high rises in the '50s, as the wealthy died, moved to the suburbs, or sold to developers.

A stroll through Chicago's Gold Coast today recalls life as it was 80 years ago, with occasional jarring modern intrusions in the form of huge signs advertising condominiums.

But before we start, let us pause for a moment to praise a political leader of this area, 42nd Alderman Burton Natarus, a true Chicago original. As of 1992, he had attempted to ban horse-drawn carriages, successfully legislated for diapering horses pulling such conveyances, called for a prohibition of horses walking in warm weather, tried to put speed limits on bicycle messengers, wanted to ban troubadours from the streets, noted that the best place to get a cheese sandwich was from a silver-sided truck, wanted to ban the word condom from a sign on Division Street (see the Condoms Now entry in the Rush-Division Pub Crawl), and called for the outlawing of parasailing on Chicago's lakefront. He claimed that Chicago did not have enough hot air to push the parasails, making the sport unsafe. Natarus also added, "I have no comment about the amount of hot air at City Hall."

Leaving the contemplation of the hot air quotient of the city to experts, this walk begins at State and Division Street. As you head east on Division, note the sandstone townhouses at 45–47 East Division. They were built around 1885. Take a left on Astor and walk north.

One of Astor Street's oldest structures is the 2½-story, red-brick, Queen Anne-style building at 1207 North Astor, which was built around 1881. You'll see a lot of Queen Anne-style homes in this area. In 1891, *Industrial Chicago* reported that that style "has met with great favor from the barbaric tastes of modern Chicago." Oh well, one man's barbarism is another man's charming city home.

Continue walking north. The art moderne apartment buildings, at 1260 and 1301 Astor, were built by Philip B. Maher in the 1930s. The Potter Palmers once lived on the top three floors of 1301. According to one critic, both buildings show the influences of Gothic revival, cubism, art deco, Eero Saarinen, Louis Sullivan, and the 1916 New York Building Code. But they just look like early high rises to me. Let's call them proto-condos.

Astor Tower Hotel

The Astor Tower Hotel, on the northwest corner of Goethe and Astor, has been the temporary home of the Hollywood Squares panelists, the Monkees, and other famous acts. According to C. Paul Luongo, who searched the world to find the best of everything from mouse traps to hot dogs, Maxim's Restaurant in the basement of the Astor Tower qualified as one of the best anywhere because he was "deluged with hospitality" while eating there. Alas, the hospitality and the restaurant are no longer available to the public.

Harriet Monroe and Poetry Magazine

Continuing north on Astor Street, the 3½-story row houses at 1308–12 were designed in 1887 by John Root, who was Daniel Burnham's partner. Root, who lived at 1310 Astor, died in 1891 at the age of 41. Root's sister-in-law, Harriet Monroe, founder of *Poetry* magazine, also lived at 1310, and died in 1936 at the age of 77 while trying to climb a mountain in Peru.

Ms. Monroe's magazine first published Vachel Lindsay's "General William Booth Enters Into Heaven" in 1913, Lindsay's "The Congo" in 1914, T. S. Eliot's "The Love Song of J. Alfred Prufrock" in 1915, and Carl Sandburg's "Chicago" in 1914.

Poetry magazine's efforts were not universally appreciated. *The Dial*, another Chicago poetry magazine, wrote of Sandburg's poem—which begins "Hog butcher for the world . . ."—that it was "nothing less than an impudent affront to the poetry-loving public." "Prufrock" wasn't much appreciated either, with Louis Untermeyer writing Ms. Monroe that the poem was "the muse in a psychopathic ward drinking the stale dregs of revolt."

The white and peach limestone buildings at 1316–22 Astor were built by Potter Palmer as a speculative venture in 1889.

The high-rise apartment building at 1325 Astor, designed by Andrew N. Rebori in 1928, was once advertised as having 11 rooms, four baths, and two wood-burning fireplaces in each apartment. Ideal for a family who enjoys being clean.

Irna Phillips, Queen of the Soaps

Irna Phillips, inventor of the soap opera, lived at 1335 Astor until her death on December 23, 1973. The Queen of the Soaps, Ms. Phillips was responsible for "The Guiding Light," "As the World Turns," "Young Dr. Malone," and others. Irna's favorite story concerned the selling of "Another World" to Proctor & Gamble. Not wanting to travel to Ivorydale, Ohio, she insisted that the company executives come to her. When they arrived in her apartment, they saw stacks of scripts and dramatic concepts. Before the P&G people could even read this material to see if they liked it, they had to give Irna $5,000. The diminutive lady was playing poker with the P&G board of directors, and the opening bid was $5,000. Miss Phillips got her money.

If you look through the entranceway at 1353–55 Astor to the doorway to the left, you'll see why it is called the Court of the Golden Hands. Vandals have been at work, and some of the door knockers at the entranceway with the graceful hands carefully holding an apple have been removed. But they are still on the doors back in the courtyard beyond the gate.

This huge home at 1353 Astor was designed for the William O. Goodman family, who donated Chicago's famed Goodman Theater as a memorial to their son, Kenneth, a Naval Lieutenant who died in World War I. The keystones above the third-floor windows are decorated by bovine skulls.

James Charnley House

We now arrive at a landmark—the 11-room, three-story, single-family residence at 1365 Astor, the James Charnley House, designed by Louis Sullivan and Frank Lloyd Wright in 1891. To understand why this home is historically significant all one has to do is look at the homes around it, designed at the same time, but decorated with Queen Anne, Romanesque, and Georgian revival facades. Charnley looks, and is, modern, a forerunner of the ranch house, the first statement by the then 23-year-old Wright that a city home could be constructed of simple shapes. One critic said that "there was no duplicate of the Charnley House anywhere in the world in 1891," and Wright said, "It is the first modern building."

Wright was an apprentice to Sullivan when he designed this home for a lumber executive. Sullivan contributed the fireplace and the leaded-glass windows.

For a couple of years in the 1980s, you could have bought this landmark from Lowell Wohlfeil, the owner, for a mere $1.25 million, provided you agreed to preserve the building. Most buyers were happy with the 30-foot-tall atrium and the unadorned wood paneling, but some people wanted to add his and her bathrooms to change the home.

It was bought by the Skidmore Owings & Merrill Foundation, thus both saving and restoring it. Daily, self-guided tours can be arranged by calling the Chicago Institute for Architecture and Urbanism.

More Astor Street Houses

Cross Schiller, noting the townhouses from 36–48 East Schiller, and notice the Joseph T. Ryerson House, at 1406 Astor. It was built in 1921–22 and patterned after pre–World War I Parisian hotels. Ryerson's grandfather founded Ryerson & Son, now a subsidiary of Inland Steel.

The William McCormick Blair residence at 1416 Astor had its moment in history. Illinois Governor Adlai Stevenson stayed there in 1952. Around midnight on July 26, Stevenson got official word from the Democratic Convention that he would be the new presidential candidate. He went to the Bowen House, 1430 Astor (since demolished), and told 2,000 supporters and newsmen, "The party has reached its decision openly. It has asked me nothing except that I give such poor talents as I have to my country. That I will do gladly. I have no feeling of exultation, nor sense of triumph." A sense of triumph also evaded Stevenson that fall when, although beloved in Illinois, he was defeated by Dwight David Eisenhower.

Across the street, the light gray building at 1425 Astor, built in 1895, was originally the residence of William D. Kerfoot, a city controller and a hero, of sorts, after the 1871 fire. On October 10, one day after the fire burned all he owned, Kerfoot, then a realtor, built a shanty near Washington and Dearborn, the first structure to be erected after the fire. He had to construct it back from the pavement and the nearby ruined walls, which were still hot from the fire. Kerfoot put up a sign, now on display at the Chicago Historical Society. It reads, "Wm. D. Kerfoot is at 53 Onion Park Place/All gone but wife children AND energy." See the Lincoln Park walk for reference to that sign.

A large, curved bay marks the G. W. Meeker residence at 1431 Astor, while 1435 Astor is a facsimile of a Georgian mansion. The H. N. May House, at 1443 Astor, was designed in 1891 by Joseph Lyman Silsbee, who employed both Frank Lloyd Wright and George W. Maher as apprentices early in their careers.

The art deco home at 1444 Astor was built in 1929, with the limestone for its facade imported from Lens, France. One critic called it "very probably the finest residential art deco design in Chicago." Everything collects its honors where it may.

The nearly flat-front building at 1447 Astor, built around 1903, was originally the home of Charles Daniel Peacock, who was born in Chicago in 1838, went to a little school house at State and Madison (now the world's busiest corner), and became a wealthy Chicago jeweler, selling shirt studs to gentlemen and brooches to ladies.

The modern high rise at 1450 Astor, soundly hated by old-line neighborhood residents, has been called a "junkyard" because of its open garage along the sidewalk.

Robert Patterson Home

We now cross Burton and see a grand home, the Patterson-McCormick Mansion at 20 East Burton, which was built in 1882. Joseph Medill, editor of the *Chicago Tribune*, gave this home to his daughter as a wedding

Robert Patterson Home: Beautiful again

present (what a father-in-law). Cyrus Hall McCormick II, son of the inventor of the reaper, bought the home in 1929 and tripled its size. In fact, the King and Queen of Sweden once stayed on its second floor. It later became the Bateman School, which defaulted on its mortgage and lost the property in 1950. The home rested in sad dilapidation until 1979 when developers bought it.

In its heyday, it was quite a home, with from 42 to 90 rooms, depending on how one defined the term. The fourth floor allegedly contained one room lined with 50 locked boxes designed to hold Christmas and birthday gifts. A room close by was set aside, naturally, for wrapping presents. That is an interesting bit of extravagance—a room permanently reserved for Christmas present wrappings.

Across the street, the red-brick home at 40 East Burton Place (alternate address—1501 Astor) originally belonged to John G. Shortall, who built it in 1909. Shortall became another 1871 fire hero when he saved 20 years of real estate records. It might seem curious—risking one's life for a bunch of papers, but Shortall's heroism allowed the city to rebuild quickly and without lengthy legal battles as to whose property ended where.

Continuing north, we pass the residence at 1505 Astor, built in 1911 in an English Georgian-style. The high rise at 1515 Astor is on the site of the home of George Frances, who once had a wine cellar with 1,300 quarts of scotch, an equal amount of bourbon, and 500 quarts of champagne. That man knew what was important in life.

Next consider the modern Charles Haffner III residence with its vine-covered cylindrical section at 1524 Astor. Built in 1968, it sympathizes well with the existing street facades.

The walk north on Astor ends at North Avenue where a bronze statue of Dr. Greene Vardiman Black looks benignly south. Before his death at age 79 in 1915, Dr. Black was the author of more than 500 books and papers, inventor of 104 different dentist's instruments, a chain-smoker of Havana cigars, and a man credited with laying the foundation of modern dentistry. While on vacation in Alaska, he was caught in a blizzard on a mountain, froze one hand, and amputated part of his own finger.

Archbishop's Residence

If you turn left and walk one block west on North Avenue, you will pass The Archbishop's Residence, at 1555 North State Parkway, the home of the head of Chicago's Roman Catholics since 1885. Don't bother to count them—there are 19 chimneys on this Queen Anne–style house. It

Some of the Archbishop's Residence's 19 chimneys

is the oldest structure still standing in the Astor Street district, and was designed by Alfred Pashley, a Protestant.

Rumor has it that there is a beautiful, high-backed, gilded chair in one room of this house. Its velvet seat is perpetually protected by a silken cord, and the chair is reserved for a visit by the pope.

President Franklin Delano Roosevelt lunched here in 1937, and Eugenio Cardinal Pacelli visited in 1936. He later became Pope Pius XII, but he didn't sit in the reserved chair.

This home was also marked by scandal. In 1982, the *Chicago Sun-Times* alleged that Cardinal Cody had diverted more than $1 million in church funds to his stepcousin and long-time "friend" Helen Dolan Wilson. There were stories about her condominiums in Florida, $100,000 insurance policies with Wilson as the beneficiary, and occasions when the Archbishop's Residence was empty except for the cardinal and Ms. Wilson. After Cardinal Cody's death in April 1982, the U.S. Attorney closed the investigation into Cody's financial dealings. No indictments were ever returned.

Now turn left on North State Parkway and head south. The high rise at 1550 North State Parkway on the corner was once the finest apartment building in the city, with 14-room apartments. Every room had its own French name and the building has an appropriate Parisian-inspired facade. It is still very grand.

Madlener House

Continue south on North State Parkway. You are going to return to Division, which is 1200 North. As you stroll, note the many beautiful older buildings on both sides of the street.

The Albert F. Madlener House, at 4 West Burton Place, is the home of the Graham Foundation for Advanced Studies in the Fine Arts. It was designed in 1902 by Hugh M. G. Garden for the president of a huge wholesale liquor firm. The home has been favorably compared to a Florentine palace.

As you cross Burton Place, look to the west at Carl Sandburg Village, which replaced a notorious slum. Its towering apartments prove that someone can live in the midst of hundreds of people and still be quite lonely.

Walk resolutely south. If it is late spring or during the summer, observe the many flower gardens in this neighborhood.

Playboy Mansion

The George S. Isham mansion, at 1340 North State Parkway, was where people of refinement went for dancing classes after it was built in 1899 for about $100,000. One early owner put human beings and horses on the black-and-white marble squares of the ballroom and played chess.

Better known as the Playboy Mansion after Hugh Hefner bought it in 1959, the mansion belonged for a time to the Art Institute, which was supposed to use it as a dormitory. In 1992, the building, which includes the famous bar in which the guests could observe bunnies frolicking underwater, was priced at $2.7 million.

In 1993, a developer had announced that he was spending $3 million in renovations and would divide the home into seven or eight condominiums priced from $675,000 to $2.1 million.

Ambassador West and East

Proceeding south, past the small home at 1328 North State Parkway, which was remodeled in 1956 for sculptress Lillian Florsheim, we quickly arrive at the Radisson Plaza–Ambassador West Hotel, on the west side of North State Parkway. If you enter, you'll see a glass doorway to the

Wall of the young and famous in the Pump Room

right just before the steps to the ornate lobby. Open the door, walk down the narrow stairs, bear left, duck your head if you are tall, follow the underground path, past a drug store facade, and walk upstairs. You have crossed North State Parkway and have entered the Omni Ambassador East.

Ambassadors East and West, once united under one owner, are now controlled by separate corporations.

The Pump Room, a famous restaurant, is directly in front of the elevators. At one time, when the railroads were important to Chicago and the town was a convenient place to stop while going cross country, being seated in Booth One of the Pump Room meant you had arrived, had made it. That tradition began in October 10, 1938, when actress Gertrude Lawrence began to sit and eat in Booth One for 90 straight days, creating an institution.

Salvador Dali doodled on the tablecloth there and it was promptly washed. Margaret O'Brien wore lipstick for the first time in public while sitting there. Elizabeth Taylor ate there with four of her first five husbands (only Eddie Fisher missed the honor). Lauren Bacall dined there with Humphrey Bogart. Lassie was refused service, but Morris the Cat ate there in 1974. In 1968, Sonny Bono became the first man to dine there without a jacket.

Celebrities do not advertise that they are there. Frank Sinatra hides within his entourage, and Kim Basinger usually wears sunglasses and a huge hat.

Today, Booth One is just to the left of the recently remodeled entrance of the dining room. It has a fancy phone, but fewer celebrities than it had in the past. The food is still terrific and the most popular dish is the roast prime rib of beef with horseradish cream, which costs about $24.

Many of the memorable moments in the Pump Room's past are preserved in the pictures of the great and near-great displayed on the walls in the hallway leading to the Pump Room. It's fun to figure out who is who and see how young they all look.

If eating where the famous folk sometimes dine isn't what you want, consider the hotel you are now visiting. It is, according to its employees, the hotel of choice of many Hollywood personalities and music stars. Dolly Parton had her exercise equipment moved into her suite when she was in Chicago for four months filming *Straight Talk*. Anthony Hopkins accepted his best actor award for *Silence of the Lambs* from the Chicago Film Critics here. Doris Day, Frank Sinatra, and Richard Gere have suites named after them, and this is where they stay when they're in town. Sinatra usually reserves an entire floor for his entourage.

Musicians who have slept here include Tom Petty, the Beastie Boys, Concrete Blonde, Smokey Robinson, and Natalie Cole.

On the 16th floor there is the Authors' Suite, where writers are welcomed. The hotel purchases their books. There are more than 400 autographed tomes in this suite, surely the most literate hotel room in town. This suite is not available for rental for any price for fear that someone with larceny in his heart may walk off with a signed book.

Incidentally, the area immediately around the Ambassador Hotels is probably the site of many forgotten tunnels. John A. Huck, who holds the unfortunate distinction of owning the last home to be burned in the 1871 Chicago fire, built a brewery here in 1867 and created two miles of tunnels to store his lager beer. They're 20 to 30 feet wide and six feet high. When the foundations for the Ambassador Hotels were dug, old tunnels were found and destroyed, but many more may be down there. Alas, all the beer is gone.

Either stop for a bite to eat or a drink at the Pump Room, or continue south, returning to State and Division. Note the older home at 1241 North State Parkway, a cottage built in 1875. The townhouses at 1234–52 North State Parkway were built around 1890. The white brick art moderne Frank Fisher apartment building at 1209 North State Parkway reflects the tastes of the 1933–34 Century of Progress Fair.

The walk ends at Yvette, 1206 North State Parkway, one of the finest restaurants in Chicago, with unsurpassed singers and jazz musicians accompanying memorable food at reasonable prices. I'd suggest trying the lightly smoked salmon.

This restaurant is open year-round, no days off, and the later the hour, the more the place jumps, with special emphasis on Bastille Day, July 14, when can-can dancers do high kicks between the tables. The street-side cafe is especially good for people watching.

Yvette is one of my favorite places in town, and it's because the owner Bob Djahanguiri has such style. He has almost single-handedly kept cabaret entertainment alive in Chicago because he keeps a steady roster of the finest singers and pianists touring his three establishments, Yvette, Toulouse (see Rush–Division Pub Crawl), and Yvette's Wintergarden (see Wacker Drive River walk).

This ends the Gold Coast tour, a quiet neighborhood of gentle tree-lined streets recalling an age when people actually needed four rooms for their servants.

9 LINCOLN PARK WALK

Three museums, one park

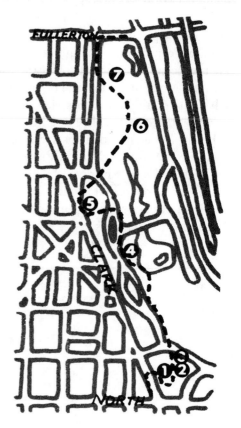

1. Chicago Historical Society
2. Lincoln Statue
3. Couch Mausoleum
4. Farm in the Zoo
5. Chicago Academy of Sciences
6. Lincoln Park Zoo
7. Lincoln Park Conservatory

Time: One to 4 hours for the walk. As many as 3 hours for the zoo, more if you are with a young child. An hour or more for the Historical Society, unless the past holds no fascination for you. At least 1 hour for the Academy of Sciences.

To get there: The #22 Clark and #36 Broadway buses both stop at Clark and North Avenue. The #151 stops at Stockton and Lincoln Park. If you are driving, take Lake Shore Drive north to North Avenue, go west to Clark Street, turn right, and go about a half block to a driveway into a Lincoln Park parking area. There are also city meters that allow you to park for up to 8 hours, if you can find an empty space.

History of Lincoln Park

Lincoln Park, between North Avenue (1600 north) and Fullerton (2400 north), is the most visited piece of greenery in the city.

It is, if the Park District keeps it clean and if visitors do not throw things in the lagoons, a lovely park, with a farm, zoo, historical museum, and natural history museum, plus statues and a botanical garden—a delightful place for a stroll. Here the casual walker can see joggers and bicyclists, catch an inning or two of a softball game, or just sit by the lagoon and watch the rowboats. It's a relaxing, expansive place—but walk carefully to avoid what dogs often leave behind despite our tough pooper-scooper laws.

Lincoln Park was a graveyard until October 21, 1864, when it was declared a park. Before that, smallpox and cholera victims from Camp Douglas, a Civil War prison camp, and from other parts of the city, were buried here in shallow graves. If the graves were dug any deeper than three or four feet this close to the lake, the diggers would strike water.

Dr. John H. Rauch, a local physician, complained about the "18,000 to 20,000 bodies undergoing decomposition at this time" in the area. This frightened folks and eventually most of the bodies were moved to other cemeteries. However, some were simply forgotten possibly under the theory that when one is moving one can't remember everything. When the basement for the Chicago Historical Society building was excavated in 1932, some old bones were unearthed, and many more may still lie beneath this idyllic park.

During the 1871 Chicago Fire, many refugees came to Lincoln Park to sit among the remaining tombstones and open graves, and watch the city burn. By 1879, so many people were using the newfangled bicycles in Lincoln Park that bikes were banned because they were "foes to the peace of mind and safety of body. . . . "

Lincoln Park also has been subject to political corruption. In 1869, the five park commissioners needed five carriages and five chauffeurs just to get to work, where fresh flowers awaited them daily. Later the park superintendent had five buddies on the payroll—and none of them knew a thing about grass, trees, or anything botanical, unless you could ferment it and drink it.

In 1904, Lincoln Park was praised as a "sylvan promenade," and an English traveler wrote that after seeing "Lincoln Park in the flush of sunset, you wonder that the dwellers in this street of palaces should trouble their heads about Naples or Venice, when they have before their very windows the innumerable laughter, the ever shifting opalescence of their fascinating inland sea." I think he meant Lake Michigan looked great!

Chicago Historical Society

Begin the Lincoln Park walk by entering through the modern doorway of the Chicago Historical Society at Clark and North Avenue. It is among the best historical museums in the country, according to its current director.

The Chicago Historical Society has a tradition of hard luck. It was founded in 1856 and, from all accounts, collected a bunch of junk, including 2,000 books of sermons. After constructing a "solid, substantial and fireproof" building in 1868, its entire collection burned (possibly a fortunate occurrence) in 1871. Whatever was left of the collection was moved to the offices of a local attorney and former society president, J. Y. Scammon, but those offices burned in 1874. Early in its history, the Chicago Historical Society just couldn't quite learn the knack of how to preserve things.

Chicago Historical Society entrance: No longer the attic for the elite

Later, there was a stroke of good fortune. When Charles F. Gunther, a local candy salesman who invented caramel, died in 1920, the society bought his collection, which included the entire Civil War Libby Prison, Lincoln's carriage, Martha Washington's thimble, and the table on which Generals U. S. Grant and Robert E. Lee ended the Civil War.

The society obviously needed a new building to house this collection, so it announced a special members meeting for October 25, 1929, to raise $1.5 million. A bad choice of dates there. The stock market crashed on October 24.

The bad luck continued. Ground was broken in 1985 for a major renovation. In July 1986, a water main flooded the society's basement and the staff, friends, and conservation experts had to work round the clock to save the collections.

The beautifully renovated Chicago Historical Society was inaugurated in 1988. They raised $15.3 million to expand 65,000 square feet by covering the 1971 limestone addition with a red-brick-and-glass envelope. Now the Historical Society is hoping that fires, depressions, and floods are strictly in its past.

One tasty addition is the main floor Big Shoulders Cafe, which serves modern sandwiches in the bull-nose, three-story, all-glass corner of the building to the far right of the main entrance just beyond the bookstore. The cafe's north wall is a 101-year-old terra-cotta arch designed for the Stock Yards Bank and Trust Co. by Daniel Burnham. The arch was first moved to the Stock Yard Inn, a South Side restaurant, and later relocated to the wall of the 135-seat restaurant. Sunday brunches are a real treat and a fine way to start a weekend walk.

This cafe is all part of a decision to modernize, an odd but necessary concept when applied to the Historical Society. Shaking off its self-assured, sleepy past hasn't been easy. In 1991, the Chicago Tribune quoted one Chicago museum professional, "Not long ago, it was a small private museum with a board that was almost entirely WASPs." The society president, Ellsworth Brown, arrived in 1981 from the Tennessee State Museum in Nashville, and the transformations began. In 1989, the long-time curator of the costume collection, who was devoted to haute couture, departed. Her replacement prepared an exhibition on Jewish immigrant and other ethnic clothing for the Becoming an American Woman show.

Recently, the museum has had exhibits examining the Chicago Street, 1860–2000; the 1919 Black Sox Scandal, when eight White Sox players conspired with gamblers to throw the World Series to the Cincinnati Reds; and a remembrance of the often violent 1968 Convention.

Permanent exhibitions include the Chicago dioramas, the Chicago History Galleries, the Fort Dearborn Exhibit, the Illinois Pioneer Life Gallery, and the American History wing devoted to the Revolutionary War and Civil War periods. One exhibit, We the People: Creating a New Nation, 1765–1820, looks at a time well before the Chicago Historical Society was founded.

In recent times, the Historical Society has received a golden-yellow suit worn by John Adams in 1780 with the back of the collar worn out by the movement of his ponytail, Mrs. Potter Palmer's diamond dog collar, and a 1908 Sears assemble-it-yourself automobile that packs in two crates.

If you walk straight into the museum from the entrance, you'll see a lobby with niches filled with many things delightful and odd, your first indication that this is no longer a museum that was an attic for the elite. The lobby boasts many ordinary things from ordinary people including a 1900 parasol, a 1950 Dad's Root Beer sign, an 1840 weather vane, a 1910 Dr. William's Pink Pills for Pale People sign, an 1896 bodice, and a 1978 beer sign for Old Chicago on Tap.

If you walk through the entrance and take a right, you'll be in the Hands-On History Gallery, where you can ride an 1890s bicycle, perform radio sound effects, figure out what the secret message was on Ovaltine's Little Orphan Annie decoder (clue: it always spelled "Ovaltine"), play with old toys, and try to figure out what the antique tools did. The toughest one to guess is the cherry pitter.

Walking straight ahead through the entrance will bring you to the current exhibits. Here, less than 2½ months after the April 1992 Chicago tunnel flood, the Historical Society mounted an exhibit of artifacts of that damp event, including videotaped news coverage of the disaster, bottles of flood water, and the suit the first diver wore when he entered the tunnels. It must have been a modern-day record for a museum that usually measures time in decades and sometimes centuries.

Beyond the current exhibit space is the Illinois Pioneer Life Gallery. The rooms show how people lived in the 1840s, and, if you're lucky, volunteers in costume will be standing in the rooms doing handicrafts and answering questions. The ladies make cloth, hand-dip candles, and dye fabrics, enlivening one of the dullest exhibits in the museum.

The Fort Dearborn exhibit is also in this area, with a model blockhouse and a view of earliest Chicago.

Next, return to the lobby area and either take the elevator, which is to your right as you face the entrance, or walk up the stairs, to the second floor where exhibits of about 15 months duration are displayed. Chicago Goes to War: 1941–45 was seen here as was the World's Fair of 1893 exhibit.

Walk straight ahead through the costume alcove into the portrait gallery.

The dioramas are to your left. These street scenes of Chicago life are so old and so beloved that they are a fixture of the museum. They may be dusty but they will never disappear. As a child, I loved the Chicago Fire of 1871 scene and all the others including the Treaty of Glenville, 1795, and the Chicago River at LaSalle Street.

If you were to walk to your right from the costume alcove, you would enter the American history wing with the We the People, 1765–1820 exhibit. Again, the emphasis is on ordinary people and their involvement in the early years of America. Perhaps the most valuable item here is the original water color rendering of the American flag. It was painted in Holland as a sketch before the actual flag was sewn.

While you're here, notice the Philadelphia street directory from 1796. Look up George Washington and notice he is simply listed as President of the United States.

Continuing your explorations, do visit the America in the Age of Lincoln exhibit, and don't be surprised if Lincoln, himself, appears. It's part of the Voices from History, a regular visit by actors costumed to look and sound like historic figures such as Frederick Douglas or Harriet Beecher Stowe.

The Civil War exhibit is one of the Historical Society's strengths. The society has the best collection of Civil War materials outside of the Library of Congress. You'll see the table on which Lincoln signed the Emancipation Proclamation, the last life mask of Lincoln and his Beatles-like spectacles, the room in which Lincoln died, and the table on which the surrender was signed at Appomattox Court House.

Perhaps the most amazing item is a sheet of lined paper framed on one wall of the exhibit. It is a copy of the 13th Amendment, which ended slavery, signed by Lincoln's vice president, Hannibal Hamlin, and the 38th Congress. This was lost until Olivia Mahoney, co-director of this exhibit, happened to be going through files in the society's basement and this rare, original, signed document fell out of a file folder where it had been consigned for decades.

If you cross through the portrait gallery, you will enter a room that has a locomotive. You can't miss it, and no child who visited the museum ever missed it either. It is the 12-ton Pioneer retired in 1874. In order to

A 12-ton locomotive in the Historical Society: It will not be moved

get it inside the museum, a second floor window and part of the wall had to be removed, the floor had to be reinforced, and a crane had to be used. It will not be moved again.

It is indestructible and generations of youngsters (myself included) have operated the levers and twisted the knobs while pretending to run the engine.

It is so big and such a shock to see a locomotive there that many people miss the fascinating display near the door of products created in Chicago. There is a picture of Marilyn Monroe on the cover of the first *Playboy* magazine, which cost 50 cents.

As you continue through this gallery, you will see an affluent living room from the turn of the century. It is interesting, but that's because there are so few such rooms in the museum which once seemed to have an endless supply of them.

Also in the Chicago History Gallery, you can see an 11-minute film about the Chicago Fire, look at the fused plates and marbles from the fire, and see Bessie the doll, which was saved from the fire by its six-year-old owner. You can also see a sign put up by one survivor of the fire, "Wm. D. Kerfoot is at 53 Onion Park Place/All gone but wife children AND energy."

This gallery ends with the sounds of old-time Chicago including jazz, blues, and the old radio show the "Breakfast Club."

On my last visit, I could not find the huge bust of Lincoln by Gutzon Borglum, who created Mt. Rushmore's heads. This Lincoln had a shiny nose because thousands of people rubbed it for luck.

Next, walk or take the elevator up to the third floor to the research gallery, which houses additional exhibits. When I last visited, it displayed the life of Chicago real estate developer Samuel Eberly Gross, who created many Chicago neighborhoods and who married a "blushing young beauty of exceptional attractiveness" when she was 18 and he was 66. And you thought Woody Allen invented the idea of older men finding younger women attractive. Unfortunately, Mr. Gross died shortly after the wedding. See the North Side Drive chapter for more information about the gentleman who created Alta Vista Street.

Also on the third floor is the library, with more than 400,000 books and other published materials. It has a helpful, courteous staff willing to get any book they have within a few minutes of the request. There is only one complaint: I have vowed that, the day I produce a bestselling book, I will replace the antiquated, balky copiers for microfilm of Chicago newspapers.

Behind the scenes, the society now has more than 20 million objects in its possession, including 1.5 million papers from architects Holabird and Root, and the entire photo morgue of the now defunct *Chicago Daily News*. The Prints and Photographs Collection has more than 1 million photos, prints, posters, videotapes, and films.

Hours are from 9:30 a.m. to 4:30 p.m., Monday through Saturday; and noon to 5 p.m., Sunday. Suggested admission is $3 for adults, $2 for students and senior citizens, $1 for children 6 through 16, free for children under age 6. Monday is free for everyone.

The Latin School

Leaving the Chicago Historical Society, turn left (going south), walk to the corner of Clark and North Avenue. The Latin School, designed by Harry Weese, is on the southeast corner. It was founded in 1888 by a group of Chicagoans who wanted to import an Eastern schoolmarm, Mabel Slade Vickery. Since then, according to one school official, this exclusive establishment has had not "a single breath of scandal," although both of my sons did try to shake it up a bit. It is also a fine school, with many important graduates, a tradition of teaching both the tough subjects and arts, and a faculty liberally sprinkled with advanced degrees.

Annual high school tuition was $10,250 in 1992. It was mentioned in *The Preppy Handbook* as THE school in Chicago, but the students are smart, nice creatures, and few of them look or talk preppy.

Walk east, following the path around the back of the Chicago Historical Society and past the 1887 statue of Abraham Lincoln, one of Augustus Saint-Gaudens' best works even though he tried to improve it with another statue, a seated Lincoln that is in Grant Park (see the South Michigan Avenue walk). The statue is now lighted at night to prevent trysting near it. There are beautiful flower gardens leading to the statue.

Couch Mausoleum

Continue walking north, moving to the left of the Lincoln statue, past a gray, forbidding mausoleum with the word COUCH inscribed on it. You'll see the word on the side facing Stockton Avenue. Ira Couch, who died in Havana in 1857, was part-owner of the Tremont House, then the finest hotel west of New York.

No one is sure how many bodies are in the mausoleum with published estimates ranging from one to 13 (the latter number might make it a little crowded). The *Chicago Tribune* reported in 1958 that the 100-ton crypt

Mystery in the park: How many bodies and why is this tomb here?

had room for only 11 bodies. The best guesstimate is that it holds three bodies: Couch, his father, and a mysterious hotel guest.

The last crypt was removed from Lincoln Park in 1895, when it completely and finally changed from burial dump to glade. Only two tombs are supposed to be there—Couch's and David Kennison's, who was the last known survivor of the Boston Tea Party. Kennison died in 1852 at age 115 and lies undisturbed near the Academy of Sciences.

No one knows why Couch is still in the park. According to one researcher for the Chicago Historical Society, there is no record of anyone going to the Park District or the courts to demand that he stay there. Current theory on the matter indicates that Couch's brother, James, probably had a quiet lunch or drink with city officials and came to a gentlemanly understanding on the matter. That sounds like Chicago, ancient or modern.

Walk through the underpass beneath Stockton Drive, where there was broken glass underfoot in the past and which now seems relatively clean; past the Lake Shore Drive exit; and past the 1896 Benjamin Franklin statue, a monument to his signature on the *Declaration of Independence*. It's been recently cleaned and looks rather new!

The Lagoon

Walk up the wide, asphalt, tree-lined path toward the Lincoln Park Lagoon. To your right was the caped statue of Italian patriot Giuseppe Garibaldi, which was unveiled in 1901. Only the base remains, a situation that has continued for at least the last six years. I'm beginning to doubt that Giuseppe will ever return.

Circle the lagoon to the left and remember the story Herman Kogan and Lloyd Wendt told in their book *Lords of the Levee*. In the 1890s, the Chicago City Council was seriously considering buying six gondolas for the Lincoln Park Lagoon. Alderman "Little Mike" Ryan stopped the debate by shouting, "Why waste the taxpayers money buyin' six gondolas? Git a pair of 'em, and let nature take its course."

Feed the ducks in the lagoon, if you happen to remember to bring some bread for them.

Farm in the Zoo

Next walk through the Farm in the Zoo, open daily from 9 a.m. to 4:30 p.m. This five-acre farm is designed to show city kids what a cow and a chicken look like. It has a poultry and egg house (the little chicks born here are rumored to be fed to the Lincoln Park Zoo snakes after-hours because the snakes need the exercise and roughage); a horse stable; a main barn with pigs and sheep; and a dairy barn, under which more skeletons were found when the foundation was dug. Thousands of people each day enter the dairy barn, look at the cows and say, "Moo." The cows do not answer.

Leave the farm from the entrance facing the lagoon, near the Dairy Barn, walk around the lagoon and under the viaduct. Pedal boats can be rented here.

Follow the path until you find Cafe Brauer, built in 1908. It was once the home of a great restaurant, where one reviewer noted "all is poetry and romance." There was an attempt to revive the old Cafe Brauer, but in 1969 the late Mayor Richard J. Daley denied the place a liquor license, and it has remained a hot dog joint ever since. But they do sell seven-inch pizzas here; there is also the Penguin Palace Ice Cream Shoppe, and bicycle and skate rentals.

That skate rental shop reminds me to insert a warning: Beware of hot-rod bicyclists and bladers, people on those new roller skates that look like hockey skates with wheels. They move fast, are very intense, and seem to be concentrating on setting a new land speed record through the park.

Go through the arches just to the left of Cafe Brauer and walk west toward Clark Street, past the statue of Hans Christian Andersen, a plain man with a big nose and a somewhat sad look on his face. The statue, complete with a former ugly duckling, was dedicated in 1896.

Chicago Academy of Sciences

Carefully cross Stockton Drive, which is the street directly ahead of you, and walk around the front of the old, but imposing building, variously called the Chicago Academy of Sciences, the Chicago Museum of Natural History, and the Chicago Museum of Ecology. It is the concrete building which looks—and is—newly sandblasted.

This is the city's oldest science institution. It was founded in 1857 by Robert Kennicott, whose heart gave out in 1866 after saving a Russian whose canoe capsized on the Yukon River. Kennicott was not an armchair scientist.

The first academy building burned in 1866. The director, William Stimpson, went to the new "fireproof" building at Wabash and Van Buren on the day the Chicago Fire started in 1871. Stimpson decided the fire wouldn't get there and, even if it did, the building would not burn. Wrong and wrong. Stimpson died six months later.

The current Chicago Academy of Sciences building was opened in 1893. It was intended to be the first wing of a huge museum, but that somehow never got to be built, especially after its competitor, the Field Museum, opened on the South Side. Where the Field Museum is a general natural history museum, the academy specializes in North America, with many exhibits on the Great Lakes region. In other words, the academy has been practicing niche marketing for over a century!

The academy was once filled with dusty, moldy, stuffed birds, a place to avoid unless one took delight in peering at mournful chickadees. The museum's former director, Dr. William J. Beecher, an ornithologist, renovated the various dioramas built by his predecessor, a snake specialist. The current director, Paul Heltne, who began in 1982, is a zoologist who has developed symposia on primates.

Today, toward the back of the main lobby, there is a small prehistoric Coal Forest, a walk-through diorama re-creating what life was like 300 million years ago.

What you will notice immediately is that the academy uses every inch of space. The stairway to the second floor is filled with exhibits including one titled "Only a few fish could adapt to polluted Lake Michigan." Inside the glass case, we see alewives (which once died by the thousands each summer, making Chicago beaches smell like a fish store gone bad), coho salmon (brought in to eat the alewives), carp, goldfish, smelt (the smelt run each spring is a Chicago fishing and frying tradition), alligator gar, and trout.

The second floor features the 1915 and 1933 dioramas showing plants and animals of our area. As you reach the top of the stairs, you'll see a huge stuffed buffalo with a moose nearby.

In the middle of this gallery, there is a reconstructed section of a canyon from Starved Rock State Park in Illinois. There are animal footprints and the shadows of tree leaves on the grassy floor around the edge of the canyon, plus a cave, a waterfall, and displays of bears, deer, wolves, owls, ducks, turkeys, shorelines, and sand dunes.

Some cases are rather small, but appear infinitely large. It's done with mirrors! See if you can tell which is the stuffed half bird or critter placed on a mirror so the reflection will create an entire fowl or animal.

Do get up to the third floor where a giant stuffed polar bear greets you. Why a polar bear? Well, it was a gift and, although it is not a local species by any means, no one had the heart to just toss the thing out. The polar bear remains.

The same principle applies to the Atwood Celestial Sphere. The night stars as seen in Chicago are inside this mini-planetarium and Earth globe.

The North Gallery features a changing variety of exhibits, beginning in 1992 with Energy: Choosing Our Future. Here an interactive computer system allows visitors to make personal choices about their lifestyles and energy consumption. Computers? In the century-old academy? How wonderful! Bring in the new, renew the old!

Other exhibits include Why Waste a Good Planet and the Vanishing Desert. Jennifer P. Stolpestad, the person in charge of audience development, said the goal of the academy is to reach out to more people, to change exhibits more quickly and to offer "more interactive displays." As a result, this small gem of a local museum will certainly find more popularity in its second century of existence than it did in its first.

In addition to everything it displays and does, the Academy directs the Chicago Peregrine Release project. See the Wacker Drive River walk to know where they nest in the Loop.

I'd suggest taking the elevator down to the main floor and then stopping at the Museum Shop. According to the lively Leslie Finn, buyer/manager, this is the "rubber snake capitol of the Midwest." The dozens of different rubber snakes are models of actual creatures, meaning that if you buy one for your 10-year-old, he will scare the little girls with life-like critters—if that is any consolation.

Other bestsellers in the shop include the $5 whining cicada key ring, the glow-in-the-dark rubber bat, giant plastic cockroaches, and the book *America's Neighborhood Bats* by Merlin D. Tuttle. The academy sponsors neighborhood bat walks at sunset several days a year.

On the serious side, the shop features native American jewelry from Navaho, Zuni, and Santo Domingo Pueblo craftspeople.

The museum is open daily from 10 a.m. to 5 p.m. Admission is $1 for adults, and 50 cents for children and seniors. Mondays are free.

R. J. Grunt's

After you leave this museum, if you are hungry, head directly west to R. J. Grunt's, across the street at 2056 North Lincoln which offers a huge salad bar and gigantic bowls of soup. Opened on June 10, 1971, it is the oldest in the Lettuce Entertain You chain of varied and fascinating restaurants.

The chain, run by the gentle and creative Richard Melman, began with a $17,000 investment to open R. J. Grunt's. It now has more than 30 restaurants in five states and Japan, employs more than 3,000 people, with sales more than $100 million in 1991. Melman, who met his wife Martha while she was waiting in line for a table during R. J. Grunt's opening night, treats eating establishments as if they were theaters: Each restaurant offers a different entertaining concept of a place to eat. They are astoundingly successful, although, like plays, they seem to close and re-open every few years as something else. R. J. Grunt's has outlasted them all. By the way, "R" is for Richard (Melman) and "J" is for Jerry Orzoff, Melman's friend and late partner.

Melman, who usually wears jeans and a baseball cap and who often uses a knapsack for a briefcase, enjoys the creativity of his life, but would probably rather be playing baseball. He plays in the Over-Forty softball league.

Lincoln Park Zoo

If you are not hungry, walk to the east, re-cross Stockton Drive, and enter the amazing and wonderful Lincoln Park Zoo. Amazing because entry is completely free—a rarity in this day and age. Wonderful because over the last few years the zoo has gone through continual refurbishment. You are about to see some spectacular displays of animals.

Lincoln Park Zoo, the second oldest and one of the smallest (only 35 acres) zoos in America, attracts more than 4 million visitors a year, and began in 1868 when the Central Park Zoo in New York gave Chicago two swans.

In 1905, when the notorious Alderman "Bathhouse" John Coughlin wanted to build his own zoo near Colorado Springs, the Lincoln Park Zoo obligingly "gave" him Princess Alice, an elephant with a defective trunk. The zoo had another elephant anyway.

There were no public feedings of the animals in the zoo during the Depression for fear that it might upset hungry humans. During the late '40s and '50s, then-director Marlin Perkins originated his "Zoo Parade" TV show from here.

Over the years, two of the zoo's most dangerous animals escaped under almost identical circumstances. Bushman, a 550-pound gorilla, wandered into the corridor behind his cage and stayed there for three hours in 1950 (see the Museum walk for the location of the now-stuffed Bushman). Sinbad, a 530-pound gorilla, entered into the same area in 1964. Both Bushman and Sinbad could bend steel bars and only a flimsy screen or two kept Chicago from experiencing its very own King Kongs.

When Bushman got loose, his keeper yelled, "Bushman, get the hell back." Bushman bit his keeper's finger. When Sinbad got loose, his keeper yelled, "Get back in there." He didn't listen either, which means that there is a long-term breakdown in man-ape communications.

Both gorillas gave up their short-lived freedom remarkably easily. Bushman was frightened back to his cage by an 18-inch-long baby alligator, and Sinbad was tranquilized and carried back. Neither of them even had a chance to pick up a beautiful girl and gently blow-dry her hair as King Kong did in the movie remake starring Jessica Lange.

The zoo once held a *Guinness* record for Heine, a chimp who died in 1971 at the age of 50 years and three months, living longer than any other primate on record, excluding humans.

This is the first zoo to have a year-round children's zoo, and today it offers visitors a new primate house, a new great ape house, and a new sea lion pool.

As you enter the zoo just east of Cafe Brauer, take an immediate right and walk around the antelope and zebra areas, walking in a big circle around Grant's gazelles, reindeer, buffalo, and others.

This long walk will eventually take you to the Lester E. Fisher Great Ape House, named after the director of the zoo who retired in 1992 after 30 years of zoo service. A plaque proclaims that during his watch "more great apes were born in Lincoln Park than any other zoo," and the zoo recorded its first gorilla birth in 1970.

It is fitting that this stunning display is named after a gentle, generous, and loving man. In it you will first see a group of gorillas swinging from large ropes. They will, I hope, be very active as they tend to be in this setting. Three of the four apes in the first group of gorillas were born at Lincoln Park Zoo, six of nine in the second group were also local births. The orangutan display boasts three of the five having been born in

Lincoln Park. You will also stroll past groups of chimpanzees and gorillas—spectacular and impressive. The Great Ape House is really great!

If you continue walking north (to the right of the Great Ape House), you'll next see the Primate House. The letters above the doorway say that it is the Small Mammal House, but a wooden sign indicates that this is the Primate House.

The 22,930 square foot, $3.6 million Primate House opened in 1992 with eight naturalistic habitats replacing 31 small barred cages that once lined the walls of the old primate house built in 1926. It is the 16th zoo building to be either constructed or renovated in the last 16 years, quite a record of renewal for what was an aging urban zoo.

The old primate house, a grim place with thick bars, was the home to three of the city's most famous captives, the Western lowland gorillas known as Bushman (1928–1951), Sinbad (1947–1985), and Otto (1963–1988). Bushman's old seat is in the new Primate House and visitors can sit where the 550-pound Bushman and the 600-pound Sinbad once roosted.

Zoo director David Hales has a cure for primate boredom, "take a pair of crickets and see me in the morning." Inside the logs or tree trunks in some of the exhibits in the Primate House are long tubes which time-

The sea lions are always active

release live crickets. They hop around the exhibit until they become a snack for a primate.

One feature of the new Primate House is that no species is alone. Black howler monkeys are joined by squirrel monkeys because research indicates that the howlers take advantage of the skittish squirrel monkeys to warn of danger. The public looks at the primates through glass to prevent viruses from being transmitted both ways. The animals have an independent air system. You won't breath in what they breath out and vice versa. The glass serves another purpose: There are almost no animal odors in this exhibit!

You will walk past black-and-white colobus monkeys, dusty titi-monkeys, red-ruffed lemurs, mandrills, and, best of all, the black howler monkey display. There is a microphone within their enclosure. May the howlers howl when you are there.

This exhibit features a sign to remember, "Extinction is forever. Endangered means there's still time."

Exit the Primate House, continue north, and walk up the path between the Reptile House and the Lion House. The Reptile House boasts boa constrictors, anacondas, alligators, snapping turtles, bullfrogs, lizards, cotton mouths, cobras, skinks, and rattlesnakes.

If the lions are outside of the Lion House next door, by all means enjoy the day. If their cages are empty, enter the Lion House, which underwent an $850,000 renovation in 1992.

Notice that piano wire, instead of bars, forms one wall of the enclosures. The wire is strong enough to keep the cats inside while making them easier to see. In fact, in some photographs, the wire disappears and is replaced with the realistic backdrops. If it works for you, you'll go home with some truly amazing pictures. You'll see mountain lions peaking out of their dens, jaguars, cheetahs, and mountain snow leopards pacing in naturalistic settings.

Exit from the west door of the Lion House, the one facing Stockton Drive, skirt around to the right, and walk by my favorite display, the Sea Lion Pool, where the creatures are always active. They are amazingly sleek and graceful swimmers.

Continue west and enter the Children's Zoo, where baby monkeys and cheetahs are sometimes in incubators and where you can see and touch guinea pigs and other animals. The garden to the south of the Children's Zoo is absolutely made for strolling.

However, if you retrace your path, going once more past the Sea Lion Pool, and take the walkway between the Lion House and the sea lions, you will eventually find a sad shed containing the ship the zoo doesn't want.

The rotting Viking Ship that sailed from Norway to Chicago in time for the Columbian Exposition of 1893 is stored here. This once-proud vessel is host to a tale both triumphal and tragic. Norway refused to allow an actual Viking ship, unearthed there in 1888, to sail to Chicago because it was a national treasure. Captain Magnus Andersen built a replica for $16,000 and named it the *Viking* (not the *Raven* as a small sign near the boat incorrectly identifies this relic). He led the dozen-man crew on a 4,800-mile ocean voyage in what was essentially an open boat.

Thousands of Chicagoans greeted the vessel and her brave crew when they arrived after a 28-day Atlantic crossing on July 12, 1893. The 20-ton longship became a featured and honored attraction at the 1893 Fair, after which no one apparently knew what to do with it.

For a while it was moored in the Jackson Park lagoon on the South Side, where it was vandalized and damaged so much that it began to sink. After repairs, it was moved to the zoo in 1920, and cleaned up again in the 1970s, when a higher fence was put around it to prevent the homeless from sleeping in the hull. The 50-foot mast and the 32 oars lie alongside the frame, while the dragon heads, sails, and shields are being kept in private homes.

It has been neglected and mostly forgotten for a quarter century. Some say it would take $250,000 to fix it up and more money to move it to a permanent home. A spokesperson for the zoo readily admitted that the zoo would love to get rid of it. Somewhere. Anywhere. Meanwhile, an artifact of the nineteenth century has the steady attention of only the pigeons.

If you return to the Sea Lion Pool, you can exit the zoo at the west entrance and walk toward the Bates Fountain (see the Gardens and Conservatory entry toward the end of this walk), or you can walk on to see the rest of the zoo.

If you walk around the Food Festival kiosks to the left, you'll find the Penguin and Seabird House. The penguins are particularly humorous to watch. Exit this house, walking by bushes shaped like various animals. The Small Mammal House and Nocturnal Exhibit are directly in front of you. The Large Mammal Area is to your left with giraffes, tapirs, and elephants.

Continue walking north and you'll see the bear and wolf habitats. Just beyond another food kiosk, you can enter the Rookery. Be careful of the flagstone here because it is uneven, and it is easy to twist an ankle while strolling through. It is a pleasant walk around two ponds.

If you went through the Rookery, exit through the north portals, take a left, making a U-turn, walk to the south, and you will find the Lincoln Park Conservatory.

Zoo hours are 9 a.m. to 5 p.m., with the Children's Zoo opening at 10 a.m. During the summertime, the zoo often will stay open until 7:30 p.m. And as I said, admission is always free.

Eugene Field

In the Lincoln Park Zoo, there is a statue in honor of bachelor Eugene Field, a *Chicago Daily News* columnist who became famous for writing such children's poems as "Wynken, Blynken and Nod" and "Little Boy Blue." It is a little-known fact that Field, who died in 1895 and who was honored as "the children's poet laureate," also wrote lascivious verse. He wrote such lines as "Ah that was glorious bangin,' good bangin' on the Rhine" and "But when my Julia breaks her wind . . ."

Gardens and Conservatory

If you exit just to the north of the Children's Zoo thus cutting short your zoo experience, walk around the 1886 statue of Johann Christoph Schiller, a German poet and dramatist. Just ahead of you is an 1887 fountain titled *Storks at Play*, by Augustus Saint-Gaudens and Frederick MacMonnies. It features three boys, three herons, three squirting fish, and lots of splashing water.

Storks at Play, also called the Bates Fountain, is in the middle of the colorful Main Garden, which has a riot of flowers in spring and summer. Across the street to the west is Grandmother's Garden, so named because at the turn of the century elderly neighborhood women would tend flowers there. There is also a statue of William Shakespeare facing the Lincoln Park Conservatory entrance. He is seated and slightly reclining, surely the least official pose for the Bard of Avon.

The building immediately in front of you, just beyond the huge bust of Sir Georg Solti, former conductor of the Chicago Symphony, is the Lincoln Park Conservatory, built in 1891–92. There is always a jungle climate in the conservatory, which is open from 9 a.m. to 5 p.m. daily, so you can see the flora from such exotic lands as India, Sumatra, Brazil, China, and Mexico. Admission is also free.

If you wish to end the walk, either go to Fullerton and Stockton Drive and take a #151 or #156 bus back to the Loop.

If you wish to continue, there are two suggested routes. You can return by walking east toward the lake and then south. If you take this route, you'll pass several signs on ridges indicating where the lake left ancient sand bars before it retreated to its present boundaries. You'll also pass an 1891 statue of Ulysses S. Grant atop a horse atop an arch, again proving that there is a statue of Lincoln in Grant Park and one of Grant in Lincoln Park.

Or you can continue onward, wandering across Fullerton, idly watching people practicing in the casting pond, and heading north through the park until you reach Diversey, a half-mile away. There isn't much that is historical for the next four blocks. It is just a beautiful, sculptured city park. You will stroll past a pretty white gazebo, walk around another lagoon, and see the Park Place Cafe with its huge, well-equipped playlot that should be a must stop for children under age six. Eventually you will reach the golden statue of Alexander Hamilton. The city driving range is about a half-block north and east of this statue. Go there, get a bucket and a driving wood, and knock some golf balls around. Very relaxing, unless you're deeply into self-criticisms.

10 OAK PARK WALK

Frank Lloyd Wright and his grand suburb

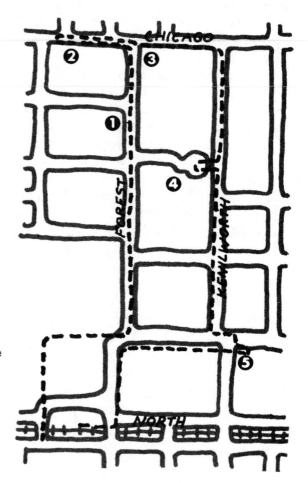

1. Nathan G. Moore House
2. "Bootleg" houses
3. Frank Lloyd Wright Home and Studio
4. Mrs. Thomas H. Gale House
5. Unity Temple

Time: 2½ hours or less, plus 40 minutes round trip for transportation from the Loop.

To get there: By public transportation, take the Lake Street rapid transit from the Loop to the Harlem/Marion stop, about a 15-minute ride past the University of Illinois, on your left. At the Harlem/Marion stop, walk to the east side of the platform (in the direction from which you came) and walk out on Marion. By car, take the Eisenhower Expressway (I-90) west, driving approximately 15 minutes from State Street to the Harlem exit, which is on the left side of the Expressway. Go north (or right) about two miles to North Boulevard, which is just beyond a viaduct. Take a right on North Boulevard and park in the Oak Park Mall.

Oak Park Mall and Visitors' Center

To walk through Oak Park is to touch genius.

Edgar Rice Burroughs wrote his stories about Tarzan in Oak Park. And Ernest Hemingway was born there and left, later scoffing that it was a community of "broad lawns and narrow minds." It must be noted that more than a few residents of Oak Park don't believe he ever said that.

But Oak Park, today, reverberates with the ghost of Frank Lloyd Wright, an architectural genius who lived there, revolutionized residential building design, and who left in the midst of a scandal after creating 25 homes, churches, and fountains in the suburb.

Except for Wright's Home and Studio and his Unity Temple, this walk will take you past private homes currently housing families. These are not museums, and the families request that you respect their privacy.

When you get off the rapid transit or after you have parked your car, the walk begins at Harlem and Marion Streets. Walk under the elevated train tracks. Go straight ahead on Marion into the Oak Park Mall, as pleasant a city shopping area as you'd ever wish to find.

If you have driven and parked in the mall lot, exit the parking area, walk to your right through the Westgate cul-de-sac and past the Unique Magic Store at 1105 Westgate. If you need juggler's clubs, buy them here. Take a left on Marion and walk to Lake Street.

The first intersection in the mall, with Barbara's Bookstore on the northwest corner, was the site of a pre-Civil War underground railroad stopping place, where slaves recuperated while escaping from the South.

Continue through the mall, taking a right on Lake at the Oak Park Trust and Savings Bank, pass the Kroch's and Brentano's Bookstore and the Lake Theater. You will shortly arrive at the corner of Forest and Lake Street.

The Visitors' Center, attached to the Mall Garage at 128 Forest, is just ahead to your left. It has taped, 1½-hour tours of Oak Park available in English, Spanish, French, Italian, German, and Japanese. The tours, updated in 1992, rent for $6, and the center is open daily from 10 a.m. to 5 p.m.

Continue north up Forest and walk past the Austin Gardens Park, with its bird sanctuary and wild flower garden.

Next, walk past the Oak Park Nineteenth Century Women's Club, which raises money for scholarships. Frank Lloyd Wright's mother and first wife were among its founders.

Thomas House

You'll see your first Frank Lloyd Wright home a little north of the Nineteenth Century Club, the Frank W. Thomas House at 210 Forest, built in 1901. (All Frank Lloyd Wright homes are named after their original owners.) Note its distinctive white-and-green-leaded-glass windows and its strong, horizontal lines. By the end of this walk, you'll be able to recognize a Frank Lloyd Wright home in a crowd of others. If not, if you ever have the opportunity to enter one of them, when you bump your head on his low doorways, you'll know you've discovered a Wright house.

Wright, who was no more than 5-foot 8-inches tall, believed that those who were taller than he constituted "weeds." He built his homes to human scale, but that meant to his measure. Any tall person living in a Wright-designed home today would know the meaning of "watch your head."

Continuing north on Forest, you'll see many Victorian homes—each unique and beautifully kept up. And each, in its own way, comment on Wright's genius. These were the homes being built at the time Wright was designing the structures you'll see on this walk. It becomes understandable why people say that Wright created the modern home.

Beachy House

The Peter A. Beachy House is at 238 Forest Avenue. The home sits at right angles to the street so Wright could use the foundation of a Gothic cottage, which formerly stood on the site. The home is on the extreme edge of its lot, something unheard of when it was built in 1906. This gave its owner a huge yard, and more grass to cut.

In 1991, this home caught fire and part of the roof was destroyed as well as extensive interior damage. None of that is visible from the street because the home was lovingly restored.

Edward R. Hills House

Moving along, and continuing to walk north, look across the street at the Edward R. Hills House, at 313 Forest. This structure was moved from 333 Forest in 1906. It was then shifted 90 degrees so that it faced north, and was remodeled by Wright. The present owner, Thomas DeCaro, took nearly 18 months off work to oversee restoration of the home at a cost rumored to be three times its purchase price.

Then the Hills home was almost completely destroyed by fire in 1976. With the help of neighbors, money was raised, and the home rebuilt almost to original specifications.

Arthur Huertley House

At 318 Forest is the Arthur Huertley House, built for a banker in 1902. Note the odd point in front of the arch—Wright often included ship prows in his homes, perhaps so they could sail the prairie.

The home is built on wooden piers so that it would settle evenly into the ground. After 70 years, I am told, there is not a single crack in the plaster anywhere in the home. Other interesting facts about this home: The main living area is on the second floor, and the arch is Wright's way of paying homage to his mentor, Louis Sullivan, who was famous for his use of arches.

Nathan G. Moore House

Continuing north, we find the Nathan G. Moore House, at 333 Forest Avenue, across the street at the corner of Forest and Superior. My original guide for this walk, Mrs. Vernette Schultz, said, "This home always brings a smile to my face." The reason is fairly obvious—the home is the result of a tussle between architect and client.

Ah, the wonders of compromise in the Nathan G. Moore House

Built by Wright in 1895 and rebuilt by him in 1923, the home is a compromise between Moore's demands for Tudor styling and Wright's interest in Japanese designs. The result is a Tudor home, with Japanese-style lower levels, or maybe a Gothic home in Oriental drag. When he first designed it, Wright needed money because of his growing family. This house proves that sometimes in his life Wright could actually design something that satisfied the client.

Copeland House

Next door, at 400 Forest Avenue, is the Dr. William H. Copeland House, which doesn't look like a Wright home at all. However, the inside of this home is immediately identifiable as a Frank Lloyd Wright, but you'll have to take my word for it. The Copeland House is not open to the public, although I saw it once during the annual Wright Plus Walk, a happy springtime trek through various Oak Park and River Forest Homes sponsored by the Frank Lloyd Wright Home and Studio Foundation. I don't think I'd bother about attempting to become part of it—for years, the walk has been sold out the same day tickets are announced for sale.

Wright built the garage in 1898, remodeled the home in 1909 giving it a typical Wright, flat-roofed dormer on the third floor and putting most of his distinctive touches on the inside of the home.

Bootleg Homes

Walking north, you will next arrive at the corner of Forest and Chicago Avenue. If you turn left and walk slightly less than a block to the west, you'll see three homes at 1019, 1027, and 1031 Chicago. These Wright Homes are small, nearly identical, and were inexpensive. However, they proved costly in a personal way to Wright.

These are called Wright's bootleg homes, although their official names are the Thomas H. Gale, Robert P. Parker, and Walter H. Gale Houses. Wright designed these homes in violation of the exclusive contract he signed with Louis Sullivan, the one man on earth Wright loved as one would a father. Wright needed money so he could experiment with the barrel-roofed playroom in his nearby home, but Sullivan learned about Wright's bootleg homes. There was an argument in Wright's drafting room, after which Wright left the firm and did not speak to Sullivan until Sullivan was on his death bed in 1925.

Return to Forest and Chicago, and you'll be standing in front of the Frank Lloyd Wright Home and Studio, a national landmark, on the northeast side of the street. It was a home of experimentation, joy, and intense emotional pain.

It was also a home that was never quite finished, as Wright continued to experiment on his own domicile by constantly rebuilding it. His first wife, Catherine, and his six children lived amid dust and workmen, and Catherine was not a very happy woman.

The Mamah Cheney Affair

She was destined to be even unhappier because of a 1903–1909 scandal which still shocks the people of Oak Park. Frank Lloyd Wright, husband and father of six children, fell in love with Mrs. Mamah Cheney, wife of one of Wright's clients, mother of two, and a "new" woman in 1903. She had an open marriage. Frank Lloyd Wright did not.

So Frank remained friendly with Edwin Cheney, but had problems with Mrs. Wright. Wright finally moved out of his home, adding a floor above his studio to create an apartment that could be rented to increase the family income. The MacArthurs moved in and their son, Charles, eventually married Helen Hayes and was the co-writer of *The Front Page*.

Wright's love story had a tragic ending. He built Taliesin, a home in Spring Green near Madison, Wisconsin, for Mamah. After the couple escaped Oak Park in 1909 to live openly and without benefit of divorces in Wisconsin, Wright completed precious few designs in Oak Park. The scandal affected his career for decades.

Mamah, the love of his mid-life, was killed in 1914, when an insane servant set fire to the home and hacked with an ax anybody who stepped outside. Within two minutes, seven people, including Mamah and both her children, were murdered. The folks in Oak Park now say that Wright, who was in his forties during the Mamah Cheney affair, was having a mid-life crisis. What a crisis!

Frank Lloyd Wright
Home and Studio

After reflecting on the triumphs and tragedies of a genius, walk toward the home on the Chicago Avenue side. Note the columns on the front

Frank Lloyd Wright's dining room: Stylish, but is it comfortable?

Frank Lloyd Wright's barrel-roofed playroom. Note the grand piano under the stairway to the left

porch, with secretary birds symbolizing wisdom (and architects), a tree of life, and a book of specifications.

The humorous message of these columns is, "Good friend, if you want to live fully of the tree of life go to a wise bird who knows his specifications to have your plans drawn up."

In 1898, Oak Park permit #34-61 was issued to Frank Wright for an $1,800 frame dwelling. He spent $5,000 to eventually create the brick home you see today. About one-fourth of Wright's life's work was done here, and it was in this studio that the Prairie House was developed.

The National Trust for Historic Preservation dramatically bought this property in 1974 when it was about to be torn apart and possibly shipped to museums room by room. Do notice how the woodwork has been lovingly restored, how the stained glass windows glow with the sunlight, and reflect on how many hours must have been spent by people who enjoy Wright's memory to bring the home and studio to the condition it is in today.

Mrs. Dawn Goshorn, one of the founders of the Frank Lloyd Wright Home and Studio Foundation, said that Wright, during a visit to his home, said that "if nothing else remains of mine in Oak Park, my home and the Unity Temple will be enough for people to understand what I was doing."

It took a dozen years of difficult work and $2.2 million to restore the home and studio. As many as 28 coats of paint covered the original plaster, and 10 layers had to be removed from the three murals on the second floor. The renovation involved raising the entire studio on concrete caissons, excavating a basement and pouring a concrete foundation to support the structure. One skylight alone required 350 hours to restore and 30 architects, 80 contractors, 350 workers, and more than 1,000 volunteers worked on the huge project.

Finally, the job was completed in the summer of 1987. It now looks like Wright's home in 1909, Wright's last year in the house, just before he left to go to Germany to create a book of his drawings that would make him an international celebrity. Mamah joined him on that trip, fueling the scandal.

Enter through the living room and notice the words above the hearth, "Truth is Life," which is an adaptation of Wright's mother's family motto "Truth Against the World." As far as Wright was concerned, the hearth was the soul of the family, the place where all should come together, thus the additional words there, "Good friends, around these hearth stones speak no evil word of any creature." I could never understand, if this place was so important, why are the benches there so uncomfortable?

Proceed to the dining room, built in 1895, which was the first room to be restored. Notice the distinctive Frank Lloyd Wright furniture designs.

Next, go up to the barrel-roofed, second-floor playroom, where Catherine Wright once set up a Montessori-type school. You enter the playroom through a narrow corridor, in keeping with Wright's notions of re-creating womb and birth experiences within the home.

On the balcony above the hallway there is a statue. Frank Lloyd Wright has several of these winged tributes to victory, and he carried them with him when he moved about the world.

Notice the stairway to the balcony. There wasn't enough space for a grand piano, which Wright needed because he required that classical music be played when he did his architectural drawings. Wright stuffed a piano under the playroom stairway and installed hooks so the landing could open up as a normal piano sounding board would. Only the keyboard stuck out from the wall.

Follow your guides and leave the playroom. In the area between the home and the studio, you'll see a honey locust tree growing out of the wall. This is as close as the restoration could get to the original tree, which was a willow, but which died around 1940. Wright believed that nature was a part of man, and he became justly famous for homes that did not disturb nature. It is said that he built his studio passageway around this tree.

On to the octagonal drafting room, where you will notice the chains around the top of the room. In 1909, those chains held up a balcony from which the Wright children would sometimes waterbomb daddy and his apprentices. The chains were buried in walls and floors and were redis-covered during the 13-year restoration. Now, because of zoning laws, they are more decorative than functional (something about which Wright might be less than enthusiastic). Here, sometimes, the children would learn almost too much about life in 1909, as they would watch Richard Bach sculpt from live nude models.

Do notice the cream Gothic-style cottage with the tan trim at 929–931 East Chicago, next door to Wright's home and studio. It was the home of Frank's mother; we leave it to the marriage counselors amongst you to determine the effect of mother's proximity on Wright's relationship with his wife.

Frank Lloyd Wright's home is open for public tours for $6 a person Monday through Friday at 11 a.m., 1, and 3 p.m., and on Saturday and Sunday at 11 a.m. and 4 p.m. The staff is energetic and helpful, but if you are lucky, perhaps you'll be guided by Lyman Shepard, who also

Could any client resist in Frank Lloyd Wright's octagonal drafting room?

performs his impressions of Wright at various gatherings. It's a little like having Frank Wright take you through his own home. There are more than 500 other enthusiastic volunteers to help keep the Wright memory alive.

This home is now the business office of the foundation. On the third Saturday in May this becomes command central for Wright Plus, a thoroughly delightful springtime tour of suburban homes. Each year some 3,000 lucky ticket holders are allowed to walk through the inside of a dozen local homes, at least several of which were designed by Wright. Guides give brief lectures and everyone comments on how modern the kitchens invariably look. Tickets, which go on sale March 1, are almost impossible to get. Call (708)848-1500 for more information.

Continue a little farther east, take a right, and enter the Ginko Tree Book Shop, which is open daily from 10 a.m. to 5 p.m. You can buy distinctive Wright-influenced coffee mugs here. I'm drinking from one as I write this. The shop also sells books about Wright, neckties, children's educational toys, unique posters, and art-and-glass reproductions. Most of the staff are volunteers.

Walk half a block to the next corner and take a right on Kenilworth, proceeding south, past a beautiful block of immaculate Victorian, Queen Anne, and Italianate homes. The white, gray, and green H. P. Young House, at 334 North Kenilworth, was a farmhouse remodeled by Wright in 1895.

Mrs. Thomas H. Gale House

You'll see the end of a cul-de-sac to your right; walk about 100 yards and you'll see the Mrs. Thomas H. Gale House. The five-bedroom home, designed by Wright in 1909, is supposed to be a series of planes floating in space. It is one of Wright's most unusual Oak Park homes and is seen as a forerunner of the homes he later designed in California.

Unity Temple

Now walk another 2½ blocks, down a pleasant, quiet, well-kept street, past the Gothic United Church to the Unity Temple at Lake and Kenilworth, Wright's first public building. This reinforced concrete masterpiece, just to the left of the post office, established Wright's

Unity Temple entrance

renown the world over, but was built amid great controversy between 1905 and 1908.

Parishioners called the design a "blasphemy to God" or a "fortress." But Wright insisted that no one could understand his design until they worshipped in the finished church, with its acoustically perfect chancery. Wright stayed home that first Sunday, but a trustee of the church quickly called and said, "You're right, Frank, it works."

Walk east on Lake until you reach the Unity Temple entrance, with its words, "For the Worship of God and the Service of Man." The chancery is upstairs, to the right. Notice that you enter and exit past the pulpit, because Wright wanted parishioners to leave by walking toward the minister, rather than away from him. The church is open to the public but tour times vary. Call (708)848-6225 for information.

In 1985, the sanctuary was completely restored to its original colors and condition at a cost of $250,000.

The chancery is a nearly indescribable space of light, rectangles and squares, art glass, balconies, and passageways. One atheist said, "It is the one place on Earth I feel close to God."

For the sake of accuracy, we should note that this structure is now called the Unitarian Universalist Church. It was the Unity Church until 1961, but there was another church with the same name in Oak Park—this church changed its name to avoid mix-ups in the mail.

Frank Lloyd Wright was perhaps the first man with sex appeal in Oak Park. Ancient ladies offering gingerbread cookies remember rushing out to stop him as he rode by on horseback. When he arrived in Oak Park the prairie grass was as high as a horseman's thigh. When he left, the prairie was dotted with his masterpieces.

The Unity Temple concludes the Frank Lloyd Wright portion of this tour. Return to Lake Street. If you turn right, you will pass the concrete Horse Show Fountain, at Lake and Oak Park, built by Wright in 1909. There is a CTA stop at Oak Park. If you turn left, you can walk west on Lake, then return to the Loop via the CTA Harlem/Marion stop. Or you can retrieve your car.

Ernest Hemingway's Museum and Home

If you're not too exhausted, stick around Oak Park a little longer. Just around the corner and up the street from Unity Temple, at 200 North Oak Park Avenue, is the Arts Center, which has a Hemingway museum. Hemingway, a third generation Oak Parker, was born in his maternal grandparents' home in Oak Park, after which his father announced the birth by blowing his cornet.

You can see Hemingway's 1915 Oak Park high school baseball season ticket, his childhood diary in which the boy marked off the days in terms of what he bought ($1 for fishing tackle, 5 cents for *Saturday Evening Post*), and the "Dear John" letter from Agnes Von Kurowsky, the nurse who tended his wounds in Italy during World War I and who became a prototype for the character Catherine Barkley in *A Farewell to Arms*. The museum also has his first story, written at age 12 and titled *The Sea Vouge*. He was not a great speller at the time. He got a 96 on a spelling test, but missed "leizure" and "arnt." There is also a map he drew of the Louisiana Purchase, which got the comment "not very neat" from a teacher, plus a notebook announcing Hemingway's intention "to write and travel." By the way, Hemingway was elected class prophet of his high school class.

The museum also offers a six-minute video on his years at Oak Park-River Forest High School.

Ernest Hemingway's home and birthplace, which now has three apartments and is privately owned, is another block and a half away at 339 North Oak Park. Hemingway's room was the center bedroom on the third floor. He would practice boxing in the 30 by 30-foot music room.

The Cheney House is at 520 North East Avenue, about four blocks east of the Unity Temple. At the corner of East Avenue and Fair Oaks, which is one block east of East Avenue, are two more streets with many Wright homes.

11 UNIVERSITY OF CHICAGO WALK

Where learning is an adventure

1. Rockefeller Chapel
2. Robie House
3. Oriental Institute
4. One quadrangle
5. Cobb Gate
6. *Nuclear Energy* by Henry Moore

Time: About 2 hours.

To get there: The Illinois Central Railroad stops at 59th Street, a short run from its Randolph and Michigan station. It is also possible to sometimes find parking close to the 59th Street station.

174

The Hebrew Professor
and the Tycoon

The University of Chicago is a miracle. It is the result of a meeting between a dumpy Hebrew professor and a rich oil tycoon, who never realized that some day he would give more than $80 million to create one of the great universities in the world.

William Rainey Harper, the Hebrew professor, was an educational dynamo who finished high school at age 10, completed college while in short pants at age 14, became a college teacher when he was 16, was in charge of a college at age 19, and could sell anybody anything.

The man never slept. He taught much of the nation Hebrew by correspondence, wrote textbooks, started scholarly journals, created summer schools and conducted five of them at once in 1885, and lectured throughout the country. He would nap whenever things got dull.

Then Harper began seducing tycoon John D. Rockefeller. Slowly, without revealing all of his plans, Harper appealed to Rockefeller's thoughts of immortality, the need for a great university, and to their joint Baptist leanings. He demanded—and eventually got—as much money as he wanted from one of the tightest-fisted American millionaires.

Harper's task of creating a university where none existed before wasn't easy. The child of one Latin professor, who had been spirited away from Cornell by Harper, was heard praying, "Good-bye, God, we are going to Chicago."

Harper even stole nearly the entire faculty of one school, Clark University. When the University of Chicago opened on October 1, 1892, its faculty included eight former college presidents; the country's first Dean of Women; the first Jewish theologian in a Christian university; three physicists who would go on to win Nobel Prizes; and the first professional football coach, Amos Alonzo Stagg. There were 594 students that first day. Harper had created a university.

In a video prepared by the Alumni Association, Loraine Richardson Green, the first black woman to get a master's degree in sociology from the school, recalled that all prospective faculty members had to have dinner with Dr. Harper. "If you didn't meet his standards as a dinner guest, you didn't get on the faculty," she recalled. Someone involved in creating the video remembered that, while in her nineties, Mrs. Green feared that her schedule was too full to allow her to participate in the video.

Other alumni recalled that students did not "have to be apologetic about reading a book or playing a violin." During prohibition when Al Capone ran Cicero, fraternity pledges would be given a lantern and sent to Cicero during Hell Week to "look for an honest man." Mike Nichols, the film director who is a graduate, thought the school was "wonderful because everyone there was a weirdo."

The University of Chicago today teaches more than 10,800 students, and tuition is about $18,000 per year. There is one faculty member for every six students and 62 winners of the Nobel Prize have been associated with the school as students, teachers, or researchers.

The U. of C. is the largest, richest and most prestigious private institution in the Midwest. Its professors have helped develop sociology as an academic discipline, discovered the various stages of sleep, created the first self-sustaining nuclear chain reaction, and discovered the jet stream, the solar wind, and uranium 235. Its alumni include novelists Saul Bellow, Sara Paretsky, Andrew M. Greeley, and Kurt Vonnegut; actor Ed Asner; the first Heisman Trophy winner, Jay Berwanger; astronomer Carl Sagan; author and interviewer Studs Terkel; the publisher of *Ebony* and *Jet* magazines, John J. Johnson; the late composer Philip Glass; David Reuben, the author of *Everything You Always Wanted to Know About Sex But Were Afraid to Ask*; and the leader of the so-called Untouchables during Prohibition, Elliot Ness.

Hyde Park

U. of C.'s campus is in Hyde Park—bastion of Chicago liberalism—an integrated community of thinkers and protesters. Shortly after the village of Hyde Park was chartered in 1861 (it wasn't annexed to Chicago until 1889), the village protested the foul odors resulting from a company which hauled "offal, dead animals, and other offensive or unwholesome matter" through the village streets to a nearby plant. When the U.S. Supreme Court decided the company must move, Hyde Park breathed a sigh of relief.

The Midway

The walk begins by going west on 59th Street. The Midway, created for the 1893 World's Columbian Exposition, is on your left. In the Midway, you'll see a statue honoring Thomas Masaryk, Czechoslovakia's first president (1851–1937). The steps to the statue are rotting and the whole area is old and ugly. Masaryk is honored because, after being a professor at the school, he returned to Czechoslovakia to become its president. Across the Midway, the first building west of Dorchester is the Sonia Shankman Orthogenic School, where Bruno Bettleheim pioneered treatment of autistic children.

International House, at 1414 East 59th Street, was dedicated in 1932, "That brotherhood may prevail." Two of the university's Nobel prize winners, Saul Bellow and economist Milton Friedman, lived in the apartment building just north of International House.

Continue walking west, past the tennis courts, and notice Emmons Blaine Hall, at 59th and Kimbark, part of the University of Chicago Laboratory Schools, where John Dewey gave birth to progressive education. Dewey founded the school in 1894 and demanded that the school encourage the child's curiosity without rote learning, that the child have self-set tasks, and that the child, not the subject matter, was the primary concern of all teaching. Ground was broken for a new $5 million Middle School on June 15, 1992.

Walk one block west along the Midway Plaisance and look to the west. The massive first Ferris Wheel stood here for the 1893 World's Columbian Exposition. Nearby, on the Streets of Cairo, visitors could be scandalized by the gyrations of Little Egypt. (More on her later.)

Turning our minds from thoughts of hootchy-cootchy dancers, at 59th and Woodlawn is Ida Noyes Hall, a three-story building resembling a Tudor English manor house and the center of both women's physical education and student activities. Do walk inside and notice the Gothic staircase, windows, and columns. This is University Gothic at its ultimate.

Ida's Cafe, on the main floor, owned by a Hyde Park favorite restaurant, the Medici, is a friendly place for a bite to eat. The Pub, which can be found by following the signs to the men's or women's rooms in the basement, has eight "great" beers on tap and costs $3 per year to join, but you have to be a student, faculty member, or one of their friends to go there. There is a cinema just off the lobby and this is the home of the Documentary Film Group, the oldest college film society in America.

There are two unfounded campus rumors as to why the Noyes family gave this hall. One alleges that Ida Noyes committed suicide after being rejected by a sorority and the family wanted to bribe the school to forever banish such women's associations (there are none at the university). The other version is that the Noyes family gave a windmill to an Iowa college, whose students promptly rolled it down a hill, causing the family to transfer its support to the U. of C. Such fictions are the stuff of campus legends.

Rockefeller Chapel

Walk diagonally across the foyer and exit, taking a right and walking through the picturesque cloisters section of Ida Noyes. Then cross Woodlawn and enter Rockefeller Chapel. There are so many things to notice and so many facts to enjoy about this place that it's hard to know where to begin.

Taking the facts in a somewhat haphazard order:

■ The chapel, donated by a rich Baptist oilman, is amazingly nonsectarian with Old Testament figures to the right of the entrance and pagan philosophers to the left. The outside is decorated with the seals of private and state universities and, over the east door, you can see figures of Teddy Roosevelt and Woodrow Wilson holding the seals of Harvard and Princeton, their respective alma maters.

■ This is a true Gothic structure, with the arches and buttresses actually sustaining a 32,000-ton load. The chapel, 265 feet long and 120 feet wide, was designed by Bertram Goodhue, who also created the Empire State Building.

■ If you go to the rear of the chapel, you'll see the ashes of four U. of C. presidents and five of their wives. People tend to stay at the university for a long, long time.

■ The tower rises 207 feet, and it takes 235 steps to reach the carillon's clavier room and 45 more to the bell tower. The carillon has a 6-octave range, less one half tone, with bells ranging from 10½ pounds to the 36,926-pounder named Great Bourdon, which sounds C-sharp. Great Bourdon is the second largest tuned bell in the world.

■ From 1928 to 1961, the bells marked every quarter hour from 9 a.m. to 10:45 p.m. by playing Wagner's *Parsifal Tune*. When the four bells playing this tune began to wear out, Easley Blackwood wrote *Chicago Tune*, which has been played since 1961. There are carillon recitals Wednesday at about 12:15 during the school year; at 7:30 p.m. Thursdays; 4 p.m. Sundays during June, July, and August.

■ A death knell is signaled by six peals for a woman and nine peals for a man. When President John F. Kennedy was assassinated, there were nine peals, plus 46 more on Great Bourdon, one for each of the years of his life.

■ The liturgical banners inside the chapel are from the 1964 New York World's Fair Vatican Pavilion. Across the balcony parapet over the doors, eight kneeling angels alternate with the coats of arms of nine private American universities including rival Northwestern, Harvard, Princeton, Yale, and Stanford. The seals of 10 foreign universities, including Oxford, Cambridge, Padua, and Calcutta, can be seen in the windows of the east facade. The seals of 10 state universities are in the windows along the west wall.

■ The chapel doors are allegedly locked in the evening because then-President Harper stopped by one night and saw "more souls being conceived than saved."

Robie House

Exit on Woodlawn, to your right if you entered Rockefeller from the 59th Street side, take a left and walk north to 58th Street. You will see Robie House before you, at 5757 Woodlawn. This walled Frank Lloyd Wright masterpiece was designed in 1906. According to architecture

Robie House: Mrs. Robie was *not* ordered to wear horizontally-striped dresses to match her house

critic Bill Newman, it is not true that Wright demanded that Mrs. Robie wear horizontally striped dresses so as not to clash with the home.

Frederick C. Robie, whose firm eventually became the Schwinn Bicycle Co., spent $35,000 on the house, plus $10,000 on Wright-designed furnishings. The home included several innovations, such as a three-car garage attached to the house and zinc-lined pockets under the bedroom windows, designed for plants and equipped with their own watering pipe. The wine cellar was under the front porch, and the Robie children could enter their recreation room and get to a toilet without passing through other rooms of the house. Robie appreciated that. This was also the first home to have controlled ventilation, a precursor of air conditioning, with fans set in the ceilings of the living and dining areas.

The Robie family only lived here for two and one-half years. It later became classrooms, a refectory, and a dormitory, but was scheduled for demolition in 1957, when a panel of architectural experts named Robie House as one of the two outstanding houses built in America in this century. The other house was Falling Water in Bear Run, Pennsylvania, also by Wright. A plaque in front of Robie House calls it "one of the most significant buildings in the history of architecture." After a series of complex maneuvers and last-minute deals, Robie House was saved and preserved in 1963. It now houses the university's Alumni Affairs office and daily tours are offered.

Walk west on 58th Street. The Chicago Theological Seminary, at 1150 East 58th Street, has a small chapel to the right of the entrance and various stones in its cloister area, including rocks from Solomon's quarries and a fragment of Plymouth Rock.

Oriental Institute

Cross the street and enter the Oriental Institute, 1155 West 58th Street (open Tuesday through Saturday from 10 a.m. to 4 p.m.; Sunday, noon to 4 p.m.). Since it was founded in 1919, the institute has conducted more than 100 expeditions. It saved Egyptian monuments threatened by the Aswan Dam, has helped date the Dead Sea scrolls, and has been working on an Assyrian Dictionary since 1921. Its collection, open free to the public, includes a copy of the Rosetta Stone; a colossal Persian stone bull that once flanked the entrance to the throne room of Xerxes; very small fragments of the Dead Sea Scrolls; a collection of the rarest, finest quality Assyrian metal art dating from the ninth century B.C.; Persian gold treasure in amazing shape; and one of the finest collections of Sumerian statues (2900 to 2330 B.C.). They are the ones with the really silly looking eyes. One sincerely hopes the Sumerians didn't look that way in real life.

One of the most interesting treasures is a 40-ton winged bull, which once guarded the throne room at Khorsabad of an Assyrian king named Sargon II (727–705 B.C.). Oriental Institute curator Karen Wilson believed that an image such as this one might have inspired the creatures described in the Old Testament's Book of Ezekiel.

The French began excavating Khorsabad in 1842; the University of Chicago entered the scene in 1929. The Iraqi government gave permission to take the bull to Chicago, but it wasn't easy. Vehicles broke down; the water level of the Tigris River fell, making boat transport difficult; railroad tunnels were too narrow in America; but finally, the bull was lowered into the museum by crane in 1931 before the roof was completed. It will be virtually impossible to give it back.

Notice the 18-foot tall, 18-ton statue of Tutankhamen, which has no name on it because it was erased and replaced with King Harmhab.

Toward the back of the huge first hall there are several mummies and skeletons, which gave me nightmares when I first visited the Oriental Institute. To this day, I am proud to say that, as a 10-year-old, I was brave enough to look at them without closing my eyes.

Incidentally, the Oriental Institute has been the subject of rapt attention by cranks over the years, such as callers who claim they once went to Egypt and discovered that they were God, folks who warn that if a certain Turkish tomb is not immediately closed all who tampered with it would die, and a fellow who sometimes performs a ritual dance in front of the King Tut statue.

Last time I toured the Oriental Institute, I met Klaus Baer, a most energetic professor of Egyptology, who took me on a whirlwind, in-depth tour, and Gretel Braidwood, assistant to the director of the institute, who laughingly said she could be Indiana Jones' girlfriend. Her father, Robert Braidwood, an archaeologist for the Oriental Institute, found the tops of 50 human skulls while excavating a 10,000-year-old building in Turkey in 1985. All the skulls had been burned. It's the sort of mysterious find that leads to notoriety. In addition, when Indiana Jones was a meek college professor in the movies, he taught at a school like the University of Chicago (according to Ms. Braidwood) where his professor was named "Ravenswood." Furthermore, Ms. Braidwood is charming and pretty enough so that she might have been his girlfriend. Farfetched? Not if you get a chance to meet her.

As you leave the Oriental Institute and cross University, you can see the modern Albert Pick Hall for International Studies to your left. *Dialogo*, a modern sculpture by Virginio Ferrari, is in front of this building.

The Renaissance Society

Continue west, entering an area surrounded by university buildings. While standing near the circle in its midst, the Administration Building, called by those who work in it "the ugliest building on campus," is directly before you. To its immediate left (south) is Cobb Hall, the first building built on campus and completed in 1892. On the fourth floor of this building is The Renaissance Society, one of the strangest and most fascinating art galleries in Chicago.

Since 1915, The Ren has been devoted to showing the most avant-garde art. It exhibited Picasso, Brancusi, Mondrian, Noguchi, Miró, Moholy-Nagy, Arp, and Matisse in the 1920s, Leger and Calder in the 1930s, and Magritte, Chagall, and Henry Moore in later years.

Director Susanne Ghez said the gallery, which does not sell its art and which does not charge admission, is "the best kept secret in town. We are only interested in the vanguard, in the way people see and think about the arts on an international basis."

But she had the last laugh on me. During one visit there were wet/dry vacuum cleaners resting on beds of neon lights encased in see-through plastic boxes, and the artist claimed that the sculptures were sexually symbolic. At the time, I had a lot of fun with the notion that people might actually pay $9,000 to own a wet/dry vac resting on neon. However, just six years later, similar works by the same artist were selling for up to $400,000!

Scientific Breakthroughs

The G. H. Jones Laboratory is to the right (north) of the Administration Building, and Room 405 of this lab is a National Historic Landmark. Here in 1942, Glenn T. Seaborg and associates first isolated and weighed plutonium.

In Room 110 of this same building, Stanley Miller, then a young graduate student working with Nobel Prize-winning chemist Harold C. Urey, sent some sparks through a test tube of gases in 1953. The gases reproduced the atmosphere of the earth billions of years ago and, when the miniature lightning display ended, Miller discovered that amino acids, the building blocks of life, had been created. Room 110 is now a mail room.

If you continue to stand near the circle in the middle of the quadrangle and face the Administration Building, the William Rainey Harper Memorial Library is directly to your left, just beyond the square at the end of the walkway/street.

On March 29, 1911, while the library was under construction, the West Tower collapsed. Sabotage was suspected because of labor unrest at the time. Some said the derrick used by workmen was too heavy. The true cause was never determined, but stronger steel beams replaced the reinforced concrete girders, and the building was completed without incident.

After most of the books were shifted to the newly opened Regenstein Library in the 1970s, the Harper Library became administrative offices.

Walk to your right, heading north, then take another right just before the ornate gate; and enter a beautiful quadrangle, done in American collegiate Gothic-style.

Look up and you'll see Mitchell Tower, a fairly close copy of the Magdalen College tower in Oxford University, England. The tower has 10 bells cast by the same English foundry that created Big Ben and the Liberty Bell, according to "A Walking Guide to the Campus," a booklet issued by the university.

Famed Athletic Director and football coach Amos Alonzo Stagg requested that the Alma Mater be rung each night at 10:05 to remind his athletes to go to bed. From 1908 to 1911, the ancient art of changing ringing, in which all the bells are rung in every possible order and permutation, was practiced. Complaints ended change ringing until it was revived in the 1960s "to mixed reviews," according to the "Walking Guide."

Cross the court area, enter Reynolds Student Clubhouse and take a left. The "C" Shop Restaurant is for a quick bite, while Morry's offers inexpensive food in the 115-foot-long, paneled Hutchinson Commons room. Observe portraits of university presidents and faculty members as you eat.

Cobb Gate: Does the griffon on top really represent seniors?

Retrace your steps; skirt the north edge of the octagon in the middle of the quad. If the area seems familiar, you might have noticed this quad at the beginning of the film *When Harry Met Sally*, as Billy Crystal left school to go to New York.

Walk up the six stairs slightly to your right, go through the low-arched cloisters, and exit past the Botany Pond, former swampland that remains at the level the land was before the university arrived. Goldfish swim here in the summer.

Take a right and go through the Cobb Gate, built in 1897 by the first campus architect, Henry Ives Cobb. Tradition has it that the ugly gargoyles at the bottom of the arch are admissions counselors, with freshmen, sophomores and juniors as figures up the sides, and seniors as the ugly, but triumphant, winged griffon at the top.

Du Sable Museum

If you take a left on 57th Street and walk about three blocks west, you will pass the huge Biological Sciences Learning Center and Jules F. Knapp Medical Research Building, which brings all biologic concerns of the university from undergraduate to post-graduate under one long, long roof. If you continue walking west, you will cross Cottage Grove and enter Washington Park. You will soon see signs for the Du Sable Museum of African-American History.

Enter through the $3 million Harold Washington Wing, opened in January 1993, the first true museum space for this unique depository of our cultural heritage. In 1961, an amazing, energetic, and far-sighted woman, Margaret Burroughs, founded the Du Sable Museum in her home. The idea, which was astounding back then and which is still pretty amazing today, was to teach black history to the community.

It has always seemed to me that, by learning the true story of any one group, especially when their history has been distorted, ignored, or denigrated, we can all learn about ourselves and our country.

Over the years, the museum became the Ebony Museum, the Museum of African-American History and Art and, finally, the Du Sable, named after Chicago's first settler, a wealthy and influential trader who married a Pottawatomie woman. Du Sable was a black Haitian who was responsible for the first baptized child born in Chicago. With his settlement, which included a smoke house, a smithy, and dairy and poultry farms, he "developed the first shopping center between the States and Canada," according to Ramon Price, the energetic museum curator.

In 1973, the museum moved from the Burroughs' home at 3800 South Michigan to its present quarters, part of which was a jail when the Park District had its own police department.

One of the most significant holdings is the 700-pound, 9-foot by 11-foot wooden mural that Robert Ames completed shortly before his death. Carved of Honduras mahogany and titled *Freedom Now*, it has 225 figures moving through the history of African Americans. If you allow your eye to snake from left to right beginning at the bottom of the mural, the story will be fairly obvious.

There is a 1775 powder horn that belonged to Barzallai Lew, a Revolutionary War hero who represents the hundreds of blacks who fought in that war. Price pointed out that, in the past, some researchers were angry because it seemed as if Negroes were denied their pensions for fighting in that war. But more study revealed that the reason they did not get their government dole at the time was because they were too wealthy to qualify!

The museum has the first aviator license issued to a black—Bessie Coleman in 1921—and Harry Belafonte's open-neck shirt, given to the founders in 1963.

There are significant displays on the life and times of Chicago's first black mayor, Harold Washington, including a kiosk that will allow the visitor to view videotapes of the mayor's speeches. He was a most persuasive and beloved person.

It costs from $1 to $3 to enter, depending on your age. I'll be willing to wager that, no matter what your race, once you go, you will learn something you never knew before.

If you have chosen to take this three-block stroll into history, exit the museum and retrace your steps, walking along 57th street until you return to Ellis Avenue. Take a left and go north.

Regenstein Library

Note the Joseph Regenstein Library, a nearly $21 million building housing more than 13 million pieces, which is directly to your right as you walk north on Ellis Avenue. Regenstein invented the cellophane window on envelopes and was smart enough to patent his idea.

The library is on the site of the original Stagg Field, home of the "monsters of the Midway," when the U. of C. played Big Ten football. In 1905, one All-American player, Walter Eckersall, could boast that the score for the season was "University of Chicago 245, opponents 5." Big Ten football was sacrificed for "the life of the mind" in 1939, when the university stopped competing with Ohio, Illinois, Michigan, and the rest. When asked about athletics, former university president Robert Maynard Hutchins said, "I, sir, am a scholar. Every now and then I feel like physical exercise. I then lie down until the feeling passes."

Moore's Nuclear Energy

Walk past the Regenstein Library, heading left (west) around the building and take a right on Ellis Avenue, going north. Stop when you reach an unmistakable, 12-ton sculpture titled *Nuclear Energy*, by Henry Moore. Almost everyone refers to it by its nickname: "The Skull."

This site brings on odd feelings of dread without hope, of silent, pervasive desperation. The plaques proclaim that here, on December 2, 1942, man achieved the first self-sustained nuclear chain reaction.

At 3:25 p.m. on that day, in a former squash court under the Stagg Field grandstands, Zip, the last control bar, was withdrawn and, for 28 minutes, Enrico Fermi's so-called suicide squad (because no one knew what risks were involved) watched the counters record the chain reaction. Zip was then slid into the pile, physicist Eugen Wigner brought out a bottle of Chianti, and everyone drank from paper cups.

It was an event that changed civilization, the equal to the invention of the steam engine or the introduction of the automobile or airplane. For the first time man was not using energy drawn either directly or indirectly from the sun. He had created his own sun, something only God could do before 1942.

On a lighter note, one alumnus recalled being so impressed with Fermi's mind that, when the alum was up to bat and Fermi was pitching in a baseball game, the alum deliberately struck out for fear of hitting the great man in the head.

Court Theater

Walk past 56th and go straight ahead to the Court Theater, 5535 South Ellis. Once this theater offered a summer of delights outdoors near the Reynolds Club, where real horses galloped through the quadrangle during *Richard III*. It is now housed in a modern, 250-seat indoor theater built in 1981. That means theater probably without both horses and mosquitoes.

Henry Moore's *Nuclear Energy*

David and Alfred Smart Museum

Walk through the iron gate and into the Cochrane-Woods Arts Center and the David and Alfred Smart Museum of Art at 5550 South Greenwood. The museum is open Tuesday through Saturday, 10 a.m. to 4 p.m.; Sunday, noon to 4 p.m. This free gallery, which opened in 1974 to display the more than 6,000 works of art given to the university, is named after the founders and publishers of *Esquire* magazine. Their foundation gave $1 million for the creation of this eclectic, 7,200-square-foot gallery.

Of special note are the windows from the Robie House and the original Frank Lloyd Wright 1909 furniture, especially the oak table with the high-backed chairs and the four lamps attached to the corners. It is spectacular to look at, but I wonder what it would be like to sit at something like that. Having an actual meal at such a table would seem like the worst possible torture.

The collection includes a cast bronze model of Auguste Rodin's *The Thinker*, Rodin's *The Cathedral*, a statue featuring two hands praying; George Segal's sensual sculpture in plaster titled *The Lovers*; plus works by Picasso, Matisse, Marcel Duchamp, Henry Moore, Alberto Giacometti, Franz Kline, Mark Rothko, Richard Hunt, and Jim Nutt. The most valuable object is the Renaissance reliquary, or container for a sacred object usually associated with a saint. Its first owner was Pope Paul III, who commissioned Michelangelo's *Last Judgment* and whose papacy lasted from 1534 to 1549. It is rare not only because it is beautiful, but because the owners of many such objects often melted them down over the last four centuries to finance armies.

Walk east again, out the other iron gate to Greenwood. Take a right (south) and go one half block to 56th, take a left to University, and then go right one block.

You are now standing at 57th and University. The private Quadrangle Club is to the east. The large building to the north is Bartlett Gymnasium, donated by Adolphus C. Bartlett in memory of his son, Frank, who died at age 20. It has been called the most lavishly decorated gym in the world. A mural showing medieval athletic tournaments is on the wall opposite the front doors. The artist was Frederic Clay Bartlett, brother of Frank and the man who donated Seurat's *A Sunday Afternoon on La Grande Jatte* to the Art Institute.

You can walk about six blocks to the I.C. stop at 57th, passing such restaurants as Edwardo's, Ann Sather's Swedish Restaurant, and the Medici, a coffeehouse that serves either the best or worst pizza in Hyde

Park, depending on which student you ask. You can also return to 59th and retrace your steps to the I.C. or your car.

Writer John Gunther has called the University of Chicago "a peculiar, miniature principality." It survived the red-baiting hysteria of the fifties, did not call police when SDS-inspired students staged a sit-in in the administration building in 1969 (some folks liked that idea, others wanted the hippies beaten to a pulp), and remembers President Harper's 1887 prediction that the university "would in ten years have more students, if rightly conducted, than Yale or Harvard has today." The University of Chicago is still chasing Yale or Harvard in other areas, but many folks think it has already passed them.

12 MUSEUM WALK

Field Museum, Shedd Aquarium, Adler Planetarium

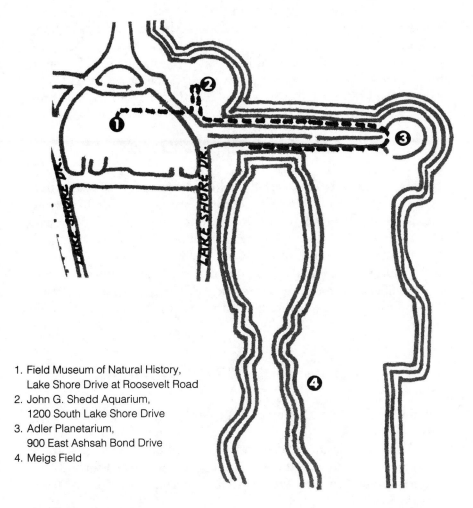

1. Field Museum of Natural History,
   Lake Shore Drive at Roosevelt Road
2. John G. Shedd Aquarium,
   1200 South Lake Shore Drive
3. Adler Planetarium,
   900 East Ashsah Bond Drive
4. Meigs Field

Time: A minimum of 1 hour per museum, and you'd probably have to be on roller skates to do any of them justice that briefly. The Adler Planetarium program takes 1 hour, the Shedd Aquarium can be seen in slightly less than 1 hour provided you forgo both the dolphin show and the coral reef feedings, which are not to be missed. The Field Museum deserves a 2- to 4-hour stay. But, remember, any exhibit could lead to a lifetime of study. Each of the museums can be the subject of a separate walk and probably should be—they are that spectacular.

To get there: By car, go south on Lake Shore Drive, follow the signs, remember that the exits to the parking lots come up quickly on the left, and park in the lots either in front of or directly behind the Field Museum. If these are filled, the Soldier Field lot is just south of the Field Museum. Or you can drive around the Field Museum, enter Lake Shore Drive heading north, and take a quick right on Achsach Bond Drive, which goes toward the planetarium. Parking at meters for 25 cents an hour, up to six hours, is often available there. Or take the #146 CTA bus daily or the #130 CTA bus on weekends and holidays to the museums.

Lakefront Explorations

There are three museums, each devoted to different specialties, within a mile of each other on Chicago's lakefront. A day spent with them brings the visitor in touch with man's natural history, aquatic life, and the stars, plus offering vistas of Lake Michigan and a chance to see private planes landing and taking off at nearby Meigs Field.

All three were founded by Chicago merchants who wanted posterity to remember them for more than just being dry goods salesmen. All three museums have had a grand past and are modernizing to prepare for the future.

History of the Field Museum

Begin with the Field Museum, a large, imposing edifice, dominating a curve on Lake Shore Drive. It was located in the Palace of Fine Arts (now the Museum of Science and Industry) when it opened in 1894. It was the outgrowth of the anthropological collections created for the 1893 World's Columbian Exposition in Chicago and moved to its present location in 1921.

By the way, in *The Package*, starring Gene Hackman, the exterior of the Field Museum became a government office building.

The museum came to life because of pure salesmanship. Edward E. Ayer raised the money for the museum from Marshall Field I, who at first said no. Then one evening, Ayer demanded to see Field, who asked how much time Ayer needed.

Ayer's memorable, and incredibly confident, reply was, "If I can't talk you out of a million dollars in 15 minutes, I'm no good, nor you either."

Ayer mentioned the name A. T. Stewart, a forgotten merchant, and told Field, "You can sell dry goods until hell freezes over; you can sell it on the ice until that melts; and in 25 years you will be just the figure A. T. Stewart is—absolutely forgotten." The next day, Field gave $1 million and the museum got started.

From the beginning, this museum has had a history of unparalleled adventure, discovery, and excitement, all with good business sense.

Consider Berthold Laufer, stiff-necked, proud, formal, Germanic, and notorious for his attempts to seduce the museum's female staff. Laufer went to China and Tibet for the museum in 1908–10 and brought back invaluable artifacts. To get them, he suffered the indignities of being bitten by Tibetan mastiff dogs, having stones thrown at him because he was a foreigner, and being beaten in front of the royal palace "for no other reason (but) because I politely expressed the wish to see the king and held presents for him in my hands." The Tibetans even refused to sell him food or fodder for his horses.

There was William Jones, born on the Saulk and Fox Indian reservation, who worked as a cowboy, and became the first American Indian to earn a Ph.D. in anthropology. Eventually, the Field Museum sent him to the Philippines where he had difficulty adjusting to tribal near nudity. He wanted to get home to see the fiancée he left in America 16 months earlier. The tribes weren't cooperating with him to help him get his collection home, and he made a big mistake—he yelled at Takadan, an elder of the Ilongots, a tribe of headhunters. He quickly learned never to yell at a headhunter. It was only because of great good luck that his body was recovered with his head still in place.

Elmer S. Riggs poked around Colorado in 1900 and found a leg bone. It was the upper foreleg of an unknown creature. And the bone was 6 feet 8 inches long. Paleontologists thought about that one for a long time and finally decided that the brachiosaurus, as the creature was called, was the largest land animal ever, weighing 85.63 tons, with, of all things, a small mouth and weak teeth. How did it ever feed itself?

Dr. Henry W. Nichols, former head of the geology department, was called Foozleduck behind his back because of his neatly trimmed full beard. He lost half of it while investigating a gold mine near Porcupine,

Ontario, in 1919. He avoided a forest fire by jumping into a nearby stream, saved his life, but lost half a beard.

Sharat K. Roy was another museum adventurer who studied in Calcutta, became an expert on the Arctic, and succeeded Dr. Nichols as head of the geology department. He set off from Chicago to collect fossils in upper New York State and didn't notice he was heading in the wrong direction until he found himself on a bridge crossing the Mississippi.

Unfortunately, some of the romance, fun, and excitement of the museum is not available to the casual visitor. It's hidden in the archives and stored in the museum's attics. Again and again, the museum's publications proudly state that it owns more than 20 million specimens and artifacts, and "less than one half of one percent of these are exhibited at any given time."

But make no mistake: This once dusty, ill-lit museum filled with silent stuffed animals has completely renewed itself over the last decade or so. Beginning with the King Tut exhibit in 1977, virtually every hall—sometimes it seems every square inch of the museum—has been renovated and modernized. In fact, where once this write-up could have been cast in stone because the museum was never going to change, now I have to warn the stroller that what I saw on any given floor may have been

Field Museum: "Only a fool would attempt to mount an elephant."

moved, changed, stored, or hung from the ceiling by the time you read this book.

It's now a museum that rocks (in addition to displaying lots of rocks, pun intended) with video displays, resounds with animal and bird calls and native chants, and reacts with interactive displays. It's now a natural history museum to visit without once yawning. Bravo! Anyone who has ever attempted to clean and organize an attic or closet knows that is difficult to accomplish. Think how much tougher it must be to bring an entire century-old museum from the nineteenth into the twentieth century! Much of the credit for awakening this giant institution must go to Michael Spock, the museum's director of public programming since 1986. Some curators hated his whiz-bang approach, and in 1990 *The New York Times* portrayed the Field Museum as an intellectual battleground.

But with millions of dollars going for renovations, with new exhibits frequently opening, and with lots of public approval, dissension within the museum has quieted. Spock told the *Sun-Times*, "we have reached a crescendo. The Field has become a vibrant institution. If you are doing the job right, people are going to disagree."

Beginning a Field Museum Trek

Enter by walking up the wide, grand stairway just behind the totem pole and facing North Lake Shore Drive. Directly ahead of you, on the main floor, you'll see the magnificent fighting bull elephants, stuffed by Carl Akeley, who created a new, complex taxidermy process for this world-famous exhibit. The job got so difficult that Akeley later said, "Only a fool would attempt to mount an elephant."

The museum store, with T-shirts, books, masks, and mugs, is to your left. Take a left, and enter the galleries near the store. Just ahead, the Resource Center is a place to rest, read, or watch a video presentation.

Beyond the center is A Place for Wonder, where children are encouraged to touch and play with toys, cooking utensils, baskets, a dinosaur thigh bone, or animal pelts. There is usually a rack of clothing on one wall. The theme changes and the costumes may be from China or India. Children can try on ceremonial horns, shawls, robes, blouses, and skirts. One eight-year-old girl exclaimed, while wearing a Mexican costume, "This place is soooo neat."

Reluctantly move along, make a U-turn and walk through the Indians before the Columbus exhibit. Nearly half the main floor of the Field Museum is devoted to displaying Native Americans' clothing and artifacts from the institution's vast collection.

The next hall is devoted to Indians of the Woodlands and Prairies with the spectacular Pawnee Earth Lodge, 40 feet in diameter and 17 feet high—the only life-size replica of a Native American dwelling. Enter and sit on a buffalo robe.

As you wander through these exhibits, you'll understand a little more about the dress and customs of the Navajo, Pima, Yuma, Mojave, Aztec, and Mayan cultures.

Running parallel to the main hall with the stuffed elephants (and perpendicular to the Indian exhibits) is the Eskimo and Northwest Coast Indian exhibit. Many of the totem poles and lodge poles shown here were brought to Chicago for the 1893 World's Fair, when an entire Indian village was built on the Midway.

Here the modern lighting, the video documentaries, and the sound effects tapes add up to a most impressive display.

Crossing the main hall (you'll be on the other side of the battling elephants at this point) by all means enter the reconstruction of the tomb of King Unis-Ankh, the last pharaoh of the 5th dynasty, 2428–2407 B.C.

Read the sign: "Look down and see the mummy of a person buried at least 2,000 years after the tomb was built." Well, it doesn't look quite like a mummy, more like the gilded wooden face put on a coffin, but it's still more than a little spooky. One youngster, peering with me into the alleged final resting place of a poor person who couldn't afford a tomb of their own, whispered, "I was dreaming about this last night."

Ground Floor Exhibits

Then, walk up the stairs to the top of the tomb and descend the spiral staircase to the ground floor and Unis-Ankh's burial chamber. Unfortunately, you'll learn that tomb robbers got there first!

Follow the tomb robbers' path into the tunnel, pass the displays of jewelry, and note the sign saying "this case is filled with fakes." Eventually you will see actual mummies. Many of them.

The Field Museum's Egyptian mummy collection has no romantic stories attached to it. A rich museum trustee went to Egypt and, instead of digging in the sand, bought a few carloads of stuff and brought them home. A guard once claimed the mummies move at night. But then he had a *lot* of time for imagination.

This exhibit includes a spell for curing a sick cat that translates, in part, "You cat here—your head is the head of Re. . . ." If you know anyone who has a sick cat, you might want to copy this down. Who knows, the spell might still have efficacy after 5,000 years.

As long as we're in the lower level, we might as well explore it. Picnic in the Field, which includes a cash station (ah, a natural history museum for the '90s!), offers excellent coffee and snacks. And there is a McDonald's on this level. And the politically correct men's washroom has a baby changing table, although the sign out front said "Baby hanging Tab" instead of "Baby Changing Table."

You'll see the magnificent sculpture of lions by Carl Akeley, chief taxidermist for the museum from 1896 to 1909.

The long-lived and popular gorilla from the Lincoln Park Zoo, Bushman (1928–1951), is stuffed and in a case nearby.

Daniel F. and Ada L. Rice Hall

Take the stairway to the main level and return to the vicinity of the Egyptian Tomb. The Daniel F. and Ada L. Rice Hall features skeletons and stuffed representations of turtles, snakes, penguins, tigers, and birds. Nearby, the major exhibit on Africa will open in November 1993.

Walking through Mammals of Asia, which somewhat resembles the way the entire museum looked years ago, you'll see displays of tigers, rhinos, deer, mountain goats, water buffalo, and primates.

A sign asks: Who is the most unusual primate? When you pull aside the red curtain, you'll see a mirror and another sign saying, "Yes, it's you." For instance, humans have more hair than a chimpanzee. I seem to remember a controversy at the *Chicago Tribune* when a book reviewer said that man is also unique among primates for the length of his penis, but that is not mentioned here.

As you walk through these displays, look above the elephant skeleton. A whale skeleton, once an awe-inspiring display, is suspended from the ceiling and almost hidden.

In the room devoted to carnivores, there are the stuffed remains of Su-Lin, the first panda in captivity. It is where she should be, but that wasn't always the case. In the first edition of this book in 1977, I told the story of the late D. Dwight Davis, Field's curator of vertebrate animals, who spent his life studying Su-Lin's body. After 25 years of work, in 1964, he wrote that "pandas are nothing more than highly specialized bears." Experts then thought the panda was a strange raccoon because the two species have similar chromosome counts. Davis said not so, but the museum had Su-Lin squatting with the raccoons for decades.

A stand in front of the current display allows the visitor to decide who are Su-Lin's relatives by comparing skull, teeth, chromosomes, and bones of bears, pandas, and raccoons.

In the World of Birds, visitors are encouraged to push buttons to hear bird calls.

More Exploring

Continue wandering through the Field Museum and you will soon find Messages from the Wilderness, a 5,600-square-foot exhibit taking visitors through 18 parks in the Arctic circle, Venezuelan jungles, Argentinean grasslands, and elsewhere. The purpose is to inform patrons about the perilous state of the planet and its environment.

But this is not merely a bunch of stuffed animals and nagging signs. You'll hear recorded messages from naturalists. And it can be politically controversial: The elk diorama includes a call for logging practices that would save jobs and forests, and the brown bear scene allows the visitor to complete a puzzle which illustrates that the bears' method of fishing is sustainable while commercial fishing is not.

The Wildlife Research Station is an East African building within the museum complete with books, computers, slides, and videotapes.

The Field Museum also has a Nature Walk, with a computer game on deer control, impressive displays of eagles and condors, and a telescope pointed at a wildlife scene. When you look through the eyepiece, you'll see videotape of waterbirds coming in for a landing.

Balcony Exhibits

Next take the stairs or elevator to the second floor balcony level.

When you see statues labeled Zulu Woman, 1931, or Pedaung Woman, 1933, you know you're looking at the portraits of humankind by Malvina Hoffman. How they got here is quite a story.

After visiting the attractive, dynamic sculptress, a museum official agreed to have her sculptures cast in bronze. They are supposed to portray

Field Museum: Maori House

typical folks from various races, but Malvina liked sculpting her vision of beautiful people. The busts and statues have been criticized as embodying the white man's ideal of beauty rather than, say, the pygmy's, and can be a bit of an embarrassment to the Field Museum. The museum tells visitors that they are interesting statues, rather than accurate depictions.

As you walk through the nearby Tibetan displays, please remember the earlier story of Berthold Laufer, who was beaten in front of the royal palace while attempting to collect some of the art you can now see merely by strolling past it.

Just beyond the Tibet exhibit is the Earth Sciences Hall, where you are encouraged to touch basalt, copper, a fossil tree, quartz, and meteors. One of my favorite displays, which has not changed much over the years, is the Benld Meteorite, which fell on Benld, Illinois at 9 a.m., September 29, 1938, and went through the roof and seat of a 1928 Pontiac coupe. The seat and dented muffler are also on display.

Next, the Pacific Spirits show allows us to walk through a men's hut and read that "the dead once watched over this house." You'll hear eerie chants, see the slit drums, and walk through a Tahitian market. Just outside the market, there is a lava flow with a television set resting in the lava and miraculously working. It is tuned to a Hawaiian station reporting the disaster.

This section of the balcony level also features the Maori House and prehistoric animal exhibits. The latter gives this museum the nickname of "the bones place." The 72-foot-long brontosaurus excelsus skeleton was actually found in two parts, with the rear collected in 1901 in Colorado and the forequarters in Utah in 1941.

Walk through the China exhibit, enter the gems exhibit and, across the hall, the jade show. Gems include the 5,890-carat Chalmers blue topaz and a model of the Hope Diamond.

Plants of the World, around the corner from the Jade display, exhibits three-dimensional, handcrafted plants. This is not only a beautiful exhibit, it takes botany and transforms it from a namby-pamby field of learning into a vital, fascinating science. Life Over Time, an exhibition on evolution, will take over almost half the balcony area in 1994.

Michael Spock, the Field's vice president for public programs, has correctly pointed out, "Museums are voluntary institutions. Attendance is not compulsory. There are no tests or grades."

However, in recent years the Field Museum has been getting very high marks indeed for becoming vital and fascinating while making learning a joyful experience.

The Field Museum is open 9 a.m. to 5 p.m. every day except Thanksgiving, Christmas, and New Year's Day. Each Thursday is a free admis-

The Shedd Aquarium's stairway to underwater discovery

sion day. Otherwise it costs $5 for adults and $3.50 for children, students, and seniors, or $13 for a family group.

History of the Shedd Aquarium

Leaving the Field Museum's north exit, turn right and walk under Lake Shore Drive, using the pedestrian tunnel. You will emerge facing the Shedd Aquarium, the largest of its kind in the world.

Founder John Graves Shedd came to Chicago after the 1871 fire and told Marshall Field he could "sell any kind of goods in the store every day." He went to work in the stock and shipping room of the linen department of Marshall Field and Co. for $10 a week, became a partner in the firm in 1893, president in 1906, and chairman of the board in 1921. When he died in 1926, he gave $3 million so the world's largest aquarium could be built.

Oceanarium

The newest addition to the Shedd Aquarium is the 3-million-gallon, 170,000-square-foot, $43 million, saltwater oceanarium, the largest indoor marine mammal pavilion in the world. It officially opened on April 27, 1991. It should be remembered that the entire adjoining aquarium cost $3.25 million when it was originally built in 1926.

The beluga whales are the big attraction here, although the oceanarium also has a terrific Pacific white-sided dolphin show; a two-level, 40,000-gallon Alaskan sea otter habitat (many of the otters here were rescued as orphaned pups after the Exxon Valdez spilled 11 million gallons of oil in Prince William Sound in 1989); and harbor seals frolicking in a re-creation of the Pacific Northwest coast.

Since the oceanarium was created when 30 million gallons of Lake Michigan were pumped out of the area, into which was dumped 22,000 cubic yards of landfill, there was some concern that its existence would raise the level of the lake. That problem was answered when it was learned that, if 165 oceanariums were plunked into the lake, it would rise .002 inch, or the thickness of a plastic bag.

Since almost nothing in Chicago is accomplished without controversy, the beluga whales were brought here after considerable disagreements. Animal rights activists demanded hearings and filed a federal law suit to prevent their import. The activists were defeated in court and in the local press with both downtown daily newspapers editorially supporting the aquarium's desire to display the animals. Yet, it remains a sensitive issue and the aquarium is careful to note in its publicity material that the whale pools "are irregularly shaped offering the animals varied and interesting swimming routes. The size of these habitats far exceeds all government regulations concerning the housing of marine mammals."

Then, on September 22, 1992, tragedy struck: Two of the beluga whales, which cost between $250,000 and $500,000 each to capture and bring to Chicago, died minutes after being given antiparasite medication.

Aquarium officials mourned the animals and said they "were devastated." Whale Number 4 (that was its only name) received the first shots and, after a short struggle, seemed to be all right. Number 6 was then given the medication, after which it was noticed that Number 4 was convulsing. Heart stimulants were administered; Number 4 seemed to momentarily recover, but then Number 6 began swimming erratically. Few words were spoken between the staff members as heartbeats, respiration rates, and eye movements were called out for each of the animals. Within 15 minutes, both died and the staff had to hold back tears.

The animal rights advocates returned with a candlelight vigil and called for a ban on capturing whales for purposes of displaying them. It was a tragedy perhaps best summed up by Andy Johnson, curator of marine mammals at the Vancouver Aquarium, which has five belugas. He told the *Chicago Tribune*, "Nothing of value is accomplished by having these animals die. It's expensive, it's bad publicity, and the animals don't like it either."

After the whale and/or dolphin show, you can walk down the steps and go to the left where you'll find the sea otter cove. The nearby tide pool has anemones, barnacles, sea stars, and mussels. The enormous whale harbor takes up most of the display. Unless there is a medical emergency, the white belugas are also here. They are among the smallest and slowest of whales and are not found in the open ocean.

If you go downstairs, the viewing galleries allow you to see the whales and dolphin underwater, while microphones let you hear their calls.

The marine mammal presentations take place at 10:30 a.m., noon, 1:30, 3, and 4:30 p.m.

Coral Reef Tank

The other major attraction of the aquarium is the $1.2 million coral reef tank, which occasionally must shut down because the parrot fish eat the fiberglass and latex coral. It's 40 feet in diameter, has 90,000 gallons of salt water held in place by windows 2½-inches thick. The exhibit features a diver feeding the 500 tropical Caribbean fish at 11 a.m. and 2 p.m.

While the diver has been engaged in this humanitarian mission, the moray eel has nipped his leg and the sharks have gone into a feeding frenzy. However, the least friendly residents are the sea turtles. The divers hate the turtles and the turtles do not enjoy the divers. Notice this relationship deteriorate as you watch the feeding.

It is quite an exhibit and you'll see staghorn and brain coral, angelfish, tarpon, sergeant majors, yellowtails, snappers, black durgeons, butterfly fish, grunts, catfish, and damsel fish. One tarpon, called "Dead Eye" because he is blind in one eye, has been living at the aquarium since 1935.

Aquarium

In the aquarium there are 203 exhibit tanks seen by more than 2 million visitors a year. Strange and beautiful fish are displayed in tanks with labels sure to tell the average visitor as little as possible about what's inside. That situation is gradually changing.

The exhibits change frequently because the average life expectancy of a fish after being acclimated to an aquarium is around 18 months.

The joy of the aquarium is that no child can ever be lost there. It is shaped like a daisy, with tanks in each of the petals. If a child gets lost, eventually he or she will wander into the central area and be found. One cold Saturday afternoon, I took 11 eight-year-old boys there as part of a birthday party celebration. I was the only adult and yet I left on time without misplacing a single child.

When you enter, walk to the first hall on the right, you'll see such Caribbean fish as moray eels, sharks, blue chromis, parrot fish, and angelfish. Look above you to see a 55-foot model of a giant squid.

Moving to the next hall, the Indo-Pacific fish there include marine jewels, tangs, clams, lobster, shrimp, and black durgeon.

The cold ocean display features a kelp forest and the sea anemones exhibit, which opened in 1980 and displays the beautiful (and the deadly to small fish) "flowers" of the sea.

Once again, look to the ceiling where a 25-foot octopus model may be found, unless it's been returned to its owner, the Field Museum.

The Great Lakes exhibits include river otters, paddlefish, sturgeon, whitefish, perch, smelt, alewives, minnows, walleyes, pike, trout, bass, gar, and crappie.

The fresh water displays include a catfish farm, the almost motionless alligator snapping turtle, and electric eels. An additional hall of freshwater fish includes stingrays, piranha, and lungfish.

Emerging from the displays, as you walk toward the exit, notice the Tributaries exhibition to your right. This was once called the balanced aquarium room. But it was never really balanced in that oxygen must be added to the water. This room has always featured tiny fish in small tanks under Chinese pagodas. Today, it is a small, beautiful display of the sorts of fish you might be able to keep in your home aquarium, including tetras, guppies, and goldfish. Of course, the aquarium's goldfish are much more spectacular than you'd win at the average church carnival.

It is not easy caring for a lot of fish. In the past, a lionfish sent one keeper into intensive care for three days after he touched one of its spines while cleaning the tank.

And, at one time, there was a problem with the octopus, which, with eight arms, could get out of anything. The solution: lining the tanks with Astroturf, which felt yechy to octopuses and which didn't give their suction cups anything to hold on to.

There are usually about 7,000 fish on display in the Shedd Aquarium, representing more than 700 species of salt- and freshwater fish. Here you can see creatures living beneath the sea in the two-thirds of the world we seldom visit.

For the record, the water system cleans the facility's 3 million gallons of water every two hours. The water in the oceanarium can be cleaned in four hours, but that isn't enough to get all the fecal matter deposited by whales and dolphins. That is why there is a slight chlorine smell there.

Aquarium hours are daily, 9 a.m. to 6 p.m. Admission to the aquarium costs $4 for adults, $3 for children ages 3 to 11 and senior citizens. Admission to the oceanarium costs $4 for adults, $3 for children and seniors. On Thursdays, admission to the aquarium only is free.

Meigs Field

As you look south from the Shedd Aquarium, you'll see Meigs Field. This was originally Northerly Island, part of the 1933 World's Fair, and was mentioned in earlier plans as a recreational facility. Merrill C. Meigs was a pilot and publisher of two Chicago newspapers. He wanted a place to land an airplane near downtown offices, so ground was broken for Meigs Field in 1947, in partial violation of the Burnham Plan. Notice that Lake Point Tower is only two miles north of the field. Pilots have said that an airplane going 120 mph could hit that tower less than a minute after takeoff.

Adler Planetarium

Walking left from Shedd Aquarium, follow the curving sidewalk and head east toward the Adler Planetarium, which sits a half-mile out into the lake on what was once an island, but is now connected to the shore thanks to a man-made peninsula. You will pass the statue of Nicolaus Copernicus, a copy of a work by the nineteenth-century sculptor Bertel Thorvaldsen. His 1823 original, which stood in front of the Polish

Adler Planetarium: Henry Moore's sundial tells the time

Academy of Science in Warsaw, was destroyed in 1944. Chicago's copy was made from Thorvaldsen's working model, which survives in a Copenhagen museum. To put it briefly, this is an American copy of a Danish model for a Polish original.

It was unveiled in 1973 at a time when many people of Polish descent were angry about ethnic jokes and wanted others to know about the greatness of Poland. The inscription reads, "By reforming astronomy, he initiated modern science."

Copernicus (1473–1543), was a Polish doctor, priest, and scientist, who was branded a heretic after becoming the first person to say that the planets revolve around the sun. At the time, everyone believed that the Earth was the center of the universe. But we haven't made much progress. Many women today say that some men *still* think they are the center of their universe.

Just before you enter the planetarium, you'll see the 12-foot high Henry Moore sundial sculpture installed in 1980. It accurately shows the time of day.

The show here is about an hour long. During the summer, it can be seen daily at 2 p.m., also Friday at 8 p.m.; Saturday, Sunday, and holidays at 11 a.m., 1, 3, and 4 p.m. Adults are charged $4; children and seniors, $2.

The program begins in the Kroc Universe Theater, which opened in 1973 as part of the planetarium's new, underground (so as to avoid ruining the view of the lakefront) Astro-Science Center. The theater introduces the spectator to the universe with a fast-moving, multimedia show, which usually includes several films being shown at once, slides projected on the ceiling, music, and narration. In 1991, a silver screen capable of showing three-dimensional images was introduced and, at some point during the presentation, you'll put on plastic glasses so you can be in the midst of the stars.

Following this, the spectator takes the Stairway to the Stars, an escalator that appears to go directly through a field of stars. You will then enter the Sky Theater, which is dominated by a contraption that looks like a rejected Jules Verne submarine. It is the Zeiss Mark VI Planetarium Projector, which weighs 17½ tons, has 40,000 individual parts, and can project views of the heavens as they would be seen from any spot on the earth at any hour of the day at any time in the past, present, or future.

The multimedia presentation in the 430-seat Sky Theater makes use of some 150 special effects projectors, a helium/neon and argon laser projector, and a video projection system. State of the art!

Ride on the Stairway to the Stars escalator at the Adler.
Photo courtesy of the Adler Planetarium

One of the main, often unspoken attractions of this presentation are the soft comfortable chairs, arranged around the projector. They allow the visitor to lean back and look at the ceiling. Unfortunately, because the air in the theater is so pure (dust interferes with the illusion) and the seats so comfy, many adults doze during the show. My dad did that every time he took us to the planetarium and, while not achieving his perfect record, I have occasionally napped.

But not in recent years since the planetarium has put together some fascinating and informative programs including Fast Forward to the Future, which looked at what life will be like 500 years from now, and Discovering New Worlds, which examined Aztec and Inca astronomy and how Columbus navigated the sea.

The programs are loaded with information and change about four times a year.

The planetarium, which opened on May 12, 1930, is a gift to Chicago by Max Adler, who retired in 1928 as senior officer of Sears, Roebuck & Co. Adler said, "The popular conception of the universe is too meager; the planets and the stars are too far removed from general knowledge. . . ." More than 22 million people have since visited the planetarium.

In addition to seeing the sky show, by all means walk around the 22,000 square feet of exhibit space. There are some breathtaking photographs of galaxies. Also, the Planetarium has early time-keeping devices, navigation aids, telescopes, an Earth globe six feet in diameter, a moon mural, a 74-gram, 4-billion-year-old moon rock collected by astronaut David Scott during the Apollo 15 mission, a scale that tells you your weight on other planets, and the world's largest map of the universe seen on the ceiling of the Universe Theater, with a fiber optic image that takes the viewer back 3.6 billion light years.

In 1992, someone offered to donate two nocturnals, which are measuring devices. They were the same nocturnals that had been missing from the planetarium's collection since 1959.

In the main level Hall of Space Exploration there are Space Transporters—kiosks in which you step on some footprints on the floor and are told "prepare for transport to Jupiter." It's a brief trip (the sun, the moon, and Mars have their own kiosks) during which you see the planet, hear some facts, and learn how much you weigh on the surface. There is also a video presentation in this hall on taking a "solar system vacation."

Doane Observatory

As you exit the planetarium, walk or drive around it, looking at the Lake and Chicago's skyline as you do. You'll see the Doane Observatory directly east of the planetarium. This houses a 20-inch computer-controlled telescope, and its views are transmitted to a classroom and exhibition area. It is the only one of its kind in the country devoted to public observing.

This ends your museum walk. The Field Museum, the Shedd Aquarium, and the Adler Planetarium are three museums specializing in different views of man and his universe, yet they are all somehow complementary. They all essentially say that there is something worth saving—and a lot worth knowing—on this Earth and in this universe.

13 MUSEUM OF SCIENCE AND INDUSTRY WALK

Please touch

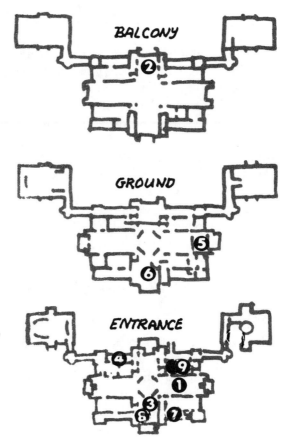

1. Santa Fe Model Railroad
2. Omnimax Theater
3. Coal Mine
4. Omni-Cam
5. U-505 Submarine
6. Colleen Moore's Fairy Castle
7. Yesterday's Main Street
8. Petroleum Exhibit
9. Food for Life

Time: 3 hours and 36 minutes (the average stay for visitors)

To get there: The Illinois Central and the Chicago, South Shore, and South Bend Railroads regularly leave Randolph and Michigan and stop at 55th/56th/57th Street station, about two blocks west of the museum. This is the safest public transportation. It is not advisable to take the

CTA Jackson Park "B" train to 55th and Garfield and transfer to the #1, #6, or #55 buses because the neighborhood there has a high crime rate. If you're driving, take Lake Shore Drive south to 57th Street, where you'll see the museum and the huge signs directing you there. Now that Chicago has erected a stoplight at 57th Street and Lake Shore Drive, formerly the most dangerous intersection in town, it's even safe to return home from the Museum of Science and Industry.

Hands On!

The Museum of Science and Industry will defeat you. There is no way you will see everything in this gigantic museum in a single day.

It houses a delightful collection of things that respond when you push a button, lights that glare when you flip a switch, or stuff you can operate with a steering wheel or throttle. The museum's first director, Waldemar B. Kaempffert, enthused in 1928, "We are going to have activity! Buttons to push! Levers and handles to turn! And nowhere any sign reading 'Hands Off!'" That promise has been kept.

Over 3 million people a year visit this mecca of education by razzamatazz—where learning is fun—where science is a multimedia experience—where knowledge and joy are not separate ideas—all in a Greek Temple dedicated to modern technology!

Palace of Fine Arts

Twice in its history this museum almost wasn't.

It began life as the Palace of Fine Arts for the 1893 Columbian Exposition. What is now the front door, facing the huge parking lot, was actually the rear of a building, that faced a lagoon (more about that later) and dozens of other structures.

The 1893 Exposition is famous for the first Ferris Wheel in America (which took folks 265 feet into the air); for Fahreda Mahzar also known as Little Egypt, a sleek, Asian beauty who entranced visitors with her dance (she married a Chicago restaurant owner and became Mrs. Andrew Spyropoulos); and for giving Chicago the name "Windy City." Chicagoans boasted a lot while trying to get that 1893 Exposition, and Charles A. Dana in the *New York Sun* wrote, "Don't pay attention to the nonsensical claims of that windy city." From that point on, Chicagoans became proud of their wind.

Before the 1893 Exposition, the Palace of Fine Arts was said to be "unequaled since the Parthenon and the age of Pericles." Because it was supposed to house fine art works by Constable, Monet, Pissarro, and others, it was a little more fireproof than its neighbors. It had foundations eight feet thick. But, as marvelous as the place looked, many of its walls were built of "staff," a mixture of plaster and chicken wire, designed to last a year or so.

When the 1893 Exposition closed, the Field Museum took over the Palace of Fine Arts, which quickly began to fall apart. By 1905, fences had to be put up around the place to protect visitors from falling mortar. By 1921, the Field Museum abandoned the old palace for newer quarters at Roosevelt and Lake Shore Drive. And the building was said to be "A scaly wormy pile that should be allowed to die!"

The Illinois Federation of Women's Clubs spent $7,000 to renew one corner of the building in 1922. In 1925, the federation held a perfectly miserable banquet in the drafty building. The *Chicago Tribune* reported "the men and women shivered and shook as they basked in the warmth of memories of the Parthenon and dodged the wind that swept through the friezes. Men's white bow ties were hidden by mufflers and overcoat collars. Women's white shoulders were swathed in last year's furs, hauled out of this year's traveling bags."

There were suggestions that the building become a branch of the Art Institute, an industrial arts school, or a convention hall.

Then, a strong champion came along to save the museum-to-be.

Julius Rosenwald, head of Sears Roebuck and Co., remembered a trip to Munich in 1911 with his son William. The boy continually got lost in The German Museum for the Preservation of the Mysterious Past in Natural Science and History of Engineering, thankfully known for short as the Deutsches Museum. Rosenwald wanted a similar museum of science and technology in which visitors could push buttons and learn. He backed his dream with $7 million in cash gifts and stocks, a fine way to turn dreams into reality.

In 1929, R. C. Wieboldt, whose company was chosen to restore the exterior of the building, threw the first brick through a window of the old building and reconstruction was under way.

The staff walls were torn down and a permanent structure was erected. The museum opened in time for the 1933 Century of Progress Fair, with the coal mine available for youthful Chicagoans who wanted to briefly neck in the dark cars on the way to the mine.

But the museum was well on its way to becoming a smashing failure, a stodgy place, old before its time. By 1940, it was spending $200,000 a year more than it was earning.

That's when Lennox Lohr became the museum's president. He had already been a success in three other careers—as editor of a military magazine, as general manager of the 1933 Century of Progress, and as president of the National Broadcasting Co. He also should be a hero to everyone who hates to wake up in the morning. Lennox Lohr never got to the office before 10 a.m.

Lohr fired part of the staff, began to woo both industry and visitors, and turned the museum into the vital, energetic, show biz, educational extravaganza it is today.

Lohr died in 1968, but by that time the Santa Fe Railroad had put in its train models (1940), International Harvester created its farm (1946), actress Colleen Moore's fairy castle opened (1949), the 16-foot-tall walk-through heart was first seen (1952), and the U-505 submarine had arrived (1954).

These days the museum gets offered lots of very strange stuff: Jesus Christ's furniture (rejected); a letter from God (accepted and filed under folklore); the airplane that flew people to and from a local nudist camp (rejected); and several sports cars, that the owners could no longer afford (rejected).

In 1992, the museum announced a 15-year, $57 million dollar revitalization plan that includes a face lift for the building, a $43 million parking facility, and some all-important roof repair. Jack Kahn, the president of the Museum of Science and Industry, told me that the museum needs internal and external remodeling. With total conviction, he added, "My classroom is the exhibits. What I worry about is how do we reach the kids who completely lose out on their preschool learning experiences because of a bad home environment. How can we use our exhibits to bridge that gap?

"We will always have good, tough, scientific, technological, and industrial exhibits. But we also want the softer displays that will work on the issue of how do we all make a contribution to society. Remember, within our classroom no one takes attendance or gives a test."

Open Every Day
(Except One)

Today, the museum is Chicago's number one tourist attraction with more than 3 million visitors a year. It sets attendance records in December, when it mounts Christmas Around the World exhibits. On December 12, 1976, a one-day record of 68,251 visitors was set for a Polish Christmas program. Over 100 million people have visited the museum since it opened in 1933.

The museum is open from Memorial Day through Labor Day from 9:30 a.m. to 5:30 p.m.; the rest of the year from 9:30 a.m. to 4 p.m. weekdays, and from 9:30 a.m. to 5:30 p.m. Saturdays, Sundays, and holidays. The museum is closed on Christmas Day.

Admission is $5 for adults, $2 for children 5 to 12, and $4 for those 65 or older. Thursday is a free day.

However, admission to Omnimax, the large-screen theater, which was showing a Rolling Stones concert in 1992 and the Academy Award-nominated film *Fires of Kuwait* in 1993, is additional. A combined museum and Omnimax adult ticket is $9, while an Omnimax only ticket for evening and Thursday shows is $5.50 for an adult. And prices are subject to change.

When the once-free museum instituted a general admission price on June 10, 1991, a 38 percent decline in attendance occurred the next year.

However, museum officials are happy with the reaction to the 89-minute film of the Rolling Stones' 1990 Steel Wheels tour. After it opened in June 1992, it played to 92 percent capacity for its first 10 weeks in the 344-seat theater. In my opinion, you have to be a confirmed Rolling Stones fan to enjoy the experience. Many seats are so close to the curved wall that the group's guitars appear seriously distorted. Furthermore, Keith Richard's face is no longer attractive in a tight close-up. There are times when Mick Jagger looks worse than Freddie Kreuger in *Nightmare on Elm Street*. But then, perhaps Omnimax was never intended to splay a human face over 40 feet of movie screen.

The Omnimax has a 5-story-tall, tilted, domed screen with the largest motion picture sound system in the world, delivering 20,000 watts of audio power through 72 speakers. You *will* hear the Rolling Stones!

If parts of the museum look familiar, it's because they became an aging medical research facility in the film *Flatliners* starring Julia Roberts and Kiefer Sutherland.

A Starting Point

The best way to see the museum is to follow a child through it. He or she may not be organized in his or her explorations, but after a few hours many of the museum's 14 acres will be covered.

■ If you need a starting point, enter and look up at the F-104 Starfighter jet suspended above you. This lobby resembles a 10-year-old boy's bedroom if his model airplane fascination ran amuck.

■ Next, you might try the Communications Exhibit, the renewed telephone company exhibit, directly to the right of the entrance. By all means go to the virtual reality area where you can play catch with a computer-generated ball. You can also tune in to satellite news programming from around the world here. Be sure to check out the whispering gallery. You can hear friends across the hall while facing the other way.

Many of the exhibits are well worth seeking out. Either museum personnel will direct you to them or free maps are available at the information booth directly in front of the entrance. The vast museum shop to the left of the entrance behind the information booth sells Einstein bags, U-505 Captain's caps, Fairy Castle sweatshirts, toys, learning devices, chemistry sets, cards, games, books, inflatable globes, puzzles, fossils, flags, skeletons, piñatas, and printed guides.

The Exhibits

■ The U-505 exhibit on the ground floor is an actual German submarine captured by Americans during World War II. It was the first enemy ship seized on the high seas since the *U.S.S. Peacock* took possession of the *British Nautilus* in 1815. Its capture on June 4, 1944, after it sank eight Allied ships, was kept secret until the end of World War II.

The sub's trek to the museum involved an almost as difficult, but lesser-known, undertaking. Before it was brought from Lake Michigan to the museum, motorists near the 57th Street Beach in 1954 saw astounding signs reading, "SUBMARINE CROSSING. DRIVE CAREFULLY."

The boat was carefully placed on a specially constructed steel carriage that rode on steel rollers and was inched across the 800 feet of Lake Shore Drive, which adjoins the museum. That last trip began on August 13 and ended September 4, 1954.

Fairy castle: Thank you, Colleen Moore

Today two-thirds of the boat's 1,120-ton weight rests on 20 pairs of eight-inch steel rollers on tracks set up in the front and back cradles. The rollers allow the U-505 to move up to 2½ inches a year, to compensate for the contraction and expansion of the boat's steel hull in Chicago's heat and cold.

■ Colleen Moore's Fairy Castle, which is near the coal mine exit on the ground floor, is a 9-square-foot, $500,000 doll house. It took 700 artists nine years to create the 1,000 miniature treasures in it. The highest tower stands 12 feet above the floor. There's a painting of Miss Moore, a film star, in the Great Hall; King Arthur's Dining Room features a solid gold dining service and crystal glasses more than 100 years old; the royal bed chamber has a bearskin rug with teeth taken from a mouse and platinum chairs set with real diamonds and emeralds; and the chapel has the world's smallest Bible, printed in 1840 and containing the entire New Testament.

Colleen Moore, whose bobbed hair was a symbol of the flappers of the 1920s, later became Mrs. Homer Hargrave, wife of a wealthy Chicago stockbroker. Lohr convinced her to give the fairy castle to the museum (after she asked, "What on earth would a dollhouse do there with all those gadgets and big machines?") when he said he wanted a few displays purely for joy and entertainment. There is another doll house with quite a different story in the museum, but you'll learn about that one in the Architecture and the City exhibit.

- The Coal Mine has been a permanent exhibit since 1933. Visitors descend 50 feet in a real hoist to the bottom of a mine shaft where the 6- to 8-foot-high walls are made of real coal. A quick but informative "underground" tour follows the ride.

- Yesterday's Main Street, near the entrance to the coal mine on the main floor, perpetually waits for the Honorable J. J. Hone to talk about "Shall Women Vote" and features a 10-cent nickelodeon (a contradiction in terms there, but who cares?). It is a re-creation of a 1910 street complete with an operating version of Finnigan's Ice Cream Parlor, which uses the furnishings of an old pharmacy that began business about a mile from the museum in 1911.

- Earth Trek, once called the Petroleum Exhibit, to the rear of the entrance floor, takes visitors for a 10-minute, hair-raising ride in the *Argonaut* where they'll discover how petroleum is formed. The exhibit cost $1.2 million to build, opened in 1986, and was renovated in 1992.

- The Food For Life section, to the left of the information booth on the main floor, includes a computer that will tell visitors how much nutrition they get out of their favorite meals. During one visit, my young son, who ate only carbohydrates at the time and enjoyed meals of tacos, pizza, French fries, potato chips, and milk shakes, learned that he was getting lots of vitamins and minerals, mainly from the tomato sauce in the pizza. It didn't help matters at home. There is also a baby chick hatchery here. After a few days, the chicks supposedly go to farms where they are raised for egg production.

- Architecture and the City has fragments of the world's first sky-scraper, the Home Insurance Building, which stood at LaSalle and Adams from 1885 to 1931; six computer games, two of which will allow you to design your own dream house; an architect's office without an angry client's wife complaining about lack of closet space; and a 16-foot-long scale model of Ralph and Janet Falk's Georgian-style house. The Falk's real home cost around $6 million, but the doll house, which took eight years to complete, cost $200,000. Ralph was the Baxter Travenol Laboratories heir. The same week the model was finally delivered by Maine modelmaker Jay Hanna, Ralph moved out of the real home "for another woman," said Janet. She added that she's glad the model was on display in the museum "where somebody can enjoy it."

- Calculating to Computing, which is to the right off the lobby, teaches the history and technology of computing while giving everyone lots of terminals with which to play. There are programs to teach sailing, inform us about our car and mortgage payments, a computer that speaks Spanish and English, another that teaches us how to throw a ball from an elevator into a box, and Beano, a mathematical bingo game that sometimes lets us beat the computer.

■ The Money Center teaches about supply, demand, the nature of money, and good old-fashioned capitalism. It's fun to get an account number from the nearest computer when you start through the exhibit and then see how much (or how little) money you make as you proceed to own a doughnut shop, and do other tasks.

■ The Santa Fe Railroad model trains have been a favorite at the museum for years. This 3,000-square-foot display has 35 diesel locomotives, 85 freight trains, and passenger trains looking like the old Superchief and El Captain choo-chooing over 1,200 feet of track. Of the eight operational trains, four are running at any given time, hauling as many as 15 cars. The trains pass through settings representing the Midwest, the Great Plains, the Arizona desert, the Grand Canyon, and California.

■ The 999 Locomotive broke the world's speed record on May 10, 1893, when it raced on iron rails at the astounding speed of 112½ m.p.h. American commuter trains only dream of doing that today. The 197-foot Pioneer Zephyr, located next to the 999, was the world's first streamlined

Railroad: It may move, but it won't disappear

passenger train. It went from Denver to Chicago in 13 hours and five minutes on May 26, 1934, making a nonstop trip of 1,015 miles and averaging 77.6 m.p.h. No train had ever traveled more than 775 miles without stopping for fuel and water. Also, the 2903 Locomotive logged nearly a million miles hauling Santa Fe trains from 1943 to 1955. All three can be seen outdoors on the east side of the museum's exterior.

■ The Kids' Starway: A Child's Path to Self Discovery, opened in May 1992, and is intended for children 7 to 12 years of age. It's designed to promote self-esteem, recognition of one's own feelings, and to help children avoid alcohol and substance abuse. And I do believe it works. The child learns that each person is special in the "self-esteem house," and that the greatest discovery is self-discovery. There's a TV set playing a cartoon rap song "I feel good about me," a mirror for the child to show his or her feelings, and a feelings room with a 15-minute presentation. The balcony-level exhibit ends with a fine display designed to keep the child from experimenting with alcohol and drugs and it includes the message "heroes don't take drugs." I entered a doubter that any museum exhibit could accomplish very much about self-image and I left a believer. Not only is it a must see, this exhibit might point to a new direction for the museum to take in the future.

■ The Curiosity Place, which opened on the ground floor in November 1990, is free for young children through six years of age, but they must have tickets. During a 45-minute play period, the child can play with blocks or Legos, operate a sand pendulum, pretend to be in a veterinary office and help sick stuffed animals, play drums, cymbals, marimba, or a unique xylophone, operate a crane, or fiddle with squirt guns. It is a smallish, slightly out of the way place that has been known to calm the overactive child.

■ The Human Brain exhibit on the balcony is designed to teach about the mysteries of the brain through touch screens, videos, and models. The first of its kind in this country, this display teaches about learning disabilities. When you stand in front of a mannequin, the television set that has replaced its head suddenly comes to life and a person tells you about their feelings and problems.

■ Prenatal Development, another balcony exhibit, displays a sequence of 40 preserved specimens showing the development of the human embryo and fetus. The controversy about showing such specimens has faded away over the years. A pathologist from Michael Reese Hospital noted that, while all of the specimens appear normal, a pathologist would be able to identify each one as nonviable due to genetic incompatibility.

In other words, these little humans could never have lived very long outside the womb.

■ Imaging Science, scheduled to open in late 1993, will allow visitors via computer to climb inside a drop of water and swim around in a water glass or travel inside the human body.

■ The new aviation exhibit, scheduled to open in fall 1994, will have an actual United 727 passenger jet cantilevered from the balcony. It, too, will have to be dragged across the Outer Drive the way the U-505 Submarine was. Visitors will also be able to take simulated takeoffs and landings from the cockpit of the 727. Some of the other airplanes dangling from the ceiling include: that F-104, which set four world records in 1958 and 1959; the Junkers JU-87B-2/Trop "Stuka", a German plane that was shot down by the British in Libya during World War II and is one of only two such Junkers in existence; the Mark 1A Spitfire, which registered 5 German kills during the Battle of Britain in World War II; the Texaco #13 Travel Airplane, which set the speed record of 13 hours, 26 minutes, and 15 seconds from Los Angeles to New York in the early 1930s; and the Coast Guard helicopter, which was the world's first amphibious helicopter.

■ The Vintage Car of the Future by the very odd British cartoonist Roland Emett is located very near the Business Hall of Fame. Emett once theorized that Chicago's Water Tower was actually a British wet-steam rocket that had never been launched. His dotty "car" here is powered by after-shave lotion, coffee spoons, and a bronze angel. A snap dragon is the antipollution device, the brakes are feet, the instrument cluster includes a crystal ball, there is a harp for background music, and a retractable barbecue for motorists who are stuck in traffic. Bizarre.

■ The Henry Crown Space Center and Omnimax Theater opened in 1986 and was the first addition ever to the museum. No one ever figured they would need additional space since the museum has almost 850,000 square feet of floor space. This is a must see, a don't miss, and absolutely a knock-out museum event. The lunar landing module is there with the legs intact, a rarity since the original left the legs on the moon. This module was used at Cape Kennedy to train the astronauts before they went to the moon, but it stayed on earth. The original, burned, and blackened Apollo 8, which carried three astronauts around the moon, is also here, plus actual astronaut suits and a rock from the moon.

There is an amazingly realistic space shuttle ride, which includes a three-dimensional movie that you see while wearing goggles, and that gives the spectators the feeling of being on the space shuttle. The secret

What else would you put in a Space Center?

is that the entire theater moves and shifts, sort of like a huge Link trainer, which was used to acclimate pilots to flying.

■ AIDS, 1994, will use interactive computers to teach about AIDS and how to prevent getting the disease.

■ Navy, 1995, on the ground floor, will allow visitors to walk on a simulated aircraft carrier deck.

A bit of final advice: Do stop frequently to see the various theaters, movies, and multimedia presentations in the museum. It's a fine way to learn while resting.

And there is a terrific place to eat: the Century Room, on the ground floor, offers salads, stir-fries, espresso, and even wine while big band music plays—the best museum restaurant in town.

Museum Grounds

Before leaving stroll to the south of the museum. Take a right as you exit, then another right to go around behind the U-505, the locomotives, and the Henry Crown Space Center to the bridge over the lagoon behind the museum.

Besides offering a stunning, often ignored view of the museum, this bridge is historically significant. In 1938, the ashes of attorney Clarence

Darrow, who won the Scopes Monkey Trial, were scattered from this bridge. Each year, on March 13, the anniversary of Darrow's death, his devotees return to this bridge to attempt to make contact with his spirit.

Don't worry if Darrow's spirit doesn't do much. It never has—and it's not supposed to. Darrow, magician Harry Thurston, and Detroit businessman Claude Noble promised each other in a Detroit hotel in 1937 that, if there was life after death, Darrow would attempt to make contact with the living here on the anniversary of his death. Darrow, who believed there was no soul, made the pact in an effort to debunk mediums and the spirit world.

For years, Noble would stand on this bridge, a hymn book in his hand, and say, "Clarence Darrow, if you can manifest your spirit to me, do it now." Darrow never did.

These days, the ceremony still takes place, a wreath is usually thrown into the lagoon (later retrieved to prevent pollution), and speeches about basic freedoms are given. Because it is often cold and miserable in Chicago on March 13, the ceremony is brief, to the point, and sometimes a spectator or two slips on the mud and falls into the lagoon.

Now I know you are tired by this time, but if you will walk just a little further south (probably away from your car and some rest for your weary legs), you will see something quite charming and special for the city of big shoulders, hog butcher to the world.

Beyond the bridge, enter the Paul H. Douglas Nature Sanctuary. Follow the winding path to an exquisite Japanese garden that is on the site of Chicago's first Japanese Garden created for the 1893 Columbian Exposition. This is a peaceful, serene place that is especially beautiful when the mock orange is in bloom.

When I last visited this garden, the moon bridge linking the two isthmuses was gone. Let us hope that the bridge is quickly restored and those who would desecrate an almost secret place of harmony in the city find other outlets for their energies.

14 BROOKFIELD ZOO WALK

A world-class zoo that should not be missed

1. Ibex Mountain
2. Lion House
3. Seven Seas Panorama
4. Baboon Island
5. Children's Zoo
6. Tropic World
7. Discovery Center

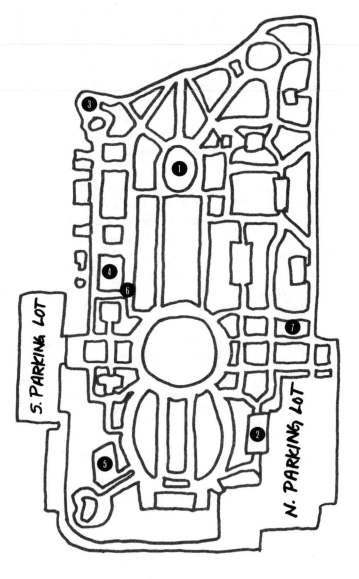

Time: 4 hours to all day for the zoo, plus 1 hour roundtrip to get there from downtown. Brookfield Zoo is about 14 miles west of Chicago's Loop, at First Avenue and 31st Street in Brookfield, Illinois. If you lose the zoo (it's got 215 acres so it's not easy to lose), call (708)485-0263.

To get there: By automobile, take the Eisenhower I-290 west to First Avenue (Exit 20), then drive south (left) on First to the zoo, or take the Stevenson I-55 west also to First Avenue. By bus, you can take the Regional Transit Authority's #304, #331, or the special #333 Brookfield Zoo bus. In Chicago, call (312)836-7000 for RTA information or 1-800-972-7000 for suburban RTA info. By train, the Burlington Metra goes from Union Station in the Loop to the Zoo Stop at the Hollywood Station, three blocks from the South Gate.

No Cages or Bars

A trip to Brookfield Zoo is a declaration that animals are important to humans. Once you are there, you will see humans looking at animals and animals looking at humans, and that's about it. There isn't much else to do.

But that's enough.

Brookfield was one of the first, large-scale American zoos to attempt to present its denizens outdoors without bars between them and the spectators. Baboons, lions, tigers, sheep, elephants, and many others loll about in the sun, with only a moat between the human and the animals.

Visitors ages 12 to 65 pay $4, children 6 to 11 and those over 65 pay $1.50. It costs $4 to park your car. Tuesdays and Thursdays are value days when admission can be by the carload.

The zoo is open Memorial Day through Labor Day, daily, 9:30 a.m. to 5:30 p.m. Labor Day through Memorial Day, daily, 10 a.m. to 4:30 p.m.

Special days include June 19, Affie the African Elephant's birthday; the first weekend in August, the Teddy Bear Picnic; October 30 and 31, Boo! at the Zoo; and every weekend in December, Holiday Magic Festival and Breakfast with Santa.

The first thing to do upon arriving at the zoo, no matter what gate you enter, is to take the Safari Train, a 40-minute guided tour of the entire park. Adults, $2; children 3 to 11 and senior citizens, $1.

This will allow you to see the entire 215-acre zoo and to begin to understand where the animals you want to see are located. Otherwise, you'll tend to wander about and get quickly tired.

Brookfield opened on June 30, 1934, after eight years of construction, which spanned the beginning of the Depression.

The country and the world didn't begin to know about Brookfield Zoo until August 22, 1937, when Su-Lin, an adorable panda who cooed, gurgled, and burped her way into America's heart, arrived. Su-Lin was the first panda in captivity, and how she got to Brookfield Zoo is shrouded in mystery, romance, chicanery, and legend.

When William Harvest Harkness, Jr., died in 1936 while attempting to capture a panda, his young wife Ruth, a New York dress designer, vowed to complete her husband's mission to bring back the first panda in captivity. Hunters had been attempting to grab the fuzzy adorables for six decades. The former Ruth Elizabeth McCombs accomplished the task only eight days after she entered the Chinese jungles.

We'll never know for sure how she did it. Floyd "Tangier" Smith, a renowned hunter, had announced he had captured three of the tykes. Did Smith sell a panda to Mrs. Harness? Did she really find the panda just sitting by an old dead tree? Was there hanky-panky in Tibet? Was "Tangier" Smith really the mysterious "Ajax" Smith, allegedly an associate of Mrs. Harkness? Who cares?

Anyhow, Su-Lin, a cuddly little girl, they said, was soon joined by another Harkness panda named Mei-Mei, who was as vicious as Su-Lin was playful. Su-Lin died at the age of 18 months (see Field Museum entry in the Museum Walk to learn where she is now), and an autopsy revealed she was a boy.

The same thing happened to Mei-Mei, who also was given a female name and who later proved to be a male, and Mei-Lan, who arrived at Brookfield in 1939. Mei-Lan, meaning Pretty Flower, died of old age in 1953. That was zero for three when it came to the zoo's panda sexing skills. But then the pandas didn't care much about that sort of thing.

Mei-Lan, the final panda to live at the zoo, bit everything in sight—newspaper photographers, radio microphones, the hand off one keeper, and the heel off another. Mei-Lan wasn't cuddly.

Ziggy

Brookfield's other star attraction was Ziggy, the oldest rogue elephant in any zoo, who died in 1975. Ziggy might have killed two men during his life (no one is very sure and Ziggy wasn't talking), and one of them might have been a midget. Ziggy was mean.

Showman Florenz Ziegfield bought Ziggy (short for Ziegfield) as a gift for his daughter in 1920. But Ziggy tromped through the Ziegfield greenhouse and that ended his career as a house pet.

Later, while starring in a midget circus, he kicked through a barn wall and uncovered $60,000 worth of bootleg booze. Still later, he got angry and allegedly threw a trombone player, possibly a midget musician, to his death.

Eventually, Brookfield bought him for $800. Then came April 26, 1941, the day that caused Ziggy to be sentenced to solitary confinement for almost 30 years.

George "Slim" Lewis, his keeper, thought it happened because the zoo wanted Ziggy mated and Ziggy wanted, well, privacy, a cow of his own choosing, romance. Who can blame him?

All four tons of Ziggy attacked Lewis, pinning the keeper between his tusks, which were buried three feet into the ground. Somehow Lewis survived those ivory pitchforks and managed to punch Ziggy's eye (the fight did not observe the Marquis of Queensbury rules) and escaped.

Ziggy was chained to the wall of his indoor pen from that day until September 23, 1970, when Lewis came out of retirement to take him for a little walk. It was part of a "Free Ziggy" campaign, and eventually enough Chicagoans donated money so a $65,000 outdoor enclosure could be built for Ziggy in 1971.

Moving from Ziggy and the pandas, animals who are no longer at the zoo, to those who are there, recall July 17, 1969, as you pass the polar bears. On that day, five inches of rain fell in about 90 minutes, clogging the drains on the polar bears' moat. This allowed seven of the polar bears to swim to freedom.

Dr. George Rabb, director of the zoo since 1976, recalled that the polar bears immediately rambled across the road in front of their enclosures and raided the concession stand, eating an unknown quantity of marshmallows, and ice cream. Two of the polar bears then visited the grizzlies in the next door enclosure, but the grizzlies hadn't invited them and chased them away.

The polar bears could not be tranquilized for fear they'd head for the moat, dive in, become unconscious, and drown. So Rabb and three others herded the polar bears with zoo vehicles until they went back to their homes. It all happened before noon on a rainy day and no spectators were in the park.

Today, in a very general way, the zoo is shaped like a huge rectangle with rounded sides. The Theodore Roosevelt Memorial Fountain and

The polar bear parade

the Ibex Mountain form the central core of the exhibits. The 2 million visitors a year can see 152 kinds of mammals, 119 of birds, 110 of reptiles, eight different invertebrates, and four fish.

Zoo Highlights

Brookfield Zoo has an enviable record for breeding (and thus conserving) such hoofed animals as Father David's deer, the addax, and the black rhinoceros. In 1959, Brookfield was the first North American zoo to breed the okapi, and several other births of this animal have occurred. Today, it is very concerned about breeding endangered species and even reintroducing the addax, the Arabian oryx, the horned black rhinoceros, and the golden lion Tamarind in the wild. Today, 95 percent of all animals in zoos are born in captivity and the main reason to bring animals in from the wild is to enhance the gene pool. Furthermore, with artificial insemination techniques, it is possible to bring the sperm to the egg rather than transport a delicate animal weighing tons for the purpose.

■ At one time, this zoo had the only herd of Dall sheep in America.

■ Wild ducks actually use the waterfowl lake called Indian Lake, at the extreme west end of the zoo, meaning that it's emptier in summer when they're farther north. Canada geese, mallards, and wood ducks nest there. The trumpeter swans were virtually extinct. Now, with a successful breeding program, they are being reintroduced into their natural habitat in Minnesota.

- The bronze statue to Olga the Walrus, near the Seven Seas Panorama, is a memorial to a very dignified mound of blubber that arrived at the zoo in 1962. Olga ate 40 to 60 pounds of mackerel, herring, squid, smelt, and clams a day and frequently spat at the customers. She died in 1988 at the age of 27, then the oldest walrus in captivity.

- Two walruses, Bulka and Basilla, occupy the 235,000-gallon pools adjoining the statue. Despite their names, they have not yet attained the bulk (or Bulka) of Olga. They were sent to Chicago from a Moscow zoo in 1991 for treatment of chronic sinusitis, which unfortunately forced the removal of their tusks.

- Seven Seas Panorama offers daily and frequent dolphin shows. The zoo spent $12 million to completely replace the marine mammal complex, including the Seven Seas Panorama, which was 25 years old. The new home for the dolphins, which opened in the spring of 1987, is four times larger than the old structure. The dolphin pools have more than 1 million gallons of water; the seating for 2,000 people is comfortable; and it is a marvelous opportunity to see (and hear) these extremely intelligent,

Either Bulka or Basilla, Brookfield's tuskless walruses

gentle creatures. Admission for the shows, which feature leaping, trick-playing dolphins, is $2 for adults and $1.50 for children and seniors.

While researching a story for the old, extinct *Chicago Daily News*, I once had the rare opportunity to swim with the predecessors of these dolphins. It was so much pure fun that I began to consider the possibility that the dolphins had evolved in the right direction (mammals returning to the water) while we went the wrong way.

■ Walking west from the North Gate, the Australian House features a brilliantly conceived "walkabout," taking you through Australian terrain in which brush-tailed bettongs, three kangaroos, and hairy-nosed wombats move in natural surroundings.

■ In the aquatic bird house is the best kiwi display in America. That isn't difficult because only five American zoos have the New Zealand-native kiwis. The earthworm-eating bird is an expensive animal to display because most of the time it just sticks its head in the burrow "so all the spectator sees is a kiwi butt," according to Dr. Rabb.

■ The Reptile House features dangerous snakes and the eight-pound goliath frog, representing the world's largest frog species. At one time, it housed the zoo's oldest resident, an alligator snapping turtle who had been there looking like a mossy rock since 1933. There was also an entire glass case filled to a disgusting point with Brazilian giant cockroaches. The zoo has an adopt-an-animal program, which allows patrons to pay for the feeding of zoo critters. The giant Brazilian cockroaches (blaberus giganteus) are often left as orphans in this program, although I adopted one as did a woman in California who, when learning that they were three inches long, said they would be perfect for her ex-husband.

■ Excellent signs throughout the zoo explain animal behavior. They are particularly informative around the wolf woods, baboon island, and the Fragile Kingdom, a renovation of the old lion house. The sign near the tiger enclosure noted that a tiger needs an area the size of O'Hare Airport to survive. The wheel of survival, across the path from the tiger enclosure, explains how many times a predator must attack before it actually finds food.

Habitat Africa

The first of a planned-for seven phase look at African wildlife is the 4.5 acre water hole exhibit called a kopje (pronounced "copy"), meaning little head, a term that describes the rock formations leading into the exhibit. Opened in on May 1, 1993, this display gives the viewers a feeling of what life is like on a rocky island in Africa as they look at apparently free-roaming wild dogs, giraffes, zebras, and birds.

You enter the fictional Makundi National Park (makundi is Swahili for a gathering place for people or animals). You'll see a jeep with its two-way radio still broadcasting. There will be items confiscated from poachers, a bar that does not serve alcohol, and television sets tuned to conversation messages. But most of all there will be the animals, separated from the public by moats that are shallow on the animals' side and very deep on your side. Thorny bushes are planted to keep the people from the animals.

In the wild dog exhibit, watch for the device that scoots from one burrow to another. It's something like the rabbit that encourages racing dogs to run at tracks. These endangered dogs will be watching very closely for it, and you can see how they hunt in packs. Also notice they tend to rest near the window for viewing. The secret is that heating elements are buried in the man-made rocks. The dogs like the comfort of the hot rocks.

A spotting scope, like the ones used by park rangers and scientists, is nearby. When you look through it, you will see an eagle's nest, but that's because a videotape is cleverly playing through the scope.

Cynthia Vernon, the manager of educational programs for the zoo, said that Habitat Africa allows the public to see animals in context and to understand the connection between animals, other animals, and plants.

Do wear a hat in the aviary, where the birds fly overhead, and the dwarf mongooses are housed. Once inside, you'll hear animal sounds, see eyes looking at you, and you can touch a lizard model or a snake skeleton. See the klip springers, a tiny antelope, and notice that the milky eagle owl does not fly free but is kept separate from the rest of the birds. That's because the owl is a predator and, if it were flying around, there might not be much of an exhibit left!

The winter viewing area for the giraffes continues the theme of the exhibit because the backdrop makes it look as if you are outside. By the way, mother giraffes have a version of day-care in the wild. They often leave their children with a maternal giraffe while they go to eat.

For a long time, zoos outside of Africa had a problem breeding giraffes. It seems that a baby giraffe drops from the mother at birth. It could be a 6-foot fall, but that's not a problem on the soft ground of Africa. However, it is not a pleasant birth experience in old-fashioned zoos where the cages had concrete floors so they could be easily washed. It

The unexpected family in Habitat Africa

took a while for keepers to observe the births and learn to put straw or soft material on the enclosure floor. There are many more successful births of giraffes at zoos these days than in the past.

The giraffe winter viewing area has a hands-on exhibit of African climbing power. You can put on gloves shaped like hydrax feet and understand how it climbs with suction cups. The gecko's feet seem like Velcro and the klip springer hoof has a spongy end that seems to give it gym shoes.

Tropic World

Tropic World. A must. What an exhibit. What brilliant planning. What pure fun for the spectator and for the animals.

Built at a cost of $10.8 million and opened in stages in 1982 (Africa), 1983 (Asia), and 1984 (South America), Tropic World is a spectacular exhibit, which is free with zoo admission.

It is one of the largest indoor zoo exhibits in the world. And remember: A rainforest the size of Tropic World disappears every two seconds.

You enter a South American jungle by walking between two 45-foot waterfalls. Birds are flying free, monkeys are casually flipping from tree branch to tree branch, and a giant anteater is exploring.

Now please do not walk quickly through this masterful exhibit. Stand there. Just look without searching and you will see more animals hidden in the nooks and among the trees.

Also wait for the thunder and the rain. You will be sprayed a bit, although stepping back a few feet along the path should protect you. The animals and the birds will scamper for shelter, although we saw the sloth come out of a tree trunk for a lazy drink of the water squirting on it from the ceiling.

Next move to the Asian exhibit and notice that without bars animals of different species are getting along quite well together. There is a distinct lack of animal odors in these exhibits. The secret is that the animals do not stay on display in Tropic World at all times. There are holding areas behind the rocks where the animals go at night. Through something called operant conditioning, each group of animals is called at the end of the day to return to their assigned areas. The siamangs hear their own bell, the macaques have their particular whistle, and so on.

Of course, there were problems when the exhibit first opened. Many of the animals were unaccustomed to any freedom and, at first, did not want to leave their cages. Later, once they tasted the heady air of Tropic World, some refused to return to their holding areas at night. Sampson,

Gorilla reaction to the author's provocation

one of the first gorillas in the then new area, didn't want to come out of his cage for days and later didn't want to return. It was difficult to reason with a 475-pound gorilla, but Sampson was convinced to return to his own area at night through the magical introduction of yogurt, which he loved.

Because the animals are fed and bedded in areas separate from the Tropic World on display for visitors, certain bodily functions are more likely to be performed away from the paying guests' eyes and noses. Only the birds, who are fed in Tropic World because they eat throughout the day, perform all their functions there. Consider keeping your hats on in Tropic World.

Carol Sodaro, lead keeper of the Asian exhibit, pointed out that little is as it seems in Tropic World. The leaves on the bushes are all hand painted and the branches are actually 16-gauge reinforced steel. The trees and the rocks are made of concrete applied under pressure, but it is the vines which are a miracle of ingenuity.

Real vines or rope would have been torn to pieces by the hard usage they would get. Furthermore, orangutans are brilliant animals who can undo, unravel, and unlock many of man's devices.

The vines are steel threads covered in an epoxy compound and rubbed with silica. At one time the vines were hooked to the ground with bolts, but the orangs unhooked anything that was so fastened. Notice that the vines are free now at their bases. As Deborah E. Cullen, former manager of marketing for the zoo, said, "They won, we lost."

Next move into the African exhibit and notice the tire tracks on the floor of your walkway. Tires were rolled through this exhibit when the concrete was wet.

Here you'll see black-and-white colobus monkeys, the pygmy hippopotamus, and gorillas. Notice the dominant mandrill, surveying his flock from behind a bush. Listen and try to find the 48 different species of birds.

But be alert. One of the big silverback gorillas has a habit of rubbing his behind with food and then throwing it at visitors.

Fragile Kingdom

Located in the renovated old Lion House and cat grottos at the northeast end of the zoo, Fragile Kingdom is another naturalistic, mixed-species exhibit.

In the Asian Rain Forest section of this exhibit, find the Rodriquez fruit bat, which is from Rodrigues Island (yes, the name of the bat is pronounced the same but spelled differently from the island). This bat, with a wingspan of up to 3 feet, was once in the Australia House. But it was moved here out of concern that the public might hurt it while it was flying free, to say nothing of the effect on the public of a sudden encounter with such a huge bat. This exhibit also houses clouded leopards, fishing cats (with webbed feet for swimming), small-clawed otters, giant squirrels, and the Burmese python.

In the Fragile Desert, you can see meerkats (a type of mongoose), African crested porcupines, black-backed jackals, caracals, rock hyraxes, fennec foxes (with hairy soles on their feet so they can run through sand), and sand cats in naturalistic settings. Look for the naked mole rats in tunnels under the exhibit. These hairless creatures are the only mammals known to live in colonies and behave like bees with one breeding queen. If she dies, all the other females fight it out to see who will succeed her.

The Fragile Hunters exhibit is also an outdoor home for African lions, Siberian tigers, snow leopards, jaguars, and Asian leopards. Rocks with hidden heat elements attract the lions for close-in viewing.

More Exhibits

■ The Discovery Center, which is very near the North Gate, has a 12-minute, free, multimedia presentation showing the zoo's many faces. There are 28 projectors offering slides on a 12-foot by 50-foot screen, and the show is easily worth the time because you'll see close-ups of animals you might miss as you wander through the zoo.

■ In the aardvark exhibit, which opened in 1986, the Brookfield Zoo teamed up with the lighting designer for Chicago's Lyric Opera to create a scene of a moonlit night on the African savannah. The lighting along with the thin pane of glass separating the exhibit from the spectator is very effective. Some people are startled to note how close they are to actual wild aardvarks eating their 90,000 ants for dinner inches from the human visitors. You can even see below ground to watch the aardvarks in their burrows.

■ The small, excellent Children's Zoo, where admission is currently $1 for adults and 50 cents for children and seniors, allows kids to pet the animals. Afterward they excitedly tell nearby adults, "I got to feed a bottle of milk to a goat. . . . I got to hold a rabbit."

Hint: It is probably better to pack your lunch, if possible, before going to Brookfield, where the commissaries offer your basic hot dogs and hamburgers, although the food service has been improving over recent years. On my last visit to the Safari Stop Restaurant, the Chicago-style hot dog was excellent, as was the chicken salad, chicken sandwich, and the fresh oatmeal cookies.

Because of Chicago's climate, Brookfield draws small crowds in winter. But I think that is the best time to visit the zoo. The animals sometimes appear to be lonely!

Brookfield Zoo allows a visitor to look face to face with a giraffe, lion, bear, tiger, rhino, baboon, Galapagos tortoise, wolf, antelope, or camel. Nonverbal communication occurs while seeing majestic animals in naturalistic settings.

Make It Live for Them

Dr. George Rabb, the director of the zoo, has a standing order: "Make it live for them"—meaning that the exhibits should involve the spectator.

But he and the zoo have an even higher goal: "The primary thrust of this zoo is relating people to the planet. We are part of a global system. We have inserted and asserted our species and now we are responsible for the world, which we can either manage or mismanage.

"Obviously, nature wasn't built by us. It is Brookfield Zoo's goal to enhance our appreciation of the natural world, to understand and value it. We want to educate the public to modify their behavior to a more sustainable relationship with the world. What you do each day at home affects that animal and ultimately determines if that elephant will be alive tomorrow."

15 LAKEFRONT BIKE TOUR

The best way to see the lakefront

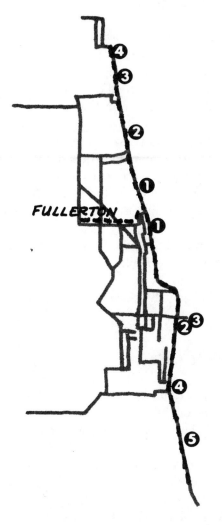

FULLERTON

North Ride
1. Diversey Driving range
2. Totem Pole
3. Waveland Golf Course
4. Graffiti north of Foster beach

South Ride
1. Chess Pavilion
2. Lake Point Tower
3. Navy Pier
4. Balbo Column
5. McCormick Place

Time: About 4 hours—longer if you love looking at Lake Michigan, shorter if you enjoy the wind streaming by your face as you pedal at full speed.

To get there: The lakefront bike path can be reached from several North and South Side areas, some of which have bicycle rental stores. For instance, the North Side starting point can be found by taking either the #36 (Broadway) or #22 (Clark Street) bus.

Bike Rentals

In the springtime, a few weeks after the first frost (actually, I'm being poetic—it starts Memorial Day) until the leaves begin to turn their multicolored hues (actually until Labor Day, except that they open on weekends when the weather is nice), Spokes for Folks operates a bike rental near the Fullerton exit of Lake Shore Drive, just east of the Lincoln Park Zoo rookery and just west of the Outer Drive bridge.

They also rent skates and even cross-country skis in the winter. They are nice people, although some of their equipment suffers from overuse. Do try out the bike or skates you rent and, if it is not up to your standards (say, with one working wheel instead of two), tell the Spokes for Folks folks and they will gladly exchange your difficult equipment for something slightly better.

You could also look up bike rentals in the consumer Yellow Pages under "Bicycles—Renting" or bring your own bike. Park, if you are lucky, just to the east of the Lincoln Park Zoo.

Whatever the trouble involved in actually getting a bike on the path through Lincoln Park, it is worth it.

The Bike Path

Bicycling along Lake Michigan is just right. It takes too long to walk the Lincoln Park paths and a car zips by too fast. With a bicycle, one can feel the wind, the sun, and the lake. There is something infinitely restful about the experience.

Unfortunately, getting to the lakefront bike paths can be a bit of an adventure. The city of Chicago has challenged the average bike rider by putting up signs indicating bike paths on dangerously lumpy streets with far too much traffic. Many Chicago bicyclists look at the city signs and immediately take them as a signal to avoid those streets.

After renting or bringing your bike, go east on Fullerton. Do not bike on Fullerton itself because the street is too narrow and parts of it haven't been repaired since the lake receded 10,000 years ago.

Biking and blading in Lincoln Park

After going through the Lake Shore Drive underpass at Fullerton, stop and test the wind. Experienced Chicago bicyclists will head into the wind at the beginning of a trip, so hopefully it will be at their backs when they are tired and heading for home. Knowing Chicago, just as they turn around, the wind shifts.

You now have two choices from Fullerton (2400 North): Take the shorter bike path by going north to Bryn Mawr (5600 north) or set off on the longer tour to McCormick Place (2200 south).

Biking South

Let's head south first, toward the downtown skyline, by taking a right along the lake. The wide walks along the Fullerton Beach are often filled with children and riders and sometimes sand or even waves waft over the path. Be careful in this area, but be sure to note the muscled males, the sleek ladies in their bikinis, and, usually, a naked child being chased by his or her mother, who is insisting that the tyke wear a suit.

This beach almost wasn't. Over 26 different methods of shoreline protection were tried beginning in the 1870s, including willow wands made into bundles and sunk as a breakwater (they drifted away); piers (washed over); oak pilings (destroyed by waves); and even transplanting sea grass from Massachusetts (didn't work). During a storm, the water beats this beach with a pressure of 250 pounds per square inch and the 100-year fight continues today.

Go to the right of the boat house at about 1700 north (the triple yellow lines on the path indicate that bicycles aren't allowed in front of the North Avenue boat house) and come to a fork in the path. The right hand fork takes you along a narrow sidewalk near parked cars, the left hand fork goes toward the lake, but both forks eventually take you by the Chess Pavilion, where serious, perpetual discussions about the game continue and where there is never a shortage of players. It is an idyllic place to pursue the royal game.

Oak Street Beach and Olive Park

Continuing south, you will pass the Oak Street Beach, Chicago's Capri, where both sexes wear the smallest of bikinis. The ladies are not top-less—the last woman to announce ahead of time that she was going to try that wore a Rudi Guernich suit in the 1960s and was arrested immediately after every newspaper photographer snapped several rolls of pictures, which were never seen in Chicago's newspapers.

Follow the curve of the lake at the south end of the beach and bicycle along the lake if that area is dry. If not, there is a narrow and rutted sidewalk at the top of the embankment all too close to Lake Shore Drive traffic.

At the end of the beach you will reach a slight hill, at the top is a bench, a water fountain, and a refreshment stand. Although the yellow line indicates that you continue south, we are going to head east, (before returning to this point), toward Olive park.

The Central District Filtration Plant is to the east. It is one of the world's largest, capable of pumping 1.7 billion gallons on a busy, dry day. Olive Park, by the way, is the site of many summer ethnic festivals.

Enter the park, ride to the end, and look back toward the Chicago skyline. The view here is unique and amazing. The curving, 70-story Lake Point Tower, which was influenced by a Mies Van Der Rohe building designed by the master in 1921 but never built, is ahead of you. This is another building that suddenly popped up on Chicago's lakefront with too little controversy over its placement.

Navy Pier

After leaving Olive Park, continue to your left until you reach Navy Pier, the edifice that juts out into the lake.

Navy Pier, designed to handle passenger and freight ships, was built as part of a deal with the federal government, which had to approve the city's plans for new parks in 1912. By the time Navy Pier was constructed in 1914, Calumet Harbor got the cargo ships, the railroads were getting popular, cars were sending passenger ships to the junkyards and few people wanted to use the theater, dance hall, and restaurant at its east end.

Navy Pier stands today as a monument to planning for yesterday's transportation innovation. After languishing, after leaking, and being filthy and rusty for decades, parts of the Pier were dismantled, leaving the entrance and the beautiful auditorium at the east end.

Leaving Navy Pier, go right, retracing your path until you get back to the yellow line by the bench near Lake Shore Drive. At this point carefully follow the path. Be especially careful crossing the streets here, and a special biking warning is in order: After you cross the first street, you will have to get around a sharp corner and travel on a narrow sidewalk. Bikers do come from the opposite way, so it is advisable to let out a whoop of some sort to let people know you are rounding the corner.

Continuing south along Lake Shore Drive, you are skirting what is almost an "S" curve. For decades, this stretch of Lake Shore Drive was called the "S" curve because of its two tight turns, which caused accidents, slowed traffic, and resulted in major traffic jams until its recent remodeling and straightening in the 1980s (oh, thank you, Chicago politicos for finally recognizing that need!). Cycle past the Outer Drive East. The geodesic dome squatting near the building is a swimming pool and private athletic club.

After you cross Randolph Street, you will cycle down a long hill, effortlessly going by Harbor Point Condominiums, the Naval Armory, Columbia Yacht Club, the Chicago Yacht Club, and Monroe Harbor, a placid body of water that stretches from the Armory to the Shedd Aquarium. Although the Lake Shore Drive traffic growls insistently, the view to the east is serene, as sailboats rock near the buoys and lovers sprawl on the grass.

Meigs Field

Biking past the Shedd Aquarium, continue south along Lake Shore Drive. Burnham Harbor and Meigs Airport are on your left (to the east). The airport, which should be a city park, was built in 1947 so businessmen could land their light planes close to the Loop. Unfortunately, the fog and winds make Meigs less than an ideal airport. Lake Point Tower is less than a minute away by airplane, a fact that makes flying in and out of Meigs an exciting adventure.

Balbo Column

Note the Balbo Column, on a white pedestal just east of Soldier Field. The column came from Ostia, the port of Imperial Rome in 1934 and, according to the inscription, is a gift to Chicago from "fascist Italy with the sponsorship of Benito Mussolini." This tribute to fascism is melancholy testimony to the fact that at times Chicago does not choose its friends well.

The column commemorates July 16, 1933, when 24 seaplanes, led by General Italo Balbo, landed near Navy Pier after a 16-day journey from Italy. There were six stops along the way and one crash in Amsterdam. General Balbo was a hero, and wherever he went in Chicago, men in black shirts and ties raised their arms in a fascist salute.

General Balbo continued to be a hero until June 28, 1940, when he was shot down over Tobruk, Libya. The Italians said the British did it, but the British denied that they had any fighters in the area at the time. It was revealed, in 1948, that General Balbo was shot down by Italian fire, indicating that either the Italians were abysmal gunners or that Mussolini didn't approve of his air marshall's popularity.

McCormick Place

After following Lake Shore Drive, bear left at the end of the McCormick Place parking lot so you can go around this huge exhibition hall and see the little-used area to the east of it.

The first McCormick Place, a concrete structure that looked like a Mayan Temple run amuck, burned in 1969. Mayor Daley promised and got a bigger, better, and more magnificent McCormick Place. The structure you are looking at opened on January 3, 1971. Throughout the

Balbo Column with Soldier Field in the background

year the hall is host for shows devoted to boats, housewares, cars, flowers, electronics, gourmet food, and even the National Gin Rummy Tournament, although over the years it has been scandal ridden and plagued by union problems.

This book contains no walks originating from McCormick Place at the request of a spokesman for the giant exhibition hall. McCormick Place is "totally business-oriented. There is no lounge area in the lobby. There aren't even any clocks in this place. The reason this place is popular with exhibitors is once a guy is here, he's stuck."

This is the largest exhibition hall in America and the second largest in the world (one in Cologne, Germany, is bigger).

Soldier Field

Turn around to head home and you will shortly see Soldier Field which is perpetually the subject of grandiose remodeling plans. According to Lois Wille in her book *Forever Open, Clear and Free*, you can't play baseball in Soldier Field; it's only 300 feet wide. And it's difficult to see a football game in this cross between a European soccer field and a Greek theater.

But this place is revered by Chicago football fans because the Chicago Bears play their home games here. They were the Super Bowl champs in 1986, finally bringing sweet victory to a city long on sports enthusiasm and short on winners. It was the most decisive win in Super Bowl history, 46 to 10 over the New England Patriots. And that victory came after the Bears won all but one game in the regular season. Quarterback Jim McMahon ran for two touchdowns and William "The Refrigerator" Perry, who normally played defense, lumbered for another one in the nationally televised rout.

In addition to Chicago Bears' football games, the two most interesting events in the field's history occurred in 1927 and 1950.

In 1927, Harold Lloyd, Buster Keaton, Douglas Fairbanks, George M. Cohan, Flo Ziegfield, Bernard Baruch, and 150,000 others saw the famous Jack Dempsey-Gene Tunney "long count" heavyweight championship. Tunney, who was guaranteed $1 million, became the first man in history to be a millionaire simply by going through a 30-minute physical drill. In 1950, a park district official was sued for divorce and his wife accused him of maintaining a trysting place under the Soldier Field stands.

Rest, enjoy the calm beauty of the scenery, and then return to Fullerton, having completed a 12-mile bike tour.

Biking North

If you chose to bike north from Fullerton, this shorter bike path is reached by turning left before the Fullerton Avenue viaduct, where a curving path takes you by a small water fountain.

You will then bicycle past Diversey Harbor, the Diversey Miniature Golf Course and Driving Range (open from 8 a.m. to 10:30 p.m.), and by a long greensward. Incidentally, Diversey is named after Michael Diversey, a Chicago brewer. According to one historian, in 1862 the Lill & Diversey brewery sold beer "from the frozen regions of the north—the rock girt shores of Lake Superior—to New Orleans, the Naples of the South—from the Falls of Niagara to the newly discovered gold regions of Pike's Peak." It would probably make a better story if we could write that Diversey was honored for his brew, but he got streets named after him because of his many donations of land and money to local German Catholic churches. When he died in 1869, his monument in St. Boniface Cemetery bore the name "Diversy," although he never spelled his name without an "e" while he lived. No one knows why his name was misspelled in death.

When you see a large tree in the middle of the now lumpy bike path, bear right and go under another viaduct, then follow the path to the left as it goes by Belmont Harbor. It is well worth pausing here because the still waters and the handsome boats often combine to make a memorable, relaxing picture.

I think some of the most colorful boats in Chicago stay at Belmont Harbor, although I am told that Jackson Park rivals its North Side cousin. Also notice the Belmont Yacht Club at the south end of the harbor.

Kwa Ma Rolas Totem Pole

Heading north, you will find the Totem Pole at Addison and Lincoln Park. This was the "Kwa Ma Rolas" pole of the Haidan Indians of British Columbia. Legend has it that it was not carved by the hand of man, but that it came floating down the Nimpkish River one day to tell the Indians the story of their tribe. It's a complicated story. Briefly, the low man on the totem pole represented a warrior whose wife was stolen by a killer whale. Now look to the top of the pole, where the Kolus, the Thunderbird's sister, sits. Under the Kolus is the steel-headed man, who was formerly a trout, who became a man, who saved the wife, who founded the tribe, and who helped everyone live happily ever after.

The steel-headed man has been troubled of late. Since J. L. Kraft, founder of Kraft Cheese Co., donated the pole to Chicago in 1929, the steel-headed man's hands have moved at least four times. Yes, Chicago possesses a totem pole infected with spirits. At one time, the steel-headed man's left hand even covered his eyes, possibly to avoid looking at accidents on Lake Shore Drive. He has held his spear directly in front of him with both hands, grasped it lightly with his right hand, and now appears to be holding a shortened pole over his right shoulder, as if he's batting for the Chicago Cubs. The movements are unexplained, although some spirit-world scoffers believe they are caused by Park District workers who regularly repaint the pole and who later put the arms back in different positions.

More than five decades after it arrived, the original pole was sent back because it was learned that it had religious significance. The Indians then carved a new pole, which was dedicated in 1986.

A Clock Without Bells

Just north of the Totem Pole, toward the lake, you will see a beautiful field house that looks much smaller than it actually is. It's virtually behind the tennis courts if you're riding along the sidewalk adjoining the parking in front of the courts.

Back in 1931, a steam leak in the Jacob A. Wolford Memorial Tower atop the Waveland Fieldhouse caused the clock tower's chimes and its four clocks to rust. Wolford was a pioneer member of the Chicago Board of Trade who died in 1917. The story goes that Wolford's eyesight deteriorated in his later years. He and his wife then vacationed in Stockbridge, Massachusetts, where he enjoyed listening to the concerts on the bell tower. After his death, with a $50,000 bequest for the purpose in his will, his widow, Annie, asked the Chicago Park Commissioners to construct a bell tower similar to the one in Stockbridge.

That's what he wanted. It's not what he got because the English Gothic tower looks nothing like the one in Stockbridge, and chimes were installed instead of bells.

For four years, starting in 1987, Curt Mangel, Chuck Askins, and Bob Boin volunteered their efforts to restart the clocks. After they entered the tower, they discovered chimes that no one knew were there. Unfortunately, the parts were so badly rusted that they were fused together. By working through freezing winters and after carrying 100-pound chimes up and down the tower's spiral staircase, the four clocks and the chimes Wolford never wanted were completely restored.

Waveland Golf Course

The bike path now passes tennis courts and goes uphill by the Waveland Golf Course. Legend has it that each hole was modeled after one of the most difficult holes in various courses throughout the country. There are 48 sand traps here and it is actually claimed that they represent the 48 contiguous states of the Union, something I am sure local golfers appreciate.

You will now approach several forks in the path. Do not panic. Go to the left and you will skirt Lake Shore Drive. Go right and you will approach the lake. Either way, you will bicycle in a large half circle and will eventually link up with the other half of the path. You won't get lost.

At the north end of Belmont Harbor, toward the lake, you'll see the fenced Bird Sanctuary where up to 125 species can be seen (binoculars and a bird book do help).

Graffiti

Continue north past Foster Beach; note the graffiti on the rocks, the concrete blocks leading to the lake. Generations of high school and college students have painted here, leaving wisdom and whimsy.

All the way at the end of rocks, as the beach turns west, there was a 200-foot mural of fish painted in 1991. Someone named Wanda proclaimed her love to Quincy on 8/19/1992, only to have someone paint over it the large word "NO." Did Quincy have a jealous girlfriend? Did Wanda change her mind? We'll never know.

In 1975, someone named Diana painted the poignant, "Albert, I may be a little screwy, but I love you." In 1972, Sue painted, "Dear Steve, when I first met you (7/17/67) my greatest dream was to some day marry you and have a family of our own. We have our family, but when our [sic] we going to marry?"

You have bicycled far enough. Turn around and return to Fullerton. Jerome's at 2450 North Clark offers hamburgers and beer, which can be eaten while sitting at outdoor tables shaded by umbrellas. There is a bike rack to the north of Jerome's.

If you do stop to eat and park your bike in a bike rack, it is advisable to securely lock it. If possible, unfasten your front wheel and lock it to the rest of the bicycle. You are in a big city where bicycles often disappear.

Here's hoping you enjoyed one of the most beautiful bike paths in the world. The benediction to this tour is: May the sun warm you today and may you be able to sit down tomorrow.

16 **NORTH SIDE DRIVE**

Milwaukee, Clybourn, and Clark:
From Machine Gun McGurn to
the Cubs

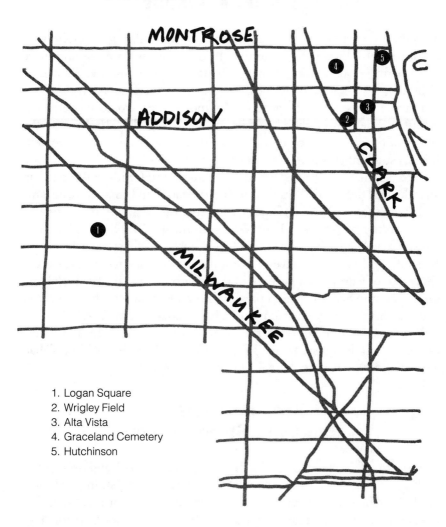

1. Logan Square
2. Wrigley Field
3. Alta Vista
4. Graceland Cemetery
5. Hutchinson

Time: About 2 hours.

To get there: Chicago has a simple grid pattern to its streets, with the corner of State and Madison being zero and the numbers increasing as you go north, south, east, or west from there. This drive starts at 800 North Chicago and Milwaukee Avenues, which is one of Chicago's rare diagonal streets.

Milwaukee Avenue

This meander through the north side of Chicago will begin by following a traditional Chicago migration route. For decades, immigrants have lived at first near the city, moving farther north or south as they grew richer.

Later, their sons or daughters or grandchildren would move to the suburbs. Then, after their children were grown, they'd return to the center of the city, buy a condominium, and tell everyone how convenient life has suddenly become for them.

The North Side Drive starts at Milwaukee and Chicago Avenues, in an industrial district. Milwaukee Avenue began as an Indian trail, became a planked road in 1849, and quickly became rutted and in disrepair.

According to *Chicago Daily News* columnist Mike Royko, "In time Milwaukee Avenue became probably the most colorful street in Chicago. Its south end became a haven for immigrants and a streetcar ride was a short tour of Europe. The street sliced through Little Italy, Little Poland, Germany, and Scandinavia. A person who walked the length of the street could hear the words 'stick 'em up' in half a dozen languages."

You can see the sign for the Como Inn, one of Chicago's fine, established Italian restaurants. In 1992 George Wendt of "Cheers" had a surprise birthday party here for his wife, Bernadette.

Strange Stuff at
Randolph Street Gallery

Just south of Milwaukee and Chicago there is the Randolph Street Gallery, at 756 North Milwaukee, home of some mighty strange exhibits. Each fall they feature the most modern of art in outdoor sculpture installation. One artist, after drinking lots of beer, created art for dogs by indicating with his own bodily fluids specific areas near the gallery where dogs should urinate.

Perhaps the most interesting exhibit occurred here in 1984, when the Ronco Show took place. There was an exhibit that made art objects of Veg-o-matics (more than 9 million sold); the Seal-a-Meal; Steam-a-Way; the Smokeless Ashtray; the Sit-on Trash Compactor "which really works"; the Buttoneer (because "everyone knows the problems with buttons is that they always fall off"); the Splatter Screen; the In-the-Shell Egg Scrambler, which solved the "French toast problem"; Mr. Microphone; an electric whisk that doubled as a flashlight; a spray gun that both fertilized grass and waxed cars; Rat Away rodent repellent; Mr. Dentist, "the plaque attacker"; the Record Vacuum; the Hula Hoe called "the weeder with a wiggle"; and the ever-popular Pocket Fisherman.

The exhibit opened just after Ronco Teleproducts Inc. filed for Chapter 11 bankruptcy proceedings, meaning it was the first Christmas in years without pocket fisherman ads on TV.

In 1939, two brothers, Sam and Raymond Popeil, founded Popeil Bros. Inc. and became millionaires. Then, Sam's son, Ron, founded Ronco, became one of the all-time great TV pitchmen and his father's business rival.

Things got even worse in that family when, in 1974, Sam's estranged wife, Newport Beach, California, socialite Eloise Popeil, and her boyfriend were found guilty of offering two guys $25,000 each to kill Sam in his Drake Towers apartment on Chicago's Gold Coast. The prosecutors called Mrs. Popeil a "practiced adulteress," but she insisted that she was only stringing along with the murderers-for-hire because she thought the two men were sent by her husband to frame her. Then Sam showed up as a surprise witness, testifying that his wife was having an affair with her boyfriend in the $700,000 Newport Beach house he bought for her as a vacation home. At the time, this was not a marriage made in heaven. It took the jury 38 hours over eight days of deliberations to find Mrs. Popeil guilty. She served 19 months of a one- to five-year sentence.

According to Sam's obituary in the *Chicago Sun-Times* in 1984, Sam and Eloise "were divorced, but later remarried." Any way you slice or dice it, their relationship "really worked" for them, when it did.

Legendary Machine Gun McGurn

Just beyond Chicago Avenue, at 805 North Milwaukee, meaning you have turned 135 degrees onto the diagonal street, where an office furniture showroom now stands, was the spot where Machine Gun McGurn was killed in a bowling alley. McGurn is generally given credit (or blame, depending on your attitude about such things) for the St. Valentine's Day Massacre. Seven years later, on February 15, 1936, three men surrounded McGurn as he was about to bowl. After they shot him, they left a comic valentine saying:

"You've lost your job, you've lost your dough,
Your jewels and cars and handsome houses!
Things could be worse, you know—
At least you haven't lost your trousas!"

McGurn, who said he didn't want to be in the rackets because "you fear death every moment," didn't laugh at the valentine. Nor did he criticize its bad poetry.

When he died, the *Chicago Daily News* said that McGurn was "reputed to have killed two dozen men." His obituary continued, "Not since the medieval days of the Italian city states has there been a hired killer as gracious, debonair, and deadly. What their velvet clad and plumed young men with Florentine daggers were to the Sforzas or the Medici, McGurn was to no less a buccaneer than 'Scarface Al' Capone, who revered him for his deadliness and his loyalty." Look, our baseball teams may not be the best, but Chicago certainly knows how to send a guy off with a well-written obituary.

You will shortly pass the intersection of the Kennedy Expressway and Milwaukee, where, according to Mike Royko, Elijah Wentworth opened an inn in 1830. Whiskey was sold for nine cents a pint, a factor that helped Milwaukee Avenue be born, grow, and prosper. A man could spend 18 cents then, and not be able to see Milwaukee Avenue at all.

You will continue driving northwest on Milwaukee Avenue for about 20 minutes. It is advisable to have a companion read about the various sites as you pass them rather than driving and reading at the same time.

Haymarket Martyrs

You will next pass a site that should be remembered and isn't. Albert Parsons and his black wife, Lucy, lived at 1129 North Milwaukee (it's now a parking lot) in 1887, and it was here that Parson's body was brought after his hanging.

Parsons was one of four men executed for allegedly conspiring to throw a bomb at police on May 4, 1886, during the Haymarket Riot. Workers had gathered to demand the eight-hour day, when many people were working 15 and 16 hours a day. Someone threw a bomb and, during the melee that followed, four workers and seven policemen were killed.

Eight men were arrested. With a prejudiced judge, a jury list chosen by a man determined to see the so-called conspirators hung, and one juror who was a relative of a policeman who died at Haymarket, the outcome was predictable.

The world protested that the trial was a way for the rich to execute the poor, but the four men were hung anyway. Wealthy folks in Chicago were still a little nervous about the matter so later they bought land north of Chicago, gave it to the Army, and eventually it became Fort Sheridan. Federal troops would be close by in case of future civil insurrections.

Ethnic Shopping

Once past Division, 1200 north, you'll enter an intense, four-block shopping area. It is crowded, dirty, boisterous, and run-down, with Latinos shops edging out the European stores that made this street famous.

A storekeeper here was once seen putting shoes on display outside his store. A reporter observed, "You sure trust your neighbor."

The man shouted, "Sure! But I only put the right shoe outside on display. The left shoe stays inside."

"Ever get robbed by a one-legged man?" asked the reporter.

"Sometimes."

Continue north past Mareva's, the city's premiere Polish restaurant at 1250 North Milwaukee.

This neighborhood has changed rapidly in the last decade. When this book was first written, you would now be passing Wladyslaw Sajewski's Music Store, Vikula's Meat Market, and Zlata's Belgrade Restaurant. Now this still-seedy area has a Latin pulse, and most of the old Serbian and Polish stores have disappeared.

Wicker Park

When you are at Milwaukee and North Avenue (1600 north), you are at another ethnic crossroads. If you take the hard left, the 135-degree turn, you'll be going south on Damen. One block away is a one-way street called Wicker. Take a left, go east on Wicker to Schiller, take a right and return to Damen, where you'll take another right and drive east on North Avenue.

With the previous maneuvers, you have gone around Wicker Park, a triangular, heavily used, little city park with quite a history. Nelson Algren sat here while dreaming up the plot for *The Man with the Golden Arm.* According to columnist Mike Royko, generations of Jews, Russians, Slovaks, Ukrainians, Poles, and Puerto Ricans have played baseball, chess, cards, and drunk wine from brown paper bags in this park. Two generations ago, Mike Todd ran the crap games in this park and he went on to produce *Around the World in 80 Days* and to marry Elizabeth Taylor. Mike Royko played marbles here, but he became a newspaperman. Who knows what he might have accomplished if he ran the crap games?

This is also the center of the Bucktown and Wicker Park areas, neighborhoods that have recently become fashionable for folks with a lot more money than the old-time residents. No one is absolutely sure how Bucktown got its name. Prevailing wisdom indicates that, when the first Polish residents settled here in the 1830s, they raised goats. Male goats are named bucks. Another story says that an early gang of Polish toughs were called the Bucks.

Germans, including 100 settlers from Schleswig-Holstein, followed the Poles, and this area became the town of Holstein in 1854. It was annexed to Chicago nine years later. During World War I, many of the German street names were changed to appease anti-German sentiment. Berlin became Medill, Hamburg changed to Shakespeare, and Holstein was switched to Oakley. Jews followed Germans and they were replaced by Hispanics in the 1960s, followed by artists who couldn't afford Old Town in the 1980s, and now, gentrification and yuppies. Homes that sold for $2,000 in the 1880s are fetching $500,000 to $750,000 now.

Clybourn Corridor

As you head east on North Avenue, the numbers on the buildings should be going down. You will cross the Kennedy Expressway, an odd, nearly diagonal street called Elston Avenue, and the north branch of the Chicago River. Shortly after that, you will see a stoplight and another diagonal street called Clybourn. Take a left on the angled street and head northwest.

This is the Clybourn Corridor, once a seedy industrial area that has been transformed in the 1990s into a vital area of bars, restaurants, and malls.

For instance, the mall at 1800 North Clybourn contains the Remains Theater, a group devoted to making drama as accessible as possible. For what must be the lowest ticket price in town, you can sit anywhere you want (there are even couches in the theater), bring in your drink or refreshments, and enjoy some of the best productions in town. William Petersen, who has been seen in many movies (*Young Guns II*) and TV shows, often appears here.

This mall also contains Barbara's Bookstore; the Goose Island Brewery, a good place to have a bite to eat and order a local beer; and an 18-hole miniature golf course designed by artists.

Continuing up the street, Bossa Nova at Clifton and Clybourn has delicious "world beat" food and Latin music. There have been several other restaurants here, including one owned by a member of the Chicago Sting soccer team. Bossa Nova has a tapas menu with 60 international appetizer dishes. The Nova margarita here is made with Sauza Mexican beer instead of sour mix. The sesame-crusted tuna is excellent, as is the margarita pizza with pine nuts, tomatoes, basil, and mozzarella. Since it opened in 1992, the Ramones, Chicago Bull Scottie Pippin, Chicago Bear Neal Anderson, and actor William Petersen have been seen here.

Continue driving northwest. Whiskey River, Chicago's first country nightclub, at 1997 North Clybourn, opened on September 23, 1992. It is a 12,000-square-foot establishment with a 1,000-square-foot dance floor devoted to the teaching and performing of country dances. There are two-hour dance lessons beginning at 7 p.m. seven nights a week, with live music alternating with disc jockeys and country music videos beginning at 9 p.m. Many city folks go to Alcala's, 1733 West Chicago, spend up to $1,000 to get outfitted in boots, hats, and jeans to look just like a Texan or Oklahoman, and then dance away the night at Whiskey River.

More Bars, Restaurants, and Shopping

Driving ever north and west, you'll see the Cafe 2191 sign, which actually looks like it's saying "Zigi"; take a right on Webster. At the corner where you turn, there is a small shopping mall and the Webster multiplex movie theater.

As you proceed east on Webster, you will notice how the many homes and apartment buildings have been spruced up.

You will pass a neighborhood bar, Charlie's Ale House, at 1224 Webster. The Kangaroo Connection, at 1113 Webster, is the one-stop place to shop for those who want to look like Paul Hogan in *Crocodile Dundee*. I got my Australian bush hat there.

Continuing east, you will cross Halsted where you'll see Glascott's Tavern on the corner. You are in the DePaul University campus area; drive by Oz Park and Grant Hospital until you reach North Clark Street.

Take a left.

If you were to take a right (don't because all that's there now is an empty lot), you would quickly arrive at the site of the St. Valentine's Day Massacre, which took place on February 14, 1929, in what was then the S. M. C. Cartage Company garage at 2122 North Clark Street. Six of Bugs Moran's men and one optometrist who liked to hang around gangsters, Dr. Reinhardt H. Schwimmer, were mowed down by machine gun fire. Two of the men were finished off with shotgun blasts to the face after they lived through the machine gun volleys.

Witnesses said that two of the gunmen were wearing police uniforms. Al Capone, who was suspected of ordering the bloody raid, was in Florida at the time giving a deposition in a lawyer's office.

Jake Gusenberg, who was supposed to drive an empty truck to Detroit that day to pick up some smuggled Canadian whiskey, was alive when police arrived.

The cops asked him, "Who shot you?" "Nobody shot me," was his tough-guy answer. He was told that his brother Pete was dead, that he didn't have long to live, and that the law would avenge him. Gusenberg's last words were, "I ain't no copper."

Frances Parker High School, just north of Webster, is a fine private school that has graduated such actresses as Daryl Hannah (star of *Splash* in 1984) and Jennifer Beals (remember her taking off her sweatshirt in *Flashdance* in 1983).

Continue north. The Reebie Storage building at 2325–33 North Clark is on the National Register of Historic Places.

Video Beat at 2616 North Clark rents music videos for everyone who is tired of renting Hollywood films.

Just beyond Diversey (and please drive straight on Clark Street—if you veer slightly to the right, you'll be on Broadway) is the Great Ace, 2817 North Clark. What a hardware store! It is bright and big and has some great buys.

Across the street, the Century Mall is in a former movie theater. Now a winding ramp takes you past many stores including the Limited and a Victoria's Secret lingerie shop.

On Toward Wrigleyville

Continue driving north. The Duke of Perth, at 2913 North Clark, is a Scottish tavern. In fact, if you go inside, you'll swear you have left America. The beer is full bodied, the fish and chips are $6.25, and the bar offers Illinois' largest selection of single malt whiskeys. Bagpipes and kilts are optional here.

Moving right along, the Organic Theater at Buckingham and Clark has had great success with home-grown productions. *Bleacher Bums*, a play starring Joe Mantegna, was about people who wager on Cubs games. It began with this theater company.

The Happy Sushi at 3346 North Clark serves raw fish, while El Jardin at 3407 North Clark is said to have the best margaritas in the neighborhood. The Ethopian Village at 3462 North Clark features that country's foods.

A little farther north, the Wild Hare is a bar devoted to reggae music. You do not have to smoke marijuana to enjoy it.

This brings us to Addison and the Cubby Bear, a bar with a changing entertainment line-up. Sometimes it presents alternative rock bands, once it offered Johnny Cash. For some reason, after the Chicago Bulls win basketball championships, many people come here to celebrate and even to riot.

Wrigley Field

But Addison and Clark is famous because here is Wrigley Field, the home of the hapless, hopeless, almost helpless Chicago Cubs.

The Chicago Cubs have not been in a World Series since 1945. 1945. They have tried everything—except getting good players. In 1976, the owner, the late Phillip K. Wrigley, publicly said the Cubs were "playing like a bunch of clowns." One wonders what he thought of them from 1945 to 1976.

The Cubs have featured a shortstop with a deformed finger on his throwing hand (Roy Smalley), the most valuable player in the National League while the team was in last place (Hank Sauer), and a relief pitcher who fell off the mound before throwing a single pitch (Jim Brosnan). Once Babe Ruth pointed to center field and then hit a home run exactly where he pointed—and he was playing against the Cubs in Wrigley Field.

One Cubs' outfielder claimed the vines in center field had poison ivy and would not follow fly balls to the wall. Another Cub long-ball hitter had only one weakness—he couldn't slug any fast ball pitched waist high and over the center of the plate.

In the past, they would have one fine player, a true superstar sentenced to forever play with losers as though for penance for some unmentionable deed. Each spring, this player (in years past it would be Ernie Banks) told everyone that the Cubs had a chance. Then they would do well during the exhibition season and even win a few games when it was cold in Chicago and no one was looking.

By the time All-Star game time arrived, the Cubs might be in second or third place. Then they would slide, skid, fade, and err their way to their rightful place in the universe—somewhere near the bottom. If the league had eight teams, they'd be near eighth place, unless they could convince the St. Louis Browns to stay in business a few more years. If the league was expanded to 10 teams, they'd find 10th place. If the leagues were divided four ways, subdivided, and parceled out (as they are today) so that the new leagues contain eight, six, four, or even only two teams each, the Cubs would be in eighth, sixth, fourth, or third—never, ever second.

And yet Chicago loves the Cubs, their field with such nice vines and grass, and that they provide a little excitement, but not too much.

The Cubs are a lesson for us all. If you had been trying to do something and had consistently failed since 1945, would you still both be popular and in there trying? The Cubs give all of us something to look down upon, and that is a public service.

And yet. And yet. Believe me, as an undying Cubs fan, I write this with hope eternal. They have been showing signs of life of late, since they were bought by the *Chicago Tribune*. This year, this year for sure, they could go all the way.

On August 18, 1988, Harry Grossman, age 91, turned on the lights for the first time in Wrigley Field, ending a 72-year, day-game tradition. That game, against the Philadelphia Phillies, was rained out in the fourth inning. Despite neighborhood protests that night games would disrupt traffic, create noise problems, and result in suburbanites urinating on local lawns after the games, night baseball has been grudgingly welcomed at Wrigley Field.

John Goodman portrayed Babe Ruth in the film *The Babe*, and Wrigley Field once again became the site of Ruth's famous called home run. Alas, the film was about as successful as the Cubs have been over the years.

Alta Vista

Take a right on Addison, travel one block and take a left on Sheffield, go two blocks north to Grace Street, take a left and go another couple of blocks to a small, one-way street called Alta Vista, which begins at 1054 west. Because Alta Vista is one way, you'll have to go around the block by taking the alley/street called Seminary, which is just west of Alta Vista. Enter another age.

Alta Vista, a Chicago landmark built from 1900 to 1904, is a street transplanted from London. A plaque at the south end of the street says that "every townhouse on one side of the street is duplicated with only minor variations at the diagonally opposite end of the block." In other words, with a few differences due to remodeling, the townhouse at 3800 Alta Vista is identical to 3847, 3802 to 3845, etc. In the middle of the street, the pairings are 3822–3825, 3824–3823, 3826–3821, and so on.

Alta Vista: "The block of 40 doors"

Alta Vista is also known as "the block of the 40 doors," and it features 20 different types of facades on each side of the street.

It was built by Samuel Eberly Gross, who billed himself as "the world's greatest real estate promoter" in the 1890s. He also achieved some literary fame when he sued Edmund Rostand, author of *Cyrano de Bergerac*, claiming that Rostand's play was stolen from his blank verse comedy titled *The Merchant Prince of Cornville*. The world laughed when the suit was filed and Rostand cried, "But there are big noses everywhere in the world." But the courts agreed with Gross, awarding him the play's royalties. Actor Richard Mansfield was prevented from performing in the play in America until the 1920s.

According to his obituary, Gross divorced his long-time wife in 1909 and one month later, at age 66, married an 18-year-old lass from Battle Creek, Michigan. His bride, Miss Ruby L. Haughey, was described by the *Chicago Examiner* as "a blushing young beauty of exceptional attractiveness" whom Gross "showered with gems, pearls, rubies and diamonds." His romance with the teenager was unknown to his ex-wife when he remarried. By the time he died four years later, much of his $5 million fortune was gone. I'll refrain from assuming that his bankruptcy, death, and misfortune are any comment on May–December marriages.

Graceland Cemetery

After driving through (or better, walking along) Alta Vista's 480-foot long facade of stained-glass transoms, and townhouses with ionic columns and Georgian features, turn right on Grace Street and go west up that potholed street to Clark Street, where you will turn right (north). Drive just past Irving Park to the Graceland Cemetery and Crematorium, 4001 North Clark Street. The entrance is virtually on the corner of Irving Park and Clark, between two ancient posts. Stop at the office to the right of the entrance, near the greenhouse, and ask for a free tour map, or just drive slowly through the cemetery, or park near the greenhouse and walk.

Graceland, dedicated on August 30, 1860, is the final resting place for many of the people who made their fortunes in Chicago before and after the turn of the century. A tour past their ornate mausoleums indicates that it doesn't matter whether you believe in life after death. For them, it was the death after life that was important.

Eerie! Lorado Taft's *Eternal Silence* in Graceland Cemetery

The most elaborate and expensive tombs are toward the northeast corner of the cemetery, near the Willowmere section, where the wealthy can rest eternally while overlooking a pond.

To get there, drive or walk to the right of the office. When you pass a statue titled *Eternal Silence*, but more commonly called "Death", by Lorado Taft, take the second left, proceed past the 10-foot-high statue of a crusading knight marking the grave of Victor Lawson (founder of the *Chicago Daily News*) and veer to the right as you pass the Schoenhofen pyramid. Peter Schoenhofen was a millionaire brewmaster of Edelweiss beer, and his pyramid-shaped tomb is decorated with Egyptian plant forms and guarded by a barefoot angel. His descendant, Graf Schenk, carried the portfolio with the bomb into Adolph Hitler's conference room in the famous unsuccessful attempt on the dictator's life.

Near the Schoenhofen pyramid is the Corinthian column marking the George Pullman tomb, designed by Solon Beman, who also designed Pullman village.

In Emmett Dedmon's book, *Fabulous Chicago*, he notes that Pullman feared his grave might be desecrated after his death. Therefore, "A pit as large as an average room had been dug on the family lot and lined across the base and walls with reinforced concrete 18 inches thick. Into this, the lead-lined mahogany casket was lowered, covered with a wrapping of tar paper and covered with a quick-drying coat of asphalt, which would exclude all air from the casket. The balance of the pit was filled to the

At rest: Graceland Cemetery lagoon looking toward the Palmer Tomb

Getty Tomb: "Close to perfection" and a hell of a tomb

level of the casket with solid concrete, on top of which a series of heavy steel rails were laid at right angles to each other and bolted together. The steel rails were then embedded in another layer of concrete. . . ." After which, the grave was covered so that it looked like all the others in Graceland. In other words, you are now standing atop a sealed concrete bunker.

The Bertha and Potter Palmer tomb is a little further down the road, and it is an example of going to one's reward as stylishly as one lived. Their sarcophagi are under 16 ionic columns, a copy of a Greek temple that somehow doesn't look out of place in a cemetery on Chicago's North Side. Nearby, on an island in the middle of the pond, are the granite boulders marking the graves of Daniel H. Burnham, father of the Chicago Plan, and his family. At his request, the island remains in a wild, if slightly littered, state.

Just to the west of the pond is the Getty Tomb, a Chicago landmark created for Carrie and Alice Getty, wife and daughter of a lumber tycoon, by Louis Sullivan. A plaque there states that the tomb "marks the maturity of Sullivan's architectural style and the beginning of modern architecture in America."

The lower half of the square tomb is rather plain, but the upper half, with its small Sullivan arches and detailed ornamentation, makes this a beautiful box with stunning bronze doors.

The praise for this tomb is almost embarrassingly gushing. Frank Lloyd Wright said it was a "piece of sculpture, a statue, a great poem addressed to human sensibilities as such. Outside the realm of music what finer requiem." One historian noted that Sullivan was never "more subtle than when he sketched the lacelike patterns circling the arches. . . ." Another writer praised it for "harmony in mass. . . ." and yet another writer said the tomb "approaches so closely to perfection that one gasps at his temerity." As you can tell, it's one hell of a tomb.

Lots of other folks—and a few of their pets—are buried in Graceland, including Cyrus Hall McCormick, inventor of the McCormick reaper; packer Philip D. Armour; architect Ludwig Mies Van Der Rohe; merchant Marshall Field; National Baseball League founder William Hulbert, whose tomb is marked by a large seamed baseball; heavyweight champions Bob Fitzsimmons and Jack Johnson; and detective Allan Pinkerton, whose tomb has a long inscription recalling his many deeds and concluding that Pinkerton was "A friend to honesty—a foe to crime." Many of Pinkerton's employees are buried in the same plot, including Kate Warn, probably America's first woman detective, and Tim Webster, hanged as a Union spy in Richmond, Virginia, on April 29, 1862.

I once attempted to find Lot 300, where Charles Dickens' brother, and the brother's mistress and children are allegedly buried in an unmarked grave. Charles Dickens was very angry because Augustus ran off to Chicago and left Augustus' wife in England, so the writer never gave the money needed to mark where Augustus lies. We couldn't find Lot 300 or even an indentation where the grave might be.

Leave Graceland by taking a right on Clark Street, going north to Montrose, where you'll take a right and go east to North Marine Drive, which is just before Lake Shore Drive. Turn right on Marine Drive, go two blocks south and take another right on a westbound, one-way street, Hutchinson Street.

Suddenly, after driving along a cemetery, after going by some fairly run-down apartments, and after skirting an area favored by Appalachian whites, you enter the nineteenth century. You are in what was Lake View, a resort and farming community in the 1850s, which was annexed to Chicago in 1889. Wealthy folks had their country homes here and, when land values increased, they began subdividing and building on their own property.

The first house on the block, called the Scales House, is in the Queen Anne-style, with a rounded turret and a vaguely English look.

Driving up this quiet street, which is a Chicago landmark, you'll see a modern-looking, turn-of-the-century home at 706 Hutchinson; the ionic columns on the William F. Monroe House (he founded a cigar store chain) at 716 Hutchinson; another Prairie School of Architecture example at 737 Hutchinson; and identical homes built for two brothers in 1909 at 747 and 757 Hutchinson.

In the 800 block, limestone is used at 803 Hutchinson; the Claude Seymour House at 817 Hutchinson was designed in 1913 by George W. Maher, a respected architect; the W. H. Lake House at 826 Hutchinson is also a Maher built in 1904; and the 839 Hutchinson may have been a Maher.

Turn right on Hazel Street and return to Montrose, where you'll take another right and go to Lake Shore Drive. If you follow the signs leading you south, you will return to the Loop. This ends the North Side Drive.

17 SOUTH SIDE DRIVE

From where the fire started to where the White Sox play

1. Dearborn Street Station
2. Chicago Fire Academy, 137 West DeKoven
3. Hull House and the University of Illinois
4. Coliseum, 14th and Wabash
5. Glessner House, 1800 South Prairie
6. Illinois Institute of Technology
7. Comiskey Park
8. The late Mayor Richard Daley's home, 3536 South Lowe
9. Stockyards Gate, near Halsted and Exchange
10. Chinatown
11. McCormick Place

Time: Less than 2 hours.
To get there: We begin at Congress and State Streets, driving south on State.

The Changing South Side

The South Side of Chicago is where the city was born, grew up, and became powerful. It was, for many recent decades, both the Irish and African-American political heart of Chicago.

During this drive, you will experience the dizzying changes a big city can offer. You will see where the wealthy lived in the late 1800s and where some of the poor live today.

Every neighborhood in Chicago can be friendly. And every neighborhood has its tough element. So be sensible during this drive and walk where it is so advised, and keep your car doors locked at all times.

The South Side is changing but then this has always been true. Originally, the area over which you will be driving was near a huge mud lake. Later, parts of the South Side became the fashionable place to live in Chicago, and still later a slum, the port of entry into Chicago for immigrants. Today, some of the slums have reverted to mud lakes, as old buildings have been torn down, to be replaced by empty lots awaiting tomorrow's bright new idea for housing. This could be the urban pattern—mud lake to settlement to wealthy folks to slum to mud lake, and then we start all over again.

Drive south on State, past Congress, past the William Jones Commercial High School, and the Pacific Gardens Mission at 646 South State, which was founded in 1877 to help drunks in what is still called Skid Row. Take a right on Polk and you'll see a red brick railroad station, built in 1885.

Dearborn Street Station

The Dearborn Street Station was once the eastern gateway for the Atchison, Topeka, and Santa Fe Railroad, and trains such as the Super Chief, El Capitan, Maple Leaf, Phoebe Snow, Blue Bird, the Wabash Cannonball, and the Georgian stopped there. Railroads using the station included the Chicago and Eastern Illinois, Erie-Lackawanna, Grand Trunk Western, Monon, and the Norfolk & Western.

The station became the focal point of the $1 billion South Loop New Town project, a community of 13,000 homes. The abandoned railroad station, the oldest surviving railroad terminal in Chicago and one of the oldest in America, has a new lease on life.

A 1922 fire destroyed the original clocktower and the ornate weather vane that was once part of this station, and the entire structure was almost demolished. But it was saved, an indication that Chicagoans are finally interested in preserving their past.

However, unless you have found a nearby parking space and need to use a cash station or need something from a hardware store, drive on, going west on Polk. The block between Polk and Congress to the north on Dearborn is the heart of Printer's Row. Many of the huge buildings here, which once housed presses of all descriptions, have become rental or sales properties for yuppies, who want a loft apartment here.

One block to the north is Prairie, an upscale restaurant that is doing a fine job creating tasty, healthy Midwest foods. I'd suggest calling Prairie for a reservation because there are delicious items on its menu that you will not find anywhere else. And it is a most romantic restaurant.

On to Wells and Jefferson

Drive west on Polk to Wells, where you will take a left. The odd structure adjoining the building with the words "Chicago Paper Company" fading on the facade is River City, 800 South Wells, with 446 apartments including some four-bedroom penthouses with three levels, 3½ baths, a gym room, sauna, and whirlpool bath.

Only a few years ago, people would have thought you were crazy to live immediately south of the Loop, an area with "vast tracts of unused railroad yards, underused industrial sites and unusable vacant lots," according to Steve Kerch of the *Chicago Sun-Times*.

Then, in 1984, $60 million was spent on the first phase of a gigantic, serpentine construction, which includes 240,000 square feet of commercial space, a 70-slip marina, a health club, jogging track, and party rooms.

The architect was Bertrand Goldberg, who also created Marina City in 1963–64 and who obviously likes curves. River City, from either the outside or the inside, has a futuristic, but humanistic, look.

Take a left on Clark, and head south. Drive up the ramp to Roosevelt Road and take a right, going west two stoplights to Jefferson.

Before you get to Jefferson, if you're in the market for a 30 percent discount on Claude Montana, Missoni, or Armani suits, stop by Morris & Sons Company, 555 West Roosevelt Road, which gets overstocks of designer suits "on the condition of anonymity and a ban on advertising," according to *Chicago* magazine. There is even an annual, secret, every-thing-at-cost sale, which is available only to customers who have pre-viously spent $350. During my last shopping trip here, the salesman proudly said he did not work on commission so it wasn't required that he see any customer more than he needed.

Also the Einstein Clothing Company, at the same address, has flawed suits for savings of up to 75 percent.

You know you have reached Jefferson when you see the Chernin's sign just ahead of you at 606 West Roosevelt Road. Chernin's is one of the largest, cut-rate shoe stores in Chicago with salesmen picked for their hyperactivity. Stop here if you want to quickly buy a pair of good, but inexpensive, shoes.

Chicago Fire Academy

Otherwise, turn right on Jefferson and drive north to the Chicago Fire Academy, at 147 West DeKoven. It's hard to miss the academy—a bronze statue, titled *Flame*, by local sculptor Egon Weiner is in front of the building.

The friendly firefighters there will be glad to show you through the academy. They'll point to a plaque on the floor opposite the library that marks the exact spot where the fire started in the Patrick and Catherine O'Leary barn in 1871, frightening Mrs. O'Leary's herd of five cows, burning 300 people to death, making 100,000 people homeless, and leveling 2,000 acres, or about a third of the city. The wind was so strong in a northerly direction that the O'Leary home, south of the barn, was untouched by the blaze.

Generally speaking, most Chicagoans accept the story printed in the *New York Herald* that the 1871 fire started in Mrs. O'Leary's barn when one of her cows kicked over a lantern. Mrs. O'Leary denied that story under oath, and there were rumors that someone who left a party next door to the O'Learys went to get milk for some punch and allowed the lantern to tip.

There are even more bizarre theories. Mel Waskin, who grew up in Chicago and who was creative director for Coronet Films, wrote the book

Flame by Egon Weiner, near where the 1871 Chicago Fire started

Mrs. O'Leary's Comet: Cosmic Causes of the Great Chicago Fire, in 1985. He blamed the fire on a comet called Biela II, part of Biela I, which split in two in 1845 and headed for parts unknown. As evidence, he cites the fact that intense fires broke out at the same time in Chicago; Peshtigo,

Wisconsin; and Manistee, Michigan. Who knows, the firefighters may be pointing to the spot where arson by comet was committed.

Because of Chicago's severe winters, the Fire Academy has a drill hall with a ceiling 64 feet off the ground. New firefighters can slide down poles and jump into nets while indoors.

Notice the concertina wire atop the fence protecting the adjoining taxicab parking lot. This is definitely a daytime drive.

Hull House

Continue north on Jefferson, while edging into the left-hand lanes, and take a left on Taylor, going west. Cross the expressway and take a right on Halsted, going north. When you notice the distinctive red brick and white columns of Hull House on your left, take a right on Polk (the next street), and park in the city lot there. Walk across the street and enter Hull House, 800 South Halsted.

This neighborhood had known waves of immigrants before the University of Illinois and expressways ended its existence. The Irish were here in the 1850s, then came the Germans, then the Bohemians in the

Hull House: A tribute to an indomitable woman

1860s. It was a Jewish ghetto in the 1890s, an Italian community in the 1900s, and later it was popular with Greeks, Mexicans, and African Americans.

Jane Addams moved into an abandoned mansion here on September 18, 1889, and changed the world of public service. She created a new form of social service. In 1910, Jane Addams wrote, "We were ready to perform the humblest neighborhood services. We were asked to wash the newborn babies, to prepare the dead for burial, to nurse the sick and to 'mind the children.'"

This, in a neighborhood where, according to an 1895 Hull House report, the tenements were filthy sheds with "foul stables and dilapidated outhouses, broken sewer pipes, piles of garbage fairly alive with diseased odors, and numbers of children filling every nook. . . ."

By 1907, there were thirteen buildings associated with Hull House, where the city's first kindergarten was established in 1889, where Benny Goodman played in the boys' band, and where Jane Addams tried to solve the social problems of her day. Miss Addams didn't like the way garbage was collected around Hull House, so she got a job as a garbage inspector. She and her associates fought for women's suffrage, unions, the National Association for the Advancement of Colored People (which she helped found), and opposed sweatshops and World War I.

In 1931, Jane Addams won the Nobel Peace Prize, which can be seen in the parlor of Hull House.

Jane Addams was a complex, modern-day saint—a fussy picture straightener; a woman who needed adoring followers; a so-called new woman, who projected a sexually pure and innocent image; the epitome of the nineteenth-century heroine; a tough woman, who often won her battles with local authorities; an angel of mercy, who was also a shrewd businesswoman; an expert public speaker; a fundraiser; and a woman who was so shy about her slender body that, even when sharing a hotel room with her long-time friend, Louise DeKoven Bowen, she would dress completely in the closet and emerge with her hair done.

While walking through the restored Hull House, realize that before Jane Addams there was poverty. After Jane Addams, there was poverty and hope. After a pioneering Hull House survey of the people in the neighborhood revealed that 19,000 humans had no bathing facilities, Jane Addams got angry, and the result was the firing of half the city's sanitation inspection bureau. Mrs. Bowen helped get the first factory inspection law, Chicago's first juvenile court, and convinced the police department to hire policewomen.

Through all these battles, all these victories (and even the temporary setback during World War I, when many people objected to Jane Addams' pacifism), there was Jane Addams' humanity. She saw an old German woman being forcibly taken to the County Infirmary as she clutched a small battered chest of drawers. Jane Addams wrote, "To take away from an old woman whose life has been spent in household cares all the foolish little belongings to which her affections cling and to which her very fingers have become accustomed, is to take away her last incentive to activity, almost to life itself. To give an old woman only a chair and bed, to leave her no cupboard in which her treasures may be stowed, not only that she may take them out when she desires occupation, but that her mind may dwell upon them in moments of reverie, is to reduce living almost beyond the bounds of human endurance."

University of Illinois Chicago Circle

Leave Hull House after touching the spirit of Jane Addams, take two quick lefts, and enter the University of Illinois Chicago Circle Campus by walking into the large building in front of you, past the bookstore, following the signs to the Lecture Center, between halls D 1 and 2 and C 1 and 6, and into the outdoor amphitheater.

This campus, now populated by nearly 25,000 students (11 percent African-American, 13.4 percent Latino) was opened in 1965. The architect, Walter A. Netsch, Jr., of Skidmore, Owings and Merrill, created an instant commuters' campus where buildings are grouped by their functions and by the numbers of people who might use them. Other campuses feature buildings devoted to engineering or biology or English. Circle Campus groups all the lecture halls in its center because they draw the heaviest traffic. The high-rise buildings on the perimeter of the campus are offices and within them, some university officials claim, even the halls gradually dwindle in width away from the central area of heaviest use.

This campus does hold a *Guinness* record. While in the campus dream laboratory, Bill Carskadon had the longest recorded dream, lasting two hours and 23 minutes, on February 15, 1967. The brothers Guinness do not report what was the subject of the dream, but it must have been quite a story.

Alumni of this school include actor Michael Gross, formerly of TV's "Family Ties," comics Judy Tenuta and Emo Phillips; jazz pianist

Ramsey Lewis; NBC news anchorman John Chancellor; former Illinois Governor James Thompson and his wife; four public school teachers who received Golden Apple Awards for excellence in teaching; and the minister of health of Rwanda, Africa. The school claims that one out of 95 adult Chicagoans is a graduate of the University of Illinois.

UIC has been buying up land along Maxwell Street south of Roosevelt Road for future campus expansion. It could be a couple of decades in the future, but it is possible that some day the colorful Maxwell Street vendors will be replaced by coeds.

In 1992 the campus was in the midst of a rebuilding program pushed, in part, by students' reaction to the old campus that they called "ugly," "wet and slippery," "windy," and, worst of all, "feels like a parking lot." When the walkways and plaza on the east side of the campus were torn down (among other reasons, because few people used the amphitheater in the midst of campus) there were protests because they were tearing down a landmark.

This is basically a commuter campus, but an important one. UIC is the eleventh largest employer in the Chicago metropolitan area, and the total measurable economic impact on Chicago from UIC is more than half a billion dollars.

After you have finished exploring the University of Illinois, if you are hungry, I'm going to direct you to a semisecret discovery of a Chicago restaurant. But be forewarned: Almost every time I have looked for Tufano's, I have lost it and have had to ask for directions.

Leave the campus by going south on Halsted until you get to Harrison. Take a right, then a left on Racine and a left on Vernon Park, until you have gone around the block and behind the campus, and you have reached 1073 West Vernon Park.

Tufano's has been a landmark in this neighborhood for more than six decades. Lawyers, judges, National Basketball Association coaches—never the players—Frank Sinatra, Tony Bennett, the entire casts of *Phantom of the Opera* and *Les Miserables*, and Jack Nicholson have dined here. A wife of a local TV weather forecaster threw spaghetti in his face in this restaurant. She is now his ex-wife.

Joe DiBuono, the owner, told me that his grandfather, Joseph, was the chef who often cooked for Al Capone because both came from the same town in Italy. A great uncle on the Tufano side of the family made stills during Prohibition. At the time, his grandmother had a bakery across the street where she would bake bread during the Depression for neighborhood residents for a penny a loaf. At the age of 91, Grandma Teresa still came to Tufano's three days a week to start the gravy, and DiBuono's mother is there daily to make sure the food is cooked correctly.

Without question, Tufano's is a throwback to the time when owners cared about the restaurants that carried their names and therefore, they stayed on the premises to make sure everything was done right.

The menu is still written in chalk on blackboards and the food is hearty and delicious. I love the big salads, the lemon chicken, the eggplant, and the homemade ravioli. It is the perfect place to go before a Bulls game because every waiter and waitress knows how to get your order on the table so you can arrive in time for the team introductions. If you want to eat where Chicagoans eat, and if you want the best of traditional Italian cooking, you must stop at Tufano's.

The Coliseum

Now retrace your drive (if you can find your way out and if you have actually eaten at Tufano's). If you weren't hungry or decided to skip the exploration of Tufano's, then leave the campus and Hull House by driving south on Halsted (to the left as you leave the parking lot) to

The remains of the Coliseum and the Libby Prison

Roosevelt Road, which is two stoplights ahead of you. Then take a left, and go east about a mile to Wabash, and take a right.

You will drive by 1255 South Wabash where the World Tattoo Gallery had an Elvis impersonators contest a few years ago. Because so many of the contestants were overweight, almost all the impersonations were of the aging rather than of the younger Elvis.

Driving farther south, you may see the Coliseum at 14th Place. The castle-like wall formerly belonged to the Confederacy's Libby Prison. In 1888, a group of Chicago businessmen brought the prison here, piece by piece, reconstructed it, and opened a museum. When the museum folded, parts of the prison were torn down and later the Coliseum was built using the walls that remained. The last time I passed the Coliseum, everything was torn down but the old Libby Prison walls. Weeds were growing and a sign warned "no defacing stone walls."

If a building has memories, this one could almost vie with the original after which it was named.

Bathhouse John Coughlin and Hinky Dink Kenna, two notorious aldermen, held their First Ward balls here. More than 15,000 people attended their 1908 fling, including every scarlet woman, second-story man, female impersonator, and dope fiend in town.

Bathhouse read a poem saying, "On with the dance, let the orgy be perfectly proper," willing women were stripped, men in women's costumes cavorted, and drunks passed out but were forced to remain standing because of the density of the crowd, according to Herman Kogan's and Lloyd Wendt's book *Lords of the Levee*.

Despite the fact that 100 extra policemen were on duty, only one person was arrested and convicted for that night's activities—for gate crashing. One brothel madame said of these parties, "Joy reigned unrefined."

Continue south on Wabash to 18th Street, take a left and go to Prairie, and park.

If you walk to the northeast corner of 18th and Prairie, you'll see a plaque marking the spot where the Indians attacked the refugees from Fort Dearborn in 1812. The home on the southeast corner, at 1801 Prairie, is the W. W. Kimball House, which belonged to the manufacturer of Kimball pianos and organs. It was designed in 1891 by S. S. Beman, who created the community of Pullman and who modeled the home after the Chateau de Josselin in Brittany.

Glessner House

Now walk across the street and enter the Glessner House, 1800 South Prairie, a home that changed all residential architecture in America. Glessner House looked startlingly different when it was built in 1887, and does so now.

John Jacob Glessner was Cyrus McCormick's competitor in the farm machinery industry, although he eventually merged with McCormick and others to form International Harvester Co. When Glessner decided to build a new home, he went to Henry Hobson Richardson, a Boston architect who liked to do his drafting while wearing a monk's costume because he weighed 370 pounds.

Glessner's diary states that Glessner asked Richardson if he could design a home, and Richardson said, "I'll plan anything a man wants, from a cathedral to a chicken coop. That's the way I make my living."

Richardson said windows were "not to look out of." He added, "You no sooner get them than you shroud them with two thicknesses of window shades and then add double sets of curtains." So he created the first true city house, almost flush to the sidewalk, with few windows facing the street, but many of them looking at an inner court.

The inner courtyard of the Glessner House: Where the windows are

The home was immediately loathed by the neighbors. George Pullman, who tried to get the house torn down, said, "I don't like it, and I wish it weren't there. I don't know what I have ever done to have that thing staring me in the face every time I go out of my door!" One architectural critic inferred "its purpose is to be not domestic but penal." After it was built, one newspaper noted that it "threw the neighborhood into a state of consternation." One passerby said, "It looks like an old jail."

Maybe that was what the Glessners wanted. It is said that, while living in their old home and going over plans with Richardson for the new, the Glessners heard explosions. It was the beginning of the Haymarket Riot, which some thought was a direct attack on the American way of life. No wonder the Glessners opted for a fortress.

But the Glessners loved the place, bringing over the fire from the hearthstone of their old home, carrying Virginia Creepers for the courtyard, and accepting Boston ivy from a friend for the outer walls.

The Glessners enjoyed entertaining, and their diary notes that Theodore Thomas, conductor of the Chicago Symphony, would often bring over a third or more of his musicians, hide them about the house, and surprise Mrs. Glessner with music for dinner. The entire symphony was secreted in the house for the Glessners' 25th wedding anniversary. No one knew they were there until they began playing a delightful concert. And you think the wealthy have elaborate dinner parties today!

Glessner House, which was threatened with demolition in 1966, has been lovingly restored by the Chicago Architectural Foundation. Visit the upstairs bedrooms, which display Glessner antiques, furniture designed by the architect Richardson, and period wallpaper. Call the foundation at (312)922-3432 for information about tours and hours.

Widow Clarke House

Next, exit Glessner House and walk south on Prairie Avenue. You'll see a cul-de-sac with photo displays of the grand homes that were once there and the Widow Clarke House about halfway up the block. This is Chicago's oldest surviving building, built in 1836 by Caroline and Henry Clarke.

But the house was unfinished when Clarke lost his money in the Panic of 1837. A visitor in 1841 noticed that the rooms were decorated with prairie chickens, plovers, and half a dozen deer carcasses. Clarke was better as a hunter than as an interior decorator, and the game was used to feed his family.

Clarke died of cholera in 1849, but his wife continued to live there. The Clarke House escaped the 1871 fire and was moved 30 blocks from its original location in 1872. When it was bought by the City of Chicago in 1977, the entire home was hoisted up and over the elevated tracks and placed in its present site, which is only three blocks from where it was originally.

Today, it has been furnished by the Colonial Dames of America so that it looks as it did between 1836 and 1860.

Tours of the Prairie Avenue District are conducted daily, except for Monday, from April through October; and daily, except for Monday and Wednesday, from November through March.

Lexington Hotel

Having understood what life was like for the wealthy in Chicago in the 1880s and being thankful that parts of this street were preserved, leave Prairie Avenue, drive west to Michigan Avenue; take a left, and go south.

Al Capone used the Lexington Hotel, at 1825 South Michigan, as a headquarters from 1928 to 1932, and that is only a few blocks to the south as you cross Michigan.

In 1986, this was the site of one of the great televised scams of all time. Inside this hotel, which was built in 1892, workers found a 7-by-10-foot vault with walls that were 36 inches thick.

This discovery led to "The Mystery of Al Capone's Vaults," a two-hour syndicated television show seen on 181 stations in America and by gangster aficionados in Brazil, West Germany, Argentina, Italy, the Netherlands, the Bahamas, the Dominican Republic, Costa Rica, and Paraguay.

After five months of publicity hype and nearly two hours of background material, host Geraldo Rivera looked into the mysterious vault and said, "It seems . . . we've struck out." There had been suggestions that the "bones of (Capone's) criminal rivals might be hidden there." Instead, during the TV program, nothing was found except dust, concrete, and a 60-year-old empty gin bottle.

But have no fear. Even if the vault was empty, the program was a success. It had the highest rating ever for a nationally syndicated show on independent stations (34 rating, 48 percent share of the audience), and it was second to the Super Bowl in ratings in Chicago (57.3 rating, 73 percent audience). The Tribune Entertainment Company figured to profit to the tune of $1 million and Rivera, on the strength of that program, eventually got to embarrass NBC with his special on satanism. Later, almost as a direct result of the Capone vault show, Rivera got his own syndicated TV talk program. Not bad for finding one old bottle.

Al Capone Territory

Not far from here, at 2222 South Wabash, was the site of the Four Deuces, a saloon where Capone got his start as Johnny Torrio's bodyguard and where a dozen murders were allegedly committed. Colosimo's Cafe was once at 2126 South Wabash, and Big Jim Colosimo ran it until he was shot there on May 11, 1920. Big Jim, who wore diamonds on his fingers, shirt, vest, belt, suspenders, and garters, fell in love with Dale Winter, a vaudeville singer. His associates didn't like his marriage to a nice girl like Dale, and so he entered gangster heaven.

You'll also be close to 2300 South Michigan, site of the Metropole Hotel. Capone had 50 rooms in this hotel patroled by gunmen. It's now an empty lot.

Next consider the historic nature of this neighborhood. But only think about it. There's not much to see and I wouldn't advise getting out of the car.

Everleigh House and the Levee

Continue south on Michigan Avenue until you reach Cermak; take a right and proceed west. You will be only a block from the site of the Everleigh House, 2131–33 South Dearborn, the finest brothel in Chicago history. From February 1, 1900, until October 24, 1911, Minna and Ada Everleigh ran a whorehouse that featured a $15,000 gold piano, 20 gold-plated spittoons, and the finest women in the land. Prices for these ladies started at $50, but newspapermen were admitted for free. However, free admission did not include free favors for the denizens.

A home for the elderly now sits where debauchery achieved new heights of sophistication. The ladies wore evening gowns and were encouraged to read. Parlors had such names as gold, silver, copper, red, rose, green, blue, Oriental, Japanese, Egyptian, Moorish, and Chinese.

There were two mahogany staircases, flanked by potted palms and statues of Grecian goddesses.

One girl insisted on having fresh cut red roses everywhere in her room. Another girl had everything in white in her boudoir with an ermine coverlet on her bed. Money was mentioned only as a guest left. Champagne was $12 a bottle. Few men paid less than $200 for the evening and many left $1,000. The sisters admitted that their personal profits per year were around $120,000.

Bawdy history was made here when Prince Henry of Russia went to the club and, during a party in his honor, one Romeo drank champagne from a lady's slipper for the first time.

The Everleigh sisters' downfall came because they decided to advertise. A tame pamphlet boasting of the club's many advantages, including steam heat, caused a public outcry and forced the police chief to close it. After drinking all the champagne they could, the girls left.

This area was part of the notorious Levee at the turn of the century, home of madams, panderers, call girls, white slavers, and other energetic folk. Emmett Dedmon's book, *Fabulous Chicago*, notes that in this neighborhood the brothel called California had 50 prostitutes; Frankie Wright's brothel had books and was called the Library; the French Elm featured walls covered with mirrors; Black May's girls boasted there was no degeneracy they would not perform; and the Dewey Hotel specialized in Russian Jewish prostitutes broken into the life by professional rapists working on the top floor.

Drive west. After crossing under two overpasses, take a left on Wentworth and cross under the ornate gates, and you will enter Chicago's Chinatown, a two-block center of restaurants, shops, grocery stores, and, at times, illegal gambling.

Illinois Institute of Technology

Unless you are hungry, continue driving south until you get to 26th Street, take a left, cross the Expressway and take a right on State Street. You will pass the St. James Roman Catholic Church, built in 1879, at 29th and Wabash; and the Dearborn Homes, one of Chicago's rare low-rise housing projects. In a short while, you will arrive at the Illinois Institute of Technology from 3100 to 3500 south on State. The present campus epitomizes the philosophy of one of its designers, Ludwig Mies

Van Der Rohe, "Less is more," with its low, simple, glass-and-steel structures.

IIT had its start in 1890 when the Rev. Frank W. Gunsaulus gave a sermon on philanthropy while meat packer Philip Armour was in the audience. It must be ranked among the world's best sermons because shortly after that Armour began donating money to create the Armour Institute of Technology, forerunner of IIT.

The baseball field where Madonna, Geena Davis, and others in *A League of Their Own* secretly practiced was behind the fieldhouse to your left at 31st Street.

Comiskey Park

Continue south on State to 35th, where you'll take a right and go past the Stateway Gardens housing project. After you cross over the Dan Ryan Expressway, you'll go by the new Comiskey Park, home of the Chicago White Sox. The old park was in the parking lot to your right.

It was here that Chicago's Fire Commissioner, the late Robert J. Quinn, ordered the city's air raid sirens to wail after the White Sox won a pennant in 1959. He forgot it was a time when people were concerned about Russian bombers and still had fully stocked bomb shelters in the backyard. Hundreds of people got frightened, some even panicked, and spent a terror-stricken night in their shelters. Quinn was a bit over-enthusiastic.

But then Quinn was always a character, causing massive traffic jams one morning when he ran his rookies down the middle of an expressway to get them in shape. Commuters were shocked to see young men in what appeared to be their underwear jogging during rush hour.

During an investigation of fire department ambulance safety, Quinn was asked why, when so many people were being injured inside them, the department insisted on having Cadillac-built ambulances. Quinn said he thought that Chicagoans would feel better knowing that, if they were going to die, they would die in a Cadillac!

Perhaps in the fleeting moment as you pass this park, you might remember Gandil, Cicotte, Jackson, Felsch, Weaver, Risberg, Williams, and McMullin, who were barred from playing baseball for life because of taking bribes in the 1919 World Series. They say that Jackson, Weaver, and Cicotte might be in the Hall of Fame now if that hadn't happened.

The scandal helped the Sox lose the 1920 pennant. They were one game behind Cleveland in September of that year, with three more games to play when Eddie Cicotte talked to a Cook County grand jury and seven of the eight players were immediately suspended. Cleveland won the pennant.

Incidentally, Charles A. Comiskey, then owner of the team, paid the Black Sox, as they came to be called, between $5,000 and $12,000 per year for their services. The ballplayers were offered that much per game by the gamblers. Sometimes a good paycheck helps folks be morally straight.

The old Comiskey Park, built in 1910, was the site of a Disco Demolition Night when Steve Dahl, a local gab host, destroyed disco records between games of a Sox double-header. Dahl's fans stormed the field and tore things up enough so that the second game had to be canceled. Dahl and the Sox survived, disco died.

One street here is named after the legendary club owner Bill Veeck (pronounced "as in wreck," he would say), the man who brought show business to baseball. Among other things, he once had a midget bat in the major leagues. The little guy had a very small strike zone.

Mayor Daley's Home

Continue up 35th about a half mile to Lowe. There's the Ninth District Police Station on the corner. In about the middle of the block, at 3536 South Lowe, a No Parking sign announces the home of the late Mayor Richard J. Daley. He grew up here in Bridgeport, spent his life here, became Mayor of Chicago in 1955, sent John F. Kennedy to the White House in 1960, orchestrated the 1968 Convention, and died in 1976.

During his term, the face of the city was changed. He helped build expressways, universities, sewer systems, O'Hare Airport, the Civic Center, and other structures. Many of his friends were indicted, the city remained corrupt, the Democratic machine got older but stayed powerful, the schools deteriorated, the streets became a little less safe, the quality of life declined, but new buildings went up, new highways went through, and old slums were torn down.

And Bridgeport, a small, predominantly white Catholic community, remained powerful in the city. Kids learned politics in the cradle here and went on to be policemen, lawyers, and judges.

Once, when we attempted to take pictures of Daley's home for this book, a policeman ordered us to stop. We did because we were in Bridgeport, a half-block from a police station. There are better places to fight for tourist's rights.

Continuing south on Lowe, turn right on 36th, go one block, take another right on Union, and return to 35th Street, where you will take a left and go to Halsted, where you will take another left, going south about a mile past Root Street.

In 1865, Halsted stunk. It was so muddy, a man had to vault across it with a pole. Hog's hair left to dry for mortar created a stupefying odor. And the Sunday sport around here was betting who could skin a steer the fastest.

Stockyards Gate

Take a right on Exchange and you will immediately see the Stockyards Gate through which more than a billion animals went to their deaths. The stockyards opened in 1865, creating Chicago's image as "hog butcher to the world." At one time, Armour, Swift, and other packers employed 40,000 people here and, on a hot summer day, the stockyards could be smelled for miles around.

But the stockyards went into decline after World War II. Wilson & Co. left in 1955, the Armour plant closed in 1950, Swift discontinued most slaughtering operations in 1958, and the stockyards themselves closed on July 30, 1971, when the last 2,000 head of cattle were sold. The last two packing houses were leveled in 1991.

This area is now an industrial park, and more than 8,000 people are employed here making ice-cream flavors, recycling fluids, and warehousing.

The stone steer's head near the top of the gate is supposed to be a likeness of Sherman, the steer who won the grand sweepstakes at the first American Fat Stock Show in 1878.

If you are a vegetarian, this is a place to quickly leave because it is the site of a billion animal deaths. If you are a steak-lover, it is a place to revere. In any case, circle the gate and return to Halsted, taking a right (south).

You will quickly pass the International Amphitheater, site of the 1968 Democratic Convention, although the police riot was northeast of here at the Hilton Hotel.

Go to 43rd and take a left (east). After you cross the bridge over the Dan Ryan, take another left on LaSalle and head north toward the Loop on the Dan Ryan Expressway. This ends your South Side Drive.

18 RUSH–DIVISION PUB CRAWL

Where the singles bars are

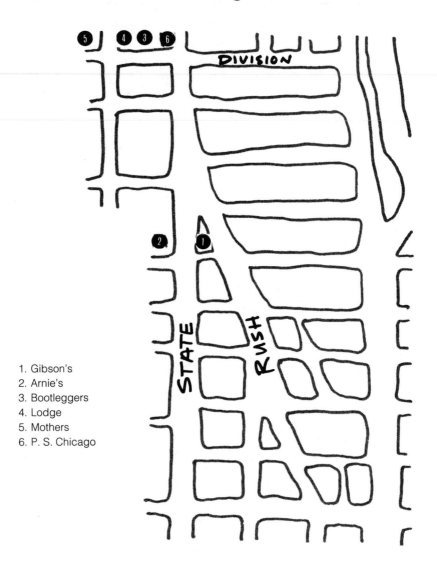

1. Gibson's
2. Arnie's
3. Bootleggers
4. Lodge
5. Mothers
6. P. S. Chicago

Time: An entire evening, plus however long it takes to recover from a hangover.

To get there: Either take the CTA subway to Division and walk two blocks east, or take the #36 Broadway bus to State and Division. If you drive, it is advisable to park in one of two nearby city lots, at 875 North Rush or 506 North Rush. You may have to wait for your car to be delivered to you when you pick it up. There hasn't been a parking place on the streets east of Rush since the day after the fire of 1871.

Formerly Infamous Rush Street

Rush Street once sat like a gigantic, hard-edged, Venus flytrap for conventioneers. Today, most of the prostitutes are gone and the whole area has become slightly more upscale.

The Division Street area, near Rush Street, has had bars for lonely single folk—or married people pretending to be single—for more than a decade now. It is by no means as pure as a church picnic, but it, too, has been considerably cleaned up.

Over the years, this entire walk has gradually changed from an excursion through prostitution and somewhat wild sex to a stroll past respectable restaurants and bars, a visit to the best of New York department stores, and a look at a world-class hotel.

It wasn't always so. I still remember with some embarrassment being sent by the old *Chicago Daily News* to interview some prostitutes on Rush Street in the mid-1970s. There had been daily sweeps of the street by police in an attempt to eliminate that sordid occupation from the area. I was working the 3 to 11 p.m. shift at the time and, to the hoots and hollers of my colleagues, had to report that I was unable to find a single fallen woman that night. The prostitutes knew the police shift times and did not begin work until 2 a.m., when one police shift returned to complete their reports and before a new shift reported.

Today, it would be fairly commonplace for a reporter to be unable to locate a prostitute in what was one of the most notorious modern vice districts in the city. The reason: What with the AIDs epidemic, hookers have become rather rare in these parts. Paul Blaney, manager of Kronies and Eliot's Nesst, two local bars, said that the remaining practitioners are really pickpockets who lure men into a position where it becomes easy to lift their wallets.

Rush Street is named after Dr. Benjamin Rush, who signed the Declaration of Independence, was a doctor during the Revolution who accepted no pay for his services, and saved 6,000 people during a yellow fever epidemic in 1793. He never visited Chicago.

Rush Street first entered the history books as a cow path. The wealthy people living on the North Side during the 1860s all had cows. They were herded by a man who looked like a cossack and who rode north on Rush Street each morning, blowing a brass horn and summoning his aristocratic cows. Except for the now-phantom cows, today Rush Street has nothing of historic, artistic, or architectural merit.

Begin to Crawl

This pub crawl begins on the southeast corner of State and Division. It should be noted that, while tracing the steps you are about to take, the author had a drink in only every third bar and then it was half a glass of beer. Despite this restraint in the pursuit of responsible reporting, he was quite tipsy when he completed only half the crawl. Pace yourself, folks, this is going to be a long night.

Begin at State and Division and walk south on the east side of State Street to Mr. Kite's Gold Coast Confectionery at 1153 North State. Dominique Gusmanos, the manager, says that this is the place where Bill Cosby comes to get s'mores, and $10-a-pound caramel clusters. This store also features custom-printed fortune cookies dipped in chocolate. These are used to propose marriage and to get attention during a job hunt. This is also the Gold Coast's headquarters for chocolate-covered matzoh during Passover. Contrary to popular belief, the store was not named after the Beatles song "For the Benefit of Mr. Kite," rather, it was named after the original co-owner.

Continue south, strolling past West Egg, a diner at Elm and Rush, and passing the Kentucky Fried Chicken; veer slightly to the left at Cedar Street, walking on Rush. You'll know you're on the correct street if you pass the Solomon-Cooper Drug Store on the corner.

The buildings here once housed a Mexican restaurant called Guadalaharry's, at 1043 North Rush, and a Parisian-like bar, Harry's Cafe, at 1035 North Rush. A bit of Mexico and Paris have left the street, but no one seems to miss them.

Take a left on Bellevue and go to Kronies, 8 East Bellevue, "home of the liter." That's what it says on their signs and matchbooks. It means that you can order a liter of Long Island iced tea for around $10. This near-lethal concoction is vodka, gin, rum, tequila, triple sec, sour mix, and Coca-Cola.

The Long Island iced tea record holder in Kronies was some guy from Tennessee who drank 14 of them. Most folks would find it very difficult to drink 14 liters of water. This visitor not only accomplished this feat, but left under his own power. This gentleman now has achieved a near-legendary status at Kronies, and returns once a year to have a few.

Eric Clapton has said that this is one of his top four favorite bars, but he likes to drink alone when he's here. Other patrons have included Christopher *Back to the Future* Lloyd, Jethro Tull's band, and members of Big Audio Dynamite.

Eliot's Nesst, a bar that has probably taken the name-pun too far, is at 20 East Bellevue, and is connected to Kronies at the back of each bar. It features a disc jockey playing '50s and '60s music, and free drinks and snacks for a $1 cover charge from 7 to 8 p.m. on Fridays. The house drink is the upside-down margarita. This drink is poured directly into the customer's mouth while he or she is lying face-up on the bar. That is why there are mirrors on the ceiling at the end of the bar.

Le Meridien

Cross Bellevue and enter Le Meridien, 21 East Bellevue, a grand, 23-story hotel with 247 rooms that opened in June 1988. This is the official hotel of the "Oprah Winfrey Show," and it is mentioned at the conclusion of every program. This connection means that a wide variety of famous and infamous people have stayed here, some in the $550 bi-level penthouse with a bedroom loft overlooking the parlor, including Janet Jackson, Neil Diamond, Mariah Carey, Gladys Knight, Marla Maples, Iman and her husband David Bowie, Cindy Crawford without her husband Richard Gere, Will Smith who plays NBC's "Fresh Prince of Bel-Aire," John Forsythe, Branford Marsalis, and Guns n' Roses. Knowing their reputation, I asked Troy I. Jones, senior sales manager, if Guns n' Roses had any special requests during their visits. Her answer, "They asked for many garbage cans lined in a special way. I don't know why."

Musicians seem to enjoy Le Meridien possibly because every room has its own CD player.

This hotel received a Mobil four-star rating in 1989. It's part of an international chain of 60 hotels owned by Air France. This means that employees must go to Paris, Dakar, St. Marten, London, and other exotic locales for training in hotel management.

The specialties at the Brasserie Bellevue Restaurant are angel hair pasta with rosemary and grilled chicken breasts ($12.95) and shrimp sauteed in white wine ($19.95).

Continuing south enter Mustards Bar and Grill at 1007 North Rush. Monday through Friday ask for the $1 bottle beer. The crowd here is mixed between students from Loyola University and business people from nearby offices.

If you go down the corridor at 1005 North Rush, you will enter The Backroom, which features live jazz.

Gibson's

Crossing Rush Street at Oak, go north, passing Hamburger Hamlet. You will find Gibson's at 1028 North Rush. This place is a throwback to the old Chicago tradition of restaurant-bars. The menu features $30 steaks, and $75 colossal "surf and turf" lobster/steak combinations, while the bar features big drinks and a nightly piano player. The bartenders are mature guys who wear aprons over their girths and mix gibsons, side cars, and large martinis. The menu also features much less expensive bar food, which can be ordered in either the dining room or the bar. Gibson's is said to resemble Fritzle's, a restaurant that once anchored the north end of State Street and attracted the famous and near-famous during the '40s and '50s.

Gibson's is an adult place where Elizabeth Taylor, Tony Bennett, Frank Sinatra, Jack Nicholson, and Tom Dreeson go when in Chicago. Lea Thompson walked in while *Back to the Future*, a movie she co-starred in, was playing. One of the bar patrons asked, "Aren't you the lady on TV?"

Tito Jackson, Michael's big brother, had his birthday celebration here, where the carrot cake is huge and excellent. This would be a place to destroy a diet.

Before it was Gibson's, this address was the home of Sweetwater, an imitation of Maxwell's Plum, a bar and restaurant in New York. Before that, it was the site of Mr. Kelly's, a legendary nightclub, which once presented the finest comics, including Woody Allen, Dick Gregory, and Mort Sahl.

Next walk a very, very short block west (left) on Bellevue, cross State Street and enter Arnie's, in the Newberry Plaza at 1030 North State. It is to the left of the lobby just beyond the entrance to the garage. Arnie's is owned by Arnie Morton, one of Chicago's great restaurateurs, who is now often referred to as the father of the man who owns the Hard Rock Cafe (see Ontario Restaurant walk).

This is an art deco bar and restaurant with an elegant, white baby grand piano at the end of the bar for the pianist or combo. The bar, with its low light and ceiling, is a friendly place usually populated by folks who dress well and can afford the best. The restaurant specializes in a standing rib roast of lamb.

Just north of Arnie's is Dublin's Pub, a bar that claims to be "a touch of Ireland in Chicago." Here, the Gate of Horn nightclub once stood. On December 5, 1962, Chicago police arrested comic Lenny Bruce for giving a "lewd and obscene" performance there. He was saying very bad words and performing anti-Catholic jokes in a strongly Catholic town, something not protected by the First Amendment in Chicago at the time. Bruce was sentenced to two years in prison and given a $1,000 fine in March 1963. The conviction was reversed in 1965, shortly before Bruce died.

Morton's Steak House

Walk slightly north (to your left as you leave the lobby) and enter the next revolving door. Morton's Steak House is downstairs. The pictures on the wall serve as proof that Frank Sinatra, Richard Burton, Arnold Schwarzenegger, Sean Connery, Roger Moore, Jackie Gleason, Bob Hope, Dinah Shore, Don Johnson, Robert Duvall, Liza Minelli, Oprah Winfrey, Dick Butkus, Dennis Hopper, Denver Bronco quarterback John Elway, sportscaster John Madden, and singer Jeffrey Osborne have eaten there.

It has been estimated that almost 22,000, 24-ounce, $28.95 porterhouse steaks, the most popular cut, have been sold here since the restaurant opened in 1980. That steak arrives with a hand-picked baked potato that must weigh at least one pound.

Morton's has won the *Travel-Holiday Magazine* fine dining award every year since 1980. *People Magazine* and *U. S. A. Today* have both called it the best steakhouse in America, and, in 1991, the *Chicago Tribune* said it served the best steak in Chicago.

Ready to serve another famous Morton's steak

Arnie Morton, a third-generation restaurateur (his son, the owner of the Hard Rock chain, is the fourth generation) opened a restaurant in 1956, became a vice president of *Playboy* in 1959, went back to restaurant ownership in 1973, and sold Morton's of Chicago to the Quantum Restaurant Group in 1989. There are now 20 Morton's of Chicago.

Memories of China is on the second floor. There are posh red couches at the entrance to this Szechwan, Hunan, and Mandarin restaurant, which surrounds an atrium with tropical trees and plants.

It is a place of quiet repose. Be sure to order one of the soongs, which is chopped chicken, lobster, or shrimp wrapped in lettuce leaves. It has been said that the Peking duck, which requires no advance notice before ordering, tastes better here than it does in China.

Continue to Crawl

Next, leave through the revolving doors on street level, and cross Maple. At one time Pat Haran's was at 12 West Maple, a bar with a sign boasting "bad booze, bum food, rotten service, great seating." Maybe that's what closed the place! The building lists toward the lake, the result of the ground settling.

The basement at 16 West Maple, a building built by a cattle baron in 1891, is called the Smiling Fish Bar and Grill and has a relaxed and fun atmosphere with fish sandwiches, clam chowder, and low prices. The Waterfront, on the second floor of the same building, has an outdoor sign proclaiming that here is "Chicago's finest clam chowder," something attested to in a *Chicago Sun-Times* article. They sell around 10 gallons of clam chowder a day here and you can purchase it to go.

Return to State. On the corner, you will find Jimo's, a large restaurant/bar with live jazz on the weekends and a very relaxed feel. It caters to younger, vaguely hip people.

Take a left on State Street, and walk to Melvin B's, at 1114 North State. In the six years prior to 1992, this location changed owners five times and was known as Melvin's, Kenny's Ribs, Tore Del Greco, Thumbs Up, and, hopefully and finally, Melvin B's. The "B" stands for Jack Binyon, of the restaurant-owning Binyon clan. That is why Binyon's turtle soup is on the menu of an eatery called Melvin B's.

The manager, Jeffrey Kalish, once made up a relish plate for his parents when they visited the restaurant, and that's why if you order a Kalish here, you'll get a relish plate.

This is the best spot to sit outdoors and watch the parade of Near North Side crazies. You may see a one-man band, or a man in a cheap hula skirt passing out advertising pamphlets, or hear a kazoo concert, or watch the local bums and madmen passing by. This restaurant intends to challenge all other eateries in Chicago for the title of best local ribs.

Continue walking north, passing the McDonald's, a discount CD store, and an always very busy cash station.

If you take a left on Elm and walk a few hundred feet west, you'll arrive at the Hangge-Uppe, with four bars, two dance floors, and a collection of 10,000 hit songs.

There is a love story here. Fred Venrick, one of the owners, fell for a pretty waitress at the Lodge, a bar you'll find a little later in this walk. Catherine O'Connell eventually became the first manager of yet another tavern owned by Fred, which she left because it became too uncomfortable dating the boss. They were married, Catherine sold wines, but dreamed of writing a novel. Fred said he'd support her as she chased her dream. After starting to write "at least" 50 novels, Mrs. Venrick was finally successful with *Skins*, a murder mystery published in 1992. Venrick said, "I'm involved in owning six nightclubs in this area, but my wife's selling of that book is the light of my life."

Meanwhile, the Hangge-Uppe is a friendly, somewhat loud bar, a place to go and consider the story of the manager who loved a waitress and how they both helped create a novel.

Returning to State Street, take a left at Ristorante Zio, at 1148 North State, which is located in a former ice-cream parlor. It remains a bright, well-lit, clean place, which is now an Italian restaurant. Walk north toward the stoplight.

The Singles Bars

We have now returned to Division and State. By taking a left at the Mrs. Field's Cookies and heading west, we will plunge into a large collection of singles bars. Look around. Notice how the energy of the area has changed, as young men look at the passing young ladies, and both sexes wonder who will get lucky tonight.

It has been claimed that the largest New Year's Eve party in the world takes place in and around this street. According to Marty Gutilla, co-owner of Eddie Rockets, P. S. Chicago, and P.O.E.T.S., "where else can you find a party, that when you put it all together has 12 men's rooms, 12 ladies rooms, and more than 480 bar staff?"

Down a flight of stairs at 5 West Division is P.O.E.T.S. (Piss On Everything Tomorrow's Saturday). The *Chicago Tribune* described this dance club as "Twin Peaks" meets *Saturday Night Fever*.

The place retains its charm from the disco days of the late 1970s, yet doesn't play disco music. It still has "hot legs" contests on Wednesday nights, and drink specials every night. It is a big open room, which seems built for a packed house, and with anything less seems empty. At one time television sets replayed the highlights of recent hot buns, bikini, swim suit, and hot leg contests. Perhaps the notion that your image would be shown after you married and became a grandmother helped end that practice. There is a mirrored dance floor, ladies drink free Sunday through Thursday, and actor Tom Cruise once had a drink here nearly a decade ago.

Upstairs at 9 West Division is Eddie Rockets, one of the few true meat-markets left on the street. (Er . . . make that meet-markets.) It is a three-tiered, glitz palace with a hi-tech sound-and-light system custom designed for the room in 1986, at a cost of $2.5 million, stainless steel tables, and old-fashioned disco strobe lights. Eddie Rockets also has hot legs and bikini contests, and manager Will Shears explained that these contests are rarely entered by party-crazed bar patrons, but rather by women who make the rounds of all the Chicago-area bars with such contests, and do so for a living.

Condoms Now

Continue west, but only go 20 feet or so and you'll find Condoms Now, at 11 West Division, which sells 5,000 to 7,000 contraceptives on a typical weekend. It has a nearly perfect location, in the very heart of Chicago's intense (nay, sometimes frantic) singles area. Yet, 42nd ward Alderman Burton F. Natarus (see Gold Coast walk) said, "I have neighbors who complain about these things and they don't like to look at the word condom out there. They find it distasteful. I have to admit, the sign does bother me, too."

The co-owner, Steven Grubart, who also runs two women's shoe stores, has asked, "Now we're in trouble because people find the word 'condom' distasteful? I'm not sure I'm believing this."

The alderman has suggested that the location be termed a "Safe Health Products Store," but Grubart feared that patrons would then believe that he was selling vitamins.

If the name is still Condoms Now, you be the judge. Offensive? Or an attempt to remove the stigma from AIDS prevention? And remember: nothing—absolutely nothing—happens in Chicago without controversy.

The owners hope to reach younger people who may not be using condoms because they are embarrassed to go to the store and buy them. This store was designed to be relaxed, friendly, and comfortable. Hoffman said that they are open until 4 a.m. on Friday and Saturday, but there are always exceptions.

One night, a guy pounded on the window at 4:30 a.m. saying he just met a woman and she was waiting in a cab out front and he really needed to get some condoms. That night they re-opened at 4:30.

More Bars

Bootleggers, at 11 West Division, is a long, dark, heavily wooded singles bar with throbbing music and goofy drinks named blue kamikaze, red lobsters, and hot pink watermelons. Because it was modeled after a Chicago speakeasy, the Rob Lowe film, *About Last Night*, was filmed in part here, although it was named "Muther's" in the movie and a basketball free-throw cage was constructed (and later torn down). This place is currently famous for its "screaming orgasms," a mixture of Bailey's, amaretto, and Vodka, served as a shot for $2.

At 15 West Division is the Alumni Club, a two-story bar decorated with pennants, football helmets, photos of college and pro sports heroes in silly old costumes, and old instruments. Only open since 1991, the Alumni Club features a Blue Skies Party on Thursdays for flight attendants and pilots.

The second floor has a dance area from which you can either see all of Division Street or have all of Division Street see you. The manager says more people like to be seen than to see.

Like almost every bar I ventured into, the folks there said it was really more of a neighborhood bar during the week. Weekends brought the crowds of college kids, suburbanites, and conventioneers. I was there one night during the week when the crowd looked like the folks who were regulars when it was still the Snuggery, certified by *Playboy* magazine in 1984 as the best singles bar in the country. Ah, Division Street.

In the '30s, it was called the North Star Inn, a joint Al Capone and his cronies enjoyed. They probably did not go up to someone of the opposite sex and ask, "What is your sign?"

A sign at The Lodge, at 21 West Division, claims that here is "Chicago's longest cocktail hour, greatest juke box, old time peanuts, and other assorted nuts." Since it started in 1957, it has given away more than 637,000 pounds of those peanuts. And most of the shells went on the floor.

The Lodge has a replica of a 1951 Wurlitzer jukebox. According to Jim Borchers, managing partner of The Lodge, the top ten songs here include Frank Sinatra's "My Kind of Town," the Righteous Brothers "You've Lost that Lovin' Feelin'," and Sinatra's "Summer Wind." The number one song for the last decade has been "Paradise by the Dashboard Light" by Meat Loaf.

As you can tell from the song selections, The Lodge definitely caters to an older crowd, over age 25, possibly because it reminds them of the bars around their college campuses. On February 24, 1992, The Lodge celebrated its 35th anniversary, making it nearly prehistoric in terms of the life expectancy of most taverns. One patron, identified only as Andy Y., said he has been a regular here for 23 years because "I'm a lazy bar-hopper." He keeps coming back despite the fact that "none of the girls here have fallen in love with me."

If you walk toward the back to the corridor called the Bull Pen, you'll see a framed picture declaring Kim Kohls as the winner of Chicago's fastest bartender contest on July 20, 1989. Kim, a pert blond, who sometimes makes drinks in the Bull Pen, then served 25 drinks in 3 minutes and 11 seconds, and won 21 cases of beer. Her friends almost immediately drank her prize in celebration.

The Lodge has, according to Dennis McCarthy's *The Great Chicago Bar & Saloon Guide*, "a drink-that-draft-beer-and-be-rowdy atmosphere." Dennis, who is probably unwise in allowing this sort of thing to happen to his lady friends, once experimented by sending a woman acquaintance alone into The Lodge before he entered. Within two minutes, she was surrounded by eight guys and "their various hustles were as rapid and multiple as you would expect from the street beggars of Calcutta."

The owner, Paul Risolia, once tossed Jonathan Winters out for playing the piano.

Pizza and Beer 'til 4 a.m.

Leaving The Lodge, take a left and continue west to Dearborn, where you will take another left. 1161 North Dearborn is the home of Ranalli's Late Night, where you can get pizza and beer until 4 a.m. (They deliver their full menu and their kitchen is open until 3 a.m.)

At the corner of Dearborn and Elm, there is Ranalli's, a two-story sports bar and grill with outdoor seating on a second-floor balcony that's slightly away from the Division Street noise. If you succeed in drinking each of the 100 beers served here, you can join the Round the World Beer Club. That entitles you to join the 902 other people who qualified for a pewter mug displayed in the entranceway with their name on it, a case of your favorite beer, and a $25 gift certificate.

O'Leary's, at 1157 North Dearborn, is an Irish pub with a real dart board (no magnets or Velcro here). This is one of the smaller bars in the area and, as a result, has a very cozy atmosphere complete with oil paintings, antique-looking mugs, violins decorating the walls, and lots of wood. Since it is nearly hidden, most of the weekend crowd misses it. Being here for 25 years makes it a genuine, neighborhood bar.

Cross Dearborn and enter Biggs, 1150 North Dearborn, a marvelous continental restaurant in the John DeKoven mansion, built in 1874. Biggs retains DeKoven's original woodwork, mirrors, and charm.

Most romantic restaurant: Toulouse. On the left, Bob Djahanguiri, owner of
Toulouse, Yvette's, and Yvette's Wintergarden

Return to Division, one block to the north, then take a left and walk
a few feet to the west.

The most romantic restaurant in Chicago, according to *Esquire* magazine, is Toulouse at 49 West Division. The piano bar is host to the finest
of singers and pianists Monday through Saturday, with no cover charge.
The French food is excellent, the wine list is outstanding. It is a small,
intimate place where my wife and I have often celebrated her birthday
and confirmed that *Esquire* was absolutely correct in its assessment.

Retrace your steps, returning to Dearborn and cross Division Street.
Houlihan's Bar and Restaurant, which was once on this corner, entered
the *Guinness Book of World Records* in 1985 for having the world's largest
St. Patrick's Day party. Actually, the 205,854 people squeezed into the
40 Houlihan's around America, but apparently they didn't stay long
enough to insure the Chicago Houlihan's continued existence on this
corner.

A Famous Bar

Downstairs at the Original Mothers, at 26 West Division, is a place mom
may not enjoy. It is a basement, Top-40 music joint, the largest nightspot
on Division Street, and it offers an annual lip sync contest (the owners

claim to be the first in the country with that), and the Thursday Cash Capsule contest (a lady grabs as much money as she can while inside a blower machine containing $5,000). The hot leg contests for the woman with the shortest shorts have been discontinued here.

Bato Prostran, the bartender, said that standing on Division checking identification cards is "the purest form of entertainment I have ever seen. Guys come by thinking they are God's gift to women, women think the same thing, and everyone is looking for Mr. Right." The co-owner, Steve Greer, called Mother's "a warped Disneyland with everything you want and don't want rolled up into one."

Not everyone finds Mr. or Ms. Right. Comic Robin Williams once came here to play pinball by himself all night. Nobody bothered him.

Mother's, which opened in 1968, was seen in the film *Class*, with Jacqueline Bisset, Andrew McCarthy, and Rob Lowe, the story of a guy who falls in love with his roommate's mother. The moviemakers thought that the audience would believe that Mother's was a place for people to pick up mommies, so the bar's name was changed to the Free and Easy in the movie. Also parts of *About Last Night*, a movie that starred Rob Lowe and Demi Moore, were filmed outside Mother's. Rob Lowe actually got paid at least twice to be near the place and returned as a customer with actor Andrew McCarthy when neither were being paid.

After a visit, Jae-Ha Kim wrote in the *Chicago Sun-Times*, "There were a lot of men in the club, but many seemed to regard dancing as a spectator sport. They seemed perfectly content sitting on their stools, watching woman dance solo. The only time they got up was when the P.A. system announced there was a fight in the men's room."

The First Singles Bar

Butch McGuire's, at 20 West Division, owns the distinction of being America's first singles bar. In 1961, Robert Emmet "Butch" McGuire first opened a bar specifically designed to encourage somewhat casual sexual encounters. On September 12, 1991, Butch McGuire was inducted into the Bartenders Hall of Fame (which, I must admit, I never knew existed) during the first Chicago Bartenders' Ball for the following civilization-altering achievements: Opening the nation's first singles bar, being the first person to put a stalk of celery in a Bloody Mary, and inventing the Harvey Wallbanger. Legend has it, McGuire was playing volleyball in Southern California with someone named Harvey when the concoction was created. Harvey drank six of them and was soon bouncing off the walls.

McGuire, who boxed and played football at the University of Michigan while pursuing a degree in architectural engineering, has mainly drunk water and hot tea since his heart attack in 1983. His secret ambition is to open a bar in Bangkok where he won't have the 18 competitors he has on Division Street.

She-Nannigans, next door at 16 West Division, claims to be Chicago's oldest sports bar, with 14 TV monitors. Its two satellite dishes allow people from out-of-town to come here to watch their home teams in action. It also has a bartender named Moose and sells sweatshirts with naughty messages on them.

Eva Marie Saint shot baskets in the freethrow cage at She-Nannigans in the film *Nothing in Common*. She was playing Tom Hanks' mother who had broken up with his father, played by Jackie Gleason.

Mothers Too, at 26 West Division, is not affiliated with the Original Mothers. The owner, Pera Odishoo, who is known as Perry Orr, was the recipient of many noise complaints when he owned two other now-closed bars.

Again moving to the east, you'll arrive at State Street. Turning left on State will bring you to P. J. Clarks at 1204 North State, based on the famous Manhattan bar of the same name. The crowd here is older and professional.

Return to Division Street, which you will cross, heading east. The Hotsie Totsie Yacht Club and Bait Shop, at 8 East Division, doesn't sell minnows. Gary DeAngelis, the owner, is friendly, gregarious, and will do everything in his power to make the customer feel at home. This is a bar where over-30 regulars walk in, and are greeted by name and with their regular drink.

Quit Crawling

This ends the Rush-Division bar crawl. If you took this walk with the intention of finding Mr. or Ms. Right for the evening, I leave you with some wise advice: A caller to one of my radio shows once said that, when cruising Rush and Division Streets, or any other singles bar area in the world, "Go ugly early." He meant that the least attractive of people should be singled out early in the evening for special attention.

On the other hand, perhaps the best approach to succeeding in the often wild and cruel Division Street singles scene is to ask a variety of people there for advice on how to succeed. The worst-case scenario for that approach would be that you could turn their responses into a movie, film it on Division, and then buy your own singles bar.

19 ONTARIO RESTAURANT WALK

Streets of food

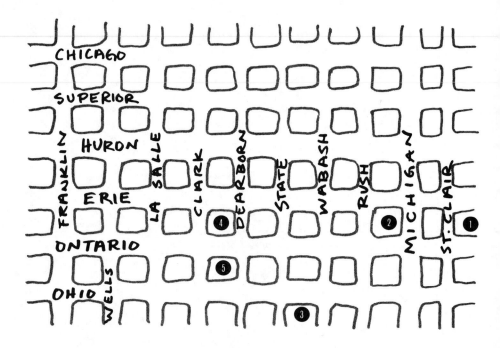

1. Richmont Hotel
2. Lawry's
3. Pizzeria Uno
4. Excalibur
5. Hard Rock Cafe

Time: An evening or a lifetime, depending on how much the walk affects your future.

To get there: The CTA buses #11 and #151 and the express buses #125, #145, #146, and #147 all stop at Michigan and Ontario.

If you drive: Many restaurants have lots adjoining them, but you should spend some money dining to qualify for the space.

Great Restaurants (with Parking)

If you drink and eat at each restaurant on this tour, you will have tried as many as 30 establishments, your stomach will have given up all hope of ever digesting anything again, and your nose may be numb.

So pace yourself. Merely look in some bars, drink at others, eat at a few, avoid any place with a long line or snooty doormen unless this book says it is worthwhile, and then only wait 10 minutes to be seated.

This is one of the rare east-west walks in this book. The Ontario Street restaurant strip wasn't zoned or planned that way, it just happened, meaning that sometimes there are traffic jams along Ontario for no reason at all.

And yet this is the one walk inside the city where you are guaranteed to meet Young Urban Professionals—Yuppies. Chicago, being a blue collar, gritty kind of town, tends to send its yuppies out to the suburbs, where they congregate in large groups at tennis clubs, which encourage them to donate their used balls to the poor—a practice I thought sure to cause the next urban riot.

The street combines superior and/or entertaining restaurants with an urban rarity: Lots of parking spaces. The *Chicago Tribune* noted, "Ontario, which leads west directly into the Kennedy and Dan Ryan Expressways, is the world's longest on-ramp or something close to it, and Ohio Street, one block south, is the comparable off-ramp. From anywhere in the suburbs, you can get to Ontario along the expressway network and never have to put up with city traffic, or even parallel park."

East of Michigan

We begin at Ontario and Michigan. Walk about a block and a half east to the Moosehead Bar & Grill, 240 East Ontario, a funky, below-street-level joint with terrific big band, swing and contemporary jazz four nights a week, 105 different beers, pizza, and a mooseburger, which is a popular hamburger with no moose in it. Within one year's time, if you are able to taste all the brands of beer for sale at the Moosehead, you can join the Hall of Foam, pun intended.

The decor constantly changes as various items are rearranged and new antique signs are hung on the walls. The redecorating is generally done on Saturday.

Exit the Moosehead and begin to return to Michigan Avenue. One block west is the Richmont Hotel, with its 191 remodeled rooms, and its Rue Saint Clair "an American bistro." The best buy here is the luncheon in the charming outdoor cafe where hamburgers are $6.25. Do notice that Rue Saint Clair is on St. Clair street. The restaurant spells out every letter, the street does not. The restaurant probably had more room on its signs.

Perhaps you feel like watching the passing scene for a few moments while drinking a good American chardonnay. Perhaps not. I have often walked down St. Clair and can't find a single reason to sit in an outdoor cafe and contemplate this nondescript street. Therefore, let us move resolutely to the west, toward Michigan Avenue. Walk by Hatsuhana, 160 East Ontario, (unless you want sushi or Japanese wine) and head on to Bice, 158 East Ontario.

Bice was formerly Charlie Chaing's, and before that it was a Spanish restaurant, Maison De Lago. Spanish to Chinese to Italian—only the address remains the same.

A manager claimed that Bice is "a clubhouse for the jet setters" and added, "We say this is the cheapest trip to Italy. Not that the restaurant is cheap, it's just that going here, with our Italian chef, is less expensive than a plane ticket."

Sidewalk sophistication at Bice

It has attracted more than its share of celebrities. Tom Selleck ate lunch at the sidewalk cafe every day for three weeks, Michael Jordan had an anniversary party here. Other diners have included Jim Belushi, Robert De Niro, Kurt Russell, Dustin Hoffman, Eric Clapton, and Robert Loggia, who insisted we dine at Bice.

Do not look for the hugely famous, they will be spirited to a back room where Madonna and Tom Hanks had an argument during the filming of *A League of Their Own.*

We next walk a few feet to Howard's Bar and Grill, 152 East Ontario. This bar and restaurant is exactly 12 feet wide so you are assured of being close to whomever is there. At one time, Howard Jones, the owner, served only one beer on tap, Leinenkugel, from Chippewa Falls, Wisconsin "because it's so good." Now you can get one other beer on tap, but Leinenkugel is still the most popular. Walk through to the back, into the patio, where various media types can often be found unwinding after a tough day.

A few feet to the west is Shuckers, 150 East Ontario, a quiet seafood restaurant with excellent clam chowder and jumbo shrimp. The second level has one room with fishing trophies on the wall and another with back-lit, stained-glass windows. This structure began as the home of Robert McCormick, the late publisher of the *Chicago Tribune*, and later became Tommy O'Leary's, the first key club in America.

Continuing to Michigan Avenue, in the lower level of the 625 North Michigan building there is the Hunan Cafe, owned by George Kuan, who also owns the nearby House of Hunan on Michigan Avenue. It is a beautiful, classy, quiet Oriental restaurant. I'd recommend the stuffed crab claws, the greaseless potato croquettes, the Szechwan duck, or the bon bon chicken in peanut sauce.

West of Michigan

Tarry there if you wish, or continue to the west. Do visit Lawry's, which was once the Kungsholm, a Danish restaurant and home of a famed puppet opera. The bar features a grand, curving staircase leading to the restrooms above. Look at the ornate decorations, consider having one of Lawry's famous spinning salad bowls (yes, the restaurant is owned by the people whose ancestors created Lawry's spices), or go all out and have a prime rib in either the English ($19.95), Lawry ($21.95), or Chicago ($24.95) cuts.

If you take a right on Rush Street and walk a very short block, you will arrive at Chez Paul, 660 North Rush. There were tunnels connecting Lawry's and Chez Paul at one time because both were homes belonging to the McCormick family, whose wealth was created by reapers (farm implements).

The Chez Paul building was built in 1875 as a mansion for Robert Hall McCormick, who was once the ambassador to Italy and who used this stately home as his ambassador's residence to entertain princes, dukes, and the elite.

The relatively new outdoor cafe features $6.25 hamburgers, but walk inside, where the original marble stairs are now carpeted, where two marble pillars have brass bands around them because they were splintered in a fire decades ago, and where other marble columns are from the Italian Exhibit of the 1893 Columbian Exposition.

The dining rooms have a sense of quiet elegance and there is a cozy bar toward the back.

Onward on Ontario

Return to Ontario and cross to the south side of the street. Ohba, at the corner of Rush and Ontario, is a fine Japanese restaurant and, around the corner to the south, you'll see Moe's Deli with one of the smallest outdoor cafes in town.

Continuing slightly west on Ontario, the Andrews Restaurant was formerly the Lenox Restaurant. If you look in the window, you'll see a review indicating that as the Lenox this restaurant once had the second best Reuben sandwich in town. Despite the name change, the review is still displayed perhaps on the theory that location is more important than nomenclature.

Once again moving west, stop at Su Casa, one of my favorite Mexican restaurants, at 49 East Ontario. There is something about the dark interior, the comfortable chairs, the strolling guitarists, the cozy bar, and the very good, salty margaritas that welcome a stranger to this restaurant.

If you walk to the corner, you will see Pizzeria Due. One block to the south, there is Uno's. Both will have waiting lines, although I sometimes like to avoid the lines by dashing into Due's and buying a frozen pizza.

Chicago's thick-crust, oozing in cheese, utterly distinctive pizzas were created here, the city's gift to the world. These pizzas are the best, revered by pizza lovers, blessed by anyone who has been away from Chicago for a long time and has had to suffer through out-of-town imitations. The pizzas weigh between four and five pounds, yet the crust is miraculously crunchy. Frankly, you have not visited Chicago and you do not know this city until you have had an Uno's or Due's Pizza (I do not distinguish between them, both are excellent).

The deep-dish pizza was allegedly created by Ike Sewell, a cattle-roper, circus manager, and vice president of Fleischmann Distillers. There are now more than 100 Uno restaurants nationwide. Americans eat about 100 acres of pizza per day.

By the way, Due's is in the Saxet Building, which a plaque says is "one of Chicago's finest examples of Victorian architecture."

Across the street from Due's, you will see the Moorish, outrageously overdone Medinah Temple just to the west. It has a stage big enough to accommodate elephants and trapeze artists during the Shrine Circus performances each spring.

But continue to walk west, to the rear of the temple, where you will see the entrance to the Tree Studios Building just east of State Street at 5 East State. It is one of Chicago's secret places, an L-shaped garden in the midst of the hullabaloo of the city, with vines growing on the wall of the temple and artists' studios facing the flowers and trees.

This is private property, and a door now completely blocks any view of the garden.

In the 1920s, this was the center for artists who embraced abstraction-ism, cubism, and post-impressionism as opposed to sculptor Lorado Taft and the traditionalists housed in the Fine Arts Building. The rebel artists' motto was "No Jury Means Freedom," and they hosted the No Jury Ball and Exhibit. One dawn, artist Rudolph Weisenborn, president of the group and a man whose painting hangs in Riccardo's Restaurant today (see Mid-Michigan Avenue walk), was routed out of bed by two Chicago detectives. They were rounding up "anarchists" and people who were against juries. Weisenborn was only released after he revealed that the No Jury art group also exhibited in Marshall Field & Co.

When you are at State and Ontario, on one corner you will see Bukhara, an Indian restaurant with terrific smorgasbords. Papagus Tav-ern, a Greek restaurant, is diagonally across the street. The restaurant serves something called patatosalata, soft potato salad laced with olive oil, perfect *after* you end your next diet.

Continuing west on Ontario we arrive at Excalibur, formerly the Limelight, a nightclub with 55,000 square feet of space because it is in a nineteenth-century mansion (called the Castle), which once housed the Chicago Historical Society.

This is the site of one of the biggest late-night errors in local history. The Chicago Limelight opened in July 1985, and too many people were invited. The doormen didn't recognize some of the guests who believed they were invited just to create an anxious crowd at the door. Once inside, they found bedlam and the Limelight (instantly nicknamed "Slimelight") got bad press. It never recovered.

The Excalibur, hoping not to repeat past mistakes, features two pool halls and as many as three live bands at once. And I've never been comfortable in this space.

The Chicago Chop House, which seats 228 people on three floors, is next door at 60 West Ontario. According to owner Henry Norton, this restaurant has 1,433 photographs, more historic Chicago pictures than "any place in Chicago, including City Hall and maybe even the Historical Society." There are pictures of every mayor, plus Chicago's famous gangsters and business tycoons. The Chicago Chop House sells a 64-ounce T-bone steak.

If you look to your left as you enter, you'll see the framed award from the Knife and Fork Club naming the Chicago Chop House as the second best steak house in America in 1992. After years as a restaurateur and advertising executive, Norton may be the most truthful bar owner in America. When I asked him what the Knife and Fork Club was, he said, "Be damned if I know. Some guy named Jack Roach owns it. I asked him who pays for the club, figuring it must be some beef group, and he said, 'No one. I got a rich wife.'"

About the popular Chop House, Norton said, "I got a great chef, good managers in front and in back. So I do the accounts and play golf three days a week. This is my retirement and it's a hell of a retirement."

Hard Rock Cafe

Next, cross the street and try to get into the Hard Rock Cafe, which always seems to have a waiting line. Walk under the neon sign saying, "No guns, drugs or nuclear weapons allowed on the premises."

This is the sixth Hard Rock, and it opened on June 27, 1986, with Robert Palmer singing "Addicted to Love" to hundreds of guests in the restaurant and under a tent erected in the parking lot.

Hard Rock Cafe: "Addicted to food"

The owner is Peter Morton, son of Arnie Morton, who owns many restaurants in Chicago. Peter is also the grandson of a Chicago bootlegger and the great-grandson of an Iron Mountain, Michigan, saloon keeper. When I asked Arnie, the father, if he was proud of his son on the night the Hard Rock opened, he said, "He's still basically a saloon keeper."

The Hard Rock and the 540 North Dearborn post office are on land once owned by the American Medical Association. The Embassy Suites Hotel at 600 North State Street is on land leased from the AMA, which also owns three parking lots in this area. The AMA's influence has helped guarantee that this is a street of restaurants rather than bars or honky tonks.

The Chicago Hard Rock cost $3.5 million to build and is supposed to resemble a rich teenaged rock music fan's bedroom, according to Peter.

As you enter, Mick Fleetwood's drums are behind you, over the door. Indiana Jones' leather jacket hangs on one wall toward the back (director Steven Spielberg is an investor) with a leather jacket belonging to the Fonz on another wall. George Harrison's original Beatles' uniform is also there. Michael Jackson's platinum records are to the right on the back wall and Madonna's "Like a Virgin" platinum records are on the second-floor balcony area. The walls are festooned with David Bowie's saxophone, plus guitars belonging to Eric Clapton, Bo Diddley, Santana, the Everly brothers, and Mötley Crüe. One corner is devoted to the Rolling Stones, with Mick Jagger's and Keith Richards' guitars.

The Los Angeles Hard Rock is famous for its 1959 lime green Cadillac sticking out of its front facade. Chicago's Hard Rock has a huge electric sign in the form of a guitar in front.

McDonald's!

Leaving the Hard Rock's rock 'n' roll museum, head west once again, cross Clark Street, and enter the world's most unusual McDonald's. In fact, if you wish to save money, avoid the crowds, and still see great rock memorabilia, go directly to the McDonald's across the street.

A perfect 1959 Corvette convertible is parked in the window and there is an old jukebox with '50s and '60s tunes (where else can you go in midafternoon to hear Chuck Berry or Dion and the Belmonts?). Life-sized statues of the Beatles dressed in Nehru jackets seem to walk in their glass case. There are framed pictures of Elvis, James Dean, John Lennon, and Marilyn Monroe. This McDonald's was the busiest in the world until the McDonald's in Moscow opened.

You are inside a pioneer. When the rock 'n' roll McDonald's opened on June 29, 1983, this entire area was deserted and even dangerous at

Rock 'n' Roll McDonald's: Life-sized Beatles' statues

night. Then-owner Angelo Lencioni, who has since sold the restaurant to the McDonalds' chain, saw "a little pocket (of property) with nothing happening to it. It was relatively inexpensive property near Rush Street and Michigan Avenue." The rock 'n' roll McDonald's was first, the Hard Rock and Ed Debevic's followed.

Both the rock 'n' roll McDonald's and the Hard Rock will have even more competition if Planet Hollywood, with investors like Arnold Schwarzenegger, Bruce Willis, and Sylvester Stallone, opens just west of here at Ontario near Wells.

Continue West

Moving to the west, you'll pass a nine-floor sports store with continual ski and tennis racket sales. You can also get baci balls (the lawn bowling game beloved by Italians) here. Hand prints of local sports celebrities decorate the walls along the sidewalk. You can see if your hand is bigger or smaller than Ryne Sandberg's, Walter Payton's, Jim McMahon's, or Stan Mikita's.

Across the street, to the south, there is Carson's for Ribs, which did win a *Chicago* magazine contest for the best ribs in town. The ribs here are meaty and the sauce is superb, but I prefer the chicken. Both the ribs and the chicken are served with bibs. Don't be shy; wear the bib. You will need it.

The bar features large-screen television and free chopped liver appetizers. Be sure to try the sweet cream cheese appetizer because my photo is directly above the cheese bowl. Once inside the comfortable restaurant be sure to order the coleslaw, which I love, or the chunky-cheesy au gratin potatoes.

Return to Ontario and Wells. Ditka's was once just to the west at 223 West Ontario. Yes, it carried the name of Chicago Bears' coach Mike Ditka. And yes, the place opened August 3, 1986, while the Bears were playing the Dallas Cowboys in a London exhibition game. And yes, it was tackled for a loss and folded.

If you wish to return to your '50s mood, cross Wells Street and enter Ed Debevic's, 640 North Wells. Thousands of dollars were spent by the Lettuce Entertain You group to re-create the high school hangout of your youth, if you are in your late thirties to fifties. Ed Debevic is fictional, but the restaurant, designed by Spiros Zakas and opened in 1984, is based on a real greasy spoon built in Atlanta in the '50s.

There are quaint slogans on the walls: "If you can find a better diner, eat there." "One at a time. The hostess has only one set of nerves." "Ed's

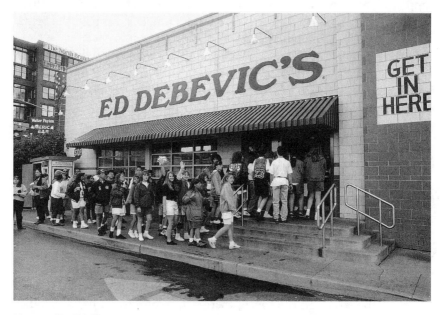

Hungry for Ed Debevic's

chili dog—the Cadillac of chili dogs." And, my favorite, "If you think you have reservations, you're in the wrong place."

You will quickly notice the gum chewing, wise-cracking waitresses and waiters, with white uniforms festooned with sloganeering buttons. The waitresses, especially, seem to audition for their roles, and many of them sport black bras under their white uniforms, slips just a tad too long for the skirts, and black-rooted blond hair.

The food here is good AND inexpensive, even though if you ask any of the help they will joyfully tell you the food is "terrible." And this is one place where you can ignore your parents' admonitions never to eat meatloaf in a restaurant and enjoy the best meatloaf in town.

Once you get inside (there is often a line), the service is fast and good, the food is excellent, and Ed Debevic's own beer is watery, but cold.

Next, walk north on Wells Street one block to Erie. Turn right and enter the Eccentric, at 159 West Erie. A sign to the left of the door advises "Visit Oprah's souvenir store," because Oprah Winfrey is an investor in this restaurant, which opened in February 1989.

To answer the most frequently asked question, I am told she actually visits the establishment every few weeks. Her fiancé, Stedman Graham, dines here two or three times a week, pays the check, and tips well. Madonna and opera star Placido Domingo have eaten here. One critic, Pat Bruno of the *Chicago Sun-Times*, suggested that the restaurant put up a sign saying "Oprah is here" or "Oprah isn't here," something the restaurant has not accepted.

Do not miss Oprah's potatoes—they're delicious. The secret of their taste, I am told, is horseradish.

This ends the Ontario east-west, yuppie bar and restaurant crawl. If you have visited and sampled each place on this walk, it is time to go home and rest. You have done enough for one night.

20 GREEKTOWN PUB CRAWL

How to "Opaa" all night

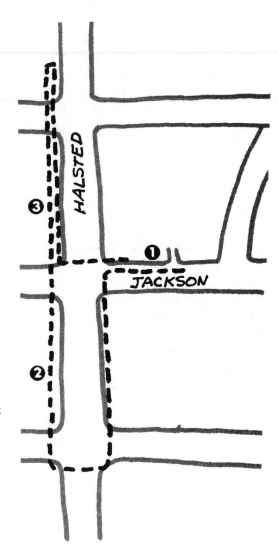

1. Greek Islands Restaurant
2. Parthenon Restaurant
3. Dianna's Opaa Restaurant

Time: All evening. Schedule at least 4 hours.

To get there: Drive or take a cab to Jackson and Halsted, which is just south and west of the loop. Many of the restaurants have nearby parking lots and, except on Saturday nights, it's usually easy to find a place to park. Via public transportation, the buses to Union Station will take you within two blocks of Greektown, and these include the #15, #38, #60, #121, #125, #128, #151, #156, and #157 buses. The #126 stops at Jackson and Halsted.

Changing West Side Neighborhood

By the end of this pub crawl, you will talk like Zorba the Greek, walk at a 45-degree angle, and maniacally yell, "Opaa" every 30 seconds or so. Don't worry. Such behavior is perfectly normal after a tour of Greektown.

Greektown is an attempt to re-create cafe life in Greece within sight of Chicago's Loop. It is one of the city's most popular areas because it features inexpensive tasty food, friendly ethnic restaurants, and cheap wine.

It is a symbol of snatching a partial triumph out of a genuine tragedy.

A true ethnic neighborhood existed for generations just south of where you are now. Then the city put through the Congress Street Expressway, and later renamed it the Eisenhower Expressway. Still later, Chicago decided to plunk the University of Illinois Chicago Circle Campus on top of a neighborhood of Greeks and Italians.

There was a fight. Oh, was there a fight. In 1962, Florence Scala, a neighborhood resident, led a round-the-clock sit-in in the late Mayor Richard J. Daley's office, but it did no good.

She told Studs Terkel, "The bulldozers were there. They were tearing down the houses . . . and Victor Cambio of Conte de Savioa, that wonderful grocery that had foods from everywhere. The fragrance . . . tearing down the buildings of Hull House. There was a Japanese elm in that courtyard that came up to Miss Binford's window. . . ."

Anthony Koclanakis, once president of the local Greek businessmen's association, said, "All businessmen here are newcomers, maybe fifteen, twenty years in this area. The whole area got smaller after the university came here. There used to be many residences, many businesses, ten different coffee shops where old men played backgammon." The university came, many of the Greek people went away. Chicago lost a neighborhood, but gained an area with wonderful restaurants.

Courtyards of Plaka

Shaking off our momentary nostalgia for what was before 1965, let us stand at the corner of Jackson and Halsted. Walk to the south on Halsted one long block to Van Buren and the Courtyards of Plaka, 340 South Halsted, to begin our trek through the Grecian islands of Chicago.

The Plaka refers to an area in the old quarter of Athens, near the Acropolis. When you are inside this restaurant you are supposed to feel as if you are under a tent (made of wood slats, although the managers claim they are aluminum, probably to avoid fire inspectors) in a courtyard.

It is a fitting place to start a Greektown tour because this restaurant is quieter and more subdued than most of the street, with a pianist quietly playing Greek songs Wednesday through Sunday. The lilting Greek melodies are a perfect accompaniment to dinner.

If you are hungry, you might try the Athenian feast, with saganaki (more about that later), shrimp salad, spinach cheese pie, eggplant salad, Greek salad, roast leg of lamb, boned chicken in cream sauce (kotopita), moussaka (a potato, eggplant, ground beef and sauce dish), rice pilaf, vegetable, creme caramele, and coffee for $14.95 per person.

In 1992 Pat Bruno, the restaurant critic for the *Chicago Sun-Times*, wrote that Plaka had the best gyros, or thinly sliced lamb, in town. Perhaps that's because the dishes are prepared slightly differently here. The moussaka and many lamb dishes are made in individual crocks rather than baked in a big pan. The chef, Pericles Stergiopoulos, was praised in no less than *Gourmet* magazine.

Notice the paper tablecloths here. With the University of Illinois nearby, many patrons would scribble their homework on the cloth. Paper tablecloths both cut the washing bills and gave the students something they could take home if necessary. It is not known if any paper tablecloths were ever submitted to the professors as a final paper.

Linda Hamilton, who defeated Arnold Schwarzenegger in the first *Terminator* and who joined with him in the second, once quietly ate here with a party of six at a table near the wall behind the pianist.

If you are hungry, eat; if not, drink a little roditys, observe the relative peace and quiet, and then press onward, passing the Athens Grocery, at 324 South Halsted and the Panhellenic Pastry Shop, at 322 South Halsted, which features kataefe, a walnut and peanut concoction with honey oozing from it.

The Parthenon

A Greektown landmark, the brightly lit Parthenon is at 314 South Halsted. Order saganaki here. The owner, Chris Liakouras, who also owns the Courtyards of Plaka, claims that he invented this flaming cheese pie in 1968 when he put brandy on caseri cheese and discovered that it helped the taste, rather than destroying it. Ask for saganaki, yell "Opaa," and duck, because the brandy brandished by the waiter does flame.

Be sure to notice the picture in the window, captioned "We created flaming saganaki." The waiter's hair is on fire! The waiter is Mr. Liakouras, who remembers giving away gyros and saganaki when the restaurant opened in 1968 to introduce those dishes to Americans.

Liakouras says that today cafes in his homeland are imitating his discovery of flaming saganaki. He adds, "Our customers enter very sober, very nice. When they walk out, after drinking the wine, they are always smiling."

The brightly lit Parthenon has also ranked among the Top Ten Chicago restaurants in several judgings. What was once a two-page menu has been expanded to four pages. We particularly enjoyed the baked eggplant dish, which we had with spinach, rice, and other vegetables.

At the Parthenon: Chris Liakouras, co-owner, and his nephew, Peter Liakouras

Former comedian Dick Gregory broke one of his anti-Vietnam fasts here. Comic-actor Godfrey Cambridge ate here while on his diet, and basketball player Bill Walton ate here while his foot was hurt because he needed fresh fruit and vegetables. Jane Russell sat in a quiet corner, ate, and made 15 phone calls.

The prices here remain amazingly reasonable: The gyros is $3.95 for the small dish and $5.95 for the regular size, while the saganaki, which is the lightest and least salty in town, is only $3.10, flames included, an increase of 40 cents in the last five years.

Many Glasses Still to Drink

Continue north (we have many glasses of roditys to drink before we sleep), past the Neon Greek Village, 310 South Halsted, which continues the Greek nightclub tradition of belly dancing and food. A few feet later, you'll arrive at It's Greek to Me, in a former warehouse and pastry shop at 306 South Halsted. This is a bright and charming restaurant with a variety of dishes that are lightly spiced. When you are inside, you are supposed to have the feeling that you are on a Greek island with blue sky overhead.

I recommend the stuffed mushrooms with crabmeat and the arni exohiko, the lamb stuffed with artichokes, pine nuts, feta cheese, peas, and tomatoes.

If he's there, ask to talk to Victor Salafatinos, the rangy, outgoing son of the owner, Dennis. He's kind of easy to recognize because he stands 6 feet 8 inches and has a big smile. Victor has quite a tale to tell.

Until a very few years ago, after playing in Greek basketball leagues in America, he became a professional basketball player, playing forward for Dafni of Athens. He describes the enthusiastic Greek fans, "Riot police with shields and billy clubs surrounded the court. During my first game, the fans were so loud that the coach had to slap me three or four times to get my head into the game! Many times we'd have to sit with chairs over our heads to protect us from the bombardment of coins being tossed through the wire mesh which surrounded the court."

He had a marvelous time, living with other basketball players in a luxury apartment, playing every Wednesday and Saturday, and enjoying the celebrity life of a single Greek-American with lots of money in Athens.

It's Greek to Me with Victor Salafatinos, former Greek professional basketball player, on the right

However, he was detained before he left the country. After two years of ball playing, Victor had stayed too long. If your father is Greek and you overstay your visa, you might automatically become a Greek citizen and be liable to up to two years service in the Greek army. He was held by customs officials in a room without a doorknob, and his American passport was of no help to him. The people on the delayed plane flight were quite upset at him because it took some time to finally reason his way out of detention. To this day, his waiters and cooks can find themselves serving 18 and 22 months in the Greek army at the end of a visit to their homeland.

Despite that experience, part of Victor's heart remains in Athens. He reads the Greek newspapers daily, gets jealous, and thinks, "I should be there, helping my team."

Traditional Greek village cooking is the specialty here, with a chef from Greece who demands to do things the old-fashioned, and extremely tasteful, way. Do try the shrimp kabob—grilled barbecue shrimps rolled in a thin slice of bacon.

Victor's mother, Antia (or Angie), is of German ancestry, and she demands strict cleanliness. Waiters have been known to report for work and see Angie scrubbing the walls and floor of the kitchen. She has declared that, if she is going to take her friends to her restaurant, it better be spotless.

Look across the street where you might see a Thai restaurant. They're everywhere, they're everywhere.

Crossing Jackson, enter The Roditys, at 222 South Halsted. It features a huge mural of a harbor. Look at the stones embedded in the wall near that mural. They are about all that remain of the original decor when the place was redecorated in 1985.

The Roditys, once rather cold and sterile, is a warm friendly place today. The decor tends to make the restaurant feel expansive and open. This is a good place to order the family-style dinner with soup, saganaki, salad, gyros, a combination plate with moussaka, pastichio, dolmades, lamb, vegetables, wine, dessert, and coffee for $9.75 per person. Actor Jim Belushi and his family were once regular diners here.

Lamb is the specialty, in all its delicious and bargain-priced incarnations, including braised lamb, roast loin of lamb, roast leg of lamb, and lamb chops.

Dianna's Opaa

Dianna's Opaa, at 212 South Halsted, just north of The Roditys, is in a former nightclub, and some customers now eat on the stage. The circle of mirrors on the ceiling is a remnant of the room's more flamboyant days.

The saganaki is excellent here, as are the gyros and the taramasalada, a fish roe salad to be eaten with Greek bread. Order them all!

Dianna's *is* Petros Kogiones, the owner and a man determined to set a Guinness record for kissing women. At last count, he has kissed more than 2 million, although one customer claimed it was more than 4 million because one kiss with that customer's wife was worth 2 million kisses with anyone else's. It's the sort of discussion one has after a bottle of roditys.

If the feeling is right and the evening is particularly happy, Petros will dance with a full glass of wine on his head, put it down and drink it, picking it up with only his teeth. Later, everyone will dance around the tables.

Petros, one of five brothers and four sisters, is from the town of Nestani in Greece—a place that has sent many sons to Chicago to create restaurants. Swarthy, long-haired, grinning, wheeling, dealing, raspy-voiced, friendly, and calling everyone "cousin," Petros has been labeled by the *Chicago Tribune* as one of Chicago's most eligible bachelors (although linked for many years to the Contessa Helena Kontos whose boutique is mentioned on the Oak Street walk). Petros is a shrewd businessman. He has created a success where others have failed, and written a cookbook titled *Petros' Famous Recipes*, which includes two references in different introductions to Dianna's being "God's gift to Chicago." Maybe it is.

At least two movies were filmed in part at Dianna's. The restaurant was closed so gambling machines could be set up here for a scene in *Next of Kin*, starring Patrick Swayze. Also, in the movie *Only the Lonely*, John Candy spoke to his girlfriend here.

As you leave, be sure to browse through the alcove in front of the cash register, where we see many pictures of Petros hanging out with or kissing the famous. Also, notice the big sign that says, "Welcome Home, God Bless America and ALL Greeks."

Greek Islands

Next walk north to 200 South Halsted, the Greek Islands Restaurant—a personal favorite of mine. I have not eaten in every restaurant in the world, America, Illinois, or even Chicago. But, of the restaurants I have tried, the Greek Islands is, without question, among the best.

I realize that reads like very, very high praise indeed, but I have never had a bad meal at the Greek Islands Restaurant. Neither have I ever had a bad evening. The feeling, the food, and the pure fun of the place combine to make it the best.

Don't take my word for it. James Ward, an often acerbic restaurant critic for the *Chicago Sun-Times*, reviewed the restaurant in 1983, just days after it moved to its present location from 766 West Jackson. He wrote, "What a revelation! What a delight! Opaa! Opaa! . . . What a setting! What a welcoming ambience! . . . And it's wonderful food, still the best. . . . Now in its new home, Greek Islands is everything that a restaurant should be in the true meaning of the word 'restaurant': This splendid, spacious establishment 'restores' the psyche as well as the soma, the spirit as well as the tum-tum. And now there's room to dance in the aisles of the Greek Islands—and dance you should!" The Greek Islands won the *Chicago Magazine* readers' poll for more than a decade and was applauded as best restaurant, best ethnic restaurant, and as having the best gyros by *Restaurant News*.

This 350-seat restaurant is a joyous experience. Although it is large, I feel intimate here in one of the five dining rooms (I prefer the balcony or the kitchen-garden). Although loud, I feel a sense of energetic quiet.

Order anything. It will be perfect.

My favorites are the taramasalada (fish roe) and tzatziki (yogurt, cucumbers and garlic) as appetizers, gyros, and a Greek salad, then the lamb chops (unsurpassed), and either the sea bass or red snapper (whichever the waiter says is fresh) washed down with the dry Cava Cambas white wine. Recently, I tasted the arni fournou, a traditional Greek Easter dish with oven-baked lamb in oregano and olive oil sauce. It was excellent.

Sometimes, I just give up and tell the waiter to order whatever he wants for me, often with some help from Mike, Nick or Gus or any of the managers. Do not worry, they will not pad the bill, they will not automatically order the most expensive items, and your meal will be the best.

I remember the night Anthony Quinn and the cast from the musical *Zorba the Greek* were eating in the balcony above the kitchen area and the waiters continually brought Quinn plates and glasses to break à la Zorba. But the plates were so sturdy that they often did not break and had to be slammed to the floor again and again. Frankie Avalon dined here after the 1992 Columbus Day Parade; Annette Funicello (without Frankie Avalon) ate here; as did Gene Hackman in a leather jacket and jeans; Jacqueline Bisset; presidential candidate Michael Dukakis (twice); and Goldie Hawn.

The Greek Islands is a happy place, where the roditys wine flows, the conversation comes easy, and the eternal truths seem to be discovered in the midst of laughter. I have gone there to cry, sing, laugh, settle differences, fall in love, introduce fiancées to parents, joke with coworkers, eat, drink, and celebrate being alive.

Santorini

Cross Adams and enter Santorini, at 138 South Halsted, where you begin to believe you are sitting in a white-washed courtyard, complete with fireplace, on a beautiful, peaceful Greek island. Steve Martin ate here with his wife Victoria Tenant; Robert De Niro, who recommended the lamb, had daily orders to go; actress Uma Thurman, Ted Danson, and Bill Murray have also dined here, as well as various local television newspeople who often come here after the 10 o'clock news. Actor Albert Finney addressed the waiters in Greek and swore in a charming way.

Half-owned by the Greek Islands, Santorini is a slightly more elegant restaurant with fresh, whole, broiled black bass and a tasteful Greek-style chicken. The last time I was there I ordered the lamb stamnas, which is a crêpe filled with lamb, carrots, peas, Greek cheeses, pine nuts, and covered with mozzarella cheese and red sauce. Delicious and amazing. We also had the eggplant spread, the fried zucchini, and the oven-baked butterfried jumbo shrimp. The only slightly more adventurous should try the charcoal-grilled octopus appetizer. It's also delicious.

Pegasus

Exit Santorini, walk south on Halsted to the next restaurant, Pegasus, 130 South Halsted. Here you will find Greektown's only roofgarden, opened in 1991, and a fine place to observe the night while eating appetizers or drinking some wine.

Pegasus' specialty is macaronada "with our award-winning saltza," which is spaghetti cooked to order for $4.95, plus Greek-style fajitas, and a tummy-filling, family-style dinner.

But, more than that, you might find love. Here is a place to begin a romance. Hundreds, perhaps as many as 5,000 marriages, have started right here.

And the instigator of all this happiness is Harriet Papastratakos or Hariklia, a matchmaker whose full-time job is being a life insurance agent. The first meeting between boy and girl or man and woman always takes place in the Pegasus, named for the mythological winged horse that carried thunder and lightning to Zeus.

I asked the wonderfully irrepressible Harriet, who is an energetic woman, whose age I would not dare to guess, and whose spirit is unquenchable, what was the secret of her success. "It's a gift. I majored in psychology, but my professor told me 'you don't need to come to my class, you were born a psychologist.' I can read people and I work hard at it.

"I do it for love. The most important thing is to find a good person with good character and for a man to be a man and a woman to be a woman. It's OK if the outside is pretty, but it's the inside that's important."

When I asked for one love story, she told me about a difficult young man with impossible ideals for his wife. Harriet introduced him to a

Harriet Papastratakos in Pegasus: 5,000 marriages!

beautiful girl from Greece via Canada. The ultimate matchmaker remembered, "So he sees her and then he wants to talk to me outside. What else does he want? He says she is beautiful, very beautiful, but he didn't see her legs! I said, John, you're something else. So we go back inside and I ask her to go with me into the kitchen. As we're leaving the room, I turn to John and say, 'Well, open your eyes.' Later, when I asked her about her boyfriends in Canada, she blushed and I knew she was a very fine girl. They went to a Greek Orthodox picnic a couple of days later. Very shortly after that they were married in court because she was only here as a visitor for a few weeks. A church wedding followed. They have two sons and one is a doctor." All this said with great satisfaction and a sense of true achievement.

So if you see an energetic grandmother and two shy people engaged in conversation, please do not interrupt. Love is a fragile experience at the very beginning, and you wouldn't want to doom some future doctor from ever being created.

What better place to end the Greektown Pub Crawl with a glass of wine in hand, toasting today and tomorrow, and just loving the fact that life can be this good.

Opaa!!!

21 OLD TOWN PUB CRAWL

Where Wells Street is better than well

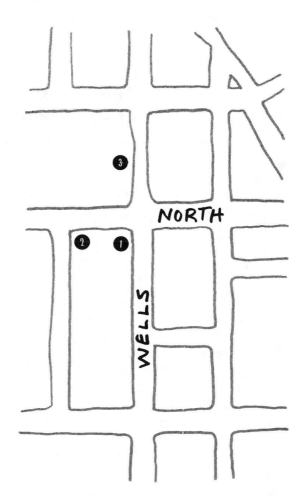

1. Zanie's
2. Old Town Ale House
3. Second City

Time: More than 2 hours.

To get there: The #22 and #36 CTA buses stop at North Avenue and Clark Street, two blocks east of North and Wells, where the pub crawl begins. The #156 LaSalle bus, #11 Lincoln, Express #135, and

Express #136 buses stop at North Avenue and LaSalle, one block east of North and Wells. The #151 bus stops in Lincoln Park at Stockton, only two blocks from the beginning of the walk. If you drive, take the Outer Drive to North Avenue, take a right on Clark Street, and enter the parking lot just north of the Robert Cavalier de LaSalle statue. Parking here is two hours for 25 cents for a maximum of 16 hours, the best buy in the area. Park in a lot rather than attempt to find a space on a side street. The streets east of Wells never have spaces and those west of Wells can be dangerous to non-neighborhood residents.

The Ups and Downs of Old Town

In the '50s, Old Town housed real artists living inexpensively in storefronts.

In the '60s, Old Town became a freak show. Long-haired hippies congregated there, and tourists and suburbanites came to observe and feed them.

After the riots in the wake of Martin Luther King, Jr.'s murder in 1968, when gangs from nearby Cabrini Green public housing roamed through Old Town smashing and grabbing at will, the area turned mean, dangerous, and unsafe during the '70s. Old Town started a comeback in the '80s, and nearly has its act together in the '90s, although the recession during the presidency of George Bush caused many businesses to fail.

The street still has its tough areas, which is why this walk does not take you too far south on Wells Street. And there are areas to the west where no one should walk alone at night. But better restaurants are opening on Wells, a few of the older establishments remain, and Second City still flourishes, offering improvisational comedy performed by the stars of tomorrow.

We begin at Clark and North, at the bus stop. Across the street, you can see the Chicago Historical Society and the Chicago Latin School, two institutions explored in the Lincoln Park Walk. The nearby Village Theater offers real movie bargains—six different films for only $2.50 each.

The Original Mitchell's, on the corner of North and Clark, is one of my favorite places for breakfast. Their omelets created from egg whites are delicious.

Cross to the south side of the street, take a right and head west on North Avenue, passing the first of several Italian restaurants on this walk, Trattoria Dinatto, at 165 West North Avenue.

When you reach Wells Street take a left, going south. Coffee Chicago is a nice place to sit and watch the day go by.

Billy "Black Snake" Wells

Incidentally, Wells Street is named after Billy "Black Snake" Wells, who died in the Fort Dearborn 1812 Massacre. Billy was captured by the Miami Indians at age 12 and was raised by Little Turtle, chief of all the Miamis. He fought with the Indians in 1790, probably killed several white men and felt guilty about that. He then fought with the white men against the Indians and finally acted as a go-between for both sides.

He showed up at Fort Dearborn because he was concerned about his niece, Rebekah, who had married Captain Nathaniel Heald, who was in charge of the fort. During the massacre, Wells rode back to Rebekah with a message for his wife, "Tell her I died at my post, doing the best I could. There are seven red devils over there that I have killed." That's a lot to say with a bullet or arrow in your lung, but Wells is supposed to have said it.

Moments later his horse was wounded. It rolled on Wells, trapping him. Wells shot one more Indian and then held up his head and shouted, "Shoot away." The Indians took his advice, beheaded him, and then ate his heart as a tribute to his bravery.

In 1870, Wells Street was so disreputable that folks thought it dishonored old Black Snake's name. So the street became Fifth Avenue. Then in 1918, despite the protests of businessmen who liked the idea of Chicago having a Fifth Avenue the way New York did, the name was changed back to Wells Street. In view of its current state, perhaps it's time to change it back to Fifth Avenue.

Shops and Restaurants

Vintage Posters at 1551 North Wells is a must stop, especially if the walls of your apartment have many, many cracks that need to be covered. The posters here sell for as much as $55,000 (antique posters have been known to fetch up to $400,000), and can be as large as 10 feet by 12 feet! The most popular size is 4 feet by 5 feet.

These are not inexpensive reproductions of old movie posters such as you'd find in many other stores. The owner, Susan Cutler, sells vintage European and American posters of bullfights, bike races, airplanes, cars, bicycles, operas, circuses, champagnes, soaps, and corsets. She boasted, "We sell museum quality posters."

At 1517 North Wells, you'll see Uno's Bizarre Bazaar, a huge, garish emporium that has changed with the times. The management once boasted that it was the "largest head shop in the Midwest." Now it sells no drug paraphernalia, no pipes, no screens. Where once it displayed 125 different brands of cigarette papers, it now stocks only 20 brands.

Instead, Uno's Bizarre Bazaar has a nearly block-long display of sunglasses, a wall filled with teddies and other underwear, tie-dyed T-shirts, incense holders, and neckties. It seems that policemen, politicians, and some members of the public did not think drug paraphernalia was quaint any more.

The second Italian restaurant of this walk, Trattoria Roma, moved from 1557 to 1535 North Wells. The most popular dish is capellini al filetto or homemade angel hair pasta in olive oil, garlic, and tomatoes. Diners here have included Jay Leno, Paul Newman, Kevin Costner, and Sean Connery. The *Zagat Restaurant Survey* named it one of the top values in restaurants in Chicago.

The Hong Kong Bay, which opened at 1531 North Wells in September 1992, features made-to-order dim sum (steamed courses). The owners met when Aries Leung found Nelson Yuen asleep on his living room couch. Nelson's sister, who was living downstairs, didn't have room for him when he arrived from Hong Kong. Her boyfriend, who is now her husband, allowed Nelson to sleep on the couch without telling his roommate Aries. When the future partners-to-be first met, one was snoring.

Walk past the Feline Inn, the shop for cats, and stop in another Italian restaurant, Topo Gigio, 1437 North Wells. Lillo Teodosi, the co-owner, said that he was fascinated by the little Italian puppet since he was five years old. Topo Gigio became famous in America after his appearances on the Ed Sullivan Show. When Lillo opened a restaurant, he discovered that he could take the name of the beloved character.

The most popular dish is Fusilli Topo Gigio, or corkscrew-shaped pasta in the restaurant's sauce, proving that it does pay to order the dish named after the restaurant.

If you continue north to Division, and I suggest you do so by automobile or cab because the neighborhood gets a little questionable in that direction, The House of Glunz is at 1206 North Wells. Established 1888 and arguably the city's finest best-buy wine shop, Glunz has a tasting room that could be comfortable in any castle in Germany. The museum there includes the top of an 1892 muscatel barrel. David John Donovan II, the manager and relative of the founder, proudly states that he still has two bottles from the wine that was in that barrel.

The founder, Louis Glunz, came to Chicago from Germany because his friends were here—Oscar Meyer, who marketed the famous hot dog, and Dr. Scholl, the foot specialist.

Today, Glunz stocks around 1,500 different wines, and is the oldest established wine and liquor shop in Chicago. Inquire about their wine tastings. For instance, in 1992, a Madeira tasting cost $20 per person, but the lucky few got to taste Madeiras from 1863 and 1864.

However, the farther south you walk on Wells the closer you get to the crime-ridden neighborhoods. Therefore, let's visit Glunz another day and cross Wells at Schiller, retracing our steps on the opposite (west) side of Wells Street.

Mirador, at 1400 North Wells, is a restaurant with very creative chicken dishes. When you have finished dining, do walk upstairs to the Blue Room, a funky bar with overstuffed furniture and a very private, intimate booth toward the back. It's just about the comfiest place to have

Mirador's Debbie Gold, chef, and Amy Morton, owner

a drink in "a '50s style retro lounge," according to Amy Morton, the owner. The Blue Room offers an eclectic variety of music, including rock, jazz, blues, and even performance art Tuesday through Saturday beginning around 10 p.m.

Continuing north, you will pass Hobo's, a basement bar next door to a custom framing shop at 1446 North Wells. The Fireplace Inn, at 1448 North Wells, claims to have "the best ribs in town." It has an outdoor dining area, weather permitting.

The Chicago Clock Co. Inc., at 1500 North Wells, has more than 1,000 clocks on display. Once this building offered very different displays. It was the home of the Ripley's Believe It or Not Museum, which had the world's largest hairball (six pounds, 30 inches around). The museum is gone, and frankly, I don't care what happened to the hairball.

But the clock company was mentioned as a "best bargain" by the knowledgeable *Chicago* magazine in 1992 because this store stocks one-of-a-kind tests, overstocks, and discontinued items. A wall clock that plays Disney tunes sells for $1,200 (regularly $1,450). The article listed several other clocks at up to $700 lower than normal prices.

When I last took this walk, Ciao, at 1516 North Wells, had a sign saying "For Sale By Owner." I guess we can say ciao Ciao.

Continue north, past the Fudge Pot, and watch the fish at the Old Town Aquarium, 1538 North Wells.

Zanie's, Cigars, and the Old Town Ale House

Zanie's, at 1548 North Wells, is one of Chicago's premier comedy night-clubs. If you haven't heard of the current stars of Zanie's, don't be put off. The standards here are very high, the comedy is always good, and you might see someone just before he or she becomes a star.

Jerry Seinfeld, Yakov Smirnoff, the late Sam Kinison, Arsenio Hall, Robert Townsend, and Chicago comedians Emo Philips, Nora Dunn, Skip Griparis, Larry Reeb, John Caponera, and T. P. Mulrooney were all seen here early in their careers. Caponera bartended between sets, Jay Leno made his Chicago comedy debut here in 1983, and Richard Lewis made his in 1984. Without warning, Robin Williams took over the hall one night, as did Eddie Murphy. Just look at the walls decorated with publicity photos from table level to ceiling and you'll know why this club is thriving.

Comics young and hopeful: Billie Maddox and Ali Le Roi at Zanies

Do stop in The Up Down Tobacco Shop, at 1550 North Wells, just to smell the heady atmosphere, if nothing else. The owner, Mrs. Diana Gits, has a smokers' paradise here and, even if you do not puff, you will appreciate the aromas, especially of her sample pipe tobaccos.

Each year she runs a pipe-smoking contest, and she will proudly show you the world's largest humidor, a 40-foot storage space for cigars. Jim Belushi has his Larranga Nationales cigars mailed to him wherever he is in the world from this store.

Mrs. Gits, an energetic, delightful, cigar-smoking woman brimming with good stories, proudly shows off the cigar named after her, the Diana Silvius, a $4 smoke from the Dominican Republic. Each Diana Silvius box is decorated with its own little diamond, Mrs. Gits said, and she added, "It's the best cigar you ever tasted."

Her Chicagoland Cigar Connoisseurs Club meets several times a year for dinner and a good smoke. With all those men and a few good women smoking cigars, I do not know if they are allowed back in the restaurants a second time.

When you get to Wells and North, turn left and go west to the Old Town Ale House at 219 West North Avenue, home of some of the more bizarre people in Old Town. It's almost as if the Beat Generation beached here 25 years ago and never moved. The wall mural features faces of Ale

House regulars. These regulars include the dean of the writers of angry letters to local newspapers, a foot fetishist, Second City regulars, and a man who enjoyed imitating Kate Hepburn.

A few blocks west, at 403 West North Avenue, was the former site of 43rd Ward Alderman Paddy Bauler's saloon. It's not there anymore, so don't bother to visit it. But it is worth mentioning because Bauler is the man who first said "Chicago ain't ready for reform." That was in 1955, after Richard J. Daley's first primary victory. He also said, "Daley's the dog with the big nuts, now that we've got him elected," but almost no one remembers that.

Return to Wells Street. Before going on, do look across the street at Walgreen's, where the first of the infamous tainted Tylenol capsules was bought in 1982 by Paula Prince, a flight attendant who died of the poison. Another poison capsule was bought at the Dominick's at 230 West North, a half-block away. Eventually, seven people were killed by the Tylenol terrorist. These murders are still unsolved crimes.

Second City

Take a left and walk north. Second City, home of improvisational theater in Chicago, is at 1616 North Wells. Walk upstairs and look at the poster just to the left of the box office. It lists the names of those who have performed with Second City in various towns as of the club's 32nd anniversary on December 16, 1991. Those mentioned include Alan Alda, Ed Asner, Dan Aykroyd, James and John Belushi, Valerie Harper, Shelley Berman, Mike Nichols, Elaine May, and Alan Arkin. Pictures of famous performers as young talents can be seen opposite the bar.

It is a little-known fact that after the regular shows (at 11 p.m. Sunday through Thursday and at 1 a.m. on Saturday), you can watch the improvisations and pay no cover or minimum. If it is late and you feel like taking a chance, you will see the gestation of future Second City revues. Sometimes the skits fail, but after all they are making things up as they go along. More often than not, they succeed, wildly, with the audience and the actors discovering the humor in the situations as they develop. Later, the successful skits become part of the regular shows.

You could end the walk at this point having seen quite a bit of Old Town night life. However, if you are still feeling energetic, hungry, or thirsty, continue walking north on Wells.

The Second City casts are never really off stage

More Walking and Shopping

Crown Books, at 1660 North Wells, is part of a large chain of discount bookstores. I am always amazed at the prices of hardcover bestsellers here. This a good place to get that gift book you've been meaning to give a relative.

Continuing north, walk and marvel at the decorated doors on the townhouses, especially at 1734 and 1738 North Wells.

You'll next pass several small shops before you reach Lincoln Avenue, a diagonal street. Two more Italian restaurants are on this corner, Cannella's, at 1820 Wells, and Topo Gigio at the Park. Walk northwest on Lincoln, taking the odd 135-degree left turn. You are walking past a row of renovated townhouses that helped change this neighborhood from near slum to old-fashioned charm.

This part of the walk takes you past one side of the Old Town Triangle, which was originally known as the Cabbage Patch, although celery was the big local crop. Johnny "Tarzan" Weismuller went to school here.

Chicago radio soap opera actors once tended to live at Whiskey Point, 1852–1856 North Lincoln. This light and darker gray apartment building once housed the stars of Backstage Wife (the story of an Iowa stenographer married to Broadway star Larry Noble), Oxydol's, "Ma

Perkins," "The Romance of Helen Trent" (which proved that "romance can live on at 35 and even beyond"), "The Guiding Light," and "Jack Armstrong, All-American Boy."

You can see the sign for The Bulls, 1916 North Lincoln Park West, one of Chicago's premiere jazz places. The Bulls has been well known among music buffs before the basketball team of the same name took back-to-back championships.

Seven nights a week for more than 28 years, this has been "the room you want to play," according to one guitarist-manager Joe Magdaleno. A keyboardist named Ghalib Ghalab was a fixture here for many years. The Bulls began as a folk club, switched to jazz, and has given a start to performers like Kevin Eubanks, who is now the guitarist with the "Jay Leno Show." It is also reasonable with a cover charge of between $4 and $7 and no minimum at the bar.

Return to Lincoln Avenue, continue walking until you reach Ranalli's, 1925 North Lincoln. Only a Chicago pizza restaurant would advertise that it was nominated for "best pig-out food." The sign proclaiming 100 imported beers is incorrect. At last count, the restaurant offered 129.

Ranalli's has the largest outdoor cafe in the Lincoln Park area, and its super-thin crust pizza is the most popular dish.

When George Wendt, who played Norm on "Cheers," dined here in a corner table on a pizza and a beer, the waiters said he behaved just like his character on television.

Armitage–Lincoln
Restaurants and Bars

If you continue this walk, you will shortly get to the corner of Armitage and Lincoln. There you will see Gamekeepers Taverne and Grill, a singles bar, and a place to go in the hopes of practicing safe sex. You might meet someone to alleviate a night's loneliness, but you may instead find a lifetime of romance.

In 1986, *Cosmopolitan* magazine named Gamekeepers one of the "top ten bars in America," called Gamekeeper's "a staggering success," and a "romantic meeting place" where "everybody looks great." That same issue had stories on "The Nonorgasmic Woman. What Is She Supposed to Do?" and a look at the possibility of loving him "in another life."

Just to the east, at 340 West Armitage, is Geja's Cafe. Walk down a few steps to the tiny courtyard to enter Geja's, which is a fondue/wine/cheese bar with a tradition of having live flamenco guitarists performing for the customers. It is just the place for an intimate glass of wine with a very, very close friend.

If you continue strolling to the east, you'll find Park West, a 750-seat nightclub at 322 West Armitage, often voted the best place to see rock music in town. A pornographic movie house was once here. In fact, I remember watching *Deep Throat* there on assignment for the now-defunct *Chicago Daily News*. I was supposed to be inside when the police arrived. They didn't close the theater until the next day, but I'll never forget the two gentlemen sitting behind me discussing the scenes during opening credits: "I'll be damned, that's Miami." "No way, ain't Miami." "Sure is, she's driving down Collins Avenue." "No way, what she's going to do in this picture, she's ain't going to do it in Miami."

Today, Park West features the best sound and light system in town and fine sight lines. Over the years, it has been host to Prince months before he became a superstar, Aretha Franklin, the Rolling Stones, U-2, Genesis with Phil Collins and Mike Rutherford, and Tina Turner. Sometimes major artists want to play here because they enjoy the feeling of a smaller club. Often acts perform here just after releasing their first album and months before they can fill a huge arena.

The Chicago Bears came to Park West to record their 1985 "Super Bowl Shuffle" rap song.

And this is a good spot to end the walk. You are about four blocks north of where you parked your car. Or you can easily find a cab or a bus from Armitage and Clark.

22 ARMITAGE–HALSTED WALK

Bar crawl, restaurant taste, and antique search potpourri

1. Old Town School of Folk Music
2. Cafe Ba-Ba-Reeba!
3. Grant's Tavern

Time: About an hour, less if you avoid all the antique stores, more if you are a serious shopper, or if you find a saloon you can call home.

To get there: The Ravenswood elevated train, which leaves from the Loop, stops at Armitage nine minutes later. Be ready to disembark, the stop arrives very quickly. The #8 Halsted bus stops at Armitage and Halsted and you can walk a couple of blocks west to the elevated tracks to start the walk. Parking is almost impossible, although I once found a space east of Halsted on Armitage. I will not reveal exactly where it was in case I decide to go back.

Overview of Armitage

This area has a little bit of everything. You might even want to take this walk twice, once during the day to stroll by the many shops and again at night when the bars are jumping.

Or you could take this walk at around 3 p.m. on a nice Saturday, as I once did, and find everything open and ready for business.

As with so much in Chicago, this area has changed over the last few years. It went from one of the toughest neighborhoods to one of the nicest. The local high school, once called Waller High, was the home of many gangs. In the '60s, a student brought a carbine to school and took over the auditorium. Now part of Waller has become Lincoln Park Academy, the home of the program that puts some students on equal footing with the best minds of their age around the world.

This walk is in the shape of an "L." You can start at any point. If you arrived by taxi or bus at Halsted and Armitage, find the entry for the Armitage Cleaners a few pages ahead.

If you arrived by train, go west to Espial, a restaurant at 948 West Armitage. Only in Chicago would a restaurant nearly under the el, with trains going by every 30 seconds during rush hour, be considered romantic and sophisticated. These adjectives apply to Espial.

It is a delightful, small, 45-seat bistro with Italian-influenced food and many choices for vegetarians. Espial offers gourmet pizzas, including one with artichokes, sun-dried tomatoes, mushrooms, mozzarella, and Parmesan and another with potatoes, leaks, provolone, and bacon. The vegetarian lasagna is a real treat.

Michelle Pfeiffer dined at the last table on the left near the wall.

The back room, called The 13th Floor, features live music with no cover charge three nights a week. In the past it has had contests for amateur torch singers.

The two partners are John Zaharakis, who has an art history degree, and Christopher Bukrey, who has a psychology degree. Their parents co-signed their first loans so they could open the original coffeehouse.

When you leave Espial, turn left, walk east, and cross the street. Sole Mio, at 917 West Armitage, has entertained Alec and Billy Baldwin, Robert De Niro, Veronica Hamel, Marlo Thomas, Madonna, Bill Murray, Diana Ross, Tom Selleck, and Meg Ryan. When asked what is the most popular main course in this northern Italian restaurant, the answer from bartender Terry Themm was, "We make the best martinis in the city."

Old Town School of Folk Music

The Old Town School of Folk Music, at 909 West Armitage, is a must stop. If you think that folk music died when the Kingston Trio's record sales faltered, think again. It is alive and well in Chicago, and this school is vital to its preservation.

Such singers as Bonnie Koloc, John Prine, the Byrds, Corky Siegel, Mahalia Jackson, Joan Baez, Win Stracke, Jim Post, David Bromberg, Stephen Wade, Ella Jenkins, and the late Steve Goodman performed here. Goodman is known for writing the best train song ever, "The City of New Orleans"; for writing a tribute to the Lincoln Park Towing Company, which protects many local parking lots by grabbing unwanted cars from the area; and for writing a perfect country song that combined mom, trucks, prison, dogs, the rain, and many other elements.

The Old Town School of Folk Music, founded in an Oak Park dining room in 1957 and the only institution of its kind in the entire country, is a great place to visit. There are always fascinating people hanging around there, the music you hear sure is good, and maybe the experience will get you interested in that old banjo or guitar that has been gathering dust for years. Instructors have truthfully boasted that, after a single hour's lesson, you would have learned at least two chords and be able to play hundreds of songs, too many for anyone to know all the words to them!

The school is the subject of a story as triumphal as any folk song about the river, the drought, or the bank. In 1982, the school was $100,000 in debt and adding $60,000 a year in deficits. Well, then, oh-lay-oh-lay-oh-lee-oh, the school turned itself around, hired a new executive director, reduced the deficit to $4,700 in *one year*, and became the school you see now. You know, that almost sounds like a conservative, do-it-your-self, don't-depend-on-government folk song—of which there have been very, very few, indeed.

In 1992, the school had 1,700 students, more than 60 instructors, and an extensive children's program. Its classes, which are at 100 percent capacity every night, include instruction in guitar, fiddle, banjo, dulcimer, harmonica, drumming, songwriting, and how to play just like the Grateful Dead. Vocal instruction is also offered, including sea shanties, Irish ballads, and doo wop.

Since 1957, the school has been interested in traditional music of the world such as blue grass, blues, Hispanic, and Eastern European music.

Every Friday night, the school has an informal gathering called Mr. Coffeehouse starting at 6:30 p.m. with a performance at 8:30 p.m.

If you have a little time, walk upstairs. To your left on the second floor is the resource center. On the walls of the stairwell you will see press clippings, photographs, and other memorabilia from the greats of the folk scene. The resource center is just a small room, but it is filled with more than 10,000 recordings and books. Paul Tyler, the curator of the center, will have to assist you, because the records, CDs, and books are shelved in an order only he understands.

My son, Joel, who enjoyed researching this particular walk, asked to hear a song or two by Big Bill Broonzy, after reading a press clipping about him moments earlier. Tyler quickly found six records and Big Bill's autobiography. Joel wrote, "The stereo is great, and I just sat there and listened to a whole stack of great folk, blues, and just interesting records."

If you can drag yourself away from all those wonderful records, as you leave, there is a store to the right in the entranceway of the school. Different Strummer sells folk instruments, songbooks, records, tapes, and CDs. There is a section of music from people affiliated with the school, whether they are teachers, former students, or hangers-on. Robert De Niro and Uma Thurman shopped for guitars here.

Antiques, Buttons, and Beads

Next door, at 907 West Armitage is Findable's, an eclectic gift store for women. It is in a building, like many in this neighborhood, that was built in the 1880s. In fact, the store's owner, David Ginople, said he had to put in a new floor to cover up the rings stained in the floor from the pickle barrels that used to sit there.

As you leave, go east, to your right, and cross the street to Turtle Creek Antiques at 850 West Armitage. This antique store specializes in textiles and fabrics, especially quilts and linens. The quilts are mainly from the northeastern U.S. and range from $250 to $2,500. Mary Pompa, the owner, opened the store in the '70s, when the area was filled with hippies, street gangs, artists, and freaks. "In those days you could open a store with a couple thousand bucks, hang a shingle, and be in business." She feels that back then younger people were more interested in older antiques, especially from the late 1800s. Now the art deco and 1950s eras are popular.

Buttons and beads on Armitage

Continuing east, cross Dayton and you will see a large, former home at 826 West Armitage. Walk up the stairs, and on your left is Renaissance Buttons, one of Chicago's best button shops. This is a store for clothes designers and those who collect buttons as a hobby. The buttons, priced from 10 cents to $80, range from a simple, normal black button to lithographed buttons from the late 1800s. In the back of the store is a large trunk, called a poke-box, filled with 10-cent buttons.

If you go to your left as you leave Renaissance Buttons, you will be in Mizepah Bead Company. This store sells all sorts of beads, as well as some finished jewelry. Although there are many beads for less than $1, some customers have been known to spend more than $200 on beads to make their own jewelry. There are also some imported, hand-painted beads for more than $10. This is a very small store, and with five or six people bead shopping, it can be quite packed.

Armitage Cleaners

Leaving the building, continue east. I feel I must mention Charlie Trotter's, a well-reviewed restaurant at 816 West Armitage. The fact that most restaurant critics are on an expense account and do not have to pay for their own meals might account for some of the praise. Fixed-price meals here run from $75 and $100 per person without wine.

If you find that affordable, enjoy. Otherwise, continue to Halsted, take a right, and cross Armitage heading south. Enter Armitage Cleaners at 1972 North Halsted, even if you don't have your dry cleaning with you.

You will quickly notice that this is one of the strangest cleaning establishments in the world. The back of the store is devoted to spot removal, the front to blue suede shoes. You are now visiting one of the city's largest Elvis Presley memorabilia stores.

In 1966, owner Max Gonzales came to America from Jovellanos, Cuba, and created the Elvis nostalgia idea in 1982, after he had already had his dry cleaning business for 15 years. The walls are covered with $11.95 cotton Elvis wall hangings, Elvis guitar clocks for $24.95, Elvis toy guitars, and the assorted James Dean and Marilyn Monroe memorabilia. Gonzales sells about 100 busts of Elvis a year at $20 per statue.

The owner proudly says, "Elvis is a good man for me. This is a potpourri business." It sure is, and it is a delightful store to visit.

Sausages, Leather, and Beer

Walking south, or right from the corner of Armitage and Halsted, Gepperth's Market is an old-world, European-style grocery store with homemade sausages, fresh Cornish game hens, and nitrite-free bacon. A sign there once read, "Just in time for mother's day—double-yolk eggs!" I've never understood what that meant.

Continuing south on Halsted, you will see Chicago Leather, at 1966 North Halsted, which sells fine imported and handmade leather goods from Europe, Asia, and Latin America, especially Colombia. Nearby, the Village Green, at 1952 North Halsted, has sent flowers to Marlo Thomas and has done landscaping for the movie *Curly Sue*.

Retrace your steps, returning to and crossing Armitage, heading north. The numbers on the addresses will now be going up. Across the street is Bellini, babyland for yuppies, with $700 designer cribs that can be folded into a bed as your child gets older.

Across Halsted, there is The Store, which may look like a normal, neighborhood watering hole, but becomes *the* neighborhood hot spot when it stays open two hours after the other bars close.

Expectations, at 2012 North Halsted, has elegant maternity clothes, which have been seen on Oprah and Jenny Jones' shows and worn by

Max Gonzales, owner of Armitage Cleaners, with Elvis busts

Ann Jillian and Mary Hart. The outfits range in price from $28 to $370 for a silk two-piece theater suit.

The Beaumont Garden Cafe, at 2020 North Halsted, does have a garden. Well, it's really an outdoor bar, usually under a tent in the back of the saloon. If the interior of Beaumont's is too loud (or if you are tired of brass, stained glass, and instant antiques), the back beer garden is a bit quieter.

Cafe Ba-Ba-Reeba!

Cafe Ba-Ba-Reeba!, at 2024 North Halsted, is a Spanish tapas bar, a concept that came to Chicago after success in New York, Houston, San Francisco, and Los Angeles.

The theory goes that we have become a nation of "grazers," people who would rather nibble on several light snacks throughout the day than sit down to a huge meal.

Tapas are Spanish appetizers which, legend says, were created when Spanish bar owners would give customers a piece of bread to cover the wine glass so flies wouldn't fall into the vino. The smarter saloon keepers would also put a piece of salty meat on the bread, making their patrons

Pouring wine at Cafe Ba-Ba-Reeba!

thirsty and producing more wine sales. Thus, a new group of appetizers was created.

Since Cafe Ba-Ba-Reeba! opened in December 1985, Chicagoans have learned to enjoy little dishes with thinly sliced octopus, squid stuffed with ground squid, mussels marinated in vinaigrette, baked fennel, goat cheese tarts, grilled Spanish blood sausage, and clams in white wine sauce.

Continuing north, you will pass Aged Experience, at 2034 North Halsted, an antique shop with chairs hanging from the ceiling. In addition to specializing in American furniture, the store also has an interesting collection of animals living in it. The owner, Terry Saunders, lives upstairs, and Betty the parrot and Magic the cockatoo are additional residents.

More Restaurants

If you walk through a corridor to the rear of 2044 North Halsted, you will discover Relish, an owner/chef-operated bistro with an emphasis on value. The most expensive entree is $15.50. Ron Blazek, the youthful owner, has said that he is trying to "bring interesting and fresh food down to a moderate price range, serve it in a casual atmosphere," while leaving the customers with change in their pockets. Blazek should know about combining value with good cooking. He has a degree in economics from the University of Michigan and another from the culinary arts program at Johnson and Wales College in Providence, Rhode Island.

I recommend the woody mushroom strudel appetizer and the fiery black bean soup, plus the rare, grilled ahi tuna or the tempura-fried soft shell crabs as main courses.

There is an outdoor garden, but in 1992 it did not have a liquor license. Only food could be served out there.

Continuing north, the Bangkok Noodle Shop, at 2048 North Halsted, is where the Halsted Street Fish Market was formerly located. The bow of a ship once stuck out over the sidewalk. Now the same wonderful restaurateurs who own the Bangkok, near Halsted and Addison and mentioned on the North Halsted walk, have this restaurant. The Noodle Shop features more than 20 Thai noodles, including my favorite pad Thai. It offers dim sum on Sunday, when a cart is rolled to your table and you can take what you want for 99 cents and up.

Cross Dickens to Cafe Bernard, a French restaurant with fresh fish daily, excellent onion soup, and a variety of fine chicken dishes.

Continue north, past the Banana Republic clothing store to the American West Gallery, which specializes in Native American art and features Navajo pottery, drums, and paintings of deserted buttes.

Nookie's Too, at 2114 North Halsted, is a clean diner.

Grant's Tavern, at 2138 North Halsted, was praised by the *Chicago Tribune* for having "an extra-ordinary women's room." It also has a magazine rack toward the front—the rare indication that people who go to saloons might also read.

Continuing to move to the north, Saturday's Child, at 2144 North Halsted, is a fine toy store, which had Greta Garbo and Carmen Miranda paper dolls. My Own Two Feet, at 2148 North Halsted, is a kiddie shoe store where tiny, tiny baby shoes can cost $30.

Otis', at 2150 North Halsted, is a sports and live music bar often featuring live local bands that sound very much like the Grateful Dead and other rock groups. Jack McDowell, a 20-game winning pitcher for the Chicago White Sox in 1992, has performed here with his rock and roll band, but the Sox front office didn't want him to.

Glascott's, at 2158 North Halsted, is a long, open, friendly singles bar.

Next, cross Webster to the east side of the street and enter Carlucci, 2215 North Halsted, an excellent Italian restaurant in a converted auto body shop. Notice the beautiful entranceway, which looks like old marble but isn't. This restaurant has a garden open in the summer.

This ends the walk. If you continue a few blocks north, you can take the #11 Lincoln Avenue bus downtown, or return to Armitage and walk west to the elevated train station there. Or you can try to remember where you parked your car.

However, if you wish to continue, the North and the South Lincoln Avenue Pub Crawls begin at this corner.

23 SOUTH LINCOLN AVENUE PUB CRAWL

From John Barleycorn to Wise Fools

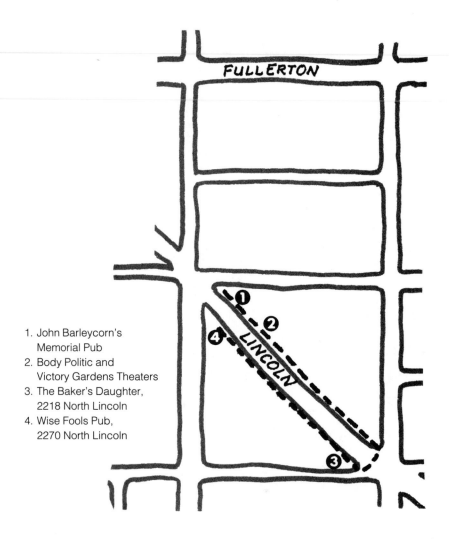

1. John Barleycorn's Memorial Pub
2. Body Politic and Victory Gardens Theaters
3. The Baker's Daughter, 2218 North Lincoln
4. Wise Fools Pub, 2270 North Lincoln

Time: An entire evening. Some people make this walk their life's work, but that's a bit excessive.

To get there: Take the CTA subway to Fullerton and walk east to Lincoln, a diagonal street. Or take the #11 CTA bus, which stops at Fullerton and Halsted, where the walk begins. By car, take Lake Shore Drive to Fullerton, then west to Lincoln, and circle the blocks for about an hour before finding a parking space.

John Barleycorn

You are in the Lincoln Park neighborhood, originally a swampy section of land settled by Germans in the 1860s. Today, the average home value around here is $360,000 (up from $125,000 only a decade ago), and two-bedroom apartments start at $1,200 a month.

Lincoln Avenue is the place to go for a mellow drink, have a bite to eat, see theater, or listen to music. It's the lively street Wells Street once was, and it's the place young Chicago goes for a good time.

The pub crawl begins at Fullerton and Lincoln. Lincoln is a diagonal street, so the directions may seem a little complicated. Walk southeast on the east side of the street past the Children's Memorial Hospital until you reach the John Barleycorn Memorial Pub, at 658 West Belden. What a bar!

Classical music constantly plays for the patrons. A screen on one wall reflects Barleycorn's collection of art slides. There is also a large outdoor garden complete with fountain and a small sidewalk cafe in the warmer months. There's as many as 16 imports on draught, including Harp, Bass, Guinness, and Moosehead. Four dart boards are in frequent operation. Model boats and a moose head adorn the walls, and the hamburgers are good! For the true aficionado of fine boozy ambience here's a tavern that lives up to one of its slogans, "Se habla Beethoven."

This place has been a tavern for more than a century! Back in 1890, an Irish immigrant on the Chicago police force opened a bar here. Legend has it that, during Prohibition, a Chinese laundry here hid a speakeasy and famed outlaw John Dillinger was a frequent patron.

Espresso or Beer?

If on your walk you choose to sober up for a moment, Cafe Trevi Espresso, once a doctor's office at 2275 North Lincoln, is a nice, low-key coffeehouse. They feature live jazz on Sunday and Wednesday nights with no cover, occasional poetry readings, short films, and even have an old upright piano they'll let you play if you feel like launching into a rendition of "Sophisticated Lady."

At 2269 North Lincoln is the Lone Star Fajita Bar featuring Southwestern cuisine. Owner Steve Liataud dropped out of the corporate world to try something new. The place obviously features grilled fajitas and buckets of Lone Star Beer. There is always a long wait for weekend dinner, but they stay open until 3 a.m. on Friday and Saturday.

These days 2265 North Lincoln is the home of Kelsey's, a yuppie bar with more than 500 bottles of liquor decorating one wall. A sign inside the door suggests that patrons remove their in-line skates (rollerblades) for safety reasons.

At one time, the Oxford Pub, at 2263 North Lincoln, sponsored "coffin races" in the spring. Alas, it could not outrace the grasp of the tax man, and so it disappeared, as did Redamaks, a hamburger joint at the same location. Ottavio Italian Tapas is now at 2263 North Lincoln and features deserts imported from Italy. It serves what is known in Italy as assaggini, in Spain as tapas, and in America as appetizers—small, reasonably priced tastes of a variety of dishes. It claims to be "the first and only Italian tapas-style dining in Chicago."

Body Politic and Victory Gardens Theaters

The Body Politic and Victory Gardens Theaters, at 2261 North Lincoln, usually have three productions going on at once. These off-loop theaters will experiment, try new playwrights, discover new actors and actresses, and succeed. Stop by and ask about the current plays, and then buy a ticket—you will not see a bad production.

These two theaters have been called the soul of Lincoln Avenue. It is amazing how important a theater can be. People who attend theaters want dinner close by and are often willing to go out for a snack or a drink after the curtain falls, meaning that a theater keeps the street alive through the evening.

The theaters also sponsor the Lincoln Avenue Street Fair in early summer, when there is food, music, performances, and the owner of a local bar dresses in his huge bunny costume and sells carrots.

The Body Politic is the oldest off-loop theater in Chicago, having begun in a church in 1969. In 1992, George Wendt, Norm from "Cheers," appeared here in *Wild Men*, a hilarious musical about men's seminars. The show's success helped alleviate the not-for-profit theater's financial woes.

For nearly two decades, Victory Gardens has been devoted to Chicago writers. In its first 19 seasons, the theater produced 173 productions, including 92 world premieres, 78 by Chicago playwrights. Some of the actors who have worked with Victory Gardens include Bill Petersen, Aiden Quinn, Shelly Berman, Esther Rolle, and Gary Cole.

Continue walking south. Look up at 2251 North Lincoln. At one time, the front half of a '57 Chevrolet stuck out of the wall above you when this was Jukebox Saturday Night. Before that, it was a cowboy bar with the first mechanical bull in Chicago. Today you'll see a pizza delivery truck driving off the roof because it has become a Carmen's Pizza restaurant. A bull to a Chevy to a pizza truck—is there any trend discernible here?

From Bamboo Bernies to Donuts

If you enter the door next to the dried grass awning at 2247 North Lincoln, you will be in Bamboo Bernies. If you think you have entered a high-concept bar like you might find in Manhattan, you are right. The owners of this bar also have a Bamboo Bernies in New York.

The bar features a 96-ounce drink called a "Shark Bite" served in a plastic fish bowl with a toy shark for a stirrer. Be forewarned, the shark bite goes for $14. The tropical island theme is complete with more than just rum drinks. There is an indoor sand volleyball court. As of this writing, the bar is so popular there is a huge line to get in on the weekends, but Monday nights you can enjoy $1 margaritas without the huge crowds.

Continue south to 2221 North Lincoln, once the home of the Drake-Braithwaite Funeral Home, where the seven victims of the St. Valentine's Day Massacre of 1929 were taken.

After one of the victims, Frank Gusenberg, was sent to the Drake-Braithwaite Funeral Home, two women claimed the body. Both Mrs. Lucille Gusenberg and Mrs. Ruth Gusenberg said they were Gusenberg's wife. We do not know exactly what Lucy and Ruth said or thought after they discovered for the first time that they were both married to the same man.

Cross Lincoln Avenue, make a U-turn, walking back toward Halsted on the other side of the street and notice Bacino's, 2204 North Lincoln, a pizza joint that introduced America's first heart-healthy pizza. It is a stuffed spinach pizza, 318 calories in an eight-ounce serving. It is the only pizza I know that lists the fat content (10.7 grams), sodium (750 mg), and cholesterol (14 mg).

The Baker's Daughter bakery, at 2218 North Lincoln, is on the site of the old Bakery Restaurant (1962–1989). It was above that restaurant that Chef Louis Szathmary, a legendary gourmet now partially retired, told me about the Chicago chefs who invented shrimp De Jonghe and crêpes suzette, two dishes created closer to State Street than to the Champs Elysses. The bakery features 25 varieties of bread.

Continue walking, staggering, or leaning north.

Sterch's

In the land of yuppie bars and glitzy food joints, you will find something unique at 2238 North Lincoln Avenue. Sterch's is a sleazy, delightful neighborhood saloon owned by Bob Smerch, who has said that he was once a carnival operator, a Paraguayan paratrooper, a lumberjack, art gallery owner, and medical researcher working on rabbits, which may be why he dresses like a bunny for the street fair.

Back in 1971, this was The Volstead Act, a bar suffering from a "personality disorder," according to Smerch, because it was a combination Indonesian restaurant, chess club, and "artsy-fartsy lounge." After he bought the place, he corrected that problem by carefully creating a sleazy, friendly place.

Smerch is one of the great talkers in Chicago, a guy who will show you "the best invisible-deck card trick in the universe," and a proprietor of "the last stronghold of the Bohemian, beatnik and mad dog Chicago drinkers," according to Dennis McCarthy's *The Great Chicago Bar & Saloon Guide*. We have a few more blocks to go before we stop, although the friendly confines of Sterch's may be attractive enough to end the walk right there.

If your choice is to continue, you will find yourself at The Big Nasty at 2242 North Lincoln. Look up and see the huge figure of Elvis Presley looming above the front window. This is the only bar I know that sells 4,000 to 5,000 cans of Silly String a week. Enter and expect to comb Silly String out of your hair all day tomorrow.

The bad publicity from the owner's two arrests for keeping a house of disorder has resulted in more customers for this bar-as-frat house.

Big Nasty and bigger Elvis

The Blues, the Cools,
and the White Elephant

Continuing north, we pass an area of small shops that tend to change owners and intent quite frequently. A few years ago something called Space Shoes was here and, after making a plaster cast of your foot, they would create the shoe just for you. They are gone now, replaced by Natural Selection, at 2258 North Lincoln, a gift shop just past Grand Slam Bagels.

The Potbelly Sandwich Works, at 2264 North Lincoln, offers vegetarian submarine sandwiches, a free jukebox sometimes playing "When a Man Loves a Woman" by Percy Sledge, and chocolate chip cookies that rival Mrs. Field's.

The Wise Fools Pub, 2270 North Lincoln, is a blues club with a long bar for drinking and a comfortable room for listening to some of the best blues bands in the city. It has a grungy, gritty atmosphere, and is often packed with blues fans and those who just like to get grungy and gritty.

Chicago's international reputation as a blues capital attracts Japanese and European tourists to Wise Fools.

Jerry's, at the corner of Orchard and Lincoln, was once a sleepy neighborhood bar. Today it is trying not to be, with a cool jukebox and low-priced beer during the week. It's got large windows facing the street making it easy to look inside to see if this is the sort of place you'd find inviting.

Across the street, there is another coffeehouse, Cafe Equinox, which features Caesar salads, quiche lorraine, iced tea, coffee, and quiet music. This was once the oldest ice-cream parlor in Chicago, and Charlie Chaplin filmed here.

Walk past the Children's Memorial Hospital garage, the parking lot of last resort in this overcrowded neighborhood. Six hours here can cost $9.

The last sight on the walk is the White Elephant Resale Shop, at the corners of Lincoln, Halsted, and Fullerton. It's probably closed if you are on a nighttime pub crawl, but look in the window. Perhaps you will see just the collapsible top hat, fur coat, or old party dress you need for $25.

If you have stopped at each of the places mentioned during this pub crawl for a drink or two, it is probably time to stagger home and lie down. If not, you may want to go back and review some of your favorite spots.

24 NORTH LINCOLN AVENUE PUB CRAWL

From a pub with ghosts to a
theater with history

1. Three-Penny Cinema
2. Red Lion Pub
3. Biograph Theater

Time: Come on now, be reasonable. How long will it take you to drink enough to call it a night and then crawl (not drive!) home? Let's say an hour for speed drinkers and until dawn tomorrow for people who like things to build slowly.

To get there: The CTA subway stops at Fullerton as does the #74 Fullerton bus. The #11 bus goes up Lincoln from Michigan Avenue. If you use the subway, exit at Fullerton and walk east a couple of blocks.

By car, take Lake Shore Drive to Fullerton, go west to Lincoln, and then good luck finding a place to park. This is one of Chicago's most congested neighborhoods. If you live here long enough, you might inherit a parking space when and if your best friend dies. Once you get a parking space, immediately convert it into a condominium.

North to Three-Penny Cinema and Lounge Ax

The area north of Fullerton along Lincoln Avenue is supposed to be more relaxed than the area south of Fullerton. At least, that's what some of its denizens say. It just might be that you have to live there to understand the subtle differences.

Suffice it to say that this is one of the shortest walks in distance because once you are north of Fullerton you'll tend to stay there. It's an interesting couple of blocks.

This walk begins at the intersection of Lincoln, Fullerton, and Halsted. Lincoln is the diagonal street, and you want to be on the west side of Lincoln, heading north. You know you are going in the right direction if you are walking past the New Seminary Restaurant, which seems to undergo remodeling every few years, adding plants and fixtures, and generally improving itself.

The Three-Penny Cinema, at 2424 North Lincoln, has had a checkered history, beginning life as an avant-garde movie house that often showed radical, politically conscious films. Later it became an X-rated film house, which upset people a lot more than the political films did. Now, although in need of remodeling, it has settled down, showing an occasional cult film, offering first- and second-run attractions, and some of the best foreign films around.

The Discover Cafe, 2436 North Lincoln, is a coffeehouse that also sells used compact discs. It has couches so you can drink coffee and pretend you're visiting someone else's living room. There are jazz brunches on Saturday and Sunday.

Next, at 2438 North Lincoln, is Lounge Ax, where you can hear new bands just before they get million-dollar record contracts and the price to see them becomes astronomical. Bands with names like Swinging Cornflake Killers, Betsy and the Boneshakers, Eleventh Dream Day, My Cousin Kenny, Poi Dog Pondering, Gear Daddies, and Timbuk 3 have played here.

Two women, Susan Miller and Julia Adams, own Lounge Ax, which is rare in the usually male-dominated club scene. Miller said that the bar is "a dream come true—not to make any money and to be exhausted all the time."

The live music is heard seven nights a week beginning around 10 p.m., and the reasonable cover charge ranges from $2 to $10. It's one of Chicago's few music bars where you can order beer by the pitcher as well as in bottles. Be sure to find out who is playing before you enter (so you can look them up on music charts a year later), and consider wearing ear protection since it is also one of Chicago's loudest music bars.

Continue going north. Uncle Dan's Army Navy Surplus Store is the Lincoln Park camouflage headquarters.

Red Lion Pub

The Red Lion Pub, at 2446 North Lincoln, is a fine place for shepherd's pie, steak and kidney pie, scones, fish and chips, and beer. John Cordwell, the owner, is central casting's idea of a British gentleman, generally walking about with an ascot, politely kissing the ladies, and happily

John Cordwell, owner, Red Lion Pub

telling stories about Nigeria, World War II, and his wife, Justine. His marital secret is "living in separate houses for 25 years."

Cordwell insists that this is a "pub" and not a tavern, meaning that it is a place for people to talk to each other. Sort of a neighborhood living room with a large and wonderful deck out back.

John was chairman of the board of one of the city's top architectural firms, Solomon, Cordwell, Buenz & Assoc. Inc., and still has his architectural office upstairs. But, when it came time to create a "pub," Cordwell claimed that "it was designed to look as if an architect had nothing to do with it."

Don't interrupt him if he's playing the piano (one of the reasons he owns the pub, since he does not drink), but do introduce yourself and listen to John's stories. For instance, there are three ghosts in this pub, two men and a woman, who have "made themselves felt from time to time by tapping patrons on the shoulder. When they turn to see who did that, no one is there." Cordwell says he was once shoved down the stairs by a ghost, causing him to hit his head and knocking him out for a half-hour. The doctors did not believe a ghost did that.

Ask about his experiences in the British Air Force in World War II, when he was a bombardier, navigator, and co-pilot. He spent 3½ years in Stalag Luft #3, the German prison camp reserved for American and British air force officers. The Steve McQueen movie *The Great Escape* retold the story of the 76 men who tunneled out. Only three made it to freedom and "50 were murdered by the Gestapo," Cordwell remembers.

Cordwell says that Englishmen who visit the Red Lion have said that it is better than the pubs in Britain because the beer and food is cheaper, and the atmosphere is more congenial.

For a while, the Commonwealth Club met here. It was a chance for local Englishmen to tell dirty stories to each other. Then, women demanded to join, so the name was changed to the Red Lion Club, which meets once a month so men *and* women can tell dirty stories to each other.

Books, Folk Music, Eating, and Dancing

If you are here during the day, and are interested in slightly avant-garde women's clothes, stop in at Blake, at 2448 North Lincoln. This boutique features American and European designed outfits from $50 to $1,200.

Continuing north, you will arrive at Guild Books, 2456 North Lincoln, which has a knowledgeable staff and a fine selection of periodicals. Many authors stop here not only to autograph their books, but to also hold discussions with their readers.

At 2462 North Lincoln is Wee Wee's, a self-described yuppie hangout. I refuse to enter any place named Wee Wee's. I have some standards.

At 2464 North Lincoln is the Montana Street Cafe, which celebrates American cuisine. At one time a folk club called Holstein's was here. Among other reasons for liking that place was that Fred Holstein, the best leader of group singing in America, was tossed out of the same high school choir I was.

The Earl's Pub, at 2470, was formerly Somebody Else's Troubles, but in either guise it is a warm, friendly bar, which usually features solo performers and never has a cover.

Jackie's, at 2478 North Lincoln, is a posh French restaurant celebrated because the hard-working owner/chef, Jackie Shen, constantly creates new and tasty dishes. Her tricolor wonton appetizer is always a favorite, and the Oriental paella or the fresh tuna are the recommended entrees. A live pianist entertains you during your elegant dinner.

Jackie Shen arrived from Hong Kong at age 17 with $1,000 from her parents. After working in several Chicago restaurants, she bought Uncle

An American success story: Jackie Shen of Jackie's

Pete's, a hot dog stand, and began working for herself. Ms. Shen was inducted into the Restaurant News Hall of Fame in 1989, the same year she organized the Chicago section of the national Taste of the Nation, the world's largest restaurant industry fund-raiser to benefit the hungry and homeless. For several years, the kickoff for that event was held at this restaurant. In 1992, Jackie's celebrated its 10th anniversary as one of the nation's few, top-rated dining establishments owned by a woman.

Right next to Jackie's is Kongomi, at 2480 North Lincoln, which features traditional African handicrafts. Looking around the small store you will see art created for tourists as well as actual religious artifacts. There has been much discussion in the art world about the so-called "airport art," and if these pieces created for tourists and not for religious ceremonies should even be considered art. Decide for yourself.

Sally Otsuji is one of the owners of Omniyage at 2482 North Lincoln, and seemingly knows everyone in the neighborhood. The store has one-of-a-kind clothing, ceramics, and jewelry, all created locally. Much of the inventory is there on consignment, since the owners take chances on new and totally unheard-of designers.

Next, cross Lincoln Avenue to get to Irish Eyes, at 2519 North Lincoln, which has a dart room and Irish entertainment without cover or minimum on weekends. The owners even assured me that if someone were to call ahead they could reserve a table on the weekend.

Lilly's, at 2513 North Lincoln, is one of the best blues bars in the city, especially on weekends. This is the place to go to hear the men who *made* the blues. You can hear what music was like before everyone plugged in and got amplified. By the way, they keep their Happy New Year sign over the stage all-year-round so they don't have to take it down and put it back.

At 2511 North Halsted is Periwinkle, an eclectic, moderately-priced restaurant, which features 25 kinds of coffee. There is an outdoor dining area and I'd suggest the Dijon chicken as a main course here.

Books and Records

Turn back and head south; you will walk by a series of bookstores. Children's Bookstore, at 2464 North Lincoln, has storytelling for children Monday through Saturday at 10:30 a.m.

In 1992, during the seventh birthday of the store, there was a 45-minute performance of a 1920s participatory Dadaist work, which featured "elaborately constructed guttural noises to suggest strange coherences." Sounds like what many children naturally do without any knowledge of the Dadaist movement. This bookstore also sells anti-coloring books, which encourage children to draw outside the lines.

Dan Behnke's, at 2463 North Lincoln, offers used, rare, and out-of-print books.

Wax Trax, at 2449 North Lincoln, is both the name of a record store and a record label, which has recorded such groups as the Revolting Cocks and Ministry. This is the place to go for obscure punk records from the early 1980s, plus industrial, dance, hip hop, acid, jazz, and alternative records. The Cult and Robert Plant shop here when they're in town.

Do talk to the clerks because almost all of them are also local musicians. They can guide you to the best records and clubs in town. According to Wes Kidd, who is both a clerk and a member of Rights of the Accused, a local band, members of the Thrill Kill Cult and Ministry have also worked here.

Or go to the second-floor boutique, the one-stop shop for punk rock clothing, where you can browse through *Outlaw Biker Tattoo* magazine, pick up the latest in bustieres, or buy a Soundgarden baseball cap.

Close by, the very best used bookstore in the city, in my estimation, is Booksellers Row, at 2445 North Lincoln, where all the books are in fine shape, where just the book you have wanted for years can often be located, and where, apparently, the people who work there have also read nearly all the books in the store.

Biograph Theater

You will next pass the Biograph Theater, at 2433 North Lincoln, which is actually three movie theaters.

Gangster history buffs will recall that the Biograph was the place where John Dillinger was shot. The notorious Lady in Red had betrayed him to federal authorities and at 10:40 p.m., July 22, 1934, after watching *Manhattan Melodrama*, Dillinger stepped into a 16-man ambush. At one time, the seat in which he sat on that night was painted silver.

Toward the south end of the theater entrance there is a sign stating, "This property has been placed on the national register of historic places by the United States Department of the Interior." There is no mention of why it received that honor, but I'm assuming Mr. Dillinger's demise had something to do with it.

Next walk past a couple of stores to Fiesta Mexicana, at 2423 North Lincoln. The patio, reachable by walking through the hallway to the toilets, is completely enclosed.

This ends the North Lincoln Avenue pub crawl, unless you want to continue past the little, triangular park to the south of Fiesta Mexicana and buy a newspaper or a magazine from the well-stocked newsstand there.

Or you might go back to one of the folk song or blues bars you passed to catch an act that seemed intriguing.

25 NORTH HALSTED WALK

Stride on the wild side

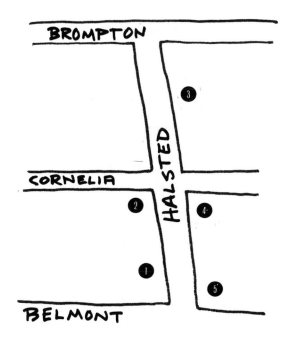

1. Yarn Boutique
2. Pergolisi Coffeehouse
3. Little Jim's
4. Chicago Diner
5. Helmand Restaurant

Time: About an hour, more if you stop to eat.

To get there: The #8 Halsted and the #77 Belmont CTA buses each stop at Halsted and Belmont. The elevated trains stop at Belmont and Sheffield about three blocks west of Halsted. Just leave the train station and take a right, heading east toward the lake. If you are driving, get off the Outer Drive at Belmont and go west to Halsted. Parking will probably be a problem because this is a most congested neighborhood.

359

Antiques, Health Food,
and a Coffeehouse

A walk along North Halsted Street today is a stroll through an area that is just becoming. We're not quite sure what it is becoming, and perhaps the neighborhood itself isn't sure. But whatever it is, it's fascinating, energetic, changing, and fun with dozens of antique stores, silly odds-and-ends stores, and a friendly group of shopkeepers and restaurant owners.

There is a Chicago feel to the area, with its profusion of ethnic restaurants, vintage clothing shops, and gay bars attracted to the street because of the low rents.

Begin on the west side of Halsted at Belmont and walk north past several sure-to-be-rehabbed flats.

The first store you will see is a weird little throwback in time called the Yarn Boutique, at 3314 North Halsted. Owner Pia Crayton studied weaving in her native Finland, and decided to have a store where people could get all the various yarns they could imagine. She thinks that knitting and weaving are still very popular and not just with grandmothers.

At 3320 North Halsted is the G-Spot, which hosts punk rock nights on Wednesday and Sunday. It seems like much of the culture on Halsted is looking back to an older time, and this place looks back to the late 1970s.

Past Mama Mia's pizza restaurant at 3322 North Halsted, which remains open until 5 a.m., is Jeffery Stephen's Limited, at 3324 North Halsted. This gift shop specializing in china, bath products, and other nice household objects is owned by two men, Jeffery Cross and Stephen Hearell. Cross was a window designer who started with the idea of a design store, and isn't quite sure how it wound up as a gift shop. Hearell's background is in retail management. The beautiful store, with fascinating merchandise, demonstrates the marriage of their talents in display and management.

The Town Hall Pub, at 3340 North Halsted, is one of the few bars on the street that caters to a heterosexual crowd. It features live entertainment on the weekends, usually of the acoustic, Grateful Dead cover-band variety. It is a very no-frills sort of place, where regulars nestle up to the bar and know each other.

3352 North Halsted is the home of the Art Mecca Art Gallery. It features functional, affordable art with an edge. This gallery has folk art, native art, and furniture in the $50-$100 range.

Roscoe's, at 3356 North Halsted, is a gay bar, which features group therapy nights when the bartender offers advice to the lovelorn and a quasi-post office box night when anyone can write messages to anyone else at the bar.

The Bread Shop, in the brown building at 3400 North Halsted, is a vegetarian, nondairy, and organic bakery and food shop. It features vegetarian lunches and dinners to-go, which are very hard to find if you are searching for such things. The highlights of the shop are the felafel sandwiches, nondairy pizza by the slice, meatless stew, and baba ganouj. It also has more than 20 kinds of freshly baked bread. If you go through the deli section to the food shop, you can find fresh pasta, healthy snacks, and packages of things called "Nature's Burger" and "Tofu Scrambler."

Pergolisi Coffeehouse and Art Gallery, 3404 North Halsted, is a survivor of the great coffeehouse days of the 1960s, when there was a profusion of such places that were the ideal shelters for starving poets and folk singers. Pergolisi is the perfect place to read a newspaper and to get upset about where the world is going.

The 99th Floor at 3406 North Halsted has everything you need for that nightclub in which everyone is wearing leather and a mean attitude. It stocks Dr. Marten's Footwear—the boots from England with more laces than are sensible—telephones with studs, and leather shirts with

Kevin Tihista and Matt Fusello at the 99th Floor, a one-story store on Halsted

chains. Mick Levine, the co-owner, says, "Come here if you want to see what people will be wearing in a couple of years." When I visited, a young chap was delighted to be buying a *Hellraiser III* T-shirt, a film he wanted to see but couldn't because he was in the midst of a two-week drug binge. First things first.

Evil Clown CDs at 3418 North Halsted is a compact disc store, which has a lot of new, alternative music. In the back are a few CD players so customers can listen to discs before they purchase them. I was told this was common in Europe. Evil Clown is bringing that idea to America and Halsted Street. They sell used CDs and specialize in European and Chicago groups, plus jazz and reggae.

We're Everywhere

Kate, the owner of We're Everywhere, 3434 North Halsted, would rather not use her last name for fear of the strange calls she might get. Her store is geared toward gays and lesbians, and sells T-shirts, sweatshirts, jackets, mock turtlenecks, tank tops, lace-up football shorts, coffee cups, and many other items emblazoned with her original sayings. Her shirts say things like "BIG FAG" or "DYKE" and her oven mitts announce "Get a grip, Mary," a saying frequently used in the gay community. British rocker Boy George has bought items here, and Kate says that Madonna gets one of her mail order catalogues. Kate's slogan, "Just be you," seems to appeal to straight friends, relatives, and parents of gays who often shop for gifts here.

Funky Stores

At 3436 North Halsted is Beatnix, which owner Keith Bucceri describes as selling "funkier vintage clothing of the '60s and '70s." Fringe vests, bell-bottoms, Superfly-style clothing, and the always en vogue platform shoes all have their place in this store. There is also a selection of disco and K-Tel records in the back room, next to the wall of shoes.

Continuing to walk north, 3438 North Halsted is the home of James Mall Antiques, which specializes in the arts and crafts movement in furniture, a pre–World War I American design movement that used heavy oak. While I was in the store, the owner was researching a piece he had just acquired, which he believed to be made in a particular shop in San Francisco by an artisan of Japanese descent. If he was correct it would be worth a lot more than he paid for it at a garage sale.

At one time 3450 North Halsted was the home of Goodies, which specialized in rubber vomit, whoopee cushions, wind-up Godzillas, and glasses with eyeballs on springs. I guess there is a limit to the marketing possibilities for rubber vomit. 3450 North Halsted is now a video rental store.

Continue north until you reach Flashy Trash at 3524 North Halsted. Harold Mandell, a former actor who now sells antique lingerie, has created the one-stop shop for girls (and, in this neighborhood, boys) who want to dress like Madonna in whatever guise she is. Mandell, who talks faster than a machine gun shoots, has owned this vintage clothing and accessories store since 1978, and now is often called upon by movie studios to supply costumes for period films.

Flashy Trash has the best collection of jewelry made from a form of early plastic known as Baccolite. The back room has racks of clothes, ranging from worn Levi's to vintage tuxedos to T-shirts of Elvis as painted by Picasso. David Bowie's ex-wife, Prince, and Bryan Adams have shopped here for feather boas, vintage eyewear, and instant tattoos.

Foreign Foods and More Shops

The Bangkok at 3542 North Halsted is one of the best restaurants in the city. It serves Thai food that can only be described as a celebration of flavor and spice. Not too hot, not too bland, a bit of Oriental perfection. The green curry dishes are quite excellent, and the Sunday buffet is a great way to try many new things for around $20 a person.

Next, cross the street and retrace your steps back to Belmont by walking on the east side of Halsted. The address numbers will be going down.

The Mexican restaurant, Las Mananitas, used to be a small, crowded, neighborhood place where the waiters knew many of the patrons. Now it is a large, crowded neighborhood place, which has expanded to three times its original size in as many years.

On your way south, back toward Belmont, you will pass Cupid's Treasures, a sex-toy boutique at 3519 North Halsted. This store features erotic items, games, novelties, lotions, magazines, leather wear, and fantasy attire. One couple entered and requested a blow-up doll. Then

Siriporn Kaiser and Piyarat Chatchawan at the Bangkok, one terrific Thai restaurant

the woman seriously asked, "What if he likes her more than me?" Everyone has self-esteem problems.

Walking south, the Ram bookstore, also called A Gay Treasure, is at 3511 North Halsted. Little Jim's, a gay bar, is at 3501 North Halsted.

At the corner of Cornelia and Halsted, take a quick left and walk about 20 yards east to Cornelia's, which sometimes has a sidewalk cafe, and which is as clean and bright as any restaurant in town. It is only open during the day on Sunday for brunch, otherwise you have to wait until 5 p.m. for cocktails and American nouvelle cuisine featuring fresh fish, steaks, and crab.

When you stop by Hobby Heaven, at 3451 North Halsted, ask the owner, Doris Kaye, about how Halsted Street has changed over the years. Doris, who has lived above her shop since 1947, can map the changes: "When I bought this building, the neighborhood was German and Polish, then it went hillbilly, then Puerto Rican, and now it's gay." There is no telling what group will come through next, although Doris, with her French and Chippewa Indian heritage, will remain.

She sells kits for embroidery, decoupage, needlepoint, beading, rug hooking, and so on. And she's glad to get the passerby started in any of those crafts.

The owners of Formerly Yours Antiques, at 3443 North Halsted, were standing around one day a few years ago trying to figure out how they could avoid working for someone else. At that moment, a man from Colorado, who did not leave so much as his name or forwarding address, came up to Ronald Holzman and Jamie Conly, and began to lecture them on how to become antique furniture brokers. They never saw the stranger again, but from that conversation, this antique store was born. Visit the store, but avoid conversations with strangers from Colorado unless you want to change your occupation.

Cheap Eats, Expensive Eats (and More Shops)

The "best of the cheap eats," according to the *Chicago Tribune*, can be found at the Chicago Diner, 3411 Halsted, which is decorated to look like a neon-lit diner from the '50s with a '90s twist. This is purely a vegetarian restaurant with the avowed intention of weaning all of us from red meat to white meat to fish and, finally, to no meat at all. The staff does not preach, and the restaurant is capable of meeting the needs of all the various vegetarians in our midst—those that eat dairy foods and those who do not—as well as those who eat sugar and those who do not.

The Chicago Diner has become the politically correct place to eat and has attracted actors John Astin, Emilio Estevez, and his wife, singer Paula Abdul.

The highlights are the big, sloppy Reuben sandwich, the miso soup, and the fresh juices. Filtered water is always available.

The Loading Zone, at 3359 North Halsted is a neighborhood bar with a deejay every night of the week. It primarily caters to gay men, but people of any sexual persuasion are welcome.

If you peek in the windows at 3347 North Halsted, you will see Chicago Trax Recording, a popular recording studio that has been the home to Ministry, Depeche Mode, and many other famous and/or hopeful groups.

The Gallimaufry Gallery, at 3345 North Halsted, takes its name from a Shakespearean word meaning a mixture of things. Michael and Pat Merkle have had this shop since 1975, but kept their day jobs for seven years.

The store began as an outlet for their own handmade crafts, but it quickly became apparent to them that they needed to expand to other artisans if they were to make a living. Now they no longer have time for their own work, but enjoy selling what they do. The store focuses on good-quality, handmade items that aren't horribly expensive. Says Michael, "Anyone can go out with a thousand bucks and get something cool, but who can do that with $10?"

The store features only stuff that the Merkles like to buy including jewelry, pottery, wooden boxes, leather bags, wind chimes, incense, candles, toys, hats, moccasins, earrings, beads, rings, bracelets, thumb pianos, and, what you've always wanted, musician-quality slide whistles.

Tari Costau constantly assembles an excellent collection of fine vintage clothes in her store Silver Moon, at 3337 North Halsted. She carries things from the late 1800s to the early 1960s. The room to your left as you walk in has a large collection of vintage wedding gowns, and Tari says she gets many soon-to-be brides who prefer something from an earlier era for their wedding.

Past the Sherwin-Williams Paint Store, you will next see Yoshi's Cafe, at 3257 North Halsted, a Franco-Asian restaurant, meaning it offers French cooking with Japanese accents and prices to match—main courses are in the $20 to $25 range, plus $7 to $9.50 for hors d'oeuvres, $6 for soup, and $5 or $6 for salads.

This restaurant, run by chef Yoshi Katsumura and his wife, Nobuko, who will greet you at the door, has had an astounding number of fine reviews and awards. In 1992 alone, Yoshi won the DeRona Distinguished Restaurants of North America Award, the Silver Platter, and the Chefs in America awards. The *Zagat Chicago Restaurant Survey* in 1991 rated Yoshi's "extraordinary to perfection," and *Chicago* magazine praised it for "spectacularly beautiful presentations."

Walk another block and a half to the large green awning at Belmont and Halsted. This is the Helmand Restaurant, which features Afghan food, meaning you can try aushak, mantwo, or bowlawni. Don't be frightened just because you do not know what those dishes are. The prices are reasonable, the staff is friendly, and they will explain their menu.

The food is delicious, if you like mild, lightly spiced curries. By all means try the outstanding eggplant appetizer. And, while you eat, reflect on the long, long trek it must have taken to come all the way from Afghanistan to Halsted Street.

Also, think about this vital, constantly changing neighborhood. Some of the restaurants and stores mentioned above may be gone when you visit, but others will replace them.

ACKNOWLEDGMENTS

Literally scores of people cooperated with this project, which was really written and rewritten by the folks of Chicago.

I am especially grateful to Emmett Dedmon, who allowed me to see his notes for his book *Fabulous Chicago*; to Herman Kogan, who knew how to write about history and how to guide a reporter; to Richard Christiansen, who let the first walks live; and to publisher Curt Matthews, who believes people can walk and read. This book was also aided by Ira Bach's *Chicago on Foot*; the Chicago Historical Society library and staff; the *Chicago Daily News*, the *Chicago Sun-Times*, and the *Chicago Tribune*; Chicago Transit Authority route maps; Chicago Park District guides to monuments; publicists and new-found friends in every museum and restaurant in Chicago; the Chicago Police Department; Mr. and Mrs. Arthur Mark; Mrs. Chloe Barrett; and everyone who told me their story or gave me directions.

INDEX